a special gift

presented to:

_____

from:

_____

date:

_____

The Women's Devotional Series

In His Presence

Carolyn Rathbun Sutton
EDITOR

Pacific Press®
Publishing Association
Nampa, Idaho | Oshawa, Ontario, Canada
www.pacificpress.com

Additional copies of this book are available for purchase by calling toll-free 1-800-765-6955 or by visiting http://www.adventistbookcenter.com.

ISBN 978-0-8163-6412-1

June 2018

About the Editor

Carolyn Rathbun Sutton finds great joy in "being there" for other women, especially those struggling to find renewed purpose after a major life setback. She particularly enjoys helping women share their own personal stories of God's faithfulness.

Dear Reader,

The North American Division (NAD) Women's Ministries team welcomes you to the 2019 edition of the Women's Devotional book. We are pleased and grateful that all proceeds from sales of the book in the NAD will be used exclusively for scholarships in our territory.

We are praying that you will be blessed this year as you read devotionals from women like you—real women with real stories of God's love and providence in their lives. We look forward to hearing from you, and we hope that you will be inspired to submit your own stories to share with others.

We have a two-person department. Carla Baker has been the NAD Women's Ministries director since 2006. Her union women's ministries and teaching background have made her the department's resource specialist. Carla is a Texan who loves living in Maryland with its four distinct seasons. She has a grown son, Brandon, and three grandchildren who have all been born in Texas while she's been in Maryland. Needless to say, Carla gets back to Texas several times a year.

Erica Jones joined the Women's Ministries Department in 2014. She didn't come far, having grown up and lived all her life just a few miles from our headquarters in Columbia, Maryland. Her background in youth ministry has given her a heart for teens and their struggles. Combined with her media experience, it was easy for her to find her ministry niche in our department—teen girls and social media . Erica lives with her four-legged children—Boots the cat and Maisy the miniature shepherd mix.

Women Helping Women

There is an aspect of this book that is unique

None of the contributors has been paid—each has shared freely so that all profits go to scholarships for women. Approximately 2,460 scholarships have been given to women in 132 countries. Recipients of the Women's Ministries scholarships are talented women who are committed to serving the mission of the Seventh-day Adventist Church.

General Conference Women's Ministries scholarship fund in the North American Division

New this year: all profits from sales of the Women's Ministries devotional book in the North American Division support women's higher education in Seventh-day Adventist colleges and universities in the United States and Canada.

Purpose of the women's devotional book

Among Friends, published in 1992, was the first annual women's devotional book. Since then, proceeds from these devotional books have funded scholarships for Adventist women seeking to obtain higher education. But as tuition costs have soared in North America and more women have applied for assistance, funding has not kept pace with the need. Many worthy women who apply must be turned down.

Recognizing the importance of educating women—to build stronger families, stronger communities, and a stronger church—each of us can help. Together we can change lives!

There are many ways to support our sisters

- Pray for women worldwide who are struggling to get an education.
- Tell others about the Women's Ministries scholarship program.
- Write for the women's devotional book (guidelines are available).
- Support women's education with a financial gift or a pledge.

To make a gift or receive materials, send us the following information:

Name _____

Street _____

City _____ State/Province _____

Postal Code_____ Country _____

Email_____

To contact us:

Women's Ministries Department
9705 Patuxent Woods Drive
Columbia, MD 21046

Phone: 443-391-7265
Email: ericajones@nadadventist.org
Website: https://www.nadwm.org/

The scholarship application and devotional book writers' guidelines are available at our website.

I'll Do It Later

I tell you that the "right time" is now,
and the "day of salvation" is now.
—*2 Corinthians 6:2, NCV*

Let me begin with a confession: procrastination has been a challenge for me all my life, and that's why I developed, many years ago, the mantra "Do it now." I've found through the years that this mantra has helped me to stay on top of the many things I had to do and kept me from being late or falling behind. But I've also found that as I get more mature (older), my mantra is harder to follow. I realize that's because my list of things to do has been increasing; and on many days, the list is just too long to fulfill. So what do I do?

Well one thing I have done is to say no a bit more often. I've also learned that I must delegate more items to my staff or my family. I can't do it all.

From conversations with other women, I've found that there are many areas of life in which we procrastinate: Beginning an exercise schedule. Pursuing higher education. Making that appointment for a mammogram that we've put off for the past few years.

We also find procrastination reflected in smaller arenas of our lives: delaying the housecleaning, not hemming a dress until wanting to wear it, or even delaying that call to a friend who may be sick.

As I thought on this topic of procrastination, one troubling question came to mind: Are we, as Christians, procrastinating when it comes to preparing for the second coming of Jesus? How many times have we said to ourselves, "I will begin my daily devotionals next week"? Or maybe we've told ourselves, "I'll start reading the Bible through at the beginning of next year so that I can start at the beginning," or "When life slows down, I'll find time to attend the Bible study group."

So many reasons for putting off spiritual preparation, and each one seems like a good reason. Yet at the beginning of this new year, I thank God that the Holy Spirit keeps calling us to a deeper and more meaningful relationship with Jesus, which brings me to our text for today.

Paul admonishes the Corinthians, "I tell you that the 'right time' is now, and the 'day of salvation' is now." I must admit to hearing and using these words in many evangelistic meetings when making an appeal for someone to give his or her life to Jesus. But I realize these words apply to all who put off salvation for another day when today is all we have.

Heather-Dawn Small

Saved by the Bell

Before they call, I will answer.
—*Isaiah 65:24, KJV*

It was the first school day after Christmas break. I was thirteen years old. I sat in my usual seat on the left-hand side of the classroom near the front. Toward the end of the class period, the teacher said, "I would like for each one of you to stand beside your desk and tell what you got for Christmas."

Oh, no! I thought. My family was very poor. A local charity organization gave gift boxes to children but only up through the age of twelve. Since I was thirteen, I had no longer qualified for a gift box that year. So all I had gotten for Christmas was a much-needed white slip!

It was decision time: *Do I tell the truth and have the kids tease me without mercy? Or do I tell a lie and keep the kids off my back?* My mother had taught me that I should always tell the truth, so this was a very hard decision for me to make.

As the teacher got closer and closer to my desk, the more anxiety and stress I felt. *What do I do?*

Then the teacher started asking students in *my* row to share what each had gotten as a gift for Christmas. At this point, I was stressed to the limit. *What do I do?*

Just as the teacher was about to question me, according to the order of our desks, I heard a loud *ring*! If you were to ask me how I would spell the relief I experienced from this tense situation at that moment, I would answer, "B-e-l-l." I was *so* relieved! In fact, I could have cried with relief as I was literally saved by the bell.

So many times as adults, we don't understand certain situations and unintentionally put children in a position that presents them with at least two equally stressful, if not undesirable, choices. The teacher thought he was doing something nice for the class by letting his students share. Yet he was unintentionally placing me in a position where I must choose between a clear conscience with a miserable social life or vice versa.

As with my mother, we must teach our children to pray for God's help in doing what is right. We can also lead them to understand that Jesus will help them in every situation. I am so glad that Christ understood my needs that day. He answered even before I called on Him.

Ruth Cantrell

Down and Almost Out!

Worry weighs us down; a cheerful word picks us up.
—*Proverbs 12:25*, The Message

Do you sometimes feel absolutely helpless, as I do, when a friend hurts? Fortunately, having a partnership with God gives us comfort in knowing that what we can't do for a friend, He can do. Yet almost always, there are a few things we can do:

- Pray for and with the friend.
- Lend a listening ear.
- Ask, "Is there is anything you *want* me to do?"
- Offer to do something that you *think* might help.

We all need friends to share in the good times and help us through difficult times. A friend told me this story about her friend Paula (not her real name), whom she met when they were teenagers. Recently, Paula, orphaned as a toddler, confessed to her, "I'd actually been contemplating suicide the very day we met. I felt I didn't fit in with anyone and was lonely. Everything was going wrong. It was difficult growing up without parents. I didn't feel wanted where I lived. But because you were friendly and offered to help me with algebra, I felt hopeful again. I really can't explain it, but for the first time I felt like someone cared about me."

Paula waited a few years to tell my friend about that dark day that turned bright because she feared my friend might consider her too emotionally unstable to be her friend. Now that both are professional adults (my friend became a professional counselor and her friend a mathematics teacher), Paula felt the time was right. My friend didn't have a clue that Paula had been feeling so down and almost out those many years ago. Yet her friendly offer to help Paula made a life-saving difference. My friend knew only that Paula was obviously struggling with her studies. So she offered to help.

"A rescued life," my friend sighed. "God allowed me to save a life—and I discovered that making friends is a blessed ministry. It provided impetus to my own profession." Hearing this story confirmed the importance of being friendly! No matter our age, there are people who come into our lives to whom we can be helpful friends. Furthermore, the story led me to this prayer: *Lord, help me discern who is discouraged and be that person's friend.*

Betty Kossick

A Time for Everything

There is a time for everything, and a season for every activity under
the heavens: a time to be born and a time to die.
—*Ecclesiastes 3:1, 2, NIV*

When I got married, I became not only a wife but also mother to two little girls. In fact, they had chosen me for their mother before their father chose me for a wife and were active little promoters until they finally had him convinced. We were a busy, happy family when little brother was born a few years later, followed by a little girl. I was sure my family was complete.

Then a few years later I got the news that I was pregnant again. My mother, who had been able to have only one child, couldn't understand why I didn't want another baby. My husband's response was, "There's always room for one more." But all through that pregnancy I worked hard and did all I could to perhaps lose the baby. Yet when little Rose was born, I loved her as much as my other children. She definitely was the missing link in our family. Since she has grown up, Rose has been a blessing to many. She became a nurse and worked for a few years as an IV therapist at a large Christian university hospital in California. When no one else could start an IV on babies, Rose could. For a while, she did blood draws on heart transplant babies.

Rose married and had two children of her own: a daughter and, later, a son. Then while her husband was studying to be a dentist and she was the breadwinner, she found out that she was pregnant again. I knew exactly how she felt, but I also knew that everything would work out for the best. Although the first few years were a challenge for this busy mother, none of the family would dream of life without her happy little girl. Later Rose started a business so that she could homeschool her children. Her business showed people how they could improve their family lives by preserving memories in photo albums. She continues doing this today, and it has been a blessing to many families, including her own children.

Life goes on, and now the little girl born to this busy mother has grown up and blessed many lives by going on mission trips to several different countries. She has also become a nurse and, in this capacity, continues to brighten the lives of others with her cheerful, caring ways.

As I reflect on our family life, I can see that Solomon was right when he said that there was a time to be born and we can just let God take care of the details.

Betty J. Adams

Who Am I?

"For without Me you can do nothing."
—John 15:5, NKJV

At my own expense, I attended our church's worldwide quinquennial conference in 1990, held in the United States. My husband, an official delegate, had his way paid. We enjoyed the various meetings as we listened to presentations by the best speakers and musicians from around the world. It was a foretaste of heaven to be among God's people from all parts of the globe.

Leadership from our part of the world church was invited to present the worship service one morning. The previous day I was surprised to be approached by our minister, who asked me to offer the opening prayer for that service. "Oh no, not me, please!" was my immediate answer. I thought, *He is an outstanding preacher from our area, but who am I?* Hearing my response, the pastor walked away to look for someone else. I felt relieved when he walked away, but remorse and shame soon took over. I felt I had sinned against God. I was scared. Moments later that same pastor unexpectedly came by, and I gave him my consent.

The next morning I found myself on the stage looking out at a sea of faces. Stage fright took over. I felt very small as I stood up by the pulpit. India has many races and languages in its many states, and I come from one of its smallest states, Meghalaya. I had been asked to pray in Khasi. Since only the half dozen of my own people present would understand my prayer, I decided to tell the audience the sentiment of that prayer before bowing my head and offering it.

First, I told the audience that it was obvious, from my image on the big screens, that I was small in stature. Then I quickly said, "Actually, in spite of being and feeling small, I have a reason to feel great." There was silence. I broke the silence by saying, "You know, if I were the only survivor on earth, Christ would still have come to die for me."* Then I pointed my hand toward the vast assembly and said, "The next reason I feel great is that you are my brothers and sisters." The audience began to clap but stopped because I had begun praying.

Friends, we all are small. Jesus said that without Him we can do nothing. Moses said, "Who am I?" when God called him to deliver Israel (Exodus 3:11). Jeremiah said he was but a child when God called (Jeremiah 1:6). But along with Paul, we can say, "I can do all things through Christ who strengthens me" (Philippians 4:13, NKJV).

Birdie Poddar

---

* See Ellen G. White, *The Desire of Ages* (Oakland, CA: Pacific Press®, 1898), 483.

God Never Says, "Oops"

All night long I flood my bed with weeping
and drench my couch with tears.
—*Psalm 6:6, NIV*

"And call on me in the day of trouble;
I will deliver you, and you will honor me."
—*Psalm 50:15, NIV*

On a very pleasant Sabbath, I woke up with a very interesting question in my mind: What if God said, "Oops"? What if, when we went to the Bible for guidance and answers to our prayers, we found a verse that said, "Oops, I didn't see that coming! Sorry." On a more serious note, I think that sometimes we subconsciously wonder whether God really knows what He is doing. Maybe we "humanize" Him, though the truth is that He is wise beyond any earthly wisdom.

If God brings us to a situation we don't understand, He will also bring us through it. If God allows for unpleasant events, serious turns of events, and life-altering drama, it is because He has a purpose for them, not only for our benefit but also for the benefit of those around us.

Nothing we encounter or have experienced in life has escaped God's knowledge. We cannot go to Him in prayer and "surprise" Him, expecting an "Oops, somehow I missed that" in return. Some days we may wish things worked that way, but be reassured that, according to His promise in Romans 8:28, all things work for the good of those who believe in, and trust, Him. Our focus must always be on God and on Christ—and never on the problem. We must never lose hope. When you feel like you cannot breathe, God is there. When you cannot see what the future will bring and the uncertainty is driving you crazy, God is there. When you don't have any strength left to keep on moving, God is there. He is with you when times are good, when times are confusing, and when times are bad and even impossibly terrible.

Be assured that when difficult situations come our way, God will not sit down with some popcorn on the sidelines, just watching while we go through pain and suffering. He will be right there by our sides because He takes each one of His children and their situations seriously and personally. What a wonderful God we have! He cares for every living thing, but He loves and cares for our lives, bodies, and souls as if we were the only ones in the universe.

God will make certain we have the victory; we just have to stay in the race, believing in His love for us. Focus on God, and He will take care of you.

Yvita Antonette Villalona Bacchus

All Things

And we know that all things work together for good to those who
love God, to those who are the called according to His purpose.
—*Romans 8:28, NKJV*

My identical twin sister was faithfully living a healthy lifestyle, so her diagnosis of nonsmoker's lung cancer came as a complete surprise, even though she knew something wasn't right. From the time she was diagnosed, she told her doctor she would accept whatever God allowed, whether healed or not, no matter what treatment plan she was to follow. God knew what was best for her. She did well for eighteen months; but after her treatment plan stopped being effective, her doctor told her she had only a few months to live. Her family called to ask whether I would come and help care for her. She wanted to stay in her home to the end. They came and got me.

I did not hesitate. My twin sister and I were very close. To help care for her would be a privilege. I would not have wanted it any other way even though the stress was great—mentally, emotionally, and physically. It was one of the most difficult nursing jobs I would ever do.

The sicker she became, though, the more her faith grew. I asked her one day, earlier in her illness, about her faith. She told me that faith was the only way to face this challenge and that faith must grow. She knew she could trust her Lord and Savior.

I sat by her bedside that last Sabbath evening, knowing her time on this earth was nearing its end. She died the next morning. Though she hoped to be healed, she had surrendered all to Jesus. Her faith remained steadfast, never wavering, to the end. Now she sleeps, waiting for Jesus to come and take her home, along with all the rest of His faithful children.

I had to ask myself about my faith. *What about my trust? What about my steadfastness?*

When troubles and trials are allowed into our lives, we need to recognize that God allows them for a reason; He doesn't waste anything regarding His children. We don't have to like our trials. I'm sure Jesus didn't enjoy being falsely accused, having nails put in His hands, or being physically abused. But He loved and trusted His Father. He knew that what came to Him was permitted for future good, no matter how painful it felt at the time. He trusted God completely.

God loves us unconditionally. He wants us to be ready for heaven so that we can live with Him throughout eternity.

Carolyn Voss

My Unbelief

And straightway the father of the child cried out,
and said with tears, Lord, I believe; help thou mine unbelief.
—Mark 9:24, KJV

Several years ago my world as I knew it was forever changed. A routine Wednesday afternoon was plunged into grief and shock by the sudden passing of a friend who could easily be classified as the brother I never had. This man had been a part of my life since I was seven years old, and then, suddenly, he was gone. Forever! My world was shaken! I asked God how this could be. This man left a young son behind. What purpose could that serve? How could God claim to be merciful and kind and allow this incomprehensible tragedy into our lives? When one of my late friend's sisters said, "God knows best," I looked at her as if she were insane and thought, *If ever God made a mistake, this was it!* I buried my friend and for two years have found little solace that grieving Christians are supposed to have. I avoided church during this time.

Though I didn't want to pray following the death, there was yet a need to lean on a Power higher than just the folks who came around to offer comfort. My friend's wife would call. Even as we questioned God, we found we still had to go to Him to ask for comfort and peace in this trying time—as a child punished for some infraction returns to the same parent for comfort.

When I was asked to speak at the funeral, I'd had to think long and hard about what to say. My thoughts had not been kind ones, yet I had sought help from the Father, even though I felt He had done us a terrible wrong. I was impressed to speak of things I was thankful for even in this time of grief and pain, such as having had the privilege of knowing my friend.

My faith in God was severely shaken by this event. And I will not pretend it has gotten very strong since. But one thing I have learned is this: God is there for us even when it seems like He is not. He does provide comfort, and He does provide solace for us, His children, when we need it.

There have been many trials and other shocking events since that sad day in October 2014. Yet every time I question God's purposes, I have to recall today's text: *I do believe in You, Lord. I believe You are there and love me. I believe You are kind and merciful. I believe You are all powerful and can do all things. So, Lord, I believe, but help Thou my unbelief!*

Raylene McKenzie Ross

Kerry's Miracle

"For nothing will be impossible with God."
—Luke 1:37, NET

I remember it as if it were yesterday. I was preparing for work one Monday when my father called. His words were cryptic: "They are about to pull the plug on Kerry." I was confused. I only knew one Kerry, my cousin, who was in her midtwenties. I tried to make sense of his statement. "Which Kerry?" I asked.

His voice cracked. "Your cousin." He explained that she'd had a seizure the previous Saturday and had been unconscious since. She had been declared brain dead because she hadn't responded since the seizure. Now medical personnel were going to remove her from life support either later that day or the next.

This made no sense, I told Dad. My cousin didn't have a seizure disorder, so I queried its cause and severity for her to be so critical. No young person in my family had ever been sick, let alone died. My father, who is not a Christian, then said, "I don't usually pray, but I'm praying now." I, too, started praying for the impossible—for God to heal my cousin and snatch her back from the cold hands of death. After praying, I took to social media and asked all my prayer warrior friends to help us pray for a miracle.

That day I asked God for a sign that my cousin would live. After going through work in a daze and praying with every breath for Kerry's healing, I made it home. I had a light fixture in my bathroom that consisted of several bulbs. One of them had stopped working more than a week before, but I hadn't found the time to replace it. That night when I turned on the light, to my amazement, that bulb shone brightly. I started crying because I believed this was my sign that Kerry would live. Oh, what an analogy! God had assured me that my cousin, who had been given up as dead, would live—just as that apparently dead light bulb had lit up and was shining again.

Kerry made a full recovery with no deficits and has since given birth to a beautiful daughter. God did the impossible for Kerry. Why not trust Him to do the impossible for you too?

Lord, I have seen You do the impossible. I ask You to do what seems impossible for us today. Grant us the patience to wait for You and the faith to know that You are working out all things for us.

Sheree Mundy

Where Are You Looking?

For man looketh on the outward appearance,
but the LORD looketh on the heart.
—1 Samuel 16:7, KJV

She looked like an ordinary restaurant manager: a little frazzled and practically running from one place to another. Her hair was a bit mussed up, and she had no smile on her face. We actually were not paying that much attention to her until the phone rang at the front desk. We heard her say, "Stay right where you are. I will come and find you and bring you here." Her words caught our attention right away because our group of six (three cousins with our spouses) had been eagerly waiting for a fourth cousin to join us.

When our as-yet-absent cousin, whom we had not seen in a while, announced earlier that she would be in our area and would like to see us, we had arranged for all of us to meet in a buffet-style restaurant because her husband was wheelchair bound. We had given her detailed directions to the restaurant as well as its phone number. But she was now half an hour overdue.

We were becoming concerned that my cousin and her husband might have been in an accident. That's when our waitress came to our table and asked whether we were expecting someone named Martha to join us. "Yes!" we responded. She informed us that Martha had called three times for directions. When she called the third time, the restaurant manager told our cousin to stay right where she was, and the manager herself would come and find her. Martha was several miles away from where she needed to be, so we waited a while longer.

After a bit, Martha and her husband came into the restaurant to join us at our table. Not only had the manager gone to meet them, but she had told the lost pair that their lunch would be free that day. We tried to pay for their lunch, but the manager would have none of it. She actually smiled and said she was glad to take care of them.

She may have looked like an ordinary manager, but we found out she was a truly caring person. How many managers would go to all that trouble to help someone? Many others might have just kept giving directions until the missing guests got there on their own. Others might not have paid for the latecomers' lunch. Truly, we had met a kind-hearted soul who recognized a need and then had gone out of her way to help. We will never forget how one restaurant manager changed how we viewed others. We are thankful she showed us her heart.

Anna May Radke Waters

The Best Example of What Jesus Said

"You know that those who are regarded as rulers of the Gentiles lord it over them, and their high officials exercise authority over them. No so with you. Instead, whoever wants to become great among you must be your servant."
—Mark 10:42, 43, NIV

Nowadays people have many individuals they look up to—such as pop music artists and movie stars. I probably, unwittingly, have some people that have some type of "authority" over me. Yet if someone asked me, "Who is the person you admire most?" I would answer, without a doubt, "My mother."

Yes, she is the one who held me in her womb for nine long months. She is the one who cuddled me every day, helping me to fall asleep. She nursed me when I was hungry. And, yes, she is the one who reprimanded me because of my bad behavior. But I can't remember her ever scolding me. In fact, I can recall only a couple of times when it was necessary for her to sit down and deliver a firm talk. Indeed, most of the time my mother taught me through her actions.

When I was eleven years old, my mum decided to start visiting the ladies in a nearby nursing home every week. And every Sabbath she invited someone who was hungry or in need to join us for potluck in our home, even though we weren't rich. When someone needed a job, they called my mum, and she helped them find one. When somebody didn't have a place to sleep because he was a foreigner, she provided him with shelter. Mum's philosophy was, "It is better to give than to receive." Only now am I realizing how much this has influenced my life.

I couldn't wait to turn eighteen—not to get my driver's license but to be able to volunteer in a nursing home. That was my dream! To this day, I continue to serve at a hospital near my school and help with disaster relief projects that help those in need of food.

Many people believe being a pop music star, with lots of perks and fans, would be very cool. On the contrary, my mum considers it a privilege to be able to help others. Her name will probably never appear on the cover of the *New York Times*. I am sure, though, that her name will be in the book of life.

For me, Mum is the best example of what Jesus said: "You know that those who are regarded as rulers over the Gentiles lord it over them. . . . Not so with you. Instead, whoever wants to become great among you must be your servant" (Mark 10:42, 43, NIV).

Lyudmyla Oliynyk

Understanding

May the Lord give you understanding in all things.
—*2 Timothy 2:7, NKJV*

I t's a disaster, I tell you. An unmitigated disaster!" Melissa paced, wringing her hands.

"Nah, it's not that bad," said her cousin while playing with the dog. "Just get over it."

"If you thought that would make me feel better," Melissa retorted, "it did *not*!"

"Hold it a minute, you two," I said, choking back a chuckle. "Melissa, I think your brain *overreacts* while your cousin's brain *underreacts* to the same situation." I went on to explain: "The brain is the first body system to recognize a stressor, and it reacts with nanosecond timing. It can stimulate the stress response for up to seventy-two hours after a traumatic incident—real or imagined—and longer, if you keep rehearsing it. Every human being needs effective stress-management strategies, but they may be critical for females. Their brains appear twice as vulnerable as male brains to some stress-related disorders."

The two cousins had left their arguing and were carefully listening, so I proceeded. "Rat-brain research revealed that in the stressed male, internal proteins pulled in some of the receptor molecules located on the surface of locus coeruleus neurons, deep in the alarm center of the brain stem."

Melissa glanced over at her cousin. He pretended not to notice.

"That meant," I continued, "fewer receptors were available to bind with the stress hormone, corticotropin-releasing factor [CRF]. This adaptation, unique to the male brain, toned down the neurons' stress sensitivity. Without this mechanism, the female brain takes the *full hit*, making it more difficult to cope with high levels of CRF, as occurs in depression and post-traumatic stress disorder, for example."

Melissa and her cousin looked at each other.

"Understanding how male and female brains respond differently to stressors gives you a choice."

Melissa raised an eyebrow.

"Instead of arguing, choose to *meet in the middle* and brainstorm a solution—together."

Fortunately, that's exactly what they did.

Lord, help me to do the same, I breathed.

Arlene R. Taylor

The Bus That Came Too Soon!

"For I know the plans I have for you," declares the LORD,
"plans to prosper you and not to harm you,
plans to give you hope and a future."
—*Jeremiah 29:11, NIV*

The other day I tried hard to complete my work in order to leave exactly at five o'clock so that I wouldn't miss my bus. All day I tried to work a little faster so that I wouldn't be stuck at the end of the day rushing to complete one last task before I could leave. I managed to complete all my work for the day and packed up my things before flying down the stairs and out of the building.

I arrived at the bus stop a full minute before my scheduled bus was to arrive—only to see it pulling away from the curb! To say I was miffed would be an understatement. I had tried *so* hard all day! I had even taken a slightly shorter lunch break so that I could finish work a few minutes early and have my things ready to go in order to be out the door at five on the dot! In fact, I'd been early! All my effort not to miss my bus that day was wasted!

Of course, I knew even then that missing the bus wasn't that big of a deal. After all, if I just waited, another bus was scheduled to arrive in less than half an hour. But it's hard to let go of our expectations and plans.

Imagine my surprise when not three minutes later, another bus appeared on my route! The first bus had not been early. It had been extremely late! So late that I had mistaken it for the bus I intended to catch. And because many people got on the first bus, stop after stop, the second bus that I boarded was practically empty! It was a much more pleasant ride than it would have been had I been squished in with everyone else on the first bus.

As I rode home, I started thinking about how God knew all along that a better bus was coming. I recalled how He always knows what He has planned and how it's always, far and away, beyond what I have planned. I know this. And yet how many times do I fret and fuss when things don't go according to *my* plan?

I thanked God for this gentle reminder that He is in control and for this example of His care in small matters as well as major ones. I resolved to do better at trusting God and His plan.

Won't you do the same? His plans are always best!

Julie Bocock-Bliss

January 14

God Always Understands

He causes us to remember his wonderful works.
How gracious and merciful is our LORD!
—*Psalm 111:4, NLT*

As I accompanied my pastor husband on his evangelistic mission trips to East African countries, I learned to greet the people in their own languages. I was quietly proud of my achievement because I am not good at learning languages. Most of these trips lasted only three or four weeks at a time, so when my husband accepted a three-year appointment to Tanzania—away from family, friends, and all the comforts of a Western lifestyle—I was somewhat apprehensive. Finally, we accepted that God wanted us to go and arranged our personal affairs. In a short time, we were on our journey to the University of Arusha.

In spite of my apprehension, it did not take long before I was teaching nursing students and enjoying the college community. My weekly trip to the local market on Friday afternoon was the highlight of every week. At first, I was bemused and spellbound by the abundant variety of fruits and vegetables all arranged in such colorful and creative ways. Women sitting on low stools at their stalls shelling beans would call out, "*Karibu. Njoo ku-nunua dada* [Welcome. Come and buy, Sister]."

Over time, my attitude about going to the market changed. You see, everyone else on campus, including my husband, was now fluent in both English and Swahili. So while I loved the atmosphere in that market, I felt somewhat saddened because, as I strolled through the buzzing crowds, I still could not speak enough Swahili to haggle for what I wanted to buy at the local price without an interpreter. This inability to speak Swahili also restricted my social activities and prevented me from mingling and bonding with the villagers as I would have liked.

In desperation, I asked God for His comfort because my heart was in anguish. As I cried out to Him, He led me to understand that the secret of joyful living is to give out to others as much as one takes in from God. Over time, through my health-education talks, a healthier lifestyle change was visible in the local community. Even though the closeness with the community that I longed for was lacking, I did not feel so isolated anymore.

Lord, thank You for being the perfect Companion and understanding our needs exactly.

Joyce Goddard

God, Turtles, and Me

"Even to your old age and gray hairs
I am he, I am he who will sustain you.
I have made you and I will carry you;
I will sustain you and I will rescue you."
—Isaiah 46:4, NIV

God miraculously brought me to work at a beautiful university campus situated between two lakes. On any given day, I can choose which of the two lakes I want to sit at as I do my midday devotion. On one of these occasions, burdened with fears and uncertainties, I cried to God for clarity and answers to the many questions whirling in my mind. I reminded Him that He promised to take care of me. Yet how dare I remind the omniscient God of His promise, for God never slumbers nor sleeps (see Psalm 121:4, NIV).

As I was chiding myself and apologizing to God, my attention was drawn to the lake. At first, I saw the usual turtle heads bobbing up and down in the water. I always thanked God for sending them to keep me company as I worshiped Him. But this time, one turtle seemed to be looking straight at me. *This is strange,* I thought. Normally, the turtles pushed their heads above the water for a few seconds and then disappeared below the surface. But this turtle's head stayed above the water a little longer than usual. As I stared, I noticed that the turtle seemed to have two heads. *What?* After I regained my composure, I realized the heads belonged to two turtles; one riding on the back of another. Tears welled up in my eyes as I watched both turtles going down and up in the water with the top turtle fastened securely on the back of the other turtle.

I discerned that God was telling me I had nothing to worry about because He always carries me through challenges. I asked His forgiveness for my doubts and fears and thanked Him for speaking to my heart through this profound object lesson from the turtles.

Have you ever been anxious before God, desperately wanting to have the assurance that He cares about you? I want to declare to you that He does. He is a personal God and will do, or use, anything to let us know that He loves and cares about us. The ultimate way He demonstrates His loving care toward us is through the gift of His Son Jesus Christ—given so willingly to die in our place. God did not stop there. He also gives us the precious gift of the Holy Spirit, who is always there to comfort and cheer us on as we advance on our spiritual journey. Trust Him.

Veon Stewart

Our Only Claim to Fame

O people, the LORD has told you what is good,
and this is what he requires of you:
to do what is right, to love mercy,
and to walk humbly with your God.
—*Micah 6:8, NLT*

She spoke barely above a whisper. "Mom, I really want to win, but I don't want to toot my own horn." In 2014, Andrea Blair, my forty-two-year-old daughter who is a middle-school music teacher in Victoria, British Columbia, was selected as one of twelve finalists in the eighth annual *Canadian Family* Teachers Awards contest (sponsored by the online magazine). In the span of three years, she had invented a completely new way to write sheet music and had taught a student, Daniel (who is dyslexic and has a writing disability), to read music via different colored squares on graph paper and to play the clarinet. Daniel's mother had nominated Andrea for the award. Should she win, her school would be awarded twenty-five hundred dollars.

Andrea continued, "Mom, in years past, the winners each got more than ten thousand online votes. The contest will run for a month, and this could become very stressful!"

Without hesitation, I blurted out, "Andee, the Lord is with you in all this! I'm pretty good at tooting other people's horns!" Her dad and I saw this as a once-in-a-lifetime golden opportunity to campaign for our precious daughter, plus share our faith in Jesus at the same time. We spared no expense in connecting with everyone we knew by either email or "snail mail." Our family is very active in both church and political affairs (as we also passionately advocate for Andee's autistic twenty-eight-year-old brother, Sonny), so we know many people.

During the contest, the teachers in British Columbia went on strike. This was depressing. But Andee kept her joy because people from all around the world were voting for her. When all the votes were cast, Andee was one of the three final winners with votes totaling more than seventy-eight hundred. From the beginning, Andee told me that the contest was a "family bonding experience" for her. Dad, Mom, and Sonny attended her victory ceremonies at the school on the day she received the check from the magazine. A lovely family photo was taken, and we shared it in our Christmas letter that year along with praise to God and appreciation to those who had voted.

Though Andee became better known as a teacher because of her win, she agrees with our pastor that the only claim to fame that our church has is that we try to walk with the Lord.

Deborah Sanders

Realizing Your Dream

"I know what I'm doing. I have it all planned out—
plans to take care of you, not abandon you, plans to give you the
future you hope for."
—*Jeremiah 29:11*, The Message

Recently, I came across the amazing life story of Gladys Aylward, who was a British missionary to China. From childhood, Gladys dreamed of becoming a missionary in China. But she encountered many obstacles that made her dream seem nearly impossible. The missionary school Gladys attended concluded her low grades would keep her from being a missionary. Disappointed, Gladys wondered why God did not intervene. Well, He did, by providing her with a job of keeping house for a retired missionary couple. But it seemed that as her dream of going to China grew stronger, so did the obstacles. The cheapest one-way train fare to China cost almost one year's salary, and she did not know anyone in China. One day in church, though, she learned that Mrs. Larson, an experienced missionary in China, needed someone to join her. After paying for her train ticket, Gladys finally embarked for China with little money and enough food for the two-week journey. During the actual two months it took her to reach Mrs. Larson, Gladys lost her money and belongings and was nearly killed along the way.

Through it all, God was with Gladys. Her dream came true. In China, God worked wonders through her. Thousands came to know about Jesus and His love. God had placed a dream in her heart. Every time she boldly stepped out in faith, He supplied all her needs.

As I listened to Gladys's life story, I was reminded of my own. God also placed a dream in my heart when I was a young girl. He confirmed it when, at the age of fourteen, I read a book entitled *The Ministry of Healing*. My dream was to share Jesus' healing around the world. I dreamed of studying abroad and then traveling the world in service to Him. Like Gladys, I could not afford to study abroad. So I worked hard for nearly one year to be able to purchase my ticket. God provided me with a visa, the needed work, and even a green card without any cost. He also provided scholarships for my master's and doctoral programs. Ultimately, He made my dream come true. Today I travel the world, extending Jesus' healing ministry in many places.

What dream has God placed in your heart? He who gave you the dream of service to Him can also make it come true. Despite obstacles, step out boldly in faith and realize your dream!

Katia Garcia Reinert

January 18

Purify Me: By Beholding, We Become Changed

Let the words of my mouth, and the meditation of my heart,
be acceptable in thy sight,
O LORD, my strength, and my redeemer.
—*Psalm 19:14, KJV*

There's a song by one of my favorite gospel artists, Donnie McClurkin, entitled "Create in Me a Clean Heart." I resonate with its words. The lyrics of the song ask God to "purify" me so that I may worship Him. Lately, I've found myself asking God, "Purify me." But before I can finish my prayer, a few things pop into my mind that are contrary to my request. For example, I suddenly visualize scenes from some of my favorite television shows or pop-culture songs play in the movie theater of my mind. Then this thought follows: *How can I ask God to purify me when I'm watching these shows and listening to that music?*

I want to be clear that nothing I watch or listen to is X-rated, and most of it is not R-rated either. Most of it is rated PG-13; to me, that means that if an audience that is thirteen years old and older is allowed to watch that movie or listen to that song, then why can't I? After all, I am an adult; it's not like I'm taking in scandalous content. But lately, I've realized that just because society says content is safe for anyone thirteen and older to take in does not mean that I should consume it. Daphanie, one of my friends, often says, "The Bible says by beholding, you become changed!" She says it with conviction and does her best to live it out in her own life. She refuses to watch television shows, listen to music, or entertain company whose lifestyle, words, or actions are contrary to what the Bible teaches. Daphanie chooses God's Word over pop culture. She tries to live by God's standards, not society's. Most of all, she realizes that in order to lead a pure life she cannot behold what may change her from walking a path of purity in the eyes of her Maker.

I realize the Holy Spirit is convicting me to follow God's rules and live as He calls me to do. He whispers words of encouragement to turn away from even the slightest suggestion of impurity, whether it is from the influence of television, pop culture, or peers. I want to live a life that's acceptable in God's sight. By beholding Him, I will become changed for the better!

My question for you today is, What are you beholding? Is what you're taking in to your mind and lifestyle drawing you closer to your Creator God, or is it moving you further away from Him?

Alexis A. Goring

Before You Call

And it shall come to pass, that before they call, I will answer;
and while they are yet speaking, I will hear.
—Isaiah 65:24, KJV

The day before I took a six-hour trip, I jumped into my minivan. My mind was racing through the personal tasks I could complete that day. I inserted the key into the ignition and turned it. Silence. My heart sank as a million questions raced through my mind. *What could possibly be wrong?* It couldn't be my battery; that was only about one year old. My friend James is a tow truck driver who leaves for work at five o'clock in the morning. It was 7:45 A.M., so he would probably be far away from my home. I felt impressed to call him.

When James answered on the first ring and informed me that he was six miles away and would be there to help me in fifteen minutes, I was speechless. "Thank You, Father, for answering the prayer I didn't even have the time to formulate in my mind," I whispered.

After hooking up and activating the battery-charging gadget, James looked at me and remarked, "It's not your battery. Your starter is dead." *Oh no! How am I going to get to work? Where will I find someone to fix this before five o'clock tomorrow morning?*

James said, "Flo, go to an auto-parts store; get the correct starter for your van. I will come back this evening and install it for you. Here are the keys to my other car. Call a taxi to take you to my house, and use it for the day." I followed his instructions, he kept his promise, and I departed the next morning as planned.

Five mornings later my van would not start. When I shared my plight with a neighbor passing by with her dog, she said, "I have jumper cables. I'll be right back." In no time, she drove up, attached the cables, and my engine fired right up.

God answered me twice in five days *before* I called on Him. As I drove to work, He brought to my memory a quote from one of my previous morning devotional readings: "To every sincere prayer an answer will come. It may not come just as you desire, or at the time you look for it; but it will come in the way and at the time that will best meet your need. The prayers you offer in loneliness, in weariness, in trial, God answers, not always according to your expectations, but always for your good."*

Florence E. Callender

---

* Ellen G. White, *Gospel Workers* (Hagerstown, MD: Review and Herald®, 1999), 258.

Never Give Up

And my God will meet all your needs
according to the riches of his glory in Christ Jesus.
—Philippians 4:19, NIV

After an initial interview with a local organization, I had been invited to complete an application for a position as an assessor. First, I needed to get two references to support my application. The first one arrived without too much bother. Getting the second one, however, became a real problem. "Leave your name, message, and number, and I'll get back to you," played the answering machine every time I called. I decided to request a reference from another manager, but the staff declined to give me the direct contact details. "She will respond."

I had already begun my training at the bureau. Every week my training supervisor reminded me, "I need a second reference urgently. You cannot observe client sessions otherwise." Nevertheless, the bureau manager permitted me to observe client sessions. Afterward, my training supervisor disapproved, saying they were unofficial observations.

Almost a month had passed since my initial interview and still my second referral had not responded. I went in person only to be told she would be in the following Tuesday.

"Thank You, Jesus!" I beamed as I walked out. I'd soon have my reference.

Two weeks later I went to the training expectantly but with no second reference. "God, is this a closed door?" I prayed. That Sunday tears ran down my cheeks as I vented my frustration. "We serve a risen Savior," my mum consoled me. Later a friend prayed with me and suggested I think about what to do. *I'm not doing anything more*, I thought.

When my training day came around again on Wednesday, my second reference had arrived! I was able to use all of my previous client observations (including those that had been discounted) when answering questions in my learning journal. I realized then that I would have struggled to write adequate answers with only my "official" observations.

This experience showed me the power of prayer and persistence when there are obstacles. Although obstacles can be frustrating, God sees what lies further ahead.

Trust in the Lord with all your heart
    and lean not on your own understanding;
in all your ways submit to him,
    and he will make your paths straight (Proverbs 3:5, 6, NIV).

Sonya Simms

The Gift of Choice

"Do not fear, for I am with you . . .
I am your God. I will strengthen you."
—Isaiah 41:10, NIV

During much of my early life, I lived with Grandma Essie Mae. When she passed, this season of loss gave birth to feelings of insecurity and the ache of abandonment. When I was nine years old, I went to live with my parents, who sent me to an elementary school a few blocks away.

The adjustment was hard and made even more difficult by Carl, the schoolyard bully. Every day during recess he would taunt me in front of the other kids and threaten that he was "going to get" me after school. I didn't know what "get" meant, but I could tell from some of the other children, who now distanced themselves from me, that it wasn't about fun and games.

True to his word, Carl would be waiting for me after school. I would start running, and he would start chasing me—for blocks on end. No grown-up, including my own mother, ever questioned me about why I was out of breath or why my hair was wind-blown.

Then one day, much to my surprise, I made a choice. As the three-fifteen bell rang, indicating that school was over for another day, I decided—somewhere between my homeroom and the exit door—that I was not going to run any more. Yes, Carl was waiting for me with his taunt, "I'm going to get you; you better run!" Although he always frightened me, on *this* day of days, I also chose not to let fear rule *over* me. I turned to face him, and with my hands over my eyes, I announced to him, "I am not going to run anymore." I waited and waited for him to start beating me up. Instead, he announced, "OK," and walked away. I didn't know whether he was telling the truth, and I wouldn't know until I took my first step toward home, walking instead of running.

The choice to speak up—and out—for myself that day was a good one, for the fear and running stopped as quickly as they had begun. I wish I could say that fear has been arrested as easily in my adult life and that trepidation was not the motivating factor for many ill-fated choices that I have taken. Yet that day I learned when I do make the good choice to look fear in the face and say, "I'm not running anymore," fear has turned and walked away with a weak "OK."

I am determined in this season of my life not to take the gift of choosing for granted. Bless God for the opportunities to see and accept the lessons that only choice can offer!

Gail Masondo

Sacred Stories

"For God so loved the world that He gave His only begotten Son,
that whoever believes in Him
should not perish but have everlasting life."
—John 3:16, NKJV

There is something sacred about our stories.

"Tell me a story." I sit next to my friend Rita, who is a hospice patient. On the surface, her story is about a car accident that left her paralyzed with a traumatic brain injury, grand mal seizures, and aneurysms. Three weeks after brain surgery, she hears that "nothing more can be done." At home, fragile, she tells me it is "the best thing that has happened to me" because now she spends her days digging through memories, praying, and being immersed in God's grace every day. "Tell me a story," she asks again in a soft voice. "A nice memory." I tell her about my aunt who fed birds and cared for plants and flowers. When Rita asks me to describe the scent of the flowers, I fumble through human words to describe the beauty of God's creation. Tears run down her face. "Now tell me *the* story," she says. "I have seen you pray at work. Tell me the story of how you got *there*."

Surprised, I realize *that* story has never been asked of me. Those who read my writing have scraps of experiences that may one day fit together in a beautiful form. Rita wants to know how all those pieces *came to be*. I tell her of a hardbound children's Bible I owned, filled with the most beautiful pictures of Jesus. The front cover showed Jesus smiling, holding a sheep in His arms. One day, understanding I was that sheep, I prayed He would be a part of my life.

"I cannot remember when I prayed that," she whispers. "I did. *I need to remember*."

It is her story, not mine, that she seeks. When death feels so near, she is asking for a memory of her faith. I see an old, dog-eared, leather Bible on her nightstand with recent writings in the margins of John's Gospel. I read, paraphrasing the notes she has made. She remembers and speaks of it all. A few hours later, as the home nurse arrives for the night shift, I pray with Rita, hold her hand, and promise to visit the next day. The next morning, during a faculty meeting, I learn that during the night Rita passed peacefully in her sleep. Amid tears I remember our last conversation: the story of how Rita met Jesus.

Thank You, heavenly Father, for the strength to share sacred stories with one another, an opportunity to edit our path with Your grace. Your presence gives us strength to serve You.

Dixil L. Rodríguez

Lighthouse

The LORD is my light and my salvation; whom shall I fear?
—Psalm 27:1, KJV

Penetrating the darkest night, the beam of a lighthouse standing on some high, isolated, and rocky coastline casts its light across the sea. It warns of perils from rugged unseen rocks that cause shipwrecks and the loss of life. The responsibility of a lighthouse keeper would be great, for he must maintain constant light to warn ships passing in the area.

The rhythmic movement of the light, as it rotates from the lighthouse, draws attention and offers reassurance to those on the sea. Both ship navigator and lighthouse keeper must be vigilant in their roles, for they share the common responsibility of protecting life.

Technology has changed the way lighthouses are operated in this age. Maritime navigation aids and newer solar-powered, automated lights have replaced quite a few of the older lighthouses. Most lighthouses now belong to various state parks or to caretakers who make weather reports and maintain the property. There are no longer any manned lighthouses in Australia; the last one to become unmanned was in Tasmania in 1995. As we pause and think of a lighthouse keeper reaching out to the endangered by his faithful keeping of the light, it's sad to see these once upstanding buildings of importance left to decay or be demolished by vandals.

Likewise, our spiritual lives need to have the light that the Savior offers to guide and save from the perils of sin and destruction. He is our constant Light Bearer in the earthly trials we must bear. In John 8:12, Jesus said, "I am the light of the world: he that followeth me shall not walk in darkness, but shall have the light of life" (KJV).

Lines from an old hymn say,

> Unknown waves before me roll,
> Hiding rock and treach'rous shoal;
> Chart and compass come from thee.
> Jesus, Savior, pilot me.*

May it be said of us, "Ye are the light of the world" (Matthew 5:14, KJV). God can use a smile, a touch, or a word to lighten another person's day. Prayer can save lives. When gazing up at the lofty stature of a lighthouse standing tall and majestic, it is not hard to associate it with the spiritual light Jesus can shed upon His people who are seeking a Savior.

Lyn Welk-Sandy

---

* Edward Hopper, "Jesus, Savior, Pilot Me," 1871.

Lots for Nothing

"For he wounds, but he also binds up;
he injures, but his hands also heal."
—*Job 5:18, NIV*

I was walking to a supermarket; and as I was crossing the road, I fell flat on my face and broke my two teeth with crowns. When I got home and looked into the mirror, I realized that I would be deformed forever. I was very sad, but all I said was, "God understands, and He knows what He is doing." I cleaned and dressed my wounds and left them to heal.

Two weeks later I visited my oncologist, and she referred me to a dentist. I did not go to see the dentist because I had no insurance. A month later I met a Christian dentist I knew. He encouraged me to go see the dentist because, with my charity care insurance, I might be able to get my crowned teeth fixed. My husband and I prayed about my seeing the dentist. Then, with faith, I went to see her.

After the dentist took x-rays and did a thorough checkup, she told me that she would give me new crowns and also clean, polish, and rebuild all the worn-out teeth, bit by bit. I could not believe my ears. So I said, "Come again, please, Doctor!" She repeated what she had told me.

"But I need to remind you that all I have is charity care insurance."

With a smile, she said, "I will fix all your teeth up for you."

"Just like that? For free?" I asked in amazement.

"Yes!" she replied. During the next six visits, she patiently fixed and polished all my teeth. I could not believe what God had done for me!

This turn of events reminded me of a Bible verse that says, "Weeping may stay for the night, but rejoicing comes in the morning" (Psalm 30:5, NIV). I had been so disturbed after my fall that I had found it difficult to go out, especially to church. Yet friends and family had consoled me, and God had healed the situation with joy. As Job 5:18 indicates, God saw me fall and become wounded. Then He led me to a kind dentist who fixed me up.

Sometimes horrible accidents come our way, and we ask, Where was God when this happened? If our faith is faint, we lose it all and give up our trust and love for God. But if we believe God's promise that He has plans for us (see Jeremiah 29:11), then we will hold on to the hand of our able and loving Father, who knows the end from the beginning.

Mabel Kwei

To Speak or Not to Speak

"For it will not be you speaking, but the Spirit of your Father
speaking through you."
—Matthew 10:20, NIV

We all have people in our lives we have been concerned about at times. They may be going through difficult times. Maybe we are concerned about a child away at school and the choices he or she is making. At other times, we pray for a heart change in someone so that he or she will long to know Jesus. Whatever our concerns for others, many of them cannot be dealt with face-to-face. After all, we might say the wrong thing, blow it, or push people the opposite way from where God would have them go. At least, these are some of the fears we entertain. So how *can* we reach these individuals?

Some time ago God gave me this thought: *You may not be able to reach them, but I can. My Holy Spirit can speak the words you cannot say. And they can't turn Me off as easily as they may dismiss your words.* Wow, how true! If we ask God to speak to individuals we care about, He will. We give God permission to save them, whatever the cost. After all, He loves them even more than we do.

Another thought that brings me comfort is that God has His eyes on the people for whom I am praying—always. His eyes are on me, too, so in a spiritual sense, He keeps me close to the ones for whom I pray. What peace I experience knowing God is watching over my loved ones!

Sin was never part of God's plan for us. When it entered the Garden of Eden, our world fell. Yet God had another plan that would restore us. Jesus would come, live the life we couldn't, face the temptations that so easily beset us, and place His robe of righteousness over us. This plan is for everyone who will accept that gift. It seems so easy: just choose. This is the choice we want our loved ones to make because "God hath from the beginning chosen [them] to salvation through sanctification of the Spirit and belief of the truth" (2 Thessalonians 2:13, KJV). There are times when we feel impressed to speak; at those times, God's Spirit will give us the words.

We should always pray for spiritual discernment to know when to allow the Holy Spirit to speak through us—and when to keep silent and let the Spirit do all the talking. And when we do speak, let our words be "full of grace" as though "seasoned with salt" (Colossians 4:6, NIV).

Sue Anderson

Gone

Precious in the sight of the LORD is the death of his faithful servants.
—*Psalm 116:15, NIV*

She is gone—forever gone. She still lives next door, but my 101-year-old mother-in-law does not converse meaningfully and doesn't know who I am. She is gone. My journey with her began forty-two years ago on a warm Michigan evening when I ate generous portions of strawberry shortcake in her humble city home permeated with familial love. She was kind, quiet, loving, and an amazing cook! Thirteen months later I was blessed to become her daughter-in-law. I soon learned that my mother-in-law's life was defined by blessing. Her heart loved, her ears heard, her arms hugged, and her hands cooked for family, friends, church, and neighbors.

Having tragically lost her loving helpmate and best friend some years prior, at the age of eighty-seven, she left her home of fifty-six years to become our neighbor. She and I borrowed eggs, shared lunches, enjoyed shopping sprees, and helped each other as needed—like good neighbors do. My husband, Ken, and I enjoyed being the benefactors of her cooking! It was a good stage, but life's stages don't last. My husband had the painful task of removing her car keys. She often needed help opening a jar; ingredients in old, familiar recipes got mixed up; potatoes burned; a Life Alert band was necessary. What? My pristine mother-in-law was skipping baths, spending all day in her robe, and making meals of pretzels, chips, or candy as she sat in her recliner.

The next painful process involved phone calls, research, paperwork, and communication with siblings regarding "programs"—programs such as Meals on Wheels, help with house cleaning, and a monitor between her apartment and our house. When she became confused at night, Ken would journey to her bedside to listen and tenderly calm her fears. Another stage arrived, with interviews, more phone calls, and more research. Then my much-loved, ninety-five-year-old mother-in-law had daily caregivers. Her independence was gone, and we ached. As her cognition slips more with each passing day, my heart grieves the enormous loss—the hideous reality of life. She is gone, and as stated in a verse of a song written by one of her caregivers, "She has returned to her childhood." This precious person who raised my husband and his four older siblings of godly character now calls for her mama. Each call deepens my desire for Jesus' soon return—she is not gone forever. "Behold, I make all things new" (Revelation 21:5, KJV).

Sandy Colburn

Plugged In

In everything you do, put God first,
and he will direct you and crown your efforts with success.
—Proverbs 3:6, TLB

We live in an age where we have so much access to technology. Our cell phones keep us connected to our friends, family, businesses, banks, music, calendars, calculators, games, maps, the Internet—oh, and they take wonderful photos! And that is just with our phones.

Our iPads and tablets do all of the above *plus* get email, store books to read or research, let us video chat with friends and family, take notes in a journal section, find one's iPhone, access Dropbox for photos, and store Bibles in a number of various translations. We also have iPods for downloading music so that we can listen to the musical selections we like. It seems as if there is some type of computerized device for almost every aspect of life. Not only can we take laptop computers with us wherever we go, but we can find other devices in our offices and at home.

Yet what happens if we forget to plug in our gadgets to recharge them? If the batteries have run down, we have no connection to anything, which usually leads to frustration!

It is easy to fill our lives with all these devices and not have much time for anything else. Sometimes our families are put "on hold," so to speak. God or our friends are put on a back burner that we'll get to—later. It is possible to wake up one day and realize that we are all alone, with no close relationships any more since we have been too plugged in to devices.

Jesus wants us to "plug in" to Him every day. He asks us to abide in Him, to be connected. Through Bible study, prayer time, and reading spiritual books, we can be recharged to face life head on. Christ has all the resources we can tap into. He has all the information we need for real life—for eternal life! We are His children, and He is willing to guide us as our heavenly Parent. Let us lift our voices in praise every day because we are told we are never closer to God than when we are praising Him. "Connection with God is connection with all true wisdom."*

Lord, You are the Life-Giver and our Sustainer. Today may we walk closer to You, who knows best how to guide our lives. You have all the wisdom, knowledge, and discernment needed to make wise decisions. Help us trust You explicitly with every aspect of our lives. Amen.

Louise Driver

---

* Ellen G. White, *That I May Know Him* (Hagerstown, MD: Review and Herald®, 2003), 135.

To Be Continued

Answer me when I call to you, my righteous God.
Give me relief from my distress;
have mercy on me and hear my prayer.
—*Psalm 4:1, NIV*

Sometimes we don't understand why tragedies happen. People may say it's for the best or maybe it was bad karma. Alex, a speaker for my school's Week of Prayer, gave me a new perspective on God's answers to prayer. He had a friend who had found the perfect woman to marry, and she believed that she'd found "the one" as well. Sometime later Alex received a call from his friend and found that his friend's soon-to-be wife had cancer. He needed Alex's support, so Alex flew to Tennessee to see the couple.

They had their closest friends constantly praying for her, hoping that she'd make it. They assumed that she would, that God would answer with a yes. But He did not. She passed away before they could get married. I was wondering where Alex was going with this story. Alex said that God doesn't always answer yes, but he believes that God wasn't answering no either. People will usually believe that God answers yes or no. Alex stated, though, that there was a "to be continued" in God's answers as well. He didn't believe God would just end it there, and I don't believe He would either.

When I was a little girl, I was abused by my father. I watched him abuse my mother and sisters as well. Hatred for him grew in my heart, and I didn't understand why God didn't take me out of that situation. Since then, I have learned a lot and realized that God didn't choose to put me in that situation, but He made sure to turn that event into a tool for me. God answered my prayers by "continuing" this event into something positive for me later on.

We should not give up on God when we feel times are rough. God will never give up on His plan for you or His purpose for your life. Whatever struggle you might be going through, don't see it as the end. See it as a "to be continued" part of your life. Give it to God, and trust Him. I've had to learn that every time I look back at the situation with my father, I must let God in and give Him the pain. He gave His Son to die on the cross to give us another opportunity. Ladies, know that your struggle isn't the end; there's more to it! God has something amazing planned—you just wait. "Be joyful in hope, patient in affliction, faithful in prayer" (Romans 12:12, NIV).

Ruth Garcia

Are You Ready for Jesus to Come?

"So you must also be ready, because the Son of Man will come at an hour when you do not expect him."
—Matthew 24:44, NIV

Susan (not her real name) prepared for two years to go on a trip to celebrate her friend's fortieth birthday. She asked me to babysit her children. On Wednesday night, she packed her suitcase with all the necessities for five days and then decided to check in online for her flight. She was traveling outside the United States, so her passport was necessary to check in. I heard a gasp. The passport had expired two years earlier! A contact in the State Department informed her she could pursue a passport in Atlanta, Georgia, the next morning. But Susan needed to be at her destination on Thursday night, so traveling to Atlanta on Thursday would be futile. How sad she was when she realized she could not travel to either place.

For many, the coming of Christ will be like the experience of Susan. Christ told a parable about ten virgins awaiting the coming of a bridegroom (Matthew 25). All ten girls had prepared for the bridegroom, but five of them found they were lacking oil for their lamps.

Ellen G. White writes, "The two classes of watchers represent the two classes who profess to be waiting for their Lord. They are called virgins because they profess a pure faith. By the lamps is represented the word of God. The psalmist says, 'Thy word is a lamp unto my feet, and a light unto my path.' Psalm 119:105."*

As in the parable, so it is now. A time of waiting intervenes, and faith is tried. When the cry is heard, "Behold, the bridegroom cometh; go ye out to meet him," many are unprepared (Matthew 25:6, KJV). Without a valid passport, preparation is of no avail. Without the Spirit of God, knowledge of His Word is of no avail. One may be familiar with the Bible; but unless the Spirit of God sends the truth home, the character will not be transformed.

May God help us to discern the times in which we live. The Holy Spirit is always ready to aid us. Let us be ready to meet Jesus.

Eveythe Kennedy Cargill

---

* Ellen G. White, *Christ's Object Lessons* (Hagerstown, MD: Review and Herald®, 2003), 406, 407.

The Cupbearer

"Father," he said, "if you will, take this cup of suffering away from
me. Not my will, however, but your will be done."
—Luke 22:42, GNT

Many glorious sunrises and sunsets have come and gone, but for eight years I observed Eddie (not his real name) doing the same thing: walking up and down the road carrying his cup.

Eddie was of light complexion and slim build. He was apparently suffering from some mental disorder as he, muttering or laughing to himself, would walk in a sprightly way down the road from his house to a shop. Occasionally, you might see him sipping from his cup or see it stuffed in his back pocket. This cup seemed to be a symbol of Eddie's joy and comfort in the midst of his friendlessness, pain, sorrow, and loneliness.

In Bible times, a cupbearer was an officer who bore great responsibility in his honorable and powerful position. He served wine to his master and tasted it for quality or poison. We read of a number of cupbearers: the jailed wine steward who had offended his master and was later released (Genesis 40); Nehemiah, the humble wine steward of King Artaxerxes and the chief restorer of the wall of Jerusalem (Nehemiah 1:11); and Jesus Himself (Luke 22:39–45). As the weight of this world's sin bore down on Him, Jesus prayed, "Father, if you will, please don't make me suffer by having me drink from this cup. But do what you want, and not what I want" (Luke 22:42, CEV). This cup was symbolic of the suffering He would bear for the sins of the whole world.

Before His crucifixion, we meet Him with His disciples at Passover in the upper room in Jerusalem. There He took a cup, gave thanks, and said, "Drink it, all of you" . . . ; "this is my blood, which seals God's covenant. . . . I tell you, I will never again drink this wine until the day I drink the new wine with you in my Father's Kingdom" (Matthew 26:27–29, GNT).

Remember that, like Nehemiah, we, too, can become a great cupbearer, not just for an earthly monarch but for the Supreme Ruler of the universe. We can also become restorers of broken lives by the way we serve others at home, at work, or in the community. We can give a cup of blessing by a prayer, a visit to the sick, or just by a cup of water, thus spreading the good news of salvation to a world dying in sin.

Won't you be God's cupbearer today?

Bula Rose Haughton Thompson

Are You Famous?

For the LORD seeth not as a man seeth; for man looketh on the
outward appearance, but the LORD looketh on the heart.
—*1 Samuel 16:7, KJV*

Every morning after devotions I turn on the radio to listen to a morning show on a very old yet popular radio station. The show's host fills me in on the weather and what is happening outside my door. It is fun to engage him with emails about some of the things he is talking about or just make comments for whatever reason.

One day he was talking about something, and I emailed him with my comments—one of which I related to him about his being famous. I got a comment back from him telling me he *wasn't* famous like I had suggested. We agreed to disagree.

The word *famous* implies you are known for some reason. Mostly it is because of something you have done or for your talent. It varies greatly from being *infamous*, which is something we probably should stay away from.

I got to thinking about being famous. When organizing my parents' fiftieth anniversary party at a hotel, where the reception was to be held, I worked with a very nice lady to plan the event. I said nothing about what religious faith I was. Yet during the planning, she asked whether I was a Christian! Being very surprised, I told her, "Yes, I am; why did you ask?" She told me she could always identify Christians in that we were the happiest and nicest people to work with and that all of our brides are the prettiest!

This happened in 1980. I am still deeply impressed by what she said to me that day. I was "famous" because I was a member of a group of people that treated others so nicely and who were kind and positive in their dealings with others. Wow, what a compliment!

I do not consider myself famous. I am sure there are those who think I am somewhat infamous. I do find myself at times thinking of what kind of character I project to others by the way I talk, act, or present myself to those around me. If I really do allow Jesus to come into my heart, do I treat others as He would? Am I kind and patient with those I deal with? Or do I gossip or tear others down with what I say? When someone else sees me, do they see Jesus' love shining out of my heart? I surely hope that is the "fame" I can show to the world.

Mary E. Dunkin

Know Whom You Are Following

Be ye therefore followers of God, as dear children;
and walk in love, as Christ also hath loved us,
and has given himself for us.
—*Ephesians 5:1, 2, KJV*

When I was growing up in California, my sister and I lived with my aunt and uncle near Fresno. Our folks worked about 150 miles away and came to visit us every other weekend. One weekend when they came, they brought a big surprise for my sister and me. It was a little terrier puppy. Scout, as we named him, was so cute! He was smart too! My sister, Priscilla, who was older than I, started to teach him tricks. He learned really fast. She taught him to sit up, beg, roll over, play dead, and, of course, fetch.

Priscilla spent a lot of time teaching him to "say prayers" with us. When we were kneeling by our bed at night, she had Scout sit by us, cross his paws and then put his head on his paws. He got very good at this and always ran to our side when we were getting ready to say our prayers every morning and night.

But my sister taught Scout one very bad habit. So what he did really wasn't the puppy's fault; he was just being led astray. My aunt was not happy about this trick at all. She would spank the puppy and get after him.

This is what was happening: My sister would find a hole in the ground and place a marble in the hole. Then she would tell the dog to fetch it. Oh, how the dirt did fly as Scout dug for that marble! The problem was that she was having the puppy do this in my aunt's flower garden. You can believe that my aunt wasn't happy with what was happening to her beautiful flowers. The puppy was following the wrong instructions.

I am glad that God has given us the freedom of choice. Sometimes, however, we let Satan lead us into making bad choices. That is the reason we need to stay close to Christ—so that He can guide us. We can make good choices when we follow Jesus Christ. We need our "power time" each day with Christ.

As my son, Pastor Terry, says, "No time—no power. Little time—little power. Much time—much power." This way we can stay close to the Lord and have Him guide us into making the right choices.

Anne Elaine Nelson

Rahab

Was not even Rahab the prostitute considered righteous
for what she did when she gave lodging to the spies
and sent them off in a different direction?
—*James 2:25, NIV*

You would think that nobody in our civilized world has to fear slavery anymore. Yet the United Nations estimates that about five hundred thousand women have been forced into prostitution in Europe. The business volume is estimated at fifteen billion euros in Germany alone. Girls are lured from eastern countries through the promise of good jobs and money. They end up in the hands of human traffickers who force them into prostitution, which is sometimes referred to as the oldest trade in the world.

In the Bible, we meet a woman who worked in this trade—Rahab of Jericho. We don't know how she landed in prostitution. But we do know that she had heard of the God of Israel and His care for His people, the children of Israel. After forty years of desert wandering, the Israelites were about to enter the Promised Land. So Joshua sent two spies to Jericho. Somebody saw them go into Rahab's house. In Joshua 2, we read that she hid these men under stalks of flax and refused to reveal their whereabouts to the king of Jericho when pressed to do so. She longed to belong to their God and give up her old life and start over with a clean slate. She hid the two spies in exchange for their promise to spare her family and herself when Israel attacked Jericho—and they were indeed spared. Rahab became a part of God's people and ended up married to someone in the lineage of David. Her name is in the genealogy of Jesus!

I have often wondered why Rahab is always identified as a prostitute though the Scriptures speak highly of her: "By faith the prostitute Rahab, because she welcomed the spies, was not killed" (Hebrews 11:31, NIV). She made it into the gallery of the heroes of faith.

Rahab experienced a total transformation of her life. God does not wait until we are perfect in order to use us. This is a story of hope for every woman. No matter what is in our past, we can turn around and live honorable and upright lives. Rahab's life story is intended to remind us that God really hurls all our iniquities into the depths of the sea (see Micah 7:19).

No matter where you are in your life or what people call you, there is only one step you should take. Put your faith in Christ Jesus, and your destiny will be changed.

Hannele Ottschofski

Mercy Needed!

He has not dealt with us according to our sins,
Nor punished us according to our iniquities.
—*Psalm 103:10, NKJV*

My levels of "righteous indignation" rose higher and higher. After all that I had done for this person—the sacrifices of my precious time when I really didn't have to, the hours and money spent, the efforts made to help—after all of that, this individual treated me very badly. And in public! Unheard of! Unacceptable! Punishable! I expressed very clearly to this individual my disappointment in the behavior I saw and how I felt about the gross ingratitude. I was justified in my response, of course. Of *course*!

How thankful I am that my faithful Friend, the Holy Spirit, did not leave me long to wallow in my state of unrighteousness indignation! Questions immediately came to my mind: *What did you read this morning? Which Bible passage have you been memorizing for the last few weeks?*

Quickly, I went over that passage in my mind:

> The LORD is merciful and gracious,
> Slow to anger, and abounding in mercy. . . .
> He has not dealt with us according to our sins,
> Nor punished us according to our iniquities.
> For as the heavens are high above the earth,
> So great is His mercy toward those who fear Him (Psalm 103:8, 10, 11, NKJV).

This beautiful picture of God moves me greatly, especially when I consider how dismally I fall short of this ideal. I ask Him to somehow enable me to extend His grace to those who are most needy of this precious gift.

And that day of expressed "righteous indignation" was my opportunity to extend grace to the aforementioned individual. At the very next opportunity when I saw the person, by the Lord's grace alone, I apologized for the way I had spoken. And the response was one that moved me yet again. The person expressed gratitude and relief in a way I had not unexpected. Again I was thankful for God's grace—which is always amazing! I continue to pray for more of it in my life.

Oh, dear Father God, please don't stop working with me. May I abound in the undeserved mercy that You extend to me daily—and offer it to all I meet. Amen.

Belinda Solomon

Our Empty House

Except the LORD build the house,
they labour in vain that build it.
—*Psalm 127:1, KJV*

Just one week after our wedding, my husband, a ministerial intern, was assigned to a new church district after having served for only one year in a previous district in Guyana.

I had also been employed by our denomination, but my husband's new assignment was far from my place of employment. Now, because of my husband's new placement—and location—I requested a one-year leave of absence from my job. But I was happy to be given a leave of absence because I was convinced that the only place for me to be was with my husband.

When we arrived at what would be our first home together following our honeymoon, we were happy. In fact, our family members had already moved our belongings into our home while we were away on the honeymoon. Yet we noticed something when we returned and entered our house. Even though our relatives had moved our belongings into the house, something appeared to be missing. As our eyes raced from one corner of our new home to the other, we couldn't help but notice that it was void of household furniture and household appliances. In other words, it looked empty.

We had just enough money in our savings to purchase a refrigerator and a gas stove. That still left the living room without furniture. As we began to settle into our new home and church district, we soon realized that our home was not empty after all. It was our marriage that had truly created our home. And it was filled with love, joy, peace, comfort, contentment, laughter, and, above all, the presence of God. As church members and family members visited us, we never felt ashamed about what we didn't have because we could still share what we did have. And our visitors always felt the warmth, love, and glory that radiated from our home.

Let's pause for a moment and take our minds away from the things we crave and desire; instead, let's look at the things God has furnished us with. He's given us the opportunity to love and be loved. He's given us peace and laughter. We could go on all day listing His blessings to us. My husband and I have learned a very invaluable lesson from our "empty" house.

What emptiness in your life do you have, and what lessons can you learn from it? I encourage you to invite God inside your life to help you build a true home.

Jenel A. N. Campbell McPherson

Pain

> Praise to God, the Father of our Lord Jesus Christ. God is our
> merciful Father and the source of all comfort. He comforts us in all
> our troubles so that we can comfort others. When they are troubled,
> we will be able to give them the same comfort God has given us.
> —*2 Corinthians 1:3, 4, NLT*

Pain has been my companion over the last six months. During this time, I learned to be more sensitive to people who live with pain 24/7. I learned that personal trials and suffering give us a new compassion for others who are in pain. When suffering, we are tempted to think we alone are experiencing severe trials. We may feel abandoned and isolated. Have you felt this way?

Listening to women's stories in many countries, I learn that pain is their companion. Many feel alone and rejected. Elijah, a familiar Bible character, also felt this way. After experiencing God's amazing display of power at Mount Carmel—but still knowing Jezebel sought his death—he ran. Elijah was experiencing intense pain (see 1 Kings 19:4).

The beauty of this story lies in how a compassionate God dealt with Elijah's pain and exhaustion. Notice how God neither answered his prayer nor condemned him for his plea. Instead, God provided rest and restoration. God had better days ahead for Elijah. And God has better days ahead for you as well. He is willing to give us new hope, new grace, and new mercies every morning.

Despite feeling isolated in times of pain and trial, we must keep God's perspective in mind, for with our hand in His, we can learn to find the blessings in our pain. Changing from our perspective to His will surprise us with beautiful insights. At one time or another, people who love and serve the Lord will suffer physical, emotional, or relational pain. Jesus said, "In this world you will have trouble" (John 16:33, NIV). But there is hope. He does not promise to save us *from* the pain, but He surely promises to save us *in* the pain.

> Let all that I am praise the LORD;
>   may I never forget the good things he does for me.
> He forgives all my sins
>   and heals all my diseases.
> He redeems me from death
>   and crowns me with love and tender mercies.
> He fills my life with good things.
>   My youth is renewed like the eagle's! (Psalm 103:1–5, NLT).

Raquel Queiroz da Costa Arrais

He Pushed Me!

For we wrestle not against flesh and blood, but against principalities,
against powers, against the rulers of the darkness of this world,
against spiritual wickedness in high places.
—Ephesians 6:12, KJV

For several weeks, I had been praying daily that Jesus would take the devil by the back of his collar and kick him down the stairs and out the door, telling him there was no place for him in my home—because Jesus was staying for the day. When I prayed this prayer, it seemed I was having freedom from overwhelming temptations. It actually felt easier to resist them.

Then came Friday, the day of preparation before the Sabbath. I had a number of things on my to-do list: cook, bake, and clean house. The night before, after cooking a potful of potatoes, I had left the potato bag on the floor beside the sink, intending to put it away "soon." About nine-thirty on Friday morning, as I was busy by the sink cutting something with scissors, I took a step sideways, and that bag of unused potatoes tripped me. I went flying across the kitchen, crashing into the garbage can and hitting my head on the doorjamb. Upset, I got up, blaming the potatoes for tripping me. I sat down to relax and get my bearings. Shortly thereafter, I went back to work in the kitchen again.

After lunch, I walked past the table to put a glass bowl into the china cabinet. Before I knew anything, I again felt myself flying toward the floor. When the dust settled, the bowl was still safe in my hand. I got up wondering what had happened. I went to check out the computer cord that was across where I had walked, thinking I had tripped on it. But it lay totally undisturbed, and the computer on the table had not been moved. Once again I sat down to get over the shock. While I sat there, God clearly showed me the answer. After two weeks of resisting Satan's attacks, he was undoubtedly getting revenge. That is not a lighthearted statement. He truly intended to hurt me and interfere with my Sabbath preparations.

Satan is determined to steal, kill, and destroy, but Jesus came to give us life and give it more abundantly (see John 10:10). So I praise God for angels that encamp round about us (see Psalm 34:7). Twice in one day I had something dangerous in my hand. Both times I fell toward a set of stairs, and both times I was able to get up on my own with no broken bones. Praise God!

Elizabeth Versteegh Odiyar

"I'll Be Back"

And if I go and prepare a place for you, I will come again, and receive you unto myself; that where I am, there ye may be also.
—John 14:3, KJV

Preparing for my husband's military departure in 2003 was the hardest thing I have ever had to do. Knowing that my soul mate and companion was going to the unknown was devastating. He would be leaving me and our children.

For the first time in my life, I would be totally alone.

My relatives lived miles away, and I could not have them come and stay with me. They had their own lives. I would have to do this alone. I did not mind spending a week away from my husband. I had done that before. But this was different. My husband was going to a place where he would have little to no contact with me. I worried about his safety and well-being.

We tried to get mentally prepared for his journey by constantly reassuring each other that we would see each other again. We took care of our bills in advance so that all I had to do was concentrate on the welfare of my children. My house seemed like a storehouse; it was full of food. We did this so that all I needed to do was to get necessities each week. We prayed every day, seeking God's counsel and guidance. We knew that God was the only one who could determine whether or not my husband would have to go.

The day finally arrived. As my husband boarded the bus, he whispered softly in my ear, "I'll be back—before you know it!"

Smiling, I kissed him goodbye. I was no longer worried. I had the hope that God would bring him back home, safe and sound.

When Christ was here on earth, He told His disciples that He was leaving to make a better place for them (see John 14:1–3). He promised that He was coming back to take them home. I believed my husband when he promised me that he would return. And if I can believe in my husband who is mortal, I can surely believe that our Savior is coming back again.

Jesus promised, "And if I go and prepare a place for you, I will come again, and receive you unto myself; that where I am, there ye may be also" (John 14:3, KJV).

I cannot wait to see my Lord in all His glory, coming back as He promised.

Diantha Hall-Smith

A Woman's Dilemma

After this, Jesus traveled about from one town and village to another, proclaiming the good news of the kingdom of God. The Twelve were with him, and also some women who had been cured of evil spirits and diseases: Mary (called Magdalene) from whom seven demons had come out; Joanna the wife of Chuza, the manager of Herod's household; Susanna; and many others. These women were helping to support them out of their own means.
—Luke 8:1–3, NIV

I boarded the bus after work and was happy to get a comfortable seat for the long ride home. Feeling tired and worn after a long day's work, I willed myself not to sleep. The bus pulled away from the terminus slowly and was just rounding a corner when I saw her, curled up near a fast-food entrance and probably asleep. A quick glance revealed the woman was young and decently clad but with recent street dirt on her clothing. Maybe she had not been long on the street. My heart grieved. In my spirit, I cried, *Lord, have mercy! Have mercy, Jesus, have mercy!*

What could have caused a young woman to fall into such a state? I wondered, *Was it drugs, a neglected mental illness, or problems in the home that became overwhelming? Was she never introduced to our loving Lord and Savior, Jesus Christ?*

I have no answer for these questions and more than likely never will. Yet I find solace in the Word of God and direct my mind back to the ministry of Jesus Christ when He met Mary of Magdala, commonly known as Mary Magdalene. She suffered much abuse and rejection, but she became a changed woman when she met Jesus.

What makes things different for women of today? We, too, have been rejected, abused, hurt, and scorned. We, too, have suffered much pain. Yet like Mary Magdalene, we have found Christ Jesus, who touched our lives, drew us into His loving care, and taught us the dignity of womanhood and how to grow in a relationship with Him.

Many dangers can befall that young woman lying on the street, but I lift my faith on her behalf, knowing that the hand of God is mighty to save and deliver. Our caring Savior can send His holy angels to protect and guide her to full redemption.

I pray that each of us will direct our thoughts and prayers toward one woman we know who is in need of the mighty hand of God at work in her life.

Elizabeth Ida Cain

God Has a Sense of Humor

For the despondent, every day brings trouble;
for the happy heart, life is a continual feast.
—*Proverbs 15:15, NLT*

Someone once said that it is hard to imagine a wonderful storyteller who doesn't know the value of humor. Jesus was a fantastic storyteller, and it is easy to see the humor in His stories and parables. I also see evidence of His humor in my own life—even practical jokes.

My mom and I share a strange sense of humor; we always find something to laugh about, even when others do not. One memorable experience with Mom occurred when I was young. Our church was holding an evangelistic series; and each evening after the meeting, our family was responsible for cleaning the church in preparation for the following meeting.

One particular night during the series, Mom and I went alone. The late night darkness in the hallway of the pastors' offices ignited our active imaginations, kicking them into full gear.

"Don't worry, Mom," I said with great bravado. "My sixth-grade gym teacher is teaching us karate, and I know exactly what to do if we are attacked. Let me show you how to kick."

Mom rolled her eyes at me, but she didn't prevent me from showing my new skill.

Thinking we were the only ones in the church, I ran down the hall at full speed and jumped as high as I could in front of the last office door while shrieking, "Kiai!"

At that very moment, the associate pastor opened his office door, and I nearly karate kicked him in the abdomen. He stared at me for an anxious second and immediately shut the door. We don't know who was more traumatized when we came face-to-face. Mom and I had no idea what was going on in his head. Was he stunned that he was nearly karate kicked as he attempted to leave the office? Did my acting crazy and yelling in the church upset him? Even with the risk that he would quickly recover from his shock and open the door to scold me, Mom and I exploded with laughter the moment our eyes met. We are certain God anticipated the scene and laughed hysterically with us that scary night in His sacred house.

Later when my own daze from nearly smashing into the pastor wore off, I discovered he was not upset. His sense of humor was tickled that night, and now we both tell a funny story.

We celebrate humor because, after all, we are made in the image of God.

Cathy Payne

In the Pit of Depression

Why art thou cast down, O my soul? and why art thou disquieted within me? hope thou in God: for I shall yet praise him, who is the health of my countenance, and my God.
—*Psalm 42:11, KJV*

In September 2015, I had just gone through a disappointment in regard to a relationship that didn't develop as I had hoped it would. I was in the United States, volunteering at a lifestyle center. Enjoying my medical missionary work, I had wanted to work there another year—and my help was really needed. A win-win situation! Unfortunately, I was feeling the dark cloud of depression pulling me down. I tried to fight it or ignore it. But as time passed, I sank more deeply into this spiral of distorted thoughts and perceptions: *I will never get married. Who would want a woman like me? The other missionaries here are all better than I am. What about my future? How will I be able to handle going back to work in Brussels next year?* I realize that I had almost every symptom of major depression except that I still wanted to live.

I couldn't talk with anybody on campus. After all, I was among those privileged volunteers in that institution who worked on the front lines, helping *others* with physical, emotional, and spiritual problems. During that time, I was somehow able to help the lifestyle-center guests through their challenges without their becoming aware of my condition.

Then my paternal grandmother passed away; I had to travel to Germany. This was the last thing I needed! Returning to the lifestyle center, I decided to just hang in there until I'd fulfilled my time commitment. One day in February, while walking through the hallways, I bumped into the chaplain of the institute. "Would you share your personal testimony next Friday evening?" he asked. I hemmed and hawed before bursting into tears. He asked me into his office, prayed, and shared Psalm 42:11 with me. From that time on, things went up for me.

Today I consider myself one of the happiest, luckiest women on this globe. Though I'm still unmarried, the Lord is my Maker and my Husband. Though I'm still not a perfect medical missionary, I know that God doesn't call the qualified—but He qualifies the called. Though I still don't know exactly what my professional future holds, I know who holds the future!

The Lord helped me out of the deepest pit of depression I had ever been in. I'm sure He can do the same for you if you trust Him!

Daniela Weichhold

The Flock

My beloved friends, let us continue to love each other since
love comes from God. Everyone who loves is born of God and
experiences a relationship with God.
—*1 John 4:7*, The Message

The church parking lot was full of Canada geese. A few were still on the school playground; some had moved across the parking lot onto grassy yards. As I watched, they gradually drifted up the church driveway onto the grass behind the church. They honked periodically. Some chased others. I thought how much like some people these geese were. Some folks like to gather around a church but never enter it. Others enter and join a church group but never participate in the activities or support the church. Little do they know how much they are missing.

Statistics show that 50 percent of church members regularly attend church. About 10 percent actively participate in church. That's a very sad statistic. What are the 90 percent missing out on? They only have peripheral vision. They are seeing only the surface of what really is happening in the church. They don't interact with groups and may be quick to criticize leaders and nitpick over mistakes and actions. They haven't put down roots to stabilize them in the trials that come their way. They can be blown away like chaff in the wind.

Church is (or should be) like family. Sometimes there are troubles in families; but with God's help, we work through the problems. We don't throw away a marriage or a family just because they have been damaged. The ideal is to work things out.

Sadly, in some churches, there are members who seem to be actively participating in tearing apart the church or other people in it. Situations like this can be discouraging to other members who may choose to attend church elsewhere as a result. Jesus talked a lot about the importance of congregations—His flocks—being safe and loving places, the kind that attract the hurting and wounded. Paul and John echoed Christ's sentiment in their letters to the church.

Helping each other—lifting each other up—brings healing to the wounded and strength to the body of Christ, which we need in order to be able to accomplish God's work for the church in the last days. Mutual support also brings encouragement to pastors who spend countless hours trying to lift members above the pits of despair into which people so easily fall when they lose hope.

May we all be encouraged in our everyday life and in our church family.

Peggy Curtice Harris

He Hears

Don't worry about anything; instead, pray about everything.
Tell God what you need, and thank him for all he has done.
—*Philippians 4:6, NLT*

When our daughter Helen went for her driver's license test, a friend of hers had to take her to Glen Burnie, Maryland. When they got there, the licensed driver realized she had forgotten her wallet and did not have identification to prove residency on her that the examiners needed.

It is our practice that when our children are about to do anything, whether big or small, we pray for them. So I called my husband, we prayed, and then I went to a seminar I was attending that day, trusting our God to do the rest.

As Helen was contemplating what to do next, a gentleman approached her and asked where she was from. He told her he was from Ghana. So when Helen spoke a few words in a Ghanaian dialect she had learned from a friend, the man began to converse with her. He asked whether she was there for the driving test. When our anxious daughter told him about her dilemma, this unknown gentleman graciously offered to help, and she got her license that day. When Helen thanked him, he just praised God for putting him in the right place. An answered prayer!

When another daughter, Maggie, was teaching English at a Christian university in Mexico, she had to come back to the United States for an interview. On her return trip to Mexico, she missed her flight and had to catch a later one. We were worried about the unrest going on in the country at the time, and the school was far from town. On our knees, we asked the Lord to find a way for her. Then we encouraged her to just go to a hotel near the airport for the night. Our brave, adventurous girl got to Mexico. She asked a police officer how to get to the campus. Maggie took the bus he suggested and arrived at the main bus stop in the city. The stop was at an open market with lots of people. She became confused. Then, from nowhere, God sent a kind gentleman who asked her where she needed to go. She told him. He got her bag, asked her to follow him, and got the ticket for her when she gave him the fare. He loaded her luggage and told her where to disembark near the campus. Another answered prayer!

Today God is waiting to hear and answer our prayers. He says to us, "Do not worry about anything, but pray about everything" (see Philippians 4:6)!

Judith M. Mwansa

February 13

The Guitar

"And remember the words of the Lord Jesus, that He said,
'It is more blessed to give than to receive.' "
—*Acts 20:35, NKJV*

During February of 2017, a longtime friend of my guitar teacher lost his cabin to a fire. Tragically, he also lost his fiancée, who had been unable to make it out of the burning cabin in time. Immediately, my guitar teacher not only became the interim keeper of this friend's dog but also organized a fund-raising benefit for him, as well as for a nearby couple whose home had also burned down on the same road on the same day. My teacher organized bands to come and play at the fund-raiser, a silent auction, and, of course, food. The event was a roaring success!

The biggest event of the evening, however, was a raffle for a really nice Fender acoustic-electric guitar that was worth four hundred dollars. Since I had already planned to donate for the cause of the fire survivors, I decided to put my donation money into raffle tickets.

I had to leave before the drawing, but, oh, how I wanted that guitar!

Later that evening my guitar teacher sent me a text: "You won the raffle!" I was the new owner of something whose value and beauty seemed almost too good to be true! Then to my chagrin, I found out that the band members had all bought tickets and put my teacher's name on them, hoping she would win the guitar. In fact, she had been planning to purchase one on a layaway plan since her own guitar—part of her livelihood—was falling apart. Before long, I *knew* what I needed to do.

The next day I sent my teacher a text: "Though I'm really excited about winning something I wanted so badly, I know how much time, energy, and personal money you spent to make the benefit a success. So . . . I am offering that Fender guitar to you." Her emotional, heartfelt thank-you message included these treasured words: "Love you like a sister."

This story isn't so much about what I did. Rather, it's about the power of God to change a person's heart. Not so long ago, I would have kept that guitar—and missed out on an opportunity to give back to someone whose *need* was greater than my *want*.

Why not experience the blessing of giving something you value to someone else in need?

Sonia Brock

"I Want to Get Close to You"

And let them make me a sanctuary,
that I may dwell among them.
—Exodus 25:8, KJV

Love is something that everybody would like to have in his or her life. And when we experience love, we always want to be in the company of the one who loves us. I want to introduce you to Someone. His name is King Loving.

In Exodus 25:8, He—God—explains His passionate desire as He tells His people that He wants to be close to them. His presence in the sanctuary in the Sinai desert was a reminder that the God who had delivered them from Pharaoh's wicked hand in Egypt was still with them. He was there to protect them from anyone who wanted to harm them. The sanctuary was also to remind them that God had come close in order to save them from their own sinful actions.

God conducted Israel to the desert to be cleansed, purified, and refined. He wanted them to become beautiful in character because of their relationship with Him. That's why He asked them to build a sacred place for Him to dwell among them out there in the desert. At the sanctuary, the people could worship and pray to Him. With the sanctuary came a system of sacred rituals and worship ceremonies so that the people could understand their need of God, be purified, and then represent His beauty to the surrounding nations and the universe. The sanctuary would especially remind the children of Israel of their need for cleansing from sin because King Loving, in whose presence they would be, is a holy God.

God wanted to be in the presence of His beloved. He said to Israel, "In the same time that I am cleansing you, I want to be with you. I want you to be with Me because I love you." When God said that He wanted to dwell with His people, it meant that He wanted to stay continually in their midst and spend time with them.

As with Israel of old, God still wants to be with His people. One day soon He will set up His own sanctuary, His throne, on the earth made new and dwell with all the redeemed. He wants us to be there with Him.

But before we can dwell in the earth made new, we have to invite the King of love to dwell in our hearts. He wants to dwell there permanently. Through the sanctuary, God says to us, "I want to get close to you."

Fabienne Maslet

Open My Eyes

"Now the hand of the Lord is against you. You are going to be blind
for a time, not even able to see the light of the sun."
Immediately mist and darkness came over him, and he groped
about, seeking someone to lead him by the hand.
—*Acts 13:11, NIV*

Have you ever stopped to think about what part of your body you consider the most important? Which one would you miss most if you lost it? Arms? Legs? Hands?

I once began to imagine how my life would be if, for some reason, I lost one of my limbs and with which loss I would suffer the most. I analyzed this and concluded that I would suffer a lot if I lost my vision.

According to some doctors, the eye is an "imperial" or "sovereign" organ of the human body. I believe that this is true. Many benefits come from the gift of sight. I will cite only a few: perception of light, shapes, and color as well as the perception of motion or direction. Through vision, we move away from danger, recognize our friends, enjoy the natural beauties of this world, and recognize love that is portrayed in smiles and looks.

Our eyes are also important because they have their own "language." Through the expression in the eyes, it is possible to identify how others are feeling. If we are concerned, our eyes often gaze intently. When we are sad, they are tearful. If we are frightened or scared, our eyes are wide open and appear agitated. When we are happy, they are brighter. And when we are in love, they are fixed on the loved one in view.

But there is a very important mission for our eyes: to really see our brothers and sisters and their pain and needs. Beyond seeing, we must act. The apostle John tells us that if we claim to live in the love of God, we must live as He lived (1 John 2:5, 6). Jesus saw the needs of the people around Him, so He sought to quench their thirst and heal their pain, even performing miracles. The church should be the most pleasant place in the world—a place where people feel seen, loved, respected, and valued. This is what the Lord expects from us. The church must be where there is the greatest manifestation of His love.

And that is our mission: seeing each other and sharing, in godly actions, the wonderful love that has reached down to touch us. This love is Jesus Christ!

Be willing to be used by the Lord in the revelation of His love to others.

Carmem Virgínia dos Santos Paulo

Meekly Wait and Murmur Not

But they that wait upon the LORD shall renew their strength;
they shall mount up with wings as eagles; they shall run,
and not be weary; and they shall walk, and not faint.
—*Isaiah 40:31, KJV*

The hymn lyric "O, wait, meekly wait, and murmur not"* has made an impression on my heart. In this modern age, we all want things to happen instantly. The times we spend waiting can be frustrating, especially if we are not sure what the end result will be. We spend time waiting for the ideal job, for Mister or Miss Right, and for the baby to come. We stand in long lines at the airport, bank, grocery store, and doctor's office. We have to wait for an examination, medical results—or healing. We wait for the prodigal son, daughter, or spouse to return. A great deal of our lives we spend waiting.

Isaiah 40:31 reminds us that we must wait on the Lord. Two other scriptures, in particular, support it. "Wait on the LORD: be of good courage, and he shall strengthen thine heart: wait, I say, on the LORD" (Psalm 27:14, KJV). Psalm 37:7 says, "Rest in the LORD, and wait patiently for him" (KJV).

"Trust in the LORD with all thine heart; and lean not unto thine own understanding. In all thy ways acknowledge him, and he shall direct thy paths. Be not wise in thine own eyes" (Proverbs 3:5–7, KJV). When we deviate from right paths, we are in trouble. We must wait and be patient. As we wait, we must trust God's timetable and not worry. He knows what is best. "My soul, wait thou only upon God; for my expectation is from him" (Psalm 62:5, KJV).

Waiting is not easy in times of uncertainty. Yet we are reminded to "be anxious for nothing, but in everything by prayer and supplication, with thanksgiving, let your requests be made known to God; and the peace of God, which surpasses all understanding, will guard your hearts and minds through Christ Jesus" (Philippians 4:6, 7, NKJV).

Worrying changes nothing and only frustrates us. God's timing is always right. He sees, He knows, and He wants His children to develop faith in Him. So as we wait on Him, we learn to trust Him. My dear sisters in Christ, all our waiting will be worth it when we finally see Jesus. "My soul waits for the Lord more than those who watch for the morning—yes, more than those who watch for the morning" (Psalm 130:6, NKJV).

Ruby H. Enniss-Alleyne

---

* W. H. Bellamy, "Wait, and Murmur Not," 1904.

Criminals Are Stupid

"You have sinned against the LORD,
and be sure your sin will find you out."
—*Numbers 32:23, ESV*

I have a theory about criminals; it is probably not new or earthshaking, but my theory is that most criminals are stupid. And most of them get caught, often by doing something else stupid. There are even websites listing stupid criminals. Maybe those who don't get caught are a little smarter, but it is still true that you may "be sure your sin will find you out" (Numbers 32:23, ESV).

The sin may take a long time to be uncovered: deep-sea explorers have found evidence among the litter of the *Titanic* that one of the couples on board was not married to each other—each was married to someone else. The woman survived, but the man did not. I wonder what happened when she got back to New York! And I'm sure Joseph's brothers were certain their sinful actions against him would never be discovered. But years passed, and their crime came to light hundreds of miles away.

Moses certainly did not believe he was going to be caught when he murdered the Egyptian, but he was seen and had to run for his life. A man in our neighboring town set up a camera in a family dressing room at a swimming pool for no good purpose and accidentally took a picture of himself! He was quickly arrested. I heard about a woman who came home to find her home ransacked. But the police had an easy arrest once again—the criminals were found asleep in the garage. And then there is the story of the man who tried to hold up a gun shop with a baseball bat. Somehow, he didn't expect that anyone there might have a gun, and he was arrested. Criminals are stupid.

Have you noticed how often a lawbreaker is arrested because of some driving infraction? I like to think that if I had broken the law, I would drive ever so carefully. But criminals are stupid.

Then I think of another text: "For all have sinned, and come short of the glory of God" (Romans 3:23, KJV). In other words, we are all lawbreakers—criminals, if you will. If we are not caught immediately, we will certainly be found out in the judgment. But what an advantage Christians have, for we have a Substitute, an Advocate, who is standing in for us rather than trying to catch us. "God made him who had no sin to be sin for us, so that in him we might become the righteousness of God" (2 Corinthians 5:21, NIV). Consequently, if we do not accept His gift of grace and salvation, we are the ones who could be called stupid.

Ardis Dick Stenbakken

It's Not a Threat; It's a Promise

May the God of hope fill you with all joy and peace as you trust in him,
so that you may overflow with hope by the power of the Holy Spirit.
—Romans 15:13, NIV

The week had gone from bad to worse. In fact, the last five years had gone from bad to worse. There were signs before I married him that I had ignored. I had left him many times only to return to what turned out to be empty promises of change.

It started with verbal abuse; then it became psychological abuse that finally escalated to physical abuse. If I left, he would follow me. If he was in one of his rages and I tried to get out of the house, he stopped me. One night, when he told me he was going to kill me and described how he was going to do it, he looked me straight in the eyes. When he added, "It's not a threat; it's a promise," I knew I was in serious trouble.

I did not get much sleep due to my fear but mostly because I was praying. I said, *Lord, I am Yours. I don't know what to do, and I am scared. If You want me to stay in this marriage, please make it normal. But if You want me to leave, then show me the way.*

I was finally able to get a little sleep. When I awoke, everything was different. I felt this amazing peace, and I knew I was leaving. I did not have to think for myself at all. I felt encircled by God and His love, and He was giving me every instruction of what to do. I left that day never to return. I was free.

After a time of healing, I met a man—when I least expected to—whom I know God meant for me to be with. My wonderful husband, Steven, is the love of my life, and I thank God for him every day. We have been married more than twenty years—years that have been the best of my life. And that is saying something because I grew up in a most loving Christian home with the best parents and sister. So, growing up, I experienced a whole lot of love.

I know God didn't want me to go through such a painful experience in my previous marriage, yet He was always with me and helped me when I called to Him. The morning I left the abusive marriage, I felt Jesus asking me to take His hand and follow Him. I did, and He gave me a new life filled with peace and joy. His hands are outstretched to all His children.

Will you trust Him today with your life? It will be the best decision you will ever make.

Jean Dozier Davey

February 19

Lessons From a Bus Ride

"I am with you and will watch over you wherever you go,
and I will bring you back to this land. I will not leave you
until I have done what I have promised you."
—*Genesis 28:15, NIV*

After only two weeks in a new country, I decided to attend a Wednesday evening prayer meeting. Leaving home, I realized the bus would have already passed the stop nearest my home, so I ran to another bus stop. Though I almost arrived in time to catch the bus, it still drove off without me. I would now have to wait twenty minutes for another bus. It was almost seven o'clock, which was a few minutes before the prayer meeting would begin.

I estimated I would be only a few minutes late if I could get another bus right away. Following my phone's GPS directions, I ran until I arrived at a busy highway. I was a few meters away from the bus stop but could not figure out how to get across the highway to the actual stop. Then I noticed a bridge overhead. Taking that route, I arrived at a bus stop, but it was the wrong one. I went to yet another bus stop, but it was the wrong one too. Upon careful observation, I realized there was another bus stop opposite a nearby roundabout. But there wasn't any pedestrian crossing on the busy highway. As I contemplated whether I should attempt crossing, a bus appeared but continued its journey without me. I gave up. On my way home, I took the risk of boarding another bus as I thought, *If tonight's meeting is like those in the Caribbean, it will start late, so I won't be too late after all.* Then I missed my stop and had to walk a longer distance to the church, where I finally arrived at 7:52 P.M. "They're almost finished," someone told me outside.

I promptly headed home. But with my phone on 5 percent battery, the mobile bus ticket would not load, so I paid the £2.80 (US$3.45) fare. Eventually, the ticket loaded. I showed the driver and asked if I could get a refund; he said no. There I was on my way home, without going to the prayer meeting and having had a "wild adventure" that cost me £2.80!

As I was getting off the bus, the driver said, "Here, I'll refund you this time." I smiled as I thought, *I didn't get a prayer meeting, but I got grace!* Then a lady who had taken the wrong bus asked me for directions, and I was able to help her! That evening I learned that I am not the only one experiencing the struggle and challenge of living in a new country, yet I can still be a blessing to others. I also learned that God is with us wherever we are and wherever we go in life.

Kimasha P. Williams

Dry Bones

Then he said unto me, Son of man,
these bones are the whole house of Israel:
behold, they say, Our bones are dried,
and our hope is lost: we are cut off for our parts.
—*Ezekiel 37:11, KJV*

Everywhere you go there are cries and groans that echo off the lips of people who are discouraged. The lives of many are laced with natural disasters and the loss of jobs, family, or dear friends. Death, sickness, and sorrow rise like never before. People's pains are horrendous. Some Christians fall by the wayside because their "bones" are no longer ignited with the Word of God, so they give in to feelings of hopelessness. Their former joy has leached out of their souls. The well of living water has dried up.

Are you one of these whose cross seems too heavy to bear? Are your bones dried up because of a lost connection with the Source of living water that alone gives energy and hope?

As a Christian, whenever my bones become dry, it is because I have lost my first love for Jesus Christ. Seeking Him early in the morning has become a ritual instead of a pleasure. The faith that was once my anchor becomes questionable. Fear and doubt step in to take up residence. Instead of calling upon Him for healing and restoration, I murmur and complain. My bones, so to speak, become frail and lose vitality, grace, and zest for life. My spiritual journey becomes restless, weak, and brittle and lacks faith and power. When I focus on my problems, I forget that "I can do all things through Christ who strengthens me" (Philippians 4:13, NKJV). I no longer hear His tender voice calling, "Come back to Me, My daughter."

When the burdens of life knock you off the path, remember you have a Savior who extends His love and care to you daily. His Word never fails. His promises are true and powerful. Do not permit the cares of this world to drain you or rob you of His joy and of the desire to share Him with others. Bring your dry bones to the foot of the cross. He told us to come to Him when we are burdened and heavy laden, and we will find rest. He has already carried your burdens for you (see Matthew 11:28).

So why not go to Christ for the life support that infuses dry bones with mercy, compassion, and beauty? In Him, we will find an everlasting well that will not run dry. Our bones will strengthen with new life, hope, and vigor that will stand firm against the wiles of the enemy.

Corletta Aretha Barbar

The Invitation

Your ears shall hear a word behind you, saying,
"This is the way, walk in it."
—Isaiah 30:21, NKJV

In 1995, Women's Ministries evolved in my denomination in Ghana. This fledgling department in our church's headquarters needed to be equipped with leaders who would carry out the new responsibilities. As a leader in my local church district, I helped with preparations for the department's opening ceremony by sending out and delivering invitation letters for this important event. About this time, I was also grappling with a personal prayer request. I wanted my son to attend a Christian college that trained teachers, but how could this be made possible? I continued to pray about this even as I delivered invitations for the women's event.

One invitation I delivered was to the president of our nearby mission. Pastor E. O. Sackey and I had a very lengthy discussion about how the opening ceremony would take place. After I left his office, I headed into the mission compound before being stopped by a sudden impression: *Go back and talk to the president about your child's education.*

Was that the Holy Spirit speaking to me? I just stood there for a few moments. Then I went back to Pastor Sackey's office. There I shared with him everything concerning the challenges surrounding my son's education and my desire that he attend the Christian teacher training college.

"It is never too late to make a change," Pastor Sackey said to me. I sat there for a moment, thinking, *He's right. It's never too late in anyone's life to make a change. We must just listen for God's voice, embrace the truth, and then act on it. God will be responsible for everything else. Jesus is just waiting for our penitent and willing hearts to turn to Him.*

The pastor directed me to the appropriate church office to gather more information regarding the prayer request that had lain so heavily on my heart. Several months later someone from the Christian teaching college contacted my son about coming in for an interview, and he was admitted to the college. About two years later, he was baptized by Pastor Kwabena Twum.

The Holy Spirit, who spoke to me when I was delivering invitations, extends to each of us an invitation. It is an invitation to attend a banquet with Jesus Christ and His redeemed children whom He will soon take home. There we will live with Jesus, never to part again.

Charlotte Osei-Agyeman

Fairbanks

Eye hath not seen, nor ear heard, neither have entered into the heart
of man, the things which God hath prepared for them that love him.
—*1 Corinthians 2:9, KJV*

One February my husband and I visited our son and his family in Alaska. Garrick and Stephanie took a few days off work, and we headed north to Fairbanks, located less than 120 miles south of the Arctic Circle.

It was a special time and the perfect occasion to visit the kids' park at Ice Alaska. Our four-year-old grandson Derion sped down the slides made from blocks of ice and finished long runs by careening across a frozen expanse; our granddaughter Avril, who was almost two, said hello to a sculpted crystalline wolf. One day we visited Chena Hot Springs, where the children splashed in the warm family pool and the adults swam with them or floated in the outdoor rock pool. Veils of mist hid—and revealed—the beauty of mountains robed in snow and trees rimmed with hoarfrost. And then it was time to eat. Delighted to learn that the vegetables and herbs were fresh, grown in the warmth of geothermal greenhouses, we ordered bowls of tomato-basil soup.

As we waited for lunch to arrive, we looked for ways to keep the children amused. Typical Alaskan hunting trophies caught our eyes. "What's that?" Garrick asked Avril.

"Boo," she announced, looking at a caribou. "And dat's a moose," Derion proclaimed, pointing to another wall.

"And what's that?" I asked, indicating a bear skin nailed to the wooden ceiling.

"Flying bear," Derion replied matter-of-factly.

At times, I have difficulties imagining heaven: John's vision in Revelation doesn't make logical sense. But like my grandson, who readily accepted the concept of a flying bear—an idea that flies in the face of the terrestrial bears he has encountered—perhaps I should embrace the assurances of beauty, care, and love found in the Bible. As I've thought of that memorable weekend in Fairbanks, I can see it as a foretaste of standing on the banks of the river of life. As I remember Derion skimming over the ice, I long to see my loved ones on the sea of glass. When I recall Avril making friends with a large carnivore, I think of the wolf and the lamb dwelling together. Picturing the sparkling hoarfrost, I look forward to walking through the gates of pearl. When I imagine the mouth-watering soup, I anticipate the fruits from the tree of life.

Denise Dick Herr

His Wonderful Face

Look to the LORD and his strength; seek his face always.
—*1 Chronicles 16:11, NIV*

As I sang "Turn Your Eyes Upon Jesus" with the congregation during the church service, we came to the phrase "Look full in His wonderful face." A question came to me: *How do I do that?* That question has been in my mind many times since.

One of the ways I think we see His face is by reading His Word. The love of Jesus is interwoven throughout the Bible accounts of His dealings with His children in the past—and even today. We contemplate the words of encouragement, inspiration, and admonition He spoke. We recall how He healed the sick, raised the dead, and cast out demons. In so doing, we see the face of a loving, caring, and compassionate Savior. His ultimate sacrifice on the cross and the promise of His return show us a face of everlasting love.

Taking time to enjoy His handiwork and beauty in nature shows us the face of an intelligent designer. The other day, while taking a half-mile walk along a country lane, I saw eleven varieties of wild flowers. Each one has a different shape and size and color of the petals and the leaves, revealing to me the face of One who loves variety and details.

The night sky with the moon in various stages of fullness and the innumerable starry hosts reveal the vastness of God's creative power. The tiny lights of fireflies penetrating the darkness bring a smile to my face. The creatures He created—from the smallest butterfly and hummingbird to the majestic eagle, water creatures, and giant elephants—show us a face that values adaptability, gracefulness, and practicality.

Other people also show me the face of Jesus. The sympathetic words spoken to those in crisis, the look of approval for a job well done, and loyalty to a friend in questionable circumstances reflect His face. Caregivers who sometimes neglect their own needs to make life better for their patients; those who give of their means to feed the hungry; and others who clothe the poor or fill a need for people who are incapable of meeting it themselves; they all imitate Him. Those who go out of their way to lift a burden for a complete stranger, the martyrs, and the servicepeople who put themselves in harm's way to secure our freedom, all reveal the face of Jesus.

What are we revealing today and every day? Do others see the face of Jesus in us?

Marian M. Hart-Gay

How to Make a Bed

*And we know that in all things God works for the good of those who
love him, who have been called according to his purpose.*
—Romans 8:28, NIV

I remember it just like yesterday, arguing with my dad about how to make up the bed. You have to understand, my dad was the most military-minded nonmilitary person I knew. First, the bed had to be stripped completely and everything pulled and tucked tightly. If you listened closely you could hear the bed cry, "Please don't pull and tuck me anymore!" Dad wanted to be able to bounce a quarter on the neatly dressed mattress. That quarter needed to turn into a gymnast, doing all kinds of flips and tricks. I had no problem with the bed turning into a trampoline, but I just didn't agree with how we arrived at the finished product.

I also had no problem showing my dad a different way that we could make the bed. Instead of removing all the sheets and covers, I would just pull everything very tightly and then reach under, pull and tuck and tuck and pull, until that quarter bounced liked a ball! I was as proud as any eight-year-old could be. While in midcelebration, I was stopped by my dad's very concerned and confused look. He said these words that have changed how I do things to this very day: "Reneé, the bed is not about the finish; it is about the process."

Queen Esther understood the process. When the lives of her people hung on her every move, she didn't go right to the king to ask for help. Instead, she prayed and fasted for three days, put on her royal robes, and *then* went before the king. Even when he said, "Ask what you will, even half of the kingdom," she didn't jump to ask for the head of Haman, her enemy. Instead, she invited the king and Haman to a banquet. Esther understood Middle Eastern culture and knew it would be very insulting to get immediately to the heart of any matter. You always beat around the bush, talk about the weather, your respective families, and perhaps current affairs, until finally you can approach the subject tactfully. She knew it would be rude to ask outright for what she wanted. God saved the Jews because Esther followed the appropriate process.

Some of us can relate to "wanting it now and wanting it fast." When we are tempted to be impatient, let us remember that all things work together for good (see Romans 8:28). That *all* means every part of the process, not just when the quarter bounces and does somersaults.

D. Reneé Mobley

The New Stove

I will abundantly bless her provision.
—*Psalm 132:15, KJV*

Household appliances are something I have always had a love-hate relationship with. If you have lived in many rental properties, you know that you don't always get what you want or, sometimes, anything at all.

I have lived in a couple of old farmhouses where nothing in the way of kitchen appliances was part of the rental agreement. The last house I lived in had been vacant for some time. I had a small refrigerator that was adequate, a microwave, and a temperamental one-burner hotplate. I got by with that for a year and then bought a house.

The stove that came with my house left a lot to be desired. It was old, and one of the burners didn't work; the oven only half worked. But it was good to be in my own home again; and because it was mine, I was glad to put up with a subpar cookstove. In fact, I put up with it for twelve years and learned to work around its deficiencies. Then one day its electrical wires started sputtering and hissing, and I knew it was time for a new stove.

Now a new stove is sitting in my kitchen, looking so beautiful. Yet I have put up with the subpar for so long that I sometimes experience a strange, almost guilty feeling for having something so nice. That feeling wants to take over—as if I really don't deserve anything as nice as this new stove.

Then a voice breaks into my consciousness and gently says, *That's right. You don't deserve it. You don't deserve any of the blessings I send you. You killed My only Son. But I forgive you, and I love you* so *much in spite of your sins that I just want to reassure you of My love.* And my heart breaks with gratitude for this wonderful gift.

If you were to ask me what I think heaven will be like, I would have to answer, "I believe heaven is a lot like a new stove." When I see heaven, I know I will be overwhelmed with the glory and beauty of it all and I will be struck with the fact that it is nothing that I deserve.

Then I will feel an arm gently slip around my shoulders, and Jesus will softly say, "I hope you like it. I bought all this for you because I love you *so* much! I'm glad you're here to enjoy your new home with Me."

Sylvia Sioux Stark

A Gentle Tap on My Window

The LORD is my rock and my fortress and my deliverer;
My God, my strength, in whom I will trust;
My shield and the horn of my salvation, my stronghold.
—*Psalm 18:2, NKJV*

It was a beautiful Sabbath morning as I started out for church; I was happy and looking forward to fellowshiping with the saints of God. As I drove on the busy highway, I was humming songs of praise and thinking how delightful it felt to be going to church.

Traveling along, I suddenly came to a stoplight. Just then I heard a gentle tap on my window. I was reluctant to open my window. Then I felt I should do so. A voice prompted me to open it, so I did.

A pleasant-sounding man on a bike beside my car said kindly, "It seems something might be wrong with your vehicle. I can see something like oil, water, or antifreeze dripping from the engine." He suggested I pull over to the side of the road and check the engine. "I fear," he pointed out, "that if you continue to drive, your engine might become damaged." I drove a few yards before pulling over to the side of the road and checking. To my dismay, the engine was covered with antifreeze. It was everywhere. I said, *Lord, what should I do? I cannot do much today, and I cannot continue going to church as it is too far away.*

"Trust and obey," the old hymn admonishes. And I was strongly impressed to trust and obey another "voice" that was now impressing me to turn around. So I turned around and started my journey home. But before I could reach home, I began to experience more problems. The car engine began slowing down. Loud noises from the engine told me that something was seriously wrong. Five minutes from my home, the car's engine began smoking profusely. I stopped and called 9-1-1. A sheriff came to assist me. God is so merciful and compassionate. He gave that man the wisdom to temporarily fix my vehicle so that I could make it home. He followed me straight home to make sure I got there safely.

I thanked both the officer and my heavenly Father. God has promised, "Fear thou not; for I am with thee: be not dismayed; for I am thy God: I will strengthen thee; yea, I will help thee; yea, I will uphold thee with the right hand of my righteousness" (Isaiah 41:10, KJV). I believe the Lord sent an angel that morning to save me from what could have been a serious accident.

Patricia Hines

The Awesome Power of Prayer

Be careful for nothing; but in every thing by prayer and supplication with thanksgiving let your requests be made known unto God. And the peace of God, which passeth all understanding, shall keep your hearts and minds through Christ Jesus.
—Philippians 4:6, 7, KJV

Being in and out of church in earlier years has shown me that being inside the will of God is the better choice. I've also learned that the power of prayer has more far-reaching possibilities than our finite minds can comprehend in this lifetime. Great men of wisdom have attempted to speculate on the almighty wisdom of God. But no one can account for His greatness and power.

I pray often during the day, thanking God for His enormous blessings. I continually ask to be always in tune with Him, focusing on Him in word, thought, and deed. I ask God's help in representing to others His character of love and forgiveness. I especially want to be forgiving—as He daily forgives me. I want to be bold in prayer and praise, speaking to others of His awesome goodness along the way.

I don't want to be a lukewarm Christian with no real prayer life. Oh, but when you taste and see how sweet it is to be loved by the heavenly Father, service to the Most High God is the ultimate choice anyone can make. When I completely surrendered my life to Jesus and experienced His unconditional love, it was more than I could imagine or ever hope for. His sweet spirit truly humbled my heart and made it willing to trust and obey. Mind you, I have fallen several times. Yet each time God extends His loving hand and again forgives me, though I don't deserve it.

God's forgiveness makes me want to obey Him. I believe that no Christian can pray—really pray—if he or she does not seek obedience to the will of God. In my closer walk with Him through prayer, I am learning that there is no tear that prayer cannot wipe away. There is no depression that it cannot relieve. When I am in earnest prayer, my heart softens, life's pressures release, and my burdens lift. There is power in prayer. That's why it is so important, as Paul wrote in today's text, to stay alert and focused, praying in seasons of prosperity or adversity, in seasons of light and darkness. For the awesome power God gives through prayer will enable us to defeat the enemy of our souls in the wonderful name of Jesus.

Sylvia Giles Bennett

Timely Answers to Prayer

"Before they call I will answer;
while they are still speaking I will hear."
—Isaiah 65:24, NIV

Our younger daughter, Amy, and a friend were traveling in South Africa. One of the activities they wanted to do was something they knew I was totally against and very fearful about. They wanted to bungee jump from a bridge; in fact, it was the highest bungee jump in the world! Why anyone would enjoy this activity was beyond me, but they were determined.

I awakened very early one morning with Amy's bungee jump on my mind though I didn't know when they planned to make the jump. Nevertheless, I began to pray for their safety. As my husband and I were getting up around five o'clock in the morning, he received a text message on his phone. It simply read, "Bungee jump safely completed." How thankful we were! As I began to think of the time difference between Colorado and South Africa, I realized they had completed the jump before I prayed for their safety. The first part of today's text came immediately to mind: "Before they call I will answer."

A number of years ago there was a time when I was concerned about an activity of one of our children. After a nearly sleepless night, I arose early and went to my husband's study for my devotional time. I was too worried to concentrate on reading, so I just spent the time praying. I remember specifically telling God that I just couldn't continue functioning unless He was with me and gave me special strength. As I opened my eyes and looked at my Bible, it appeared very blurry except for one text that stood out crystal clear. Had I been looking for a "comfort" text that morning, I may have gone to Psalms or the New Testament. But this text was Exodus 33:14, which says, "The LORD replied, 'My Presence will go with you, and I will give you rest' " (NIV).

I don't believe I could have been more comforted had I heard an audible voice speaking to me. I knew God had heard and answered my prayer for His presence and strength. In the coming months, He gave me rest as well when the situation resolved.

I am reminded of what God told Isaiah to tell King Hezekiah: "I have heard your prayer and seen your tears" (Isaiah 38:5, NIV). God hears, He sees, and He answers—not always immediately but always right on time. What a precious, awesome God!

Sharon Oster

Soul Batteries

In Joppa there was a disciple named Tabitha (in Greek her name is Dorcas); she was always doing good and helping the poor.
—*Acts 9:36, NIV*

Therefore, as God's chosen people, holy and dearly loved, clothe yourselves with compassion, kindness, humility, gentleness and patience.
—*Colossians 3:12, NIV*

It was just before Christmas when my husband and I were shopping at a mall. As we passed by a jewelry store, my husband stopped in to ask the jeweler to replace my watch battery. In just a few minutes, the watch was running again.

We were filled with great surprise when we heard the manager say with a smile, "No charge. Merry Christmas! Come back to shop for your jewelry needs!" This was a random act of kindness and a wonderful gift in the spirit of the holiday season.

As a watch battery can stop working, just like mine did, our human batteries can also stop. Our human batteries run down for many reasons: hard financial times, a family crisis, or an illness or death in the family.

Today I have within my power the capability of recharging someone's soul battery. You have that capability too. Recharging someone's soul battery might take a little of our time, a little but genuine smile, or a little but gentle touch. We may recharge the soul battery of another when we go out of our way to sit by a lonely person at church, offer the person an invitation to share a meal with us, or be present at a bedside when someone is not feeling well. Any little random act of kindness (such as the replacement of a watch's battery at a mall store—for free) can recharge someone's soul!

When my soul battery is running low and needs recharging, I am thankful for others who are generous with their time and expertise on my behalf! It may be just a little thing, just take a little time, or cost only a little, but the effects of that small, kind act can be huge!

I propose that we "pay it forward" by being present for someone today (and at any time of the year) through even a *little* act that shows we care.

I am so grateful that there are people on this planet who, in the spirit of kindness, take care of the little things for others and recharge soul batteries in the process.

Bonnie R. Parker

The Wedding Gift

Ask, and it shall be given you; seek, and ye shall find; knock, and it shall be opened unto you. For every one that asketh receiveth; and he that seeketh findeth; and to him that knocketh it shall be opened.
—Matthew 7:7, 8, KJV

Some years ago when my fiancé and I decided to get married, I went shopping for the all-important wedding dress that I had seen many times—in my head. Considering that we were on a tight budget, it was necessary that I give myself enough time to find the dress of my dreams; therefore, approximately eight months before our wedding, I started my search.

After searching for three months, I still had not found the dress. As I continued my search, it became apparent that finding it wasn't going to be as easy as I had expected. The months marched on. Six *weeks* before the wedding I still had no dress and began to feel so desperate that I started shopping in stores I didn't like and trying on dresses I didn't want.

Two weeks before the wedding, while on my bus ride home from work, I began to pray hard about my dress. In desperation, I asked my heavenly Father to help me. I humbly apologized for not having asked His help sooner. Suddenly, as clearly as if I had heard it on the radio, a voice said, *Go to Carson's [Carson Pirie Scott & Company] on State Street.*

I've been to Carson's five times, I replied in my heart. Yet the voice simply said I should go back. Stepping out in faith, I got off the bus at State Street, walking and running back four blocks to the store. As I stepped off the escalator and turned around, I saw three dresses hanging on a rack at the sales associate's counter. I could not believe my eyes. Each was the exact dress I had wanted for my wedding—in three different sizes. The sales associate told me those three were the only wedding dresses in the store, delivered just fifteen minutes earlier. She was preparing to put them on the floor to sell. Since one dress fit me, I immediately bought it, thanking the Lord God again and again for His generous, affordable wedding gift to me: a tea-length, ivory-colored satin dress with just enough delicate pearls and lace around the neck and on the sleeves to look attractive but not overdone. *Thank You again, my Father. The dress is simply beautiful!*

With what do you need His help today?

Cynthia A. HartKnott

You Won't See Them Anymore

And Moses said unto the people, Fear ye not, stand still,
and see the salvation of the LORD, which He will shew to you to day:
for the Egyptians whom ye have seen to day,
ye shall see them again no more for ever.
—*Exodus 14:13, KJV*

For the past couple of weeks, I have been trying to leave my job. In Canada and most Western countries, this is a fairly simple process. Where I am now (in Asia), doing so has been nearly impossible because my boss has refused to allow me to work anywhere else in this city despite my contract time limit expiring. This situation, among other challenges, has contributed to this being a frustrating and difficult year. Yet I am grateful in some ways for all that has happened because God has used it to shape me and bring me closer to Him. But even with all God has done in me, I still have moments of fear. Moments like yesterday when my boss threatened to blacklist my passport in this country, thereby barring me from being able to work here. Listening to this threat, I felt the fingers of fear take hold of my heart. Yet I am in this country because I believe God called me here for His purpose. I have done nothing wrong and nothing that would deserve my being blacklisted. But could someone else's actions change God's plan for me?

With this conversation still fresh in my mind, I went to teach a Bible student. Our current Bible story is about Pharaoh's refusal to let God's people go. I couldn't help but compare it to my boss's refusal to let me go from his company. We stopped our study at the part where Pharaoh finally lets the people go. But this morning when I woke up, God continued the story in my heart, pointing me to Exodus 14:13: "Fear ye not, stand still, and see the salvation of the LORD . . . : the Egyptians whom ye have seen to day, ye shall see them no more" (KJV).

The interesting thing about this is that the people are told not to fear *before* they are given the miracle—before the waves start to part and before Moses even stretches out his hand. They are to be fearless in the midst of chaos and apparently imminent destruction.

In my situation, I don't see the miracle. But I believe God's words to the people are His words to me: Fear not; no matter how hopeless it looks, even when things only seem to get worse. Instead, stand still, and see the salvation of the Lord. Wait for Him to remove your "Egyptians." He did it for the Israelites. He will do it for me. And He can do it for you too.

R. Bowen

The Very Last Turn

And do this, knowing the time,
that now it is high time to awake out of sleep;
for now our salvation is nearer than when we first believed.
—*Romans 13:11, NKJV*

It is seven o'clock in the evening. I get off my shift at a rural hospital emergency room and head home. I live in a suburb a little over one hour's drive away from where I work. On my way, I must drive along a rural road. This route is lined with trees, desolate, and full of deer and other critters that sometimes jump out, unannounced, onto the road.

It's already dark by the time I get into my car. I buckle up, say a prayer, and head toward home. I am looking forward to getting home and getting into my warm bed.

As I start my drive along the rural road, afraid a deer or critter will jump out from the woods on either side of the road, I put my headlights on high beam so that I can see better and farther. I sit upright in my driver's seat, place both hands on the steering wheel, and glue my eyes to the road and immediate surrounding woods. I am on high alert.

I make it to the double-lane roads that lead into the suburb from the rural area and start to let down my guard. I turn the headlights down from high beam to regular beam. I breathe a word of prayer: "Thank You, Lord, I'm almost home." I can see the lights from the homes in my subdivision. I lean back in my seat and make the very last turn with only one hand on the steering wheel.

Suddenly, from the small patch of undeveloped land just to the left of the road, two fully grown deer jump out—one right behind the other! I manage to miss the first one but cannot miss the second. The front end of my car is damaged, and I have to pull over to the side of the road.

I learn a great lesson this night. The enemy of our souls is not relaxing because we are almost home. He strikes when we least expect, where we least expect, and in the manner we least expect.

Beloved, do not let your guard down yet. Keep your eyes on Jesus. Keep your light shining brightly.

By faith, we can see the lights of our heaven. God is with us all the way home.

Chinwe Ubani-Ebere

March 5

Rose and Thorn

There was given to me a thorn in the flesh.
—*2 Corinthians 12:7, KJV*

And the desert shall rejoice, and blossom as the rose.
—*Isaiah 35:1, KJV*

My favorite flower is the rose, and I could never understand why such a beautiful flower would have thorns. Later I learned that the thorns on roses are a defense mechanism to keep them from being harmed. After moving from a big city to the country, I would send mail home with a colorful rose I had drawn on the envelope. My husband, who is legally sightless, and I usually have worship in the evenings after supper. One day I presented him with a new idea to add to our worship. After we finished singing, we would each say something about our day in the form of a rose and a thorn. Whenever we had company, we included them in this practice, and they always looked forward to worship. This sharing became a tradition at the Johnson household. We even had family members continue to do the same thing after they went back home.

One day during worship, my husband's thorn was, "We haven't heard from Serita [our daughter]; I hope she's OK." This thorn lasted for three days. On the fourth day, our daughter called. She said, "Just checking in. I'm OK. How's Dad?" That put a big smile on his face. He'd heard from his baby girl. That thorn had finally turned into a rose.

Days passed. Then at worship about a week later, my husband's thorn was, "We haven't heard from Tiger [our son] in three weeks. I hope he's doing OK." Well, this situation remained a thorn for the next two days. Then on the third day, right after we had finished sharing with each other that day's roses and thorns, the phone rang. As you have probably guessed, it was Tiger, our oldest son. I told him he had been his dad's "thorn" for three days.

He laughed and said, "Tell Dad I'm fine—just working two jobs and trying to take care of my family." We talked for about thirty minutes before hanging up.

In his amazement, my husband said, "Sweets, God really does answer prayers. When Serita called, I thought it was a coincidence. But the phone call from our son was like an answer to prayer—as sweet as a rose."

My rose for you today is to always remember you have a God who acts as a "defense mechanism" and hears your prayers and keeps Satan's thorns from harming you.

Elaine J. Johnson

With Prayer, the Pain Left!

I will say to God my Rock,
"Why have You forgotten me?
Why do I go mourning because of the oppression of the enemy?"
As with a breaking of my bones,
My enemies reproach me,
While they say to me all day long,
"Where is your God?"
—Psalm 42:9, 10, NKJV

It has been more than a year since my friend, who is the prayer ministry leader of our church, fell. In the fall, she suffered multiple fractures of one ankle, a contusion on her lower back, and other minor injuries. These injuries have triggered other health issues, resulting in her inability to work and function effectively.

On one occasion, our church was enjoying a great Week of Prayer. Sabbath was supposed to be a "high day in Zion," but my sister was cast down in pain. I noticed her absence during the Friday night meeting. Based on her health challenges, I figured she was not well. Very early on Sabbath morning, she called and stated, "Sis, I cannot be in church today; I am in agony. My back and other areas of my body are affected. That's why I was not there last night."

Her voice expressed the stress of the pain she was experiencing. I suggested pain medication and a heating pad. Then I encouraged her, decided to proceed with the program despite her absence, and promised that we would pray for her. I was also impressed to pray with her before we finished our conversation.

Later that morning at church, I was overjoyed when she came to the worship service. She shared her testimony with joy that someone prayed with her and her pain just "went." Later she said to me, "Soon after you prayed for me, the pain left." After giving God the glory, I thought about some of His marvelous promises.

Why are you cast down, O my soul?
And why are you disquieted within me?
Hope in God;
For I shall yet praise Him,
The help of my countenance and my God (Psalm 42:11, NKJV).

"If you ask anything in My name, I will do it" (John 14:14, NKJV). Praise God for His promises!

Sonia Kennedy-Brown

March 7

Remember Rahab

The LORD seeth not as man seeth; for man looketh on the outward
appearance, but the LORD looketh on the heart.
—*1 Samuel 16:7, KJV*

A more unlikely candidate for greatness would be hard to find. And yet the Bible singles out Rahab, a prostitute living in a house on Jericho's wall close to a gate, as a worthy ancestor of Jesus. Her business thrived because she was close to that gate. The constant coming and going through her door was hardly noticed by the citizenry and the soldier guards, but the night two Hebrew spies knocked on her door was different. Something inside of Rahab warned her to hide these men. Just as the king's soldiers knocked on her door to inquire about the visitors, she ushered the spies up the stairs and under a pile of drying flax. She raced down to the door. She must have breathed a sigh of relief when the soldiers hurried out the gate in hot pursuit of the spies, following Rahab's misleading instructions. She sped back up the stairs. Then she shocked the two Hebrew spies by her knowledge of what was about to happen to Jericho.

Rahab boldly negotiated a promise to save her family and herself in return for the spies' safe deliverance from Jericho. The deal was sealed with the scarlet cord that she used to lower the men to freedom. She begged her family to join her until the day of deliverance. When the walls of Jericho came down, Rahab's family was led to safety by the very men whose lives she had saved. Rahab and her family were accepted by the Hebrew community. In due time, Rahab and her Hebrew husband, Salmon, had a child, whom they named Boaz. Boaz was born forty-two generations before Jesus came along to save us from our sins. The apostle Paul writes in Hebrews 11:31 that Rahab's faith led her to deliver the spies and thus save all her family and herself. The apostle James states that Rahab's righteousness saved her (James 2:24, 25).

Rahab's story demonstrates that God is the one who chose Rahab for a specific role in the plan of salvation. As I remember her bravery and trust in God, despite the foreboding circumstances, I am encouraged too. Her story proves to me, beyond a doubt, that God is not a respecter of persons. Anyone who accepts the call to serve Him is certain to be accepted by Him no matter what may be hidden in his or her past.

It is as simple as saying, "Here am I, Lord. Send me" (see Isaiah 6:8).

Patricia Cove

God Never Ceases to Amaze Me

Delight yourself also in the LORD,
And He shall give you the desires of your heart.
—*Psalm 37:4, NKJV*

An email informed me I was being transferred from my university's extension campus in my country to the main campus in another country. Excitement and nostalgia engulfed me. I was excited because I was going to complete my studies and nostalgic because I had less than a month to spend time with the people I love.

As soon as I made this big move, the devil wasted no time in attacking me. A day after my arrival in this foreign land I was robbed. In that moment, I wanted to forget all my academic plans, pack up my belongings, and leave for home. But after crying and praying, I heard God's voice pointing out that I could have lost more than a pair of sneakers. That is when my personal journey with God began. The semester began, and trials came hurtling at me from every direction. My daily mantra became, "The closer you try to get to God, the more the devil pays attention to you." And I went through the entire semester believing that.

It wasn't until my final exams that I knew God was standing right next to me. Just before my last exam, I was told that I had a D in a certain class. There's nothing like a D grade to shatter your ego! When I should have been studying for the test, I was crying. I cried because I had been trying so hard to get my grade above a C. And here I was with a D! *Has God finished giving me all the blessings He has for me?* I wondered. *Have I exhausted the windows of heaven's of blessing?*

The morning of the test I opened my daily devotional book, *Altogether Lovely*. I was guided to a story of a little bird fighting with a squirrel to protect its young. The story encouraged me to keep fighting. If I didn't give up, victory would be mine. I couldn't help but wonder whether God had prepared the reading especially for me that day or if He had permitted me to face this particular academic challenge so that I would connect with the reading. God never ceases to amaze me, and I'm more than happy to be amazed by Him. The author had written that we can "never admit to failure when we know there is a God who always steps in." I'm happy to share that I got a B—not the grade I had wanted, but it was better than what I'd had before!

I encourage you to do your best today and then watch God work out the rest for you.

Renauta Hinds

March 9

The Value of Time

Walk in wisdom toward outsiders, making the best use of the time.
—*Colossians 4:5, ESV*

Twelve statements under the heading of "Life Principles" sit within a frame in our home. The first principle is "The Value of Time."

On November 27, 2015, I was given a deadline to submit a case note as part of my law degree. Wanting to submit my best work, I started the assignment steadily—after all, the deadline was months away. By January, I had formed my first draft to finalize by the deadline of one minute before midnight at 11:59 P.M., Wednesday, March 9, 2016.

March 9 arrived. On this day, I was confident I would submit my paper in time, even though Wednesdays were training days in my new job. I added more details to the note before leaving home at 11:00 A.M. Back home by 4:30 P.M., I continued redrafting my note. It outlined every issue in turn and then the three judges' individual conclusions to each issue, based on previous similar cases, together with the lower courts' judgments in the same case. Under pressure but still confident, I returned to work after dinner at 8:30 P.M.

Eleven o'clock came and went. I typed frantically, pausing to double-check citations and make sure my work was error free. My heart raced. The consequences of not completing on time entered my mind while I shouted, "I can do this," to silence my own thoughts. But my thoughts were reasonable, as there was a real possibility of not meeting the 11:59 P.M. deadline.

With less than ten minutes remaining, I desperately entered my username and password on my online portal. After a few urgent clicks, my file uploaded at 11:56 P.M., with three minutes to spare, by God's grace. A lapse in the internet connection, a typo, or a wrong click could have meant submitting within seconds at best and a missed deadline at worst.

Time is a finite resource. When each measure of time passes, we cannot get it back. "I can do all things through Christ who strengthens me" (Philippians 4:13, NKJV). But I have learned that I must value my time by spending it wisely. Not doing so can lead to unnecessarily stressful situations or missed goals. I ask God, the Creator of time and Giver of wisdom, to help me make the best use of time.

Sonya Simms

The Decision

The LORD says, "I will guide you along the best pathway for your life.
I will advise you and watch over you."
—*Psalm 32:8, NLT*

It was a clear, but cool, sunshiny day. My seven-year-old daughter and I were excited about visiting family members we seldom see, after completing a six-and-a-half-hour trip!

As we advanced, clouds rolled in, covering the sun; it became dreary. It wasn't the prettiest sight, but it wasn't intimidating either. So we continued our travels, and gradually the clouds dissipated.

A couple of hours later we spotted more clouds ahead. This time we were greeted with snow flurries and a falling temperature. This weather change was a little worse than the first one; but after a half an hour, we reconnected with the sunshine and blue skies.

Subsequently, more clouds appeared. This time the temperature dropped to nineteen degrees Fahrenheit, and snow began plummeting down. As we persevered, the snow got so thick that we could barely see the car ahead of us. We went from seventy-five miles per hour down to twenty miles per hour on the highway. My mind instantly recalled the last time I drove in conditions this treacherous: I hit a patch of ice and lost control of the car. I wanted to panic, give up, and turn around because of what I remembered. I felt blind again. As if being on the highway wasn't enough, we were in the mountains, and on the other side of the rail was a cliff!

The car ahead abruptly slowed down. When I tried to react, my tires were no match for the snowy conditions. I began to complain to God, "This is only a weekend trip. Is it really worth our lives?" The response was gentle: *If you turn back, what good will that do? You fret at the conditions you see right now, but this is a lesson about life! Will you trust Me, even though you cannot see the road or the boundary lines? Will you trust that even if you do lose control again, I still have control over the whole situation? Will you trust that because you prayed for My guidance and protection, I will get you through the storm by guiding you with My eye?*

As soon as I decided to trust God through the storm, the sky cleared for the remainder of the trip. That's just the way God works in our lives. He gives us a choice and guides us along the correct path when we accept His direction.

Rachel Privette Jennings

Welcome Inconvenience

"Be still, and know that I am God!"
—*Psalm 46:10, NLT*

This morning on the way to school, my daughters and I were stopped by a train. You should know this precious gem about me: I don't aim to be early. If I'm early, you should check my temperature, take my vitals, or maybe just skip all that and take me straight to the emergency room because something would be terribly wrong. So we weren't exactly running early, and now here was this train, *choo-chooing* by, halting our progress. For a moment, I was tempted to get anxious and irritated, along with other emotions that surface when I'm faced with that ever-devastating, impatience-causing problem of inconvenience! But this morning I didn't! Why? Because God just turned my head to the side of the road, where I saw mounds of purple morning glory flowers that bloomed following a gracious day of Texas rain earlier that week. The flowers were all sunlit and sparkling with dewdrops. Behind them were glowing sunflowers and breathtaking dew-covered plants (probably weeds, but they looked like crystallized art).

My girls and I enjoyed *every single moment* of our delay! We praised God for slowing us down to take in just a little of His beauty and to remember that He'd put those plants there for His glory and our joy. He wanted to turn our thoughts toward Him.

We all need a train stop. School, sports, and music lessons are in full swing. Our supposed workweek reprieve called the weekend is full of endless activity. The wheels on our buses go round and round at dizzying speeds. But we need moments to be still and know that He is God. We need to let His heart speak to ours and direct our attention, our thoughts, and our *purposes* toward Him.

Join me in relishing the God moments, the divine appointments, whether two minutes, hours, or days in duration. Let Him be a welcome "inconvenience" in our schedules until He becomes the *reason* we keep a schedule! Stop and smell the morning glories with me today. It will be worth every single moment.

He wants to get our attention through nature. "For since the creation of the world God's invisible qualities—his eternal power and divine nature—have been clearly seen, being understood from what has been made, so that people are without excuse" (Romans 1:20, NIV).

Mary K. Haslam

Doing What People Said You Couldn't Do

No one's ever seen or heard anything like this,
never so much as imagined anything quite like it—
what God has arranged for those who love him.
—*1 Corinthians 2:9*, The Message

Doing what people said you couldn't do—never even imagined, in fact—is exactly my experience of how God works.

In my midteens, I was approaching the end of compulsory school life. It was time to choose a career. Although my life at secondary school hadn't been particularly happy, there was an option. Some students could stay on for an extra couple of years to further their education. After some thought, I considered this to be my only choice. My parents seemed satisfied that I had a plan for my future, so a meeting was set up with the school headmaster.

I don't recall ever seeing my dad as angry as he was that day when we sat in Mr. Jones's office. The head teacher glared across the desk and without hesitation told us that I wasn't capable of doing a secretarial course.

It was probably at that point that I decided differently. From then on, things fell into place. Looking back, I was glad that I didn't stay on at that school. After being turned down, I applied to a local college.

My mum and dad had already said that if I was offered a place at the local college, they could finance me for only one year. As we waited for an interview and the possibility of a placement, a leaflet came through the door at home. It advertised an evening course and the option to buy a typewriter, which could be paid for in installments. This was an opportunity not to be sneered at. Taking the evening class would not only give me a way to go forward but also not be a huge drain on my parents' finances.

By the time I left secondary school some months later, I had been offered a place at the college and was already—thanks to the evening tutoring course—able to type. I took my end-of-first-year college exam the following spring and a further exam that summer, which was virtually unheard of. When I left college after just one year, I had good grades in all my subjects and was able to secure a position as a junior secretary at a local company.

With God, *all* things are possible!

Laura A. Canning

March 13

What a Mighty God We Serve

*"Ah, LORD GOD! Behold, You have made the heavens and the earth
by Your great power and outstretched arm.
There is nothing too hard for You."
—Jeremiah 32:17, NKJV*

On Friday, December 11, 2015, I went to fetch my blood test results. At the age of forty-two, I was expecting my fourth child.

When I entered the consultation room, I was silently praying that everything would go well. When the doctor showed me the test results, my heart sank in despair. They showed that my unborn baby had inherited an extra copy of chromosome 21, known as trisomy 21. This meant my baby was at high risk for Down syndrome. The doctor told me that there is no cure for Down syndrome because it is a genetic condition rather than a disease. Many people choose to terminate such pregnancies. I was supposed to have a sample of the amniotic fluid tested to confirm the condition of the baby. Unfortunately, this test carries a slight risk of miscarriage. I decided not to undergo this invasive test because I was not going to terminate the pregnancy, no matter the test results. I was facing five more months of anxiety, uncertainty, and unanswerable questions. Forgetting that the future lies in God's hands, I wondered, *Do I have strength to handle this situation? How would a Down syndrome baby impact my family both now and in the future?* The blood test results greatly disturbed my family. We prayed for a miracle, and that night I slept in tears. My faith was severely tested because this seemed to be more than we could bear. We solely depended upon divine intervention.

The following morning I woke up a little bit encouraged. I told myself that if having a baby with Down syndrome would help to prepare us for heaven, I would accept whatever God willed. I clung to many Bible verses, including 1 Corinthians 10:13, which says that our God will not allow us to be tempted more than we can bear. My pregnancy was filled with mixed emotions. One day I would be full of hope, and the next day I would be crying in agony and despair. Our friends and church family prayed for us throughout the remaining months. Then, praise God, I gave birth to a bouncing baby girl—*without* Down syndrome!

We serve a mighty God. He is indeed bigger than all our problems. He is the Creator of the universe, and nothing is too hard for Him!

Zandile Mankumba

Queen Esther and My Mother

I will say of the LORD, "He is my refuge and my fortress;
My God, in Him I will trust."
—*Psalm 91:2, NKJV*

As was Queen Esther, my mother was a woman of courage who trusted God. After years of physical and verbal abuse from my father when he came home drunk, she knew it was time to end the terror of threats on her life. She had to think about how she would take care of her three daughters, who were ten, seven, and five years old. She had been a homemaker and was unskilled for work outside our home. But the Lord provided her with work in a factory and cleaning a doctor's office. He also provided her with a safe apartment where my aunt and grandmother lived.

She taught us the practical duties of life: cooking, baking, cleaning, and sewing. She gave us chores to do after school and in the evenings. A woman of great love, she sacrificed her own needs and wants, sending us to church school, academy, and college. We girls worked summers and during the school year to help as much as we could. My mother wore her one winter coat and other clothes for many years before being able to buy new ones. Never did she complain.

A woman of prayer, Mother led out in our morning and evening worships when we studied the Bible and memorized scriptures. At church, she often helped with the children's classes. No Sabbath afternoon naps for her as she joined with my aunt and cousin to play Bible games. Our meals may have been meager on other days, but our Sabbath lunch was always special.

My sisters and I have all become successful in our respective fields. The youngest is a member of a child study team, sometimes working with children with disabilities. The middle sister works as a registered nurse. I have worked for my church's educational system as a teacher and school principal for thirty-five years. I have done my best to follow my mother's example as I, along with my husband, have raised our own children. They, too, have become successful in their careers and are active members in their churches.

All this has come about because of a young mother's courage years ago. Though a mother to three, she had the courage to trust in God and step out in her faith, leaving an abusive home life, so she could raise her daughters to know and love the Lord. I can hardly wait for Jesus' soon coming, when we will be reunited with our mother and spend eternity together.

Patricia Mulraney Kovalski

Ye Are My Witnesses

And this gospel of the kingdom shall be preached in all the world for
a witness unto all nations; and then shall the end come.
—*Matthew 24:14, KJV*

Behold, I have given him for a witness to the people,
a leader and commander to the people.
—*Isaiah 55:4, KJV*

In recent years, the church affiliation of individuals running for high offices in government has become part of the discussion in political news. When people hear that certain candidates have certain religious views, they often become interested and research what adherents of those various denominations believe.

When a candidate is identified as belonging to the same denomination as those of us in everyday life, people who are interested in learning more about that denomination often look to see how we are living *our* lives.

What would change if we knew we were being watched by those wanting to know more about our beliefs and how they impact our lives? Would we make different lifestyle choices than we currently do? Would we interact differently with others? Would we learn to become more comfortable discussing our personal beliefs with coworkers, neighbors, and family members?

If there were ever a time to grow in our faith and exercise it, that time is now. If there were ever a time to walk in (rather than just talk about) a personal, faith-based relationship with Christ, that time is now. Now—during this exciting and awesome period of earth's history—is the time to be a witness for Jesus.

So are we willing, right now, to put our trust in Jesus who promised that He would speak through us as His witnesses? Do our daily choices reflect what we believe about a loving God?

People learn more about someone's belief system from what they observe in one's daily life than from visiting the person's church or attending evangelistic meetings.

" 'Ye are my witness,' says the God of heaven. . . . We are to be a demonstration of the kind of people God . . . will have in His eternal kingdom. We should walk the streets of our home town just as we expect to walk the streets of the New Jerusalem."*

Gyl Moon Bateman

---

* Denton Edward Rebok, *Believe His Prophets* (Washington, DC: Review and Herald®, 1956), 249.

It Is Not Over Until God Says So

I, even I, am the LORD; and beside me there is no saviour.
I have declared, and have saved, and I have shewed . . . :
therefore, ye are my witnesses, saith the LORD,
that I am God. . . . I will work, and who shall let it?
—Isaiah 43:11–13, KJV

We will have to operate," said the doctor. "You could lose part or the entire uterus. You will need blood—screened, tested, and held for thirty days. Yet we cannot guarantee its purity, so you may have an allergic reaction. Finally, we cannot guarantee you will survive the surgery as this is a dire emergency. Do you understand, Mr. and Mrs. Richards? Please sign here."

I had headed home after a full day at church. Not sleeping well that night, I was exhausted by morning and did not feel well. I slept through the day but felt no relief. By evening, I was at the doctor's office. Despite prescribed medications, natural remedies, and analgesics, I had another sleepless night. The second morning found me in unyielding pain and great abdominal distress, and I felt increasingly ill. I could scarcely walk and couldn't eat or sit. Lying down brought no relief. At 3:00 P.M., we left the house and stopped at a laboratory, the doctor's office, the radiologist's, and the doctor's again. This time I received an immediate hospital referral.

In the hospital's emergency room, my mind swirled. I'd gotten up for work that morning and now here I was on my back in the hospital. Looking up, I saw I was at station 7. I prayed throughout my blood tests, x-ray, CT scan, and other tests, while being quickly monitored for the results. When my hemoglobin level was determined to be 3.5 (the normal range is 11.5–16.5), I was rushed to the preoperative room.

I silently prayed, *Just like this, Lord? Not even a will, a phone call, or last instructions to anyone?* I confessed my sins and committed myself to Him. In the pre-op room, while being prepared with great haste for the scalpel, I opened my eyes to see that I was at station 7. In the Bible, the number seven denotes wholeness. I smiled inwardly, sensing God's assurance and presence. The Great Physician took over. Though diluted blood was removed, I lost no organ. My body accepted the four units of blood. My situation was idiopathic (spontaneous disease of unknown cause). What next? We continue to pray.

But I do know in whom I believe—the God of station 7!

Keisha D. Sterling-Richards

City Lights

And the city has no need of sun or moon,
for the glory of God illuminates the city.
—*Revelation 21:23, NLT*

Recently, someone sent me a four-minute video montage of a sunset over Los Angeles followed by vibrant nighttime beauty when all the shimmering city lights turn on. One four-second segment in the montage, however, blindsided me. It was the aerial view of a sprawling nocturnal grid made up of lighted streets stretching for miles. It came alive as throughout the grid flowed living ribbons of diamond liquid composed of a million automobile headlights.

Then a powerful flashback struck. It carried me back to all those times I had flown into the Los Angeles International Airport at night from wherever I was living at the time—Oregon, Africa, Maryland. Often I flew in with baggage in addition to what I'd placed in the overhead compartment. Heart baggage: a heavy spirit, fear, a frightening medical diagnosis, uncertainty about a scheming coworker, or a marital breakup. Whatever blow life had dealt me, or was dealing, prior to any trip to Los Angeles, I always knew that "down there"—somewhere in those billions of city lights—was an old auction-purchased Buick bearing a stooped, wrinkled, silver-haired father on his way to pick up his daughter and take her *home*! Those nighttime city lights always assured me that soon everything was "going to be OK again," as Dad would put it. Nothing else in my life has ever duplicated the rush of heart warmth that the first brilliant glimpse of the panorama—below the left wing's window seat—unfailingly elicited when touchdown was only fifteen minutes away.

You have felt that rush too. I know you have: In the obvious answer to a desperate prayer, or when a word from a concerned mentor suggested new purpose for your wayward spirit. Or the time an obscure Bible promise lifted your thoughts—and your chin. Those were glimpses of city lights—lights from the Holy City where dwells the heavenly Parent who willingly comes to meet us at any point in time with help and promises renewed. At each "reunion," we sense a surge of heart warmth, realizing anew we never ever really were alone. He has *always* loved, waited for, accepted, forgiven, and welcomed us to Himself no matter what we have, or haven't, done.

City lights—harbingers of hope that we'll someday look into our Father's eyes when He comes to take us back home with Him where everything really *is* "going to be OK again."

Carolyn Rathbun Sutton

Choices

> "I am gathering a few sticks to take home and make a meal
> for myself and my son, that we may eat it—and die."
> Elijah said to her, "Don't be afraid. Go home and do as you have said.
> But first make a small loaf of bread for me from what you have and
> bring it to me, and then make something for yourself and your son."
> —1 Kings 17:12, 13, NIV

I had a choice to make. The due date on the bill for my children's church-school tuition was quickly approaching. At the time, ours was a single-parent household, and I understood what the additional stability of a Christian education could offer these children. The combined total of what I planned to give as tithe and offering was the exact amount needed for the tuition bill. This was God's money, yet the enemy conveniently whispered, "But you only have to use it once. After all, these are God's children, and He will understand."

Despite all the bad things that happened during the last year, God had been too good for me to give in to the devil now. I would return the tithe and offerings and pray for a miracle. Like the widow of Zarephath, I chose to banish uncertainty and trust God.

Friends, God does not disappoint. Within days, my boss informed me that I would receive an unexpected salary adjustment. For some reason, my salary had fallen below a new range for my position, and the organization was correcting the problem. But that was only the beginning. A few months later I was promoted to a new position and then promoted again in less than two years. No longer was I faced with how the children's tuition would be paid; the funds for their education were always there. Like the widow who fed Elijah, "the jar of flour was not used up and the jug of oil did not run dry" (1 Kings 17:16, NIV).

From elementary school, boarding academy, and on through college, even as the tuition increased, God increased my income so that at the end of the school year there was never an unpaid balance. In some cases, money was left over for the next year's tuition. My children were able to complete all their education through undergraduate school with no loans. In addition, God provided in such a way that I was able to complete a graduate degree tuition-free.

Friends, when you are faced with choices that involve your loyalty to God, keep Him first. He will always see you through with more than enough!

Yvonne Curry Smallwood

The Son of Another Woman

Gilead's wife also bore him sons, and when they were grown up,
they drove Jephthah away. "You are not going to get any inheritance
in our family," they said, "because you are the son of another woman."
—*Judges 11:2, NIV*

In some traditional African societies, illegitimate children have been viewed as problems. In the past, such children have sometimes been left on their own or in forests to die.

In the early 1980s, a teacher, who lived in the small town of Homa Bay, Kenya, married a woman who worked as a secretary in a government office. She already had a two-year-old boy. After a while, the man began to resent this child. Every time his wife went to work he would beat the little boy for no good reason. The abuse of the child increased until the man's wife had the child's biological grandparents come and take him elsewhere in the village—away from the stepfather. Though the boy's mother and stepfather cared very well for the two daughters and the son they'd had together, the illegitimate boy was neglected. But he became educated and secured a good job. Later, when his stepfather turned into a drunkard, beating his wife and neglecting their children, the illegitimate son came to their rescue.

The Bible teaches us that God has a place in His work for anyone who is willing, no matter the circumstances of his or her birth. Jephthah the Gileadite was rejected by his siblings because he was "the son of another woman" (Judges 11:2, NIV). But when their fortunes took a turn for the worse, they traveled to the desert of Hob to bring him back home as their leader. Jephthah became a mighty warrior who conquered the Moabites and who kept his promises to God.

Friends, sometimes we suffer for the sins of others. That little boy born out of wedlock suffered for the sins of his mother, but he never abandoned his family. He took courage, worked hard, and was able to help his mother despite the alcoholism and abuse in that home. Jephthah had not only a heart for God but also a heart for his family.

Let us be encouraged that our God is no respecter of persons. The apostle Peter shared that "God does not show favoritism but accepts from every nation the one who fears him and does what is right" (Acts 10:34, 35, NIV). No matter our circumstances, what truly matters is that we have a close, intimate relationship with our Father in heaven.

Monica Koko Asca

Who Is in Your Mirror?

"GOD judges persons differently than humans do. Men and women look at the face; GOD looks into the heart."
—*1 Samuel 16:7*, The Message

In today's world, it is difficult not to look in the mirror and wonder, Am I beautiful? Do I look good enough? Will people like how I look? I know I have had those questions. I must admit that aging does not eliminate the questions. The challenge is increased by the voices heard everywhere: "You should do this; you shouldn't wear that." You know the voices because I believe that you have heard them as well. It's difficult to have a healthy self-esteem if we just look around us. First Samuel 16:7 reminds us who we are and, most important, *whose* we are.

I have learned over the years that I was created in God's own image. There is not another me in all God's creation. He gave me gifts and talents in a package (me) that is unlike any other in the world. When I realized God needed me just as I am to represent who He is—that I did not have to be anyone else or do what someone else did—I just had to glorify my God. What a freeing concept!

Too often, well-meaning mothers, aunts, grandmothers, and older church members seek to mold others into their images! They want everyone to be just like them. Molding others into who we are does not work, and it does not reflect the love and grace of our God. He allows *all* of us to grow and develop at our own rate in our own time, all the while helping us to show His glory and grace. When I read God's Word, I hear Him tell me that I am His. He loves me so much He sent His only begotten Son, Jesus, to save me. I am important enough that He catches all my many tears in His vessel, and He's preparing a place for me to live with Him throughout eternity. *I am valuable!*

I'm so glad that God sees my heart. He realizes that sometimes, though I mean well, I don't do things well. He encourages me to learn from those experiences and to treat others with the same grace and patience He uses with me. Although I love those who wish to direct my development, I can remember that God sees my heart, and He is patient with me as I grow.

I am set free to look in the mirror and smile! I remember that thought as I see the reflection others will see throughout the day, and I can smile. God sees my heart!

Wilma Kirk Lee

Help These Women!—Part 1

I urge Euodia and I urge Syntyche to be of the same mind in the
Lord. Yes, and I ask you also, my loyal companion, help these
women, for they have struggled beside me in the work of the gospel,
together with Clement and the rest of my co-workers, whose names
are in the book of life.
—*Philippians 4:2, 3, NRSV*

Have you ever been distressed when two people you respected and loved came to a point on their respective life journeys where they just couldn't see eye to eye anymore? The apostle Paul experienced this very distress when he learned about two friends of his who were no longer "of the same mind."

In Philippians 4, the apostle Paul appeals to a coworker and, by extension, to the church members in Philippi to address a conflict that has arisen between two highly valued workers for the Lord.

Evidently, these two women disagreed about something and found themselves possibly not speaking to each other, or avoiding each other, or worse yet, speaking ill of each other. We know that others were aware of their conflict because somebody shared the news of their situation with Paul. No one in the church could plead ignorance about the tensions between Euodia and Syntyche.

It is amazing how fast news gets around about someone else's problem!

What is it about religious communities and gossip? Is it that we feel the perceived gravity of another's "sin" somehow diminishes the severity of our own? And if we do run to the aid of a brother or sister in conflict, it's all too often to take sides, not to bring people together. Understand me: we often do this with the best of intentions, wishing to be in solidarity with the person we believe has been wronged.

Even so, this can add more fuel to the fire if we aren't sufficiently informed about the issues. So Paul calls on the members of the church in Philippi to get involved with a conflict that has, at least temporarily, ruined a healthy relationship.

Likewise, how important for us, in a spirit of humility and with the cause of God on our hearts, to come alongside those in conflict and do what we can to help bring resolution.

Lourdes E. Morales-Gudmundsson

Help These Women!—Part 2

This is what I have asked of God for you: that you
will be encouraged and knit together by strong ties of love,
and that you will have the rich experience of knowing Christ
with real certainty and clear understanding.
—Colossians 2:2, TLB

The apostle Paul, in Philippians 4:2, 3, is calling on the members of the church in Philippi to get involved with the conflict that is keeping two valuable female associates in the work of the gospel from having a healthy relationship.

Church members are not to take sides or trash another but are to find ways of helping the disputants resolve differences, loving them both enough to hear each of their stories. Paul's is not a call only to involve the pastor or the elders; he wants the church members to feel a responsibility toward these women who have been serving them and blessing them with their ministry. He understands that conflicts, if left to fester, can turn into irreversible walls of noncommunication.

There is a debt of gratitude we owe our leaders who are, in fact, our servants. Their self-sacrificing work deserves our respect, and that debt is a debt of love. Once we understand this fact, it will not be so difficult for us to get involved in ways that will bring reconciliation and restoration when conflicts arise among spiritual servants.

The same applies to conflicts between members. We are invited to speak the truth in love so that conflicts are not prolonged and create irreversible damage. Matthew 18 lays out a process for potential healing that has often been misunderstood and misapplied, but it still plays a vital role in resolving conflicts. First of all, go directly to the persons, individually and in private, inviting them perhaps to share a meal so that you can express your concern over the conflict in a safe environment, while assuring them of the confidentiality of this encounter. Not keeping confidentiality could spell disaster for those in conflict as well as for those seeking to help.

After speaking to both parties and identifying the issues, you may choose to invite them to meet together at a neutral place to work out their differences. This may be all the parties in conflict need—the loving concern of another sister in the faith. There are certainly other options when this is not enough, but we should always begin with this initial act of loving and prudent concern.

That's what Paul meant when he invited the Philippians—and us—to "help these women" (Philippians 4:3, NRSV).

Lourdes E. Morales-Gudmundsson

Miracle at the Fund-Raiser

Before they call I will answer;
while they are still speaking I will hear.
—Isaiah 65:24, NIV

There were torrents of rain all week, which caused flooding in most of the surrounding areas. Farmers lost millions of dollars in water-soaked crops. Parts of nearby cities also experienced flooding. The weather forecast predicted even more doom-and-gloom weather. This did not bode well for my fund-raising event, a garage sale and fish fry, which was scheduled for the following Sunday. It appeared to be destined for failure.

I started earnestly praying for a miracle. Everyone involved in this fund-raising event was suggesting that we cancel. On Saturday night, those who had volunteered to clean the fish never showed up. I was able to grab one lady to help me when I saw her at a nearby youth meeting. So just three of us—the cook, the sister from the youth meeting, and I—cleaned all the fish. But we did get the job done in record time and were able to go home about eight o'clock in the evening. That was a blessing because we were scheduled to be at the fund-raising site again by five o'clock the next morning to cook and have the garage sale ready to begin at seven o'clock. Due to the weather, however, everyone was prepared for the event to be canceled. But I was looking and praying for my miracle. I kept beseeching the Lord to hold off the rain until after the sale, which was scheduled to end at two o'clock in the afternoon.

Though I love the Lord, I'd always felt something was missing in my relationship with Him. Perhaps He would work a miracle and strengthen my faith. One of the sisters whom I spoke to about the situation said to me, "Holding off rain like this would have to be a very big miracle."

"My God is a big God," I responded. Early the next morning I arrived at the site with a prayer in my heart and began unpacking containers for the garage sale. So far, no rain! It was forecast to move in a bit after nine o'clock. I just smiled, knowing in my heart that my God is a great God and I would be receiving my miracle today. Hour after hour went by as those around me kept looking anxiously at the sky. Not one drop of rain fell all day! My God *is* an awesome God!

The fund-raising event was a success. The Lord gave me my miracle. I know He truly loves me and is no respecter of persons, answering all our prayers according to His will.

Trust in the Lord, my sisters. Have faith, and believe that nothing is impossible for God.

Maureen Ferdinand

Child's Play and Consequences

When I was a child, I spoke and thought and reasoned as a child.
But when I grew up, I put away childish things.
—1 Corinthians 13:11, NLT

When I was a child, every day my three younger brothers and I played with children in the neighborhood. We rode bikes, built go-carts, roller-skated, and played hide-and-seek.

Sometimes we ventured to a wooded area with a brook near our elementary school. In the brook, we'd look for tadpoles, chase frogs, walk on rocks, or jump across the brook itself. One day we went to an area near the brook where we rarely played. It had a ledge with a drop of about five feet. Boards of various sizes were stacked below. Challenging each other, my friends began jumping off the ledge, seeing who could jump the farthest and land without falling. Since I was too scared to jump, they decided to "help" me by grabbing my hands and feet and carrying me to the edge, from which they threatened to drop me. Because of my screaming and kicking, they couldn't get a good grip on me and gave up. I ran home, crying.

Mother, seeing my red eyes, asked what was wrong. I told her everything. She called my friends' parents about their children jumping off the ledge, mentioning they also had planned to throw me off because I was scared to jump like they did. I'm sure they all got in trouble, but none of them ever threatened me afterwards, stopped speaking to me, or ended our friendship because of it. In childhood, we have all done foolish or dangerous things, often without considering the possible consequences. We were just children having fun. But as we grew up, we stopped doing those childish things because we saw everything had consequences: minor, serious, or deadly.

Our religious experiences are much the same. As children, we didn't realize or understand the many consequences of our reckless behavior; and as grown-ups, we may have realized but not cared. Reckless behavior, thoughtless decisions, and foolish choices have shaped all our lives.

As adult Christians, however, we've learned the pitfalls and are choosing safer paths, better alternatives, and responsible decisions that won't lead to devastating consequences or eternal damnation.

As we continue to grow in our spiritual walks, may we reaffirm that putting away childish things was the best decision we ever made.

Iris L. Kitching

Prayer Partners

"For where two or three are gathered together in My name,
I am there in the midst of them."
—*Matthew 18:20, NKJV*

"Whatever you ask the Father in My name He may give you."
—*John 15:16, NKJV*

Wow! Another miracle occurred! Kathy, a sweet prayer partner of mine, phoned with a prayer request and a Bible promise to claim. Each time she phoned, it always seemed that God was already waiting in the wings to perform a fantastic miracle. This time God was opening an opportunity for a new and rewarding ministry for our little "church in the wildwood."

Kathy had felt impressed to order seminar materials from a ministry that helps people recover from various kinds of addictions. This seminar was just what our community needed! Though Kathy had ordered the books and materials in plenty of time, they had failed to arrive, and the program for the community was to start in just two days.

We had been advertising all over the area. News of a fourteen-week seminar program with four break-out groups had resulted in a large number of anxious souls coming to register in anticipation of being helped. Now we were only two days away from our starting date but still had no materials. We contacted church members, initiating a season of earnest prayer for the seminar director and my dear prayer partner. Then—praise God!—the day before opening night, a large box arrived from that ministry, filled with all our much-needed workbooks and other necessary materials.

Kathy, suffering from painful spasms radiating up and down her spine, wore a smile on her face as she greeted the room filled with participants. How eager they were to end their struggles with addiction! While Kathy was standing bravely before the class, I slipped out and began to pray for this dear prayer partner. She was instantly relieved and able to complete her teaching of the class! Many miracles occurred during that seminar.

Truly God still works miracles when prayer partners spend time with each other and with their Lord. "Two are better than one, because they have a good reward for their labor" (Ecclesiastes 4:9, NKJV). If you don't have a prayer partner, find one, and then witness what God does in response to your faithful, persevering prayers.

Patty L. Hyland

To See Jesus' Face

And we know that all things work together for good to them that
love God, to them who are the called according to His purpose.
—*Romans 8:28, NKJV*

Romans 8:28 came to my mind on Sabbath morning, March 26, 2016. My church was celebrating Operation Reach Back, one of its outreach ministries for young students. The mass choir would be singing for church service. I had been rehearsing and looking forward to singing with the choir. But the day before we were to sing, I was smitten with a severe cold and could not attend church.

In my disappointment, I decided to read from my favorite book, *The Desire of Ages*; a book written by Ellen White about the life of Christ. I turned to the chapter titled "By the Sea Once More." While reading this chapter, my disappointment abated, and not being able to attend church turned out to be a blessing.

Reading about the love Jesus showed toward His disciples in their time of need and His tender forgiveness to Peter—despite Peter's denial of Christ—brought tears to my eyes. This chapter, as never before, gave me the desire to see Jesus as He really is. There are portraits of Jesus that have been painted; there are Bible descriptions of Him. But none can reveal Him as clearly as He reveals Himself through His love.

Before reading "By the Sea Once More," I would try to imagine how the new earth, the New Jerusalem, the tree of life, and the river of life will look. But after reading about the compassion and love shown by Jesus, my thoughts and greatest desire are only to see Him face-to-face. If, He looks as kind and loving in person as He truly is, He will be most beautiful!

Sometimes we take for granted the love and compassion Jesus has for us. Yet He died the most horrible death to save us from our sins. He deserves our praise and gratitude—so much more than we give Him.

There are times (and my time was on March 26, 2016) when we must be reminded who Jesus really is: our Creator, Sustainer, Redeemer, Mediator, and compassionate Friend. Truly, Jesus is our everything!

My prayer is to see Jesus' face and experience His peace in person. What about you?

Moselle Slaten Blackwell

Gossip Equals Hurtful Words

Speak not evil one of another, brethren.
He that speaketh evil of his brother, and judgeth his brother,
speaketh evil of the law, and judgeth the law:
but if thou judge the law, thou art not a doer of the law, but a judge.
—James 4:11, KJV

The tongue can do so much damage. It can ruin friendships, cause misunderstandings, and put a wall between brothers and sisters. We must be ever mindful that what we say, and the ways we criticize, can cause damage and division. Some things are better left unsaid.

We had thirty ladies in our Women's Ministries group. Every Saturday we met and then visited homes in the evening, sharing together.

This prayer group went on well until one lady started to criticize, gossip behind backs, and make fun of the ladies who actively took part. By doing this, she disheartened some in that group. They were no longer comfortable and became discouraged about participating. Slowly, the group dwindled to three or four members. So one day we spoke to this woman about how her gossiping and making fun of others who were doing God's work was actually damaging His work and hurting people. We urged her to encourage others instead of criticizing them.

Yes, we need to be careful about what we share about other people. Someone once said, "There is only one thing as difficult as unscrambling an egg, and that's unspreading a rumor." Gossip can be destructive because it is often subtle. It's hard not to be caught up in a discussion, however, when someone says, "Did you hear . . . ?" And we must not believe everything we hear. I've heard that "a gossip usually makes a mountain out of a molehill by adding some dirt." Some words are just not proper—or right—to speak. We also need to be aware that someone who shares gossip *with* us will, undoubtedly, share gossip *about* us one day.

Having a gossip-filled or foul mouth is not something to be proud of. Jesus said, "But let your communication be, Yea, yea; Nay, nay: for whatsoever is more than these cometh of evil" (Matthew 5:37, KJV). Gossip destroys our credibility.* But God can forgive us and restore our credibility.

Heal us, Lord, from painful words. Let Your love overflow our hearts.

Shakuntala Chandanshive

* Rick Smith, "Sermon: Taming the Tongue—Matthew 12," LifeWay, January 1, 2014, https://www.lifeway.com/en/articles/sermon-taming-the-tongue-matthew-12.

Little Plus Little Equals Much

And whatever you do, do it heartily,
as to the Lord and not to men.
—*Colossians 3:23, NKJV*

My friend Kathy and her grandson, Jacob, were enjoying some special time together one afternoon. In the middle of the conversation, Jacob suddenly announced, "Grandma, I really love Jesus."

"That's wonderful," she replied. "Tell me about it."

With the enthusiasm of a typical five-year-old, Jacob explained, "Everyone can tell I love Jesus because I love potlucks!" When Kathy shared that conversation with me, we both had a good laugh. Later, when I replayed the words of Jacob in my mind, I wondered how people can tell when someone loves Jesus. We know it's more than loving potluck luncheons or even going to church. My thoughts were drawn to Dorcas, also known as Tabitha, who was a beloved believer in Jesus. She is mentioned in the Bible book of Acts (Acts 9:36–41). Dorcas lived in Joppa and was known for good deeds and acts of charity. The Bible tells us that she made tunics, shirts, and cloaks for others. She seemed to pay special attention to the needs of the poor. They all loved her.

There were probably other ladies in Joppa who sewed, but what made Dorcas so different? I suspect that every garment was stitched with love. Nobody had to ask whether she loved Jesus. When she died, those whose lives she had touched were deeply distressed. The believers heard that Peter was in a nearby town and summoned him. He came immediately to Joppa. Seeing the sad mourners already preparing Dorcas's body for burial, he asked everyone to leave the room. He then prayed earnestly that the Lord would restore her life, and his request was graciously granted.

I learned three valuable lessons from Dorcas. First, she used her talent for the Lord. Next, she put self aside and did all she could do with what she was given. Finally, she treated all, even those less fortunate, with unconditional Christian love. Although we would like to do some great work for the Lord to show our love for Him, the reality is that's not going to happen for most of us. And God doesn't require it. But He has given us many opportunities for small things to be done that are, to Him, every bit as valuable.

Perhaps that's what I've known all along. I just need to watch for opportunities.

Marcia Mollenkopf

Church in the Wildwood

The LORD is nigh unto all them that call upon him. . . .
He will fulfil the desire of them that fear him.
—Psalm 145:18, 19, KJV

Each year, in the early spring, our small church plans an outing that we call the church in the wildwood. We plan an outside Sabbath morning worship service followed by a picnic lunch. We are privileged to have our outing at the nearby Pisgah National Forest. This park has numerous picnic tables, a large pavilion, and a beautiful grassy meadow. It is an ideal spot for us to worship our Creator God in the natural setting He Himself made for us to enjoy.

This year when I reserved the pavilion, only one Saturday was available, so I reserved it. When the announcement appeared in the church bulletin, everyone was excited. I suggested the church members dress casually, bring a comfortable chair, picnic food, and a happy heart. The seven-day forecast was ominous though—a 70 percent chance of rain. I began to petition to our dear Lord. *Please let us have decent weather. I don't care if it's not full sunshine, but at least don't let there be a continuous downpour on us. Thank You, and I seek Your will only.*

Each day my husband checked the forecast, and I became more hopeful as the week progressed. By Friday, the chance of rain was 25 percent. I was very encouraged!

The appointed day dawned damp and foggy, but my spirits were not to be dampened. We got up early and gathered our chairs, food, bright-green tablecloths, and flower vases for the tables. As the church members began to arrive, the sun was peeking through the clouds. Our worship service began, and the warm sun continued to make its presence known. After the wonderful service together, we spread food on the tables and began to enjoy the feast our wonderful cooks had prepared. We had pleasant fellowship with our church family and visitors. By midafternoon, everyone began to gather up their belongings and leftover food to head home. When someone remarked about the weather staying nice for us, I hastened to tell them that several of us, including my neighbor, had been pleading with our heavenly Father for a break in the weather. As we were loading up our cars to head home, the raindrops began to fall.

Our congregation had profound proof that God cares and does answer the requests of those who fear Him.

Rose Neff Sikora

The Maze

Lead me in the right path, O Lord,
or my enemies will conquer me.
Make your way plain for me to follow.
—Psalm 5:8, NLT

One day my husband and I went to a maze not far from where we were staying while on holiday. The maze was made up of wooden panels with four towers you were meant to go to—in the proper order. We were told, "If you get stuck, you can always go to the platform above the maze." We worked out the only way to get to the first tower—by using the viewing platform.

I thought of how God is our viewing platform. We may run into dead ends and take wrong turns; but when we look at our challenges from His perspective, we see our way clear to get to our objective.

As my husband and I went through the maze, we finally approached the last tower we needed to go to. We had gone through every single path, and it seemed there was no way to get to the last tower. That is until someone else showed us a wooden panel that could be swung from a hinge! That made me reflect on how Satan can make us think that there is absolutely no way to get to life's final destination. Yet God always has a way prepared; we just have to look at all the possibilities He provides. Eventually, He will help us see the way—the panel on which He has put a "hinge." He may even use others to show it to us.

Our lives may seem like mazes at times. Yet through it all, God makes our way clear.

He never leaves us alone in life's complexities. He had provided everything we need to make it safely to the end.

Not only does God want us to look at obstacles in life from His perspective—His viewing platform—but He also puts godly people in our lives to help us fight off Satan's deceptions. He uses them to encourage us that there *is* a way through our dilemmas, even when it appears there is not.

God, please show us how to view our lives from Heaven's point of view. Help us to remember we do this by reading Your Word and listening to Your voice. Help us to know when to heed the counsel of others who will give us wise, godly direction. Thank You for Jesus, who came to this earth to provide a path for us and show us how to lead our lives.

Melanie Carter Winkler

Eye Has Not Seen

But as it is written:
"Eye has not seen, nor ear heard,
Nor have entered into the heart of man
The things which God has prepared for those who love Him."
—*1 Corinthians 2:9, NKJV*

My friends have homes edged with well-trimmed shrubbery and colorful flowers, artistically arranged to show off the best features of each variety. In contrast, the shrubs outside my windows have become so overgrown that they almost look as if they could devour my fifty-year-old house. I stand at the kitchen window and gaze at two long pine tree trunks resting in my front yard—the result of a recent storm that took them down. One of these days the insurance claim will be settled, and it will be enough to repair the damage to the carport and at least help pay to have the trees removed.

Yet there is beauty: Two graceful does and speckled fawn graze in my backyard. Two male wild turkeys, their long tail feathers spread in showy fans, strut haughtily around the flock of a dozen or so outside the big picture window of the study. I see tiny but fierce hummingbirds dart crazily at each other in competition for the feeder that hangs outside the dining room window, and the tall, gangling crepe myrtle flaunts coral blossoms as it reaches for the sky. I notice the unkempt azalea hedge abloom this spring, the crimson blooms on the rhododendron, and the reflection of the setting sun as it lights up the sky and the clouds with an interplay of pink, orange, and gold. I contemplate the beauties that the new earth will hold. I try to imagine the lovely sights, the harmonious sounds, and the wonderful flavors of foods.

My mind turns to the One who left the most glorious place imaginable, where He was worshiped and adored by heavenly beings. He knew the path that He would follow on this fallen planet; the path that would lead through untold suffering, deprivation, torture, and death. And yet He came. And now He calls. He calls me, and He calls you. He calls all His created beings. Will we heed the call? He leaves the choice to us. What is my answer? What is yours?

The new day will dawn; the storms of life will be no more. The redeemed will gather around the throne with the assurance of eternal life and inexpressible joy and gladness. And the Father and the Son will rejoice over the prodigals who are prodigals no more.

There's a longing in my heart for Jesus; do you have that longing too?

Lila Farrell Morgan

April Fools' Day Emergency

Be anxious for nothing, but in everything by prayer and supplication,
with thanksgiving, let your requests be made known to God; and the
peace of God, which surpasses all understanding, will guard your
hearts and minds through Christ Jesus.
—*Philippians 4:6, 7, NKJV*

During my spring break one year, April 1 dawned uncharacteristically stormy and rainy. Two days earlier I had flown home to St. Thomas in order to accompany my recently hospitalized mother in an air ambulance from an intensive care unit to a hospital in Miami, Florida.

Because she was experiencing sporadic breathing and arrhythmia (AFib), she had to be intubated for the flight. A mass in her lungs (scar tissue from pneumonia or, perish the thought, something worse) appeared to be the cause of her medical issues. On the way to the airport in an ambulance, we passed another ambulance involved in a vehicle accident in the heavy storm.

Though the rain prevented us from boarding the tiny jet right away, the medical personnel finally covered Mom to keep her dry as they lifted her into the plane. I sat directly behind the copilot, next to Mom's stretcher and across from the three medics, also in tight quarters, who were on the pilot's side of the plane. I prayed as the plane made a bumpy ascent through the thick, dark, rain- and wind-whipped clouds up into the sunshine. As the plane leveled out, I thanked God and eventually dozed off. Sudden beeping sounds awakened me. Mom's breathing monitor had stopped working.

The nurse hit it a couple of times. It restarted—and then stopped again. The nurse tried to replace a cord, but it was stuck. The medics tried to work with it, then the copilot, and finally the pilot. But it was stuck! The nurse began to bag (manually ventilate) Mom, and we were only two and a half hours into our four- to five-hour flight! *I must be dreaming*, I thought. *This is not happening!*

Lord, You say that You do not give us more than we can bear. Should I demand they return to St. Thomas? Stop in Puerto Rico? God's peace descended upon me and kept me calm, assuring me that we must continue the flight. Miraculously, the numbers on Mom's heart monitor stayed steady throughout the remaining three hours of that flight.

Today Mom is alive, alert, and well after her bout with pneumonia, three weeks of intubation, and months of rehabilitation.

May the peace of God keep us all as we go through the storms of life.

Wanda Van Putten-Allen

Lord, Save Our Family

"If My people who are called by My name will humble themselves, and pray and seek My face, and turn from their wicked ways, then will I hear from heaven, and will forgive their sin and heal their land."
—*2 Chronicles 7:14, NKJV*

God wants members of all families to love, teach, and take care of one another. He gave us family because He never wants us to be alone. In fact, God is our Father and the foundation of loving families who work together, show love for one another, and readily forgive. God's purpose for families includes their being a blessing to others and sharing a sense of belonging.

It hurts when I hear concerns from people whose family members don't spend time with them and help build a sense of belonging. Ellen G. White wrote, "The family tie is the closest, the most tender and sacred, of any on earth. It was designed to be a blessing."*

When Satan, because of his rebellion, was cast out of heaven to this earth, he attacked the first family. He still does everything in his power to distract our children from their families and from knowing God. For family members, nothing should have more value than our children and their souls. God has given us this promise: "Train up a child in the way he should go, and when he is old he will not depart from it" (Proverbs 22:6, NKJV).

Growing up, I used to watch a weekly television show about a family. What I liked about the family in *Father Knows Best* was that they did everything together as a family. They ate meals together, solved problems together, and supported one another in the activities; and they also went to church together. They had their share of problems, but they learned to solve them without holding on to them. Neither the parents nor the three children were too proud to seek forgiveness when they offended one another. Unfortunately, many real-life family members don't forgive the wrongs of others, fix the problems, or let go of them.

Recently, I saw a young father and his three young children in a restaurant. They held hands and prayed over their food. It wasn't just grace; it was a long prayer. This impressed me so much that I had to go over and commend the father and encourage him to keep teaching his kids in the Lord. I encourage us all to make each and every moment with family members into happy memories that last forever.

Camilla E. Cassell

---

* Ellen G. White, *The Ministry of Health and Healing* (Nampa, ID: Pacific Press®, 2005), 201.

God to the Rescue

God is our refuge and strength,
A very present help in trouble.
—*Psalm 46:1, NKJV*

But I will sing of Your power;
Yes, I will sing aloud of Your mercy in the morning;
For You have been my defense
And refuge in the day of my trouble.
—*Psalm 59:16, NKJV*

It was a beautiful evening; the sun was moving toward the western sky but and still shining brilliantly. The sunshine was accompanied by a gentle breeze that seemed to caress my face as my husband and I went for a leisurely walk through the neighborhood where we live.

Halfway through the walk, we approached an incline. We saw a family of three, two adults and a teenage lad. They appeared to be examining the engine of a car that was parked in the garage. As we passed, I noticed that both the door leading to the house from the garage and the garage door were wide open.

Suddenly, a very large dog rushed past the individuals attending to the car and ferociously charged at me! The dog was within inches of me when I yelled out, "Stop!" Only when I yelled did the owners look up. They immediately called the dog and forcefully pulled it inside the house.

By this time, I was so shaken that I fell onto the grass by the sidewalk. My husband was slightly ahead of me, unaware that I had fallen. The individuals in the garage never came to help me. They simply yelled, "Are you all right, ma'am?" Then with the dog inside, they closed the door of the house. I truly believe that God was my defense at that moment (see Psalm 59:16). I am convinced that had the Lord not interposed and stopped the vicious attack of this dog, I could have been bitten and even mauled.

At the time this event occurred, I was so frightened and scared that I forgot to pray. But at the beginning of the day, I had asked the Lord to guide, guard, and protect me from harm. He answered just when I needed Him.

We should always make it the first duty of the day to seek the Lord and commit our lives into His care.

Thank You, dear Lord, for being a very present help to me in my trouble.

Kollis Salmon-Fairweather

Am I There Yet?

There is a time for everything,
and a season for every activity under the heavens:
a time to be born and a time to die,
a time to plant and a time to uproot.
—*Ecclesiastes 3:1, 2, NIV*

I felt it was always in me to care for others, but it wasn't really brought out in me until my son became a registered nurse—and a very good one, at that.

I worked in electronics for almost thirty years. My husband knew I didn't feel fulfilled doing this. One day he found an ad in the newspaper that stated applicants could have free training if they committed to working six months for a nursing home. The organization was accepting only ten applicants. Praying for God to lead me, I nervously quit my job and filled out an application. I was surprised I was picked because I was already fifty-nine years old. I learned I had been one of the selected applicants *because* of my age!

During the training, I asked God to help when I went to class and took tests. God was with me, and I did very well. I fulfilled my nursing-home obligation, working there for a year and a half. Then I went into in-home care. There my heart was filled with love and care for others.

My husband eventually retired, and we moved to a small town in northeast Colorado. Even at my age, I still felt God calling me. I looked for in-home care jobs but found nothing. During my prayers one morning, I felt as if God said, *Go to the nursing home.*

I said, "God, You know that's not what I want." Yet He had told me to go. Although I was in town that day, I planned to put off applying for a position at the nursing home. But God was right there, pushing me. Well, I got the job.

When asked why I wanted to work at a nursing home, I responded, "I just want to make these people's last days nice." And I do my best. Before I leave one lady's room at the home, she always says, "I love you." Talk about feeling fulfilled! She asked me one day when I was going to retire. I told her, "God sent me here, and He will tell me when it is time to leave."

"Good for you," was her response.

I'm getting close to seventy years old and am still going strong. I feel God has put me where I am and will let me know when I am finished.

You see, God can still use us—even long after we feel we're supposed to be through.

Florence L. Ashby

Trapped or Free?

It is for freedom that Christ has set us free.
—*Galatians 5:1, NIV*

The Bible-study group I coordinate meets in a conference room at a hospital adjacent to our church. At the close of our study time, I turn out the lights and ensure that the electronic security system has locked the door. This simple routine usually works well.

Recently, after locking up, I followed the rest of the group across campus, but as I arrived at the church, a group member asked, "Have you seen my wife?" Oh no! I hadn't realized that my elderly friend had entered the restroom at the rear of the conference room before we left. I rushed straight back, hoping to meet her on the way because I knew that she could use the door-release button to let herself out. The button was right next to the door on a small panel with a green light and the words "Press Here to Exit." But did she know to look? After a quick search, I finally checked the long corridor linking the conference room to the nearby consulting suites, which were all closed and dark. There was my friend, still looking for a way out!

Only ten minutes had elapsed since she'd been missed, but she was tired and stressed when I reached her. Of course, she felt rather foolish when she realized that she hadn't been trapped at all. If she had only pressed that little button, she would have been free!

Have you had the experience of trying to convince a small bird that has gotten inside a building that it is not trapped but free to go? You usher it toward an open door, but it flies against a closed window. How frustrating! If only it could understand that you are trying to set it free!

I wonder whether Jesus experiences a similar sense of frustration in dealing with human beings. He has paid the price for our sins and set us free. But the devil delights in convincing us that this can't be true, and so we go on struggling. Then there is the opposite problem: the devil entangles us in sin but tells us we are free—free to do as we please or that we don't need God or that religion ties us down. Satan doesn't mind which deception we fall for, as long as he keeps us from experiencing true forgiveness and freedom in Jesus.

But praise God, we have His promise: "If the Son sets you free, you will be free indeed" (John 8:36, NIV).

Jennifer M. Baldwin

Our Creative God

In the beginning God created the heavens and the earth.
—*Genesis 1:1, NKJV*

When I read the words "God created" and I look at the world and the many different living things around me, I know our God is creative. He could have designed all the animals to be one kind. But instead, there is variety and creativity all around. God is an artist par excellence. No Sistine Chapel or sculpture comes close to what our God made for us in the world to enjoy.

"Then God said, 'Let Us make man in Our image, according to Our likeness' " (Genesis 1:26, NKJV). I look at this verse and realize that every good thing in me reflects my God. So I have concluded that if God has a creative side, so do I, and I discovered it some thirteen years ago. It was quite an eye-opener for me to realize that I could make a card or scrapbook a page in an album when all my life I thought I did not possess one creative gene. In the past two years, this creativity has transferred to my spiritual life. Some of you may have heard of Bible art journaling or creative spiritual journaling. The first is creating art in a Bible, and the second is creating art in a journal. What do I create? Well, let me first say, I may have some of God's creativity in me, but it's very small, and I put much effort into what I do. That said, when I have my daily worship and read my Bible, I spend time meditating on what I have read and try to find a visual image that brings my thoughts to life.

For example, when I read, "He who dwells in the secret place of the Most High shall abide under the shadow of the Almighty" (Psalm 91:1, NKJV), the image that came to mind was that of a mother hen protecting her baby chicks under her wings. What a comforting picture! My Father covers me with His wings when I abide with Him. I googled "mother hen and chicks," found a drawing, printed it, colored it, and put it in my Bible by this verse.

When I read about of the woman at the well, I knew I could not draw a waterpot. Again I googled what I needed and found the image of a beautiful black-and-white waterpot that I printed out, colored, cut out, and stuck in the wide margin of my Bible with my thoughts written next to it.

Using visual imagery in my Bible study time with God has deepened my relationship with Him. Now the words on the page are not just beautiful words, they are words of life—words I see reflected in my everyday life.

Heather-Dawn Small

What's in a Name?

The name of the LORD is a strong tower:
the righteous runneth into it, and is safe.
—*Proverbs 18:10, KJV*

Terry was just two years old when we moved next door to her and her parents, Jerry and Mary Lee. She loved to come to our house even though our boys were several years older. In spite of all Mary Lee's efforts to have her call me Mrs. Graves, Terry persisted in calling me Mary Jane, which was fine with me. One day she went home feeling quite indignant and said to her mother, "Do you know what Mr. Graves calls Mary Jane? He calls her Mary Jane!"

"Well," Mary Lee said, "I think that's awfully familiar!"

Almost four years ago my granddaughter, Rachele, and her husband, Brad, blessed me with my first great-grandchild, a healthy, happy boy. The name they chose seemed a very big one for such a very little baby: Theodore Julian Epperson. This name has special meaning to the family. The name *Theodore* is for his great-grandfather, Theodore "Ted" Graves, and his great-uncle, Ted Graves Jr. The name *Julian* is for another great-grandfather. But we call our great-grandson Teddy J. He has recently been joined by a baby brother, Landon Bradley Epperson.

In Bible times, names had special meanings. I can imagine that Jacob (meaning "the supplanter") felt better about himself when his name was changed to Israel (because he was an overcomer). On the other hand, when Naomi lost her husband and both sons, she said she should be called Mara, "for the Almighty hath dealt very bitterly with me" (Ruth 1:20, KJV). But Naomi's story had a happy ending when her beloved, widowed daughter-in-law remarried and had a son, and Naomi became his nurse.

I had a college friend whose name, Malda, was unusual and often mispronounced as Maulda. So in later years, she officially changed it to Chris, which is short and simple! Although I have never been too happy with my name, it is part of my identity. Yet someday, if I'm faithful, I will also have a name change. "To him that overcometh . . . I . . . will give him a white stone, and in the stone a new name written, which no man knoweth saving he that receiveth it" (Revelation 2:17, KJV). I have no idea what my new name will be, but I do know that I will be perfectly happy with it because it will be chosen by One who knows me and makes no mistakes!

Mary Jane Graves

April 8

When Prayers Were Answered

Do not be anxious about anything, but in every situation, by prayer
and petition, with thanksgiving, present your requests to God.
—*Philippians 4:6, NIV*

As I was about to go through the door, my cell phone rang. It was my sister who lived with my parents. "What are you doing?" she asked. "Dad just fell, and the ambulance is taking him to the hospital in your area." I could feel my heart pounding in my chest; and for a moment, I could hardly breathe. She was talking about our father, whom I love dearly!

Daddy was an independent; five-foot, eleven-inch; eighty-five-year-old. Always the life of the party, he knew how to make people feel comfortable and loved. He was trained in first aid and lived to see others happy.

But all this changed on the morning of April 2, 2013. Daddy had left home early that morning to pick up his eye medication at the health center, which was only one street away from his home. But on the way, he was attacked by two dogs. The attack caused him to fall backward off a curb and hit his head.

The x-rays showed he had not suffered any broken bones; but because blood was flowing from his nostrils, he was transferred to a general hospital for further examination. An MRI revealed he had sustained a small blood clot. Doctors said it would dissolve, so Dad was discharged.

The next morning when Dad awoke, he was unable to speak or recognize anyone. He was rushed to a Christian hospital to be seen by a neurosurgeon. Yet, after seven weeks of hospitalization (six of those in the intensive care unit), Daddy peacefully fell asleep on May 21.

We had prayed day and night for Daddy's health to improve, but he died.

His death, however, did not mean that our prayers were not answered. You see, I had always told God that I wouldn't be able to handle any sudden death in my family. While Dad was in the hospital, we prayed that God would answer our prayers as He saw fit as well as grant us His peace that passes all understanding. This He did.

Sisters, we serve a mighty God who is more than able to take us through any circumstance. We can be sure God will work out everything for our eventual good. Moreover, He has promised that before we even call on Him, He will answer (see Isaiah 65:24).

Jill Springer-Cato

Sunshine in My Soul

"As I was with Moses, so I will be with you.
I will not leave you nor forsake you."
—Joshua 1:5, NKJV

As I sit on my parent's veranda in Zimbabwe, the warm sunlight beating down on my back, I feel really warm and comforted. I know that this same warmth was felt by my husband, Errol, the last time he was here. He might have even sat in the exact spot that I am sitting in now.

After thirty-seven years of marriage, I have lost the love of my life. One year and two months later I've come to our home in Africa to grieve with my parents and, hopefully, heal my heartache.

Today I gave away most of his clothes that remained in our wardrobe. I am numb—have no emotions really—but feel guilty that I am giving away the last traces of him. I know I have to let go and continue my journey without him in my life, but this is much easier said than done. People do not really understand how I feel unless they are walking in my shoes: the void caused by his absence from my life, the loneliness I feel, the emptiness when I want to ask his advice on decisions, especially when our kids are driving me crazy. When I have to make plans without him, I feel like canceling all of them.

I avoid mixing socially with other couples. Even food doesn't taste as nice anymore. I miss his smile, his mischievousness, his cooking, and all that he used to do for me. I want him back but know that is impossible.

For now, I am learning to nurture my relationship with God. Yes, there are times when I question my loss. I wrestle with my impatience for answers, and sometimes I doubt His ability to provide for me. But then I feel the warmth of the sun on my back and am reminded of how He sent a cloud by day and the fire by night for the children of Israel. I then understand what He means when He says that just as He was with Moses, so He will be with me.

He will never leave me nor forsake me (see Hebrews 13:5). He is my strength when I am weak, and He loves me unconditionally.

I trust Him completely, for He knows what's best.

I live in the hope of the resurrection morning.

Valerie Fisher Green

April 10

Queen Vashti Was Right

"My sheep hear My voice, and I know them, and they follow Me."
—John 10:27, NKJV

When we read the story of Esther, we may quickly bypass Queen Vashti; but if there had not been a Vashti, there may not have been a Queen Esther. Because Vashti exhibited discretion, Esther was able to stand before the king on behalf of her people.

All creatures have some sort of self-protection. Lions have their bite; skunks, their distinct odor; rats have a keen sense of smell; and men have upper body strength beyond what we women have in comparison. So what did God give women to protect themselves with? The most beautiful defense of all: a large portion of His Holy Spirit. We may call it by different names: intuition, sixth sense, mother wit, or our gut. No matter what we name it, it is "God with us."

By the edict of King Xerxes, no limits were placed on the drinking at his feast; the servants had been instructed to give guests as much as they wished. On the seventh day of nonstop drinking, the king ordered that Queen Vashti be brought in to be gazed upon for her beauty.

Vashti, fully understanding that the penalty for disobeying the king could mean her life, declined. The Bible doesn't say she sent any explanation or apology. She didn't concern herself about her standing in the community, what her girlfriends would say, how she would pay her bills, or the possibility of people calling her crazy. She didn't go into a season of prayer and fasting to try to get God to honor what He had already stated was wrong. She didn't even ask for confirmation for her choice and actions. She was confident she was doing what was right.

God says, "My sheep hear My voice, . . . and they follow Me" (John 10:27, NKJV). Even when we think we don't know God, God knows us. The problem is that many of us have been taught from a young age to dishonor our intuition (I like to think the *in* portion of *intuition* is God's Spirit with us). Sometimes we've been forced to hug someone who makes us feel uncomfortable. Or we feel distraught about a situation but can't explain why. So we dismiss our intuition and later find out we should have followed it. God loves us so much that He gave us intuition.

Don't allow yourself or anyone else to talk you out of listening to your Shepherd. You may be saving a nation and, like Queen Vashti, not even know it until you are in God's kingdom.

D. Reneé Mobley

Feeling God's Pleasure

Whatever your hand finds to do, do it with all your might.
—*Ecclesiastes 9:10, NIV*

God made me to run, and when I run I feel His pleasure." This was the motivation that made Eric Liddell break a world record in the 1924 Summer Olympic Games in Paris. This young Scottish athlete was a Christian who would not race on the day he thought was the Sabbath. He chose between his religious beliefs and competing in an Olympic race. His race day was changed, and he broke an Olympic record pursuing the gift he felt God had given him.

While she wasn't an Olympian, God certainly gifted Deborah with unique gifts—especially in her day. The pendulum of the Israelite nation's behavior swung back and forth between obedience to God and evil choices. It was during one of those evil swings that Deborah was chosen as a prophetess and a judge to bring Israel back to God and out from under the oppression of Jabin, a Canaanite king. Deborah's judgment was sought to settle disputes, so God had obviously given her a discerning heart as well as compassion and leadership. Deborah's courage was remarkable as she was commissioned to go into battle with the Israelite army general to rout the Canaanite enemy. At the end of this battle, Deborah rejoiced as she sang, "So may all your enemies perish, Lord! But may they who love you be like the sun when it rises in its strength" (Judges 5:31, NIV). When she was using the gifts God had given her, she felt His pleasure!

Paul tells us, "There are different kinds of gifts, but the same Spirit distributes them. There are different kinds of service, but the same Lord. There are different kinds of working, but in all of them and in everyone it is the same God at work" (1 Corinthians 12:4–6, NIV).

How do you know for sure what gifts you've received from God? Think back over your lifetime, and jot down things you've done that really brought you happiness.

If doors open and opportunities arise to do something different, don't hesitate. If this is something God is nudging you to do, His Spirit will give you divine energy to help you succeed, even if you're stepping out of your comfort zone. As you consider your God-given talents, don't be timid and reluctant.

When you feel successful, you'll know you're doing what God has gifted you to do, and you can bask in the warmth of His pleasure.

Roxy Hoehn

April 12

Let's Share the Inspiration!

My heart is overflowing with a good theme;
I recite my composition concerning the King;
My tongue is the pen of a ready writer.
—Psalm 45:1, NKJV

Constantly, I'm inspired by spoken or written words. Yet it isn't always a well-written message or vocal delivery that alerts my thoughts. Usually, it's a simple word linking that provides my pause for reflection. Oftentimes the words are never forgotten.

Ten-year-old Julius made my day when he answered a question I asked him. He and his teenage sister, Chloe, were taking a summertime writing-skills class that I developed just for kids: The Fun of Writing.

My question was, "Since you started this class, have you found that your writing is harder or easier than before?"

With profound enthusiasm, Julius stood up from his chair and announced with confidence, "It's easier!"

When I inquired why, he responded, "Because I didn't know what I was doing before!" His mother, who sat in on the class, beamed. She alerted me when she contacted me about the classes, "Julius doesn't enjoy writing." She had hoped that might change.

Before this, I'd not shared writing skills in a class setting with a child younger than twelve. Thus, I expected this child to present a challenge to me by his age and by possessing no interest. I'd even requested prayers from my prayer-warrior friends about my upcoming challenge named Julius. Instead, he and his sister both delighted me by being human sponges. They were brave enough to submit their work for publication, and they received a spread in *KidsView*. Julius's confident reply—words that inspired me—stays with me. We all teach in one way or another; and when we see evidence of inspiration making its circle, it's rewarding.

Most of my inspiration comes from the Bible. Yet I want to return that inspiration to God by writing for Him and speaking for Him. "But sanctify the Lord God in your hearts: and be ready always to give an answer to every man that asketh you a reason of the hope that is in you with meekness and fear" (1 Peter 3:15, KJV). Surely that puts a smile on God's face.

Sisters around the world, I'd like to request that we make that shared inspiration!

Betty Kossick

Parable From the Pantry

Taste and see that the LORD is good;
blessed is the one who takes refuge in him.
—*Psalm 34:8, NIV*

I began collecting big glass jars when my mother-in-law pointed out how ideal they were for food storage. I am indebted to her for quite a few good ideas, but this was a gem for several reasons. One is that I can see what is in them at a glance. One day I decided to use up some softening apples in the fridge and make pie. I peeled the apples, put together the filling, put it in the pie crust and popped it into the oven, baking it to a golden brown. It looked scrumptious. When my kids came home from school, they wrinkled up their noses and said, "What is that wonderful smell? Are we having pie for supper?" My husband asked the same questions.

So when the evening meal had been cleared away, I brought that beautiful, fragrant pie to the table. We lifted the first mouthwatering bite to our mouths. But a clamor of dismay quickly replaced our anticipation! Something was wrong. The pie was salty! I jumped up and ran to look at the big glass jars in the pantry. I'd used salt instead of sugar! Fortunately for me, we had a small but undiscriminating herd of cows just over the back fence that didn't consider a pie made with salt instead of sugar a disaster.

I got to thinking about how delectable that pie looked—until I took the first bite. God invites me to "taste and see that the LORD is good" (Psalm 34:8, NIV). He doesn't say, "Look and see how great the Lord appears." God is into the tasting part. The proof of the pudding is in the eating part. He invites me to experience the whole pie, so to speak. Notice the last part of this verse seems to flow from the first part. "O taste and see that the LORD is good: blessed is the man that trusteth in him" (verse 8, KJV). When I taste of the Lord, my knowledge of the Lord becomes personal. I've actually taken Him into my very being—He's become a part of me. Then it becomes natural for me to trust Him because I've experienced Him myself. I know what He tastes like, and it's good.

There are a lot of distractions in my world begging to be tasted. Things that look good or smell good, but often I find that they don't satisfy and may even bring a clamor of dismay.

But I've tasted of the Lord, and He's consistently the same. He is *good*! I'm glad I know that because blessed, or happy, is the woman who trusts in Him.

Rhonda Huffaker Bolton

The Power of God

"Be strong and courageous. Do not be afraid . . . , for the LORD your
God goes with you; he will never leave you nor forsake you."
—*Deuteronomy 31:6, NIV*

I heard the screams. I couldn't discern what I was hearing, but it was an alarming
sound. I kept listening.* I was living in an apartment, and a friend and I were
sitting on my balcony. I heard the screams of what sounded like a child. Now
I am not a confrontational person, and I don't like conflict. But I knew I had to
do something, and the power of God is the reason I could pursue this mystery.

The sounds were coming from the basement. Each apartment had an assigned
storage area that was concrete with no windows and a cage-type door. To my
horror, I discovered a child was screaming from within one of these storage areas
and was in the dark. He was terrified and locked in. I told him I was getting help
and knocked on the door of the closest apartment. A woman opened the door. I
asked whether the screaming child was hers.

"He's being punished," she said. I told her that she needed to let him out. She
refused, so I said I was calling the police. I was very firm, and this was not like
anything I had ever done. I was in my early twenties, and this wasn't my comfort
zone.

Finally, she agreed to let him out. My friend had come down at this point,
so we left but made sure the little boy was released. Other than being extremely
upset, he appeared to be physically OK. But who knows what type of emotional
scar was inflicted that day?

I went to work the next morning. The following day, when I inquired at the
apartment complex, I was told that the family with the little boy had moved to
their country of origin. It was then that I remembered there had been another
child in the apartment that fateful day. He was in diapers, and I remembered that
he had a cast around his arm. My heart sank. All I could do was say a prayer of
protection for these little boys.

Sometimes we may find ourselves in situations where we don't know what
to do. I know God doesn't want to put us in harm's way, but if we feel the Holy
Spirit moving in us like I felt that day, then He will lead us to do what we must.
I am glad I followed His strong impressions and found the courage to act. God
was with me every step of the way. And He is with you too.

Jean Dozier Davey

---

* This event happened forty years ago.

Like the Birds

"Look at the birds of the air;
they do not sow or reap or store away in barns,
and yet your heavenly Father feeds them.
Are you not much more valuable than they?"
—Matthew 6:26, NIV

The minute I heard the elated *cheerily, cheeriup, cheerio, cheeriup* series of musical whistles, I knew a robin had just found my garden. Following the bird's loud, melodious chirrups, I searched the blossomed branches of the Callery pear tree with hopeful eyes, trying to locate my happy soloist. There he was—peachy orange feathers and a song, sweet and wild. "Look at the birds of the air." Astonishment and wonder filled my heart. God's promises became flesh right that moment, breathing a new song of joy and praise into my heart.

How I wished then to be able to hold this magnificent living creature of the air in my opened hands and retain his songs of trust and conviction forever in my heart! I wanted him perched, but instead, as if in an attempt to preserve that sense of wonder in me, the bird stopped singing and, with an almost soundless swiftness of wings, flew away.

We might think that Jesus was only trying to help us alleviate our anxieties when He talked about the value of birds, but He was actually trying to let us see that worrying about them is really a lack of trust in God. I like to think that perhaps Jesus was also trying to bring our attention to the practice of everyday mindfulness. You see, nothing is worth more than this day. The present is a precious gift from God that too often is taken for granted. As the saying goes, "Yesterday is history; tomorrow is a mystery." We have only today. And that's what Jesus wants us to see.

We have the tendency to take things for granted. God's beautiful creations, such as birds, flowers, and the rainbow after a rainy day, often go unnoticed or unappreciated. The many blessings by which we are surrounded, including the ones we love, become invisible to us. Living each moment mindfully—paying close attention to our surroundings and to those we travel with along this road called life—makes us understand that worrying about the past and the future can only bring and aggravate stress, anxiety, depression, addiction, and chronic pain.

"Do not worry. Look at the birds of the sky!" says Jesus. So give me meadow flowers and waking up to the first flock of robins in the garden. Give me the little things that bestow joy and peace to my heart. "With singing lips my mouth will praise you" (Psalm 63:5, NIV).

Olga Valdivia

Judge Not!

Judge not that ye be not judged.
For with what judgment ye judge, ye shall be judged:
and with what measure ye mete, it shall be measured to you again.
—Matthew 7:1, 2, KJV

Even many non-Christians sense that one shouldn't judge others. It is often said, "What goes around comes around!"

Usually, our five-year-old Rick and nine-month-old Julie behaved well in church. But on this Sabbath, Julie occasionally shrieked. It was not a good day to be fussy because our new pastor, Sharpton Crabbe, and wife, Angela, were at our church for the first time, and Mrs. Crabbe was sitting in the pew with us.

"God is not pleased when His sanctuary is filled with noise!" Mrs. Crabbe hissed under her breath. "You haven't taught your children to be reverent in church. You should go to the mother's room."

That hurt—a lot! Struggling to keep my voice even, I said, "I will check to see what's wrong. But I can't stay in the mother's room because I play piano for church and my husband, Carl, has elder's duty today. The children must be close to me and cannot stay in the mother's room."

Mrs. Crabbe left, and I concluded that she was a real grouch!

I noticed Julie only cried out when she turned her head a certain way. Was something about her new little dress hurting her? She had a small red spot on her neck. New garments often contained many straight pins. Alas, we missed one! "I'm sorry, Baby," I soothed. "The only way you can say something is wrong is to cry."

After church, I explained to Mrs. Crabbe what had happened. She said, "I'm sorry. I sounded off without knowing all the facts."

After that, she and others took turns keeping both Rick and Julie happily occupied when Carl and I had to be up front.

While we are busy sizing up others, they may be doing the same to us. We shouldn't decide from a bad first impression that a person is no good. We need to think before we act. Unkind words or acts may come back to bite us. And so we shouldn't judge.

Bonnie Moyers

Meticulous Father

"But seek first the kingdom of God and His righteousness,
and all these things shall be added to you."
—Matthew 6:33, NKJV

My husband and I have lived in the United States for more than six years without a car due to some uncontrollable circumstances. By God's grace, we got some money from our tax return this year and decided to purchase a used car. We asked friends to help us find a good one. Personally, I would have preferred a Nissan Altima GLE, but with limited funds, one cannot be selective. So I left it in God's hands and forgot about it.

About three months later, a church elder told me that he had found a car, but the owner would have to fix the windshield.

A week later the head deacon, Emmanuel, also told me about another good car. I suggested he consult with Elder Evans so that they could test and select the best car for us.

They did all the necessary homework and chose one for me to buy, knowing neither my expectation nor the particular car I had really desired.

I paid for the car through Emmanuel. Then I bought automobile insurance online, registered the car, and acquired all the necessary papers. Emmanuel brought the car keys to me and said, "Come and look at your car." To my amazement, I found myself looking at a Nissan Maxima. And it was the GLE model with a sunroof, leather interior, and seats that can be warmed in the winter! After coming out from my shock, all I could say was, "Oh, my God, how great Thou art!"

I am talking about a meticulous God who is able to meet our needs.

Friends, the God we serve knows our hearts; and if we rely on Him with a mustard seed of faith, He will bless us with our hearts' desires. Elder Evans and Emmanuel did not know my desire for a certain type of car, but my able Father led them to the exact one that I wanted and with a bonus—it was a Maxima instead of an Altima. It was a luxury car.

Jesus said to seek God and His righteousness before anything else, then "all these things" would be given to us (Matthew 6:33, NKJV). I simply prayed for a used car, and the One who knew my heart gave me my heart's desire. I am in awe. How does He do it? You tell me.

Mabel Kwei

April 18

Saved From Deception

"You will not certainly die," the serpent said to the woman. "For God knows that when you eat from it your eyes will be opened, and you will be like God, knowing good and evil."
—*Genesis 3:4, 5, NIV*

On the evening of February 15, 2017, I had just finished a refresher training program on adult literacy at Repalle, Andhra Pradesh, India, and was waiting for a bus to take me to another village. I would conduct a women's ministries meeting there later in the evening.

Suddenly, I received a phone call from an unknown number. The friendly caller started asking me about the details of my debit-card account from our bank (SBI). "Madam, we are calling from SBI to let you know that your debit card will expire in a few months. We can renew it for you if you will kindly give us the four digits of the number on your card." Now I knew that bank personnel would never ask for such account details over the phone and became suspicious.

"I am not able to do so at this time," I responded, "but tomorrow I will come to SBI and provide you with all the necessary documents." The person on the phone became very angry.

"If you don't give us the last four digits on your card right now, we will have to cancel your card. Your account balance will shrink to zero!" While listening to his words, I was confused and thought, *Are my debit-card details really with that person?* God impressed me, *No!*

"I can't comply with your request because my husband has the debit card, and he's not with me at the moment," I said to the caller. He then ordered me to give him my husband's number. When I stated my belief that this was a scam call and suggested that I might have recorded it as evidence that would be turned over to the police, the caller immediately disconnected. Not only could I not call the number back, but SBI personnel confirmed they did not make such calls.

This incident reminds me how Satan deceived Eve and caused destruction to the beautiful world that was created by God. Satan's words at first sounded very cordial, as did the scammer's. But they were intended to further his interest, not Eve's. "But evil men and seducers shall wax worse and worse, deceiving, and being deceived" (2 Timothy 3:13, KJV).

Thank You, Lord, for giving us the presence of mind and timely knowledge so that we can avoid being deceived.

Uma Chinnaiah

Magnificent Deity

For in him the whole fullness of deity dwells bodily, and you have
been filled in him, who is the head of all rule and authority.
—*Colossians 2:9, 10, ESV*

While reading my devotions this morning, the following quote from Oswald Chambers tore at my heart and grabbed my attention: "One of the most amazing revelations of God comes to us when we learn that it is in the everyday things of life that we realize the magnificent deity of Jesus Christ."*

Lord, You brought this to my attention. I realize that my focus is on my stuff. It is not on You being the "magnificent deity" in my life.

What a mind-boggling concept that one God, one Lord, one Savior, one Redeemer came down from heaven to become a Baby—but also the Son of man. This Son of man was ridiculed, brutally beaten, and spat upon; He suffered horrible treatment and was rejected (even by His own disciples). Yet He chose to endure it all anyway because He loved us, even just me.

If I had been the *only* one alive on this planet, He would have died for me. This is the story I choose to tell over and over again. *Jesus loves me; this I know* (period)!

I want the knowledge of God's love for me to grow in my prayer life when I am bewildered from working with people that just don't "get it" or when I am unfortunately stumped, callously stubborn, tactlessly criticized, and ridiculously ridiculed.

The Son of man, the God, the Holy One can resolve and absolve issues that only the presence of Jesus can orchestrate. Who am I to think that I can come up with the solutions?

I confess before You, Lord Jesus, I have taken the role of the Holy Spirit, thinking I can convict or resolve someone else's problems. I choose to focus on presenting before You God's people. Soften hearts; speak through Your Word. Bring the presence of the living Jesus to blanket our people with Holy Spirit firepower. May this holy fire burn within our hearts—the presence of the real, live Jesus—so that we choose Him every minute of each day. It is through the Holy Spirit's presence that I accept and receive this in Jesus' holy and precious name. Amen!

Mary H. Maxson

---

* Oswald Chambers, *My Utmost for His Highest*, ed. James Bermann (Grand Rapids, MI: Discovery House Publishers), entry for February 7.

Easter Blessing

"He is not here; for He is risen, as He said.
Come, see the place where the Lord lay."
—Matthew 28:6, NKJV

After my family moved to Montreal, my grandparents lived with us. As they got older, they traveled back and forth to Trinidad to escape the cold. My grandfather, whom we called Papa, eventually took his last trip home and died on the Monday after Easter when he was eighty-six. Several years later my younger brother, Haisley, died of cancer when he was thirty-seven—also on an Easter Monday. When we attended Papa's funeral, my mother, Edris, contracted a virus that enlarged her heart. Mom lived with congestive heart failure. Her heart stopped beating one night when she was eighty years old—on an Easter Sunday. As you can imagine, Easter took on a new meaning for my family.

Yet I remember that before sin reared its ugly head in Eden, God had put a plan of salvation in place. But a sinless "man" needed to conquer sin and death. "For God so loved the world that He gave His only begotten Son, that whoever believes in Him should not perish but have everlasting life" (John 3:16, NKJV). So Jesus, God's Son, put on humanity and came to earth. He had a humble beginning and became a carpenter like His earthly father. Jesus grew in knowledge and stature (see Luke 2:52). In constant communion with His heavenly Father, Jesus often went off to a quiet place to pray.

The time came for the plan to be fulfilled. While Jesus' heart was heavy, He prayed to His Father for strength to endure the trial. He was nailed to an old rugged cross, and like a sheep going to the slaughter, He opened not His mouth (see Isaiah 53:7). After being crucified and dying for us, He was placed in a tomb, which was sealed. Satan hoped he had won. Yet after the Sabbath, on the first day of the week, Mary Magdalene and the other Mary went to the tomb, and the tomb was empty. A mighty angel had rolled away the sealing stone. The angel told the women that Jesus had risen just as He said He would. "O, death, where is thy sting? O, grave, where is thy victory?" (1 Corinthians 15:55, KJV). He is risen!

I thank God for Easter, the plan of salvation, and the empty tomb of Jesus that gives us hope that the tombs of our sleeping loved ones will also, someday soon, be empty as well.

Sharon Long (Brown)

"He Is Not Here"

Then they remembered that he had said this.
So they rushed back from the tomb to tell . . . everyone.
—*Luke 24:8, 9, NLT*

Very early in the morning the women arrived at the tomb, carrying myrrh, cassia, and other spices to embalm the body of their beloved Master. It had seemed the Sabbath would never end—and the night! Had there ever been a night so dark or so long? With their still broken hearts, they'd made their way to the tomb, relieved finally to have something to do that would keep their hands busy, even if their minds still grappled with the unspeakable horror of the Crucifixion.

But when they reached His tomb, instead of finding Jesus, they saw an angel who asked, "Why are you looking among the dead for someone who is alive?" Then, seeing the confusion on their faces, he continued, "He isn't here! He is risen from the dead!" (Luke 24:5, 6, NLT). Oh, can you imagine how those precious women felt just then? A moment passed. Then another. And suddenly the angel's words, "He is not here!" became their rallying cry. "He is not here! He is risen!" Now they remembered Jesus' words! Turning from the tomb, they ran to share the good news with the world.

In spite of having read this story so many times, we still turn toward the tomb. In our brokenhearted longing for Jesus, we linger at the place we image Him to be, only to find He is not there. We search among the dead for that which is alive. Have you ever been sure you knew exactly what God was calling you to do with your life? Have you pursued ministry only to discover that He was not there? Like our sisters, we move quickly to the place we think we'll find Jesus and are devastated to find an empty tomb.

Jesus knew how much those women loved Him. He knew they would go to the tomb, so He sent an angel to encourage them. He does the same for us. His Word is filled with messages of hope and instruction that remind us of our calling—to make Him known. If you find yourself weeping at the tomb today, just be still for a moment, and remember His promise: "And if I go and prepare a place for you, I will come again . . . that where I am, there you may be also" (John 14:3, NKJV). He is risen! He is returning!

Now, *run* and share the good news with the world.

Karen J. Pearson

Driven!—Part 1

"Martha, Martha," the Lord answered, "you are worried and upset about many things, but few things are needed—or indeed only one. Mary has chosen what is better, and it will not be taken away from her."
—Luke 10:41, 42, NIV

Christ's description of Martha reminds me of myself. I'm sure many of you can relate. It seems like life is so busy, and there are constant demands from every direction. How is anyone supposed to find time to relax?

My stepfather, for all his faults, taught me the lessons of hard work, perseverance, and striving for excellence. He may not have intended to teach me all those things—and he didn't necessarily live them out in his own life—yet they are lessons I gleaned from the childhood I had under his rule.

Unfortunately, he did not teach me moderation or balance. Even though he's been deceased for many years and I have not been under his control since I was sixteen years old, I can still hear his voice at times echoing in my head. Maybe it isn't even his voice anymore; maybe it is now just a deeply rooted pattern of thought and behavior molded by his words and treatment of me.

You see, nothing I did was ever good enough for my stepfather. I was a straight-A student. Yet, if an exam had ten extra bonus points and I failed to get them, that wasn't good enough for him. If I got a ninety-eight instead of one hundred on a test, that wasn't good enough either.

"Why didn't you get one hundred?" "Why didn't you do better?" "You're so stupid!"

Those words, along with abuse and other things taking place as I was growing up, led me to strive for scholarly perfection and also drove me to control the one thing I could—my eating. I became severely anorexic, but I had perfect grades! I learned to mask the pain I was in, emotionally, physically, and spiritually. I learned to put on a smile and keep pressing on.

The words *pressing on* make me think of a different—and better—kind of pressing on that I need to focus on as "I press toward the mark for the prize of the high calling of God in Christ Jesus" (Philippians 3:14, KJV). Only He can help us find balance for our lives.

Samantha Nelson

Driven!—Part 2

"Martha . . . one thing is needful, and Mary hath chosen that good
part, which shall not be taken away from her."
—Luke 10:41, 42, KJV

Though I could never measure up to the standard of excellence my stepfather demanded of me, I still strove to do so, becoming anorexic in the process. God, however, has blessed and healed me from the pain of past abuse, the anorexia, and the need to be "perfect."

Yet something still lingers of the "lessons" I learned from my stepfather. This is very evident whenever I become sick or even when I'm just extremely tired. I have failed to learn the lesson of being balanced and resting when I need to do so. Maybe my stepfather's words from long ago—or maybe just the ingrained patterns from all those years of trying to please—have caused me to always push myself. Why else would I work twelve hours in the office while battling a major infection when I should be in bed resting?

I no longer perceive myself as trying to please my stepfather or anyone else other than God and my husband. Yet clearly, I have not been able to balance the demands of work and ministry with my body's demands for rest and health!

Jesus said, "Come unto me, all ye that labour and are heavy laden, and I will give you rest" (Matthew 11:28, KJV). Oh, how I long to be able to rest more often without guilt—without my stepfather's "You're lazy!" rattling around in my mind.

May his words be replaced by my Savior's words: "Come ye yourselves apart into a desert place, and rest a while: for there were many coming and going, and they had no leisure so much as to eat" (Mark 6:31, KJV). Perhaps that was Martha's problem, too, before Jesus invited her to stop her rushing and rest in Him (Luke 10:41, 42).

My greatest desire is to know God on the deepest level possible and to be still and know that He is God (see Psalm 46:10). May He help me achieve the greatest thing I need right now: balance and rest in Him. Work can wait. It will *have* to wait. My health and my time with Jesus are more important!

What about you? Where do you stand? Do you need to come apart and rest a while? If so, I pray you will choose "that good part, which shall not be taken away" (Luke 10:42, KJV).

Samantha Nelson

Remember: Be Strong; Be Very Courageous

Be strong and of a good courage. . . . Only be thou strong
and very courageous. . . . Have not I commanded thee? Be strong
and of a good courage; be not afraid, neither be thou dismayed:
for the LORD thy God is with thee whithersoever thou goest. . . .
Only be strong and of a good courage.
—*Joshua 1:6, 7, 9, 11, 18, KJV*

In the biblical account of Joshua, who was called to lead the petulant children of Israel into the Promised Land, we may find parallels with our own lives and words from God that may serve as a source of encouragement when we feel we're being tested to the limit.

First, the Israelites had wandered for forty years. Sometimes our lives seem to take us in circles. For others, life feels like a treadmill—constantly moving, toiling, and expending highly taxed energy but going nowhere. Sometimes our petulance causes us to wander.

In many instances, however, it's the things life hands to us that have us seemingly going around in circles. I doubt that every single member of that wilderness band was cantankerous, yet, because they were part of the throng, they ended up wandering too. Sometimes we appear to wander and struggle through life, not so much because of anything we personally did wrong, but we wander because of "association." For example, our families were disenfranchised; our social, ethnic, or gender group was marginalized. Life takes us in circles and we wander; but God has a plan, just as He did for the children of Israel.

Despite our circumstances, God is working to bring us through the challenges that make accomplishing our goals and life purposes so elusive. God knows. We will occupy the promised territory—whatever that looks like for each of us. We will occupy if we do not faint, give up, or turn away. Keep moving. God knows the way.

Second, there is something encouraging about God's repeated reminders to Joshua: be strong; be courageous. Opposition and discouragement will come. Our human strength may fail us. Yet at every step along our journey, let us remember God's repeated admonition to Joshua (and to us also): "Only be strong and very courageous" (Joshua 1:7, NKJV). Let us not be dismayed, for the Lord our God will be with us to bear us out!

Dear God, please help me to be strong and courageous—and remain faithful. Amen.

Stacey A. Nicely

The Unexpected Mission Trip

"But you shall receive power when the Holy Spirit
has come upon you; and you shall be witnesses to Me in Jerusalem,
and in all Judea and Samaria, and to the end of the earth."
—Acts 1:8, NKJV

Professional development was something I had on my to-do list. But the exorbitant costs of attending Harvard University for a one-week course made everything look bleak. Bleak, that is, until God asked me one day during my devotional time, *Are you doubting that I can provide?* Thousands of dollars for a one-week course seemed impossible and outrageous to me. At least, I could apply for the course and a government scholarship. I was accepted into the program—a miracle and sign from God that if He brings me to it, He will take me through it.

My application for a scholarship, however, was turned down because living in Trinidad and Tobago made me ineligible. Disappointed, I wrote the university, informing them of my inability to pay for the course but asking whether they could hold my place until the following year. The answer was no. I would have to reapply, although a small tuition assistance of about 30 percent of the fees was available. Of course, I would also have to submit my plan to pay for the course, along with the amount I still needed, which I did. To my amazement, the university personnel wrote back and offered to help with 68 percent assistance of my tuition fees!

With a grateful heart, I asked the Lord to use me during the course to be a witness for Him to my roommate. But the course was time intensive, leaving me little time to socialize outside of class. Yet God works in mysterious ways. He had plans for me to witness instead to a young non-Christian student who sat next to me in the class.

"What do you do when you have problems?" she asked me one day. I told her that I prayed to God. I listened to her and then shared how God had helped me in the past. I found an old *Signs of the Times* tract titled "A Love Letter From Jesus" and offered it to her before we parted ways. She sent me a text message saying, "Thanks for sharing the love from God."

I am still humbled to think that God made a way for me to go all the way to Harvard University from Trinidad and Tobago to witness to a young daughter of His who needed to meet Him through prayer. I pray that this planted seed germinates to His honor and glory.

Lebrechtta N. O. Hesse-Bayne

The Inyam Tree

When I was a child, I spoke as a child, I understood as a child, I thought
as a child; but when I became a man, I put away childish things.
—*1 Corinthians 13:11, NKJV*

My parents were pioneers in one of the colleges in the Philippines. One of my favorite activities was to roam the hills beyond the school compound looking for inyam fruit.

One day the kids from the village decided to harvest inyam fruits. Hoping to gather much fruit, I had a bright idea! I would take my father's saw with us. We headed to the hills.

Climbing a big tree, I sat on the target branch that was bearing much fruit. Making myself comfortable, I sawed at the branch with all my might, never considering my location on the branch in relation to where I was sawing. Suddenly, I heard the cracking sound of the branch as it broke and fell—fruit and all. The "all" included this little girl who, just an instant earlier, had been perched on that branch, sawing. When I came to after losing consciousness, I realized that I was on the portion of the branch that fell when cut off.

You may chuckle at this naïve decision of a little girl. Yet my experience reflects some choices we adults make during our quest to reach goals in life. Some people, of course, play it safe and stay within their comfort zone. When obstacles come, they give up on the goals they were working toward. Other people take risks, working hard to achieve their dreams. They think ahead, persevere, and are determined to overcome obstacles. But there may be times when we find we have been sitting on the wrong side of the branch because of a hasty decision. Not being close to what would keep us secure and safe, we fall hard, and our dreams seem to be shattered. But if we get up after a fall and reposition ourselves to be close to the tree, we will be able to recover and move forward.

Jesus is our strength and security. His hand, as with the trunk of the inyam tree, is strong and steadfast. The psalmist wrote,

> The steps of a good man are ordered by the LORD,
> And He delights in his way.
> Though he fall, he shall not be utterly cast down;
> For the LORD upholds him with His hand. (Psalm 37:23, 24, NKJV)

Today let us hold to the strong, secure hand of Jesus.

Evelyn Porteza Tabingo

Chaos!

And as many as walk according to this rule,
peace and mercy be upon them.
—Galatians 6:16, NKJV

I was on a European bus tour some years back and saw the ultimate chaos on the streets of Rome. In a three-lane road going one way, there would inevitably be five cars abreast. In fact, it was rarely clear just where the lanes of traffic were, if indeed there were any. I soon quit gasping when someone cut directly in front of us, pulled out to drive into the oncoming traffic lane (with cars advancing), or decided to turn around right in the middle of busy traffic. After all, no one seemed to hit anyone. I chalked it up to a few extra legions of angels hovering over us.

Then came the first major intersection—fifty to one hundred little cars all packed into that intersection like sardines in a can. Vehicles were going every which way! I gasped in horror and marveled that anyone got anywhere at all. Again, I was amazed at the scarcity of accidents since traffic lights seemed to serve no other purpose than being street ornaments.

Finally, our tour guide unraveled the mystery. "They have their own rules of the road," he explained. "They are unwritten rules, yet every local knows and follows them. The trouble comes when a foreigner enters in who doesn't know these rules. That's when horns start to blow and fists to shake. That's when things get dangerous and accidents happen."

The apparent chaos wasn't really chaos at all. There were rules—unwritten— but they were there; and when followed, things went well. Rather like God's rules, I think. They aren't flashed on billboards but are available in His Word. And as long as they are followed, things run smoothly. But even one person out of order, one bad "driver," can really cause chaos.

Sometimes we're tempted to think that God has left this world to its own chaos. Yet, as we entered the highway leading to Rome's airport, I was reminded that He has not: I saw two great cedars of Lebanon standing, one on each side of the road, as if these tall, stately trees were guarding the "eternal city of Rome." Somehow, they appeared to symbolize our God standing constant guard over His world. "I will never leave you nor forsake you," He promises (Hebrews 13:5, NKJV).

That means He is with us in Rome, Toronto, Los Angeles, Singapore, Brasília, or wherever we may find ourselves in this wide world of His—today and always.

Dawna Beausoleil

April 28

The Rose's Story

He shall see of the travail of his soul, and shall be satisfied.
—*Isaiah 53:11, KJV*

Throughout the centuries, there has probably been no other flower that has so captured the imagination of poets, musicians, and romantics as the lovely rose. It has become a universal symbol of pure love and lasting devotion. Many have undertaken to cultivate this beautiful flower, bewitched by its loveliness, its endless kaleidoscope of color, and (for some varieties at least) its hauntingly intoxicating perfume. Some years ago I decided to try to beautify the church garden in Thessaloniki with the addition of not one, but one hundred rosebushes.

There was no money available to buy plants, so I would have to grow my own from cuttings. First, of course, I needed suitable parent stock. I started wandering through parks and peering into gardens as I searched for the most breathtaking roses in as many colors as possible. Soon dozens of tiny cuttings—leafless, little more than two inches long, and bearing no indication of their great potential—were planted in shallow soil under individual jam jars.

The sun became weaker and the weather colder as we slipped into a long, dark Macedonian winter. Could my tiny, sticklike rose babies possibly survive? Spring came again, but the little cuttings showed no signs of life. That is, not until the day when, almost imperceptibly, their tiny "eyes" began to open in the form of tender green leaves. My rose plants were alive! Many weeks later, when they already had several new leaves, they started to grow roots, and I was able to transplant them gently into the flower beds. But not until many months later did tiny buds herald the final stage of a miraculous transformation—the birth of new rosebushes in all their exquisite beauty.

That year, as I "babysat" my little rosebushes, I gained a new insight into the continuous, patient, and loving care with which Jesus watches over us, His children. He leads us from ugly, unpromising, and sinful beginnings to the point where He can see the beauty of His glorious character perfectly reflected in us. When we first came to Him, we had nothing to offer except our desperate need and utter helplessness. Yet one day, by grace alone, His heart will overflow with joy as He presents to His heavenly Father yet another child of His saving love who beautifully reflects the loveliness of His character—to His glory—throughout eternity.

Revel Papaioannou

God's Leading Hand

"For I know the plans that I have for you," declares the LORD.
—*Jeremiah 29:11, NIV*

N o more school! You're a big girl now, and girls shouldn't study," pronounced my dad.

That was the saddest day of my life, but God had a plan for me.

A Christian neighbor came into our butcher shop one morning to buy meat and saw me grinding some. While I was trying to push a piece of meat into the big, manually operated mincing machine (electric grinders weren't available at the time), the ring finger of my left hand got briefly caught in the machine. Blood freely flowed from the cut. When my neighbor saw the profuse bleeding, she tried to help me.

"Why isn't this girl in school?" she asked my dad with apparent anger. "That's where she should be."

"I don't have the money to send her to school," my dad replied.

The next day the neighbor returned and took me to the Christian school affiliated with her church. Neither were very far away. "Let's have a chat with the principal," she suggested.

The principal was so kind and caring as she thought about how I might be able to afford the school fees. Then she offered, "Would you be willing to clean the restrooms after school each day and also clean our church once a week in exchange for being able to study here?"

Of course, I would be willing! So it was at that school where I came to know more about Jesus and His love through the loving care of the local church members.

Some years later two American missionary nurses who worked at a Christian hospital in Baghdad visited our school. They were seeking qualified students who would be interested in attending nursing school. Surprisingly, I was one of the girls they chose! Thus began my journey in the footsteps of Jesus. I never thought I would be so blessed as to see my life take a 180-degree turn—from a butcher shop to an education in nursing! Had it not been for that Christian neighbor of ours, I would not be here today sharing my testimony with you.

God loves me. He loves you too. Just trust Him, and He will lead you in the right paths.

I am seventy-three years old now. Yet every day I still experience the hand of my loving Jesus leading me. I trust His promise when He says, "I will never leave you nor forsake you" (Hebrews 13:5, NKJV).

Elizabeth Atamian

Eyelid Cancer!

"Be strong and of good courage, do not fear . . . ;
for the LORD your God, He is the One who goes with you.
He will not leave you nor forsake you."
—Deuteronomy 31:6, NKJV

I was shocked! I had just been told that I likely had a basal cell skin cancer on my lower right eyelid! How fearful this thought was to me!

I was sent to an ocular oncologist in Vancouver, British Columbia, to have a biopsy confirmation. There I was told that I did, indeed, have a basal cell carcinoma on my eyelid. It would have to be surgically removed, followed by a second surgery to repair the eyelid.

Now I remembered rubbing my itching eye until it felt as if the eyelid was almost turning inside out. Not seeing myself very well in the mirror, I had not noticed how the cancer had already taken away my eyelashes on that lid. Yet once I had become suspicious that something was desperately wrong, a look in the magnifying mirror confirmed what I didn't want to see.

Though not wanting surgery, I needed to have the skin cancer removed before it spread even more. In prayer, I asked the Lord to guide me through this ordeal. I told Him this was too big for me to handle on my own. I didn't know what to expect or how things would work out. What would my eye look like when the surgeries were all over?

I can assure you that our God answers prayers. After leaving my problem in His hands, I saw the Lord working on my behalf. The surgeries were quickly arranged for the month following my biopsy. I was sent to one of the best eyelid surgeons in the city. (I didn't even know that there were specialists for eyelids!) I just saw God working out the details for me and walking with me the whole way. He even provided my sister and her husband to care for me all the way through my ordeal. They lived closer to Vancouver than I did and gave me free room and board for the entire six weeks that I needed to be near the specialists.

My sister told me that I was "brave."

But I knew in my heart that I wasn't brave at all but simply relying on the Lord and His promise that He would be with me all the way to the end. And the result? It was so good that most people, when they look at me, can't tell I ever had surgery!

God is faithful! You can know His faithfulness too!

Martha "Marty" Cunnington

Hearing but Not Listening

Then they said to one another, "We are truly guilty concerning our brother, for we saw the anguish of his soul when he pleaded with us, and we would not hear; therefore this distress has come upon us."
—*Genesis 42:21, NKJV*

I finally figured out why I like memes (cultural content in the form of humorous images, videos, or sayings rapidly shared on the internet). Memes give people a voice. You can be candid, open, and even sarcastic, and people aren't exactly sure on what level you are speaking your mind.

I just wish Chuckie could have known memes. I was in the sixth grade, and Chuckie was always bringing me roses from his mom's garden and laying them on my desk. He was a nice, skinny kid who sported his pants up to his sternum. His sincere blue eyes and curly blond hair didn't tell his story. No one really knew his story until it was too late. His mom had divorced his father and married his father's father—and had two kids with him. Chuckie probably spent his days wondering what fraction to label his little brother and sister. Half? Quarter? Whole? Maybe some sort of meme could have served as an outlet for his frustrations. I didn't see his frustrations. All I saw were flowers on my desk from a boy that I didn't know, didn't understand, and didn't need. Shame on me. I was too busy trying to be popular and promoted. And then it was too late.

I remember that it was a Sunday morning. My mom came home looking very serious. I was standing inside the open garage when she told me that Chuckie had hanged himself. I shook my head in disbelief. I sobbed, and then I was quiet for the rest of the day as I remembered all those flowers. It was the same at his funeral. I wondered, *What if those flowers on my desk had been words?* What if he had been trying to talk to me, to have a friend, to have someone understand? What if he'd had a voice that I could have listened to? I didn't hear the flowers. Yet the beautiful display of carefully arranged blooms on his casket were screaming at me.

Listen to the memes, read between the lines, and discern the message. Take time not only to hear but to *listen* to the message that may be carefully spoken but in an unconventional way.

Maybe someone is just trying to find a voice. Let us be the ears of Jesus.

Nicole Mattson

Kindness Returned

You will always harvest what you plant.
—*Galatians 6:7, NLT*

After our permanent return in June 2001 from mission hospital work in Zambia, my husband, Roger, and I volunteered for two years at a Christian high school in the Philippines before being called to work at a Christian university in Madagascar. There he became the maintenance director and helped build churches in the area around the university. The first church was in Ansotany and the latest was the Ambalavao Miracle Church. It was a miracle that the latest church could even be built because money for the beginning of the construction project had to be solicited from fellow missionaries, friends, family, and church members.

Dada Be was not of our denomination, though his two sons were. Because of the church's good influence on them, the father became interested. Visits, care, and concern shown for him—especially when he fell sick—began to soften his heart. We tried to show kindness by visiting and praying with him and his family. That kindness also positively impacted the community as he was well respected in the area. In fact, his desire was the community's command.

As our relationship with Dada Be developed, he began to donate what funding he could when the school or the church-building project needed financial help. He said, "These Christian people are different. I want to be one of them. I want to serve my people."

At the church, children learned to recite Bible verses and read from Bibles that were given to them. They learned to sing songs about things in the Bible. The parents were so happy for their children's progress. The *poktan* (village leaders) were especially proud to have their children perform in Bible reenactments portraying the stories of Noah, Esther, and other Bible characters. The parents were happy to hear the church choir present music for the community.

Ambalavao Miracle Church became a blessing to the community. One year the whole community participated in the miracle church's Christmas party.

Our kindness to Dada Be had been repaid in donations and financial support. Now he wants others to know the Savior. If you give away kindness, it will come back to you. "Cast your bread upon the waters, for you will find it after many days" (Ecclesiastes 11:1, NKJV).

Today's kindness may become tomorrow's blessings. Let us live our lives accordingly.

Evelyn Gabutero Pelayo

Sit at the Welcoming Table

Let us be glad and rejoice, and give honour to him:
for the marriage of the Lamb is come, and his wife hath
made herself ready. And to her was granted that she should be
arrayed in fine linen, clean and white: for the fine linen is the
righteousness of saints. And he saith unto me, Write, Blessed are
they which are called unto the marriage supper of the Lamb.
And he saith unto me, These are the true sayings of God.
—*Revelation 19:7–9, KJV*

Christ's mission to earth (John 3:16) should encourage each of us. He mingled with everyone despite their backgrounds. He did not look down on anyone regardless of their past sins and shortcomings. His will was to save lost sinners and bring them back to His fold.

But Satan also has a mission: to convince sinners that they are not worthy of Jesus' saving grace. Yet Christ is loving and just. He knew you before you before you came out of the womb (Jeremiah 1:5). No sin is too great or small for Him to forgive.

In my journey as a Christian, I had many bouts with Satan. I was tested but failed numerous times. Satan constantly reminded me of the wrong I had committed yesterday, last year, and the year before. He played mind games that pushed me into a corner of dismay, full of regrets, hopelessness, and an unforgiving spirit. He reminded me of my filthy, sin-stained garment. I felt too unclean to sit with Jesus. I hung on to the pain that Satan wreaked upon me. I believed his tricks and listened to the lies that robbed me of my connection with Christ and family. I missed out on the Word of God. Yet I thank God for His promises not to leave nor forsake me (Deuteronomy 31:8). That assurance eventually got me "home" to sit with Him.

Sisters, do not listen to the lies of Satan. His time is running out. Listen instead to the voice of Jesus. Live in His presence daily, accepting His forgiveness for all your dark sins and secrets of the past. Jesus can and *will* set you free. He died for you, rose for you, and is interceding on your behalf. Now He bids you to sit at the marriage table and dine with Him as His bride. He offers you a special wedding garment of righteousness to replace your filthy garment of sin. In accepting it, you choose to give up all that does not represent His character.

You are wonderful to Him. He knows your name and calls you by it. He knows all about you. Why not come and sit and dine with Him? You are most welcome there!

Corletta Aretha Barbar

Persist Until Something Happens

I can do all things through Christ who strengthens me.
—*Philippians 4:13, NKJV*

As I look back on my entire life, I realize that it's not been an easy road for me. I've also come to realize that at my very core, I'm not a quitter! Whenever life punches me in the gut, I may double over in pain, but I refuse to roll over and die. One of my creeds is, Quitting is not an option. I would be lying if I said that life hasn't been a struggle. I am a PUSH-er, which means I *persist until something happens*. How have I been PUSH-ing?

After experiencing the devastation of divorce, I went back to graduate school and completed a five-year doctorate degree in family therapy. This meant long, tiring days and many all-nighters. But I would repeat to myself, *Quitting is not an option, and I refuse to pay back student loans for a degree I don't have.* In addition to persistence, prayer and encouragement from the Scriptures kept me PUSH-ing. When professors tried to break me, I kept PUSH-ing. When depression and loneliness enveloped me, I PUSH-ed, prayed, and persevered.

PUSH-ing isn't easy to do. It takes energy you sometimes don't have. Sometimes simply waking up, putting your feet on the floor, and walking forward is PUSH-ing. Moving forward produces a trajectory for *that* day. As long as you *push* through *that* day, you can make something happen. Don't focus on what you didn't get done. Don't beat yourself up over what you haven't checked off your to-do list; simply get up the next day, put your feet on the floor, and move forward one step at a time.

One of my favorite texts is Philippians 4:13: "I can do all things through Christ who strengthens me" (NKJV). Right now I am persistently praying as I seek a job. So far my education has not helped me; only God and my PUSH-ing will. To paraphrase another author, our responsibility is to keep putting one foot in front of the other. Then one day we will look back and see that we have climbed a mountain!

Whatever challenge you are facing right now, I encourage you to keep PUSH-ing!

Joan Collins-Ricketts

Changes

For I am the LORD; I change not.
—*Malachi 3:6, KJV*

As we get older, it's easy to start reminiscing about the many changes the years have brought us. It seems only yesterday that our two boys, with endless energy, were running carefree around the property. Today both are married with families of their own, and we have even graduated to being great-grandparents.

Our home is on a hill overlooking the Murray River, and my husband and I have been here for more than sixty-eight years. When we moved here, our farmhouse was situated well outside of the town. We had considerable pastureland around us, where we ran a dairy farm and milked cows. Today housing estates have gradually developed around us, along with schools and places of business. Our once-busy dairy farm now stands as a silent memory for us; a place where birds now like to roost.

From Creation week and then throughout the ages, our heavenly Father has watched the changes taking place in this world that He created to be so perfect. The changes we've seen in our comparatively short life spans are nothing compared to what God has seen. And though seeing humankind's fall from sinlessness, God, in His grace and mercy, still offers sinners forgiveness and hope. Over and over in Scripture, we read the abundant promises given to God's people *if* they would choose to change. From Ezekiel 36:26 comes one such offer made to the rebellious Israelites: "I will give you a new heart and put a new spirit within you; I will take the heart of stone out of your flesh and give you a heart of flesh" (NKJV).

Reading through the Bible stories, my attention is drawn to the apostle Paul and the immense changes manifested in his life. He changed from "breathing threats and murder against the disciples of the Lord" to being baptized and then becoming someone who "preached the Christ in the synagogues, that He is the Son of God" (Acts 9:1, 20, NKJV). Like Paul, we all experience changes in our lives; some of which we cannot control. Yet if our minds are in harmony with Jesus, Satan cannot change *us*.

I look forward to the change described in 1 Corinthians 15:52: "In a moment, in the twinkling of an eye. . . . The trumpet will sound, and the dead will be raised incorruptible, and we shall be changed" (NKJV). Let us trust the Word of our God who never changes (Hebrews 13:8).

Joan D. L. Jaensch

The Truth About Failure

Blessed are those who dwell in Your house;
They will be still praising You.
—*Psalm 84:4, NKJV*

I have heard it expressed that failure is a dead end—a wrong turn. But when we consider failure to be a dead end, we have no way to turn around at the end of the failure road. We have no hope for getting out of the city of lost dreams and ruined plans.

I choose to disagree with this concept of failure. I think failure is more like the sprawl of an urban housing project. It is a place you must endure for an undisclosed period. During that time of waiting, you can suffer inside the dismal walls for as long as you must, making everyone else miserable. You might even abuse the house of failure. You may adjust to the neighborhood and become comfortable with the inadequate housing. Or you can choose to spend the waiting period in the housing project by using your time constructively in reflection.

You may never return to the life you once had—that body, that job, or that soul mate. With an aching heart, you may long for lost dreams and ruined plans. Yet do not despair. It is possible to adjust to the new "normal" and regain a sense of balance.

It takes some people longer than others to get their "want-to" attitude back while living under failure's roof. Yet the house of failure is a good place to comfort yourself by creating better goals and brighter hopes.

Housing-project pitfalls can cause you to lose hope for the future. Beware the many too-good-to-be-true sponsors paying your rent. If you become dependent on their help and stay locked in the house of failure forever, you will lose your desire for a better life.

Avoid projecting your past failures upon your future. Don't cling to the memories you love, or cherish them, or open your arms to more pain.

When you eventually escape from the housing project, you will want to return to failure's house simply to guide others out of despair.

Your true sponsors will pay and support you so that you can build better shelters for others.

Grab your spiritual gifts and tools today, and begin building the right home for someone else.

Wendy Williams

Mood Changer

Knowing their thoughts, Jesus said,
"Why do you entertain evil thoughts in your hearts?"
—*Matthew 9:4, NIV*

My mood wasn't pleasant; I was depressed. I struggled with the thought of some of my life choices and where I currently was. I fought to see myself the way God sees me—victorious, lovable, and worth the time and effort. The thoughts of shame and brokenness would not go away, and all I could think about was how I got here and what happened along the way. I had the audacity to believe that others saw me the same pitiful way.

Have you ever been there? Have you ever been in a place where you thought people only see your mistakes and shortcomings? Have you ever been defensive and guarded because you were tired of getting hurt or opening yourself up only to feel rejected or overlooked? How do you compensate for those feelings?

I realize I compensate for those harsh feelings by withdrawing and putting a wall up. Sometimes I can be mean and dismissive of others in an effort to protect myself, only to find myself in an emotional prison more than anything else. But instead of helping, my self-protection only makes things worse.

On that evening, I decided to exercise. In the process, I played the song "Free Worshipper" by Todd Dulaney; and before I knew it, I was bouncing around, believing I *could* be free! Free to love, free to shake off what I am projecting on myself that others have no time to think about. Free to believe that grace is a gift given from God and that He doesn't look at me and see my faults, misjudgments, or ignorance. He sees His child and how He chose to be beaten, spat upon, and wrongfully hung on a cross to die so that I don't have to live in the torment of my shame. He conquered death to show that there is absolutely nothing that can separate us from His love and that He has *all power and authority*, no matter what.

You can change your mood. Set the atmosphere. Listen to music or something that edifies Christ, reminding you of your worth to Him. Fill your mind with the truths that He is not willing that any should perish, but all come to repentance (see 2 Peter 3:9). He will blot out our transgressions and love on us as if nothing had ever happened. What you believe becomes the foundation for your mood.

Rachel Privette Jennings

May 8

Absolute Nothingness!

Each time he said, "My grace is all you need. My power works best in weakness." So now I am glad to boast about my weaknesses, so that the power of Christ can work through me.
—2 Corinthians 12:9, NLT

I became fascinated with the number zero when the chaplain at a Christian academy where I worked added me to a discussion with one of our coworkers. From a spiritual perspective, he was passionately making the case for the number one being the most important number. After all, one represents unity—"one Lord, one faith, one baptism" (Ephesians 4:5, NIV). As I listened, the concept of zero popped into my head. I quipped, "Zero is the most important number from a spiritual standpoint." Mathematically, zero is a placeholder that gives our real number system meaning. It also carries the meaning of absolute nothingness. Negative and positive real numbers cannot be defined unless compared to a true zero. A slight movement to the right of zero yields positive numbers and to the left we have negatives.

Spiritually, the entire plan of salvation is centered on my absolute nothingness. I cannot save myself. Scripture affirms that. "For it is by grace you have been saved, through faith—and this is not from yourselves, it is the gift of God—not by works, so that no one can boast" (Ephesians 2:8, 9, NIV). Zero self! When I am empty of self, I make way for the Holy Spirit to use me according to the will of God. Relying on self pulls me to the negative side. Yet if I invite Jesus to fill my emptiness, He moves me to the positive side. "My old self has been crucified with Christ. It is no longer I who live, but Christ lives in me. So I live in this earthly body by trusting in the Son of God, who loved me and gave himself for me" (Galatians 2:20, NLT). My mind was whirling with the number zero and its potential spiritual significance. For even if we find ourselves with zero dollars, friends, job, or spouse, we still have precious promises from God. For example, "And my God will supply every need of yours according to his riches in glory in Christ Jesus" (Philippians 4:19, ESV). "The Lord has appeared of old to me, saying: 'Yes, I have loved you with an everlasting love' " (Jeremiah 31:3, NKJV).

Allow my God to save you from your absolute nothingness. In your weakness, He will be your strength.

Veon Stewart

Hungry for the Word

Thy word is a lamp unto my feet,
and a light unto my path.
—Psalm 119:105, KJV

One day each week a group from our church works with the local food bank to distribute food to low-income residents. During my half-hour drive to the church, I pray that we may meet more than just the physical needs of people coming to the food bank that day. Although we aren't allowed to give out literature, I do keep an assortment of Bibles for children, youth, and adults at my desk where the clients register. If interest is expressed, I offer a free Bible.

When Julie, a middle-aged mother, came in, she mentioned that a few years back she had given her Bible to a young man who was having trouble with drugs. "I just hope that he read it, and that it helped him. I really miss having a Bible." I reached down and brought out a nice leather-covered study Bible I'd brought from home. Tears started rolling down Julie's cheeks as she realized that she might become the owner of this beautiful Bible. Tears came into my own eyes as I saw her emotional reaction to this gift. For the next few minutes, she smothered me with hugs as well. I realized that it wasn't just an accident that I had decided to bring that Bible with me that morning. God knew there was somebody who needed that Bible that day. I shared that thought with Julie. When Julie left my cubicle to get her food, she was proudly showing her new Bible to the others who were waiting. Although they may not have appreciated the value of this gift, it was something very special to her.

Several weeks passed, and there hadn't been many requests for Bibles, so one morning I prayed that there would be people wanting Bibles that day. One of the first clients that morning asked for the youth Bible that had been right on top of my stack of Bibles for a few weeks. A short time later another client picked up a small Bible and hugged it as she said, "This Bible is just the right size and has nice print that I can read. And I just love the King James Version!"

Before the morning was over, not only had two more women selected Bibles they were happy to take home, but a Hispanic lady had also found I had a Spanish Bible for her as well. I was overwhelmed by the ways God had answered my prayers!

Thank You, God, for helping us to meet more than just the physical needs of those who come to us.

Betty J. Adams

Waiting for Answers

"But as for you, you meant evil against me;
but God meant it for good."
—Genesis 50:20, NKJV

I remember going through difficult situations in my life when it seemed hard to find God. Many times it is too easy to blame Him for them. *He is God, so why doesn't He do something about this? He must not love me; can't He see my pain?*

Some of our questions will have to wait for answers, just as they did for Joseph, a Bible character I love. Yet God has promised to be with us and never leave us. He also knows what is best for us and those we love. We can become strengthened because of trial, which also gives us a testimony that can help someone else experiencing a similar problem. Trial can turn us toward God when we realize that He is the only one we can trust to see us through.

On this sin-filled planet, there will be pain. We have an enemy, Satan, and he is responsible for all the bad things we experience here. One day God will wipe away all our tears—no more sadness and no more pain (see Revelation 21:4). We are part of a much bigger picture. Angels that remained faithful during Satan's rebellion didn't understand what sin was (see Isaiah 14:12–15). So when Satan slandered God, accusing Him of being unfair, doubt arose in the angels' hearts. But how could the angels see truth when they had never before experienced a lie? Sin had to be allowed to reveal its true darkness; Satan had to be shown for the proud liar that he is.

If God mercifully wiped away every tear now, healed every wound, stopped every war, and fixed every wrong, how would we know the whole truth?

If we love God and trust Him, He will take us through our trials to the end. We are not alone; He walks beside us. And when we hurt, our loving God feels the pain. He knows how cruel sin is because He had to stand back and watch His own innocent Son suffer and die in our place. That was the only way to meet the demands of His law. He, in His great love, wants to save as many as possible. When the angels in heaven beheld their beloved Creator spat upon, ridiculed, beaten, bruised, and hanging on a cross while Satan stood by in exultation, hoping he had won, they knew—without a doubt—what a lie was. They also understood that God *is* love!

So Joseph's words to his brothers resonate with me, and I hope they will for you: "But as for you [Satan], you meant evil against me, but God meant it for good" (Genesis 50:20, NKJV).

Sue Anderson

A Light in the Darkness

When Jesus spoke again to the people, he said,
"I am the light of the world. Whoever follows me
will never walk in darkness, but will have the light of life."
—John 8:12, NIV

Think about the darkest place you've ever been. Spelunking in a cave? Diving in the deep ocean? Hiding in a closet?

As children, we often associate darkness with being frightened—we are afraid of what we cannot see. As we mature into adulthood, darkness often becomes less about our environment and more about our inner selves.

Two years ago I found myself in darkness—not in a cave or a closet—but in a state of being. I had been struggling with anxiety and panic attacks without even knowing it. I have always been a happy, upbeat person who handles stress well. Unbeknown to me, I was struggling with a disorder and coping by ignoring the symptoms.

As my anxiety grew and my panic attacks happened more frequently, I slowly slipped into the abyss of depression. To my friends and family, I seemed like a completely changed person—the joy in my heart had disappeared—and they felt helpless as nothing they did brought comfort to me. In those weeks, I truly felt as if life would never be the same. I desperately hoped that I would feel happiness again.

Covered in a dark cloud, I finally confessed to a friend that I couldn't find the words to pray. She gently placed her hand on my arm and assured me, "God understands. You have friends and family who are continually praying for you."

I thank God for hearing and answering those prayers of petition. When I couldn't find my voice, He heard theirs and, I believe, the silent prayers of my heart.

Over the course of several weeks, the dark cloud began to lift, and I slowly began to feel like myself again. My prayers were often short and conversational: "I can't do this without You. Walk with me today."

And He did. The clouds parted, and the sun shone through.

I am forever grateful for the prayers of those who asked for my healing when I could not and for my Father whose love for me shone like a light in a time of darkness.

Erica Jones

The Storm

"The LORD will guide you continually,
And satisfy your soul in drought,
And strengthen your bones;
You shall be like a watered garden,
And like a spring of water, whose waters do not fail."
—*Isaiah 58:11, NKJV*

It was Mother's Day. That is the day when my family purchases a gift for me that we can plant together in our yard. One year we planted a dwarf burning bush. Another year it was a forsythia. Our yard is filled with various hostas, lilies, and irises. I love how these plants bloom and add such beauty and color to our home.

This year I decided to purchase some annuals: marigolds, begonias, and impatiens. My daughter, Pami, and I spent the afternoon digging, separating the plants, and placing them in just the right spots in the garden areas and pots. They were small, but with loving care they would grow beautifully.

Little did we know that two days later, a storm would hit in the middle of the night. During the storm, I ran to the front door and opened it. It looked as if snow had fallen all over our yard!

The next morning I surveyed the damage. Hail had ravaged all my plants. The hostas were the hardest hit. The flowerpots were completely filled with rainwater, and it seemed literally impossible that anything would survive.

Little by little, as the water subsided and the summer heat came on, the plants began growing and, much to my surprise, even blooming! The damage done to the hostas had mostly affected the leaves, not the roots. So these plants eventually bloomed even though their leaves looked like Swiss cheese!

Likewise, storms of life also batter us at times. During these storms, we wonder whether we will ever bloom again. Or even survive! Yet God tells us in Isaiah 58:11 that the Lord will make us new again—like a well-watered garden. His creative power can bring new life into us. We may, at first, not be able to see what He is doing. But if our roots are solidly planted in God's Word, He can restore the damage that the storms have caused.

Karen M. Phillips

Living for His Glory

Oh that men would praise the LORD for his goodness,
and for his wonderful works to the children of men!
—*Psalm 107:8, KJV*

To the praise of the glory of his grace,
wherein he hath made us accepted in the beloved.
—*Ephesians 1:6, KJV*

By him therefore let us offer the sacrifice of praise to God continually,
that is, the fruit of our lips giving thanks to his name.
—*Hebrews 13:15, KJV*

I would like to share an experience that occurred in Pune, India.

Sometime in the late fifties, a young mother from Hyderabad was preparing to deliver her first baby. The doctor was her own mother, who was a renowned gynecologist and a graduate from a Christian medical college in Ludhiana. She was a brilliant lady named Mrs. Kamala Sudhi.

The young mother planned to have her baby in Kachiguda, where her younger sister lived, so that is where she traveled to. Then one evening the young woman went into labor. In only a little more than two hours, she delivered a beautiful baby girl. But it appeared the baby was stillborn, for when the baby was picked up and turned upside down, she did not cry as is the normal reaction for most newborn infants.

The doctor was about to hand the motionless baby to the nurse when she suddenly heard a very faint sound, rather than a cry, coming from the baby. She noticed an obstruction in her throat. Quickly, she inserted a tube and extracted phlegm that had accumulated.

That tiny baby girl, delivered on that long-ago evening by my grandmom, was none other than me. When I grew old enough to understand, Grandmother always told me that God had a purpose for me and that is why He had given me new life just moments after my birth. God did have a plan for my life, as He does for yours. Not only have I been a teacher for thirty-five years, but I also carry the joys and responsibilities of being the wife of a pastor and church leader.

I am so thankful to the Lord that He spared my life so that I could testify to others about *Him*. I will always praise the Lord as long as I have breath. Amen.

Rhoda Shinge

Mrs. Job

"Are you still holding on to your principles? Curse God and die!"
—Job 2:9, GOD'S WORD

Mrs. Job was married to a world leader who must, in his day, have had the combined wealth of Aristotle Onassis, Bill Gates, and Donald Trump. Mr. Job was a good man who was faithful in marriage, provided for his family, and conducted his business dealings honestly.

I can only imagine, therefore, Mrs. Job's devastation and frustration with all the calamities that befell her husband, her children, and the family's wealth (see Job 1; 2).

Women are designed to be fixers, helpmates, and caregivers. When Mrs. Job was unable to do any of this, it must have been devastating to her. She had no choice but to bear the disasters that befell her family. Apparently, the final straw was seeing her husband trying to clean the oozing, itching boils all over his body. Her only words recorded in the Bible asked a question and made a statement: "Are you still holding on to your principles? Curse God and die!" (Job 2:9, GOD'S WORD). She may have been so moved by her love for Mr. Job that she wanted his acute suffering to end.

I find it notable that Mrs. Job did not curse God herself but only suggested that Mr. Job do so. But Mr. Job did not. What an amazing story of Job's faithfulness to God, even though he didn't understand why this was happening. Furthermore, through his faithfulness, his wife was also saved and went on to enjoy the increase God later gave them both, which included ten more children and more wealth than ever before.

The Job family's tragedy must have been the talk of the community where they lived. After all, their "good friends" had come during the troubles to commiserate with Mr. Job and point out to him what they thought he might have done to deserve divine punishment. Most of the conversations in the book of Job involve his talking either to God or with his so-called friends. Now all can see that family's restoration. Their story is a witness to many.

What is your story telling the world? Even though you may not understand all God's plan for your life, do you trust Him with your life and your future? Do you believe that He will work all things together for your best good (see Romans 8:28)?

We now see through a glass darkly, but one day God will make all things clear (1 Corinthians 13:12)!

Peggy Curtice Harris

Potato Salad and a Prayer

Whatever you do, work at it with all your heart,
as working for the Lord, not for human masters, since you know
that you will receive an inheritance from the Lord as a reward.
It is the Lord Christ you are serving.
—*Colossians 3:23, 24, NIV*

It's good to be cautious; however, God sometimes puts people in our path for a reason. He puts them right there in our path, leading us to a choice: stay on that side of the road and help, or cross over to the other side and don't help.

My three-mile-long road is an excellent place for loving people and talking about Jesus. One day while I was walking I was chatting on the phone with my friend Georgia when a man pulled his truck up to the edge of the road from his long gravel driveway. He rolled down his window and hollered out, "Do you know my wife, Kelly?"

"Just a second," I said to Georgia, "a man is yelling at me. I need to go over to his car."

"I'll be praying," she replied as we ended our conversation. The man repeated his question to me. I said I didn't think I did.

Not deterred, he continued. "My wife, Kelly, was just diagnosed with cancer and is going into treatments."

"I'm sorry to hear this. Would it be all right if I came to visit in a few days?" I asked.

"Yes, you can," he replied, then drove off.

It is nice to take something along on a visit, so I decided on potato salad. I made my salad and headed out with a friend a few days later. The man, T. J., met us at the door with his children and sister-in-law.

T. J. said, "Potato salad is my favorite thing, and I rarely get it." (Score another one for the Holy Spirit's inspiration!) Kelly was too sick to get out of bed and not up for visitors.

I asked, "Would you like for me to have a prayer?" We held hands around the circle, and I prayed. It was a nice connection that we made with this family on our road. And we have maintained the connection. Several months later Kelly stopped her car on the road and thanked me. She was doing well. Another time she stopped to report she was healed. A couple years after that I again knocked on their door to share that my book had come out. The children especially were excited to tell me their own God-moment stories and let me hold their pet chinchilla. It is rewarding to work for the Lord and meet people on the road that God puts in our path.

Diane Pestes

Crocus Counsel

Beloved, let us love one another, for love is of God; and everyone
who loves is born of God. . . . In this is love, not that we loved God,
but that He loved us and sent His Son to be the propitiation for our
sins. Beloved, if God so loved us, we also ought to love one another.
—1 John 4:7, 10, 11, NKJV

The frigid winter eased. Crocus bulbs pushed little green spears toward the
sun. Days later, a patch of purple-and-white delight greeted us. Then the
sun warmed the temperature enough for the blossoms to open like bowls.
Bees buzzed around yellow stamens, gathering pollen. The pure-white blossoms
shone in the bright sunlight. That evening, as the sun dropped toward the
horizon, I stood at a window admiring pink painting the sky and purple polka-
dotting the flower bed. The crocus petals had pulled together in tight cylindrical
buds.

The next morning the flowers were still wrapped as tight buds. "Thank You,
God," I whispered, "for the beauty of spring."

The blossoms will open again when the sun warms them, I seemed to hear.
*The crocus are like My children that don't know me. They'll open their hearts to the
warmth of love.*

I pondered the parallel. A line from an Edgar Guest poem came to mind:
"I'd rather see a sermon than hear one any day." Some people misunderstand
God's character. Some have gotten the impression that God is a big bully
seeking evidence to condemn. For some, their relationship with father—or other
authority—figures have made them feel unworthy of love. They can't conceive
of godly love. That's where Christ's followers come in. When I open my heart
to see people as God's precious, cherished children; when I show acceptance to
those who condemn themselves; when I consistently treat people with respect,
even when their behavior doesn't inspire respect; when they feel the warmth of
divine love flowing through a human, they may begin to open their hearts to the
love of God.

Later in the day, the sun came out. The temperature warmed. The purple-
and-white blooms opened and displayed their beauty. *Dear God*, I prayed, *plant
Your love in me. Live Your love through me. Warm some struggling soul through me
today so that this person can begin to open his or her heart to You.*

Helen Heavirland

Joy of Adoption

For you did not receive the spirit of bondage again to fear,
but you received the Spirit of adoption
by whom we cry out, "Abba, Father."
—Romans 8:15, NKJV

It was late. We had just locked up the church after a very busy night of Vacation Bible School. One of the other leaders came up to us and showed us a poor little ragamuffin of a kitten she had found in a thicket. The poor little thing had been crying for help when he was found. My daughter and I quickly agreed to take the little guy home. We named him Pogo because the cat character in the Vacation Bible School program was named Pogo.

We stopped on the way home and bought some kitten food. Because he was dirty and half starved, we gave him a bath and fed him. He would eat anything and everything he could find. He filled up on the cat food and our dogs' food and begged for treats just like our dogs did. In fact, our new little family member acts a lot more like a dog than a cat. He "talks" to us, bugs us to scratch his ears, and plays with the frisky dogs—all being careful not to seriously hurt each other. When the play gets too rough for him, Pogo yowls at the dogs and runs off. The dogs do the same when Pogo gets too rough on them!

We love Pogo so much and are so glad we adopted him because he brings us so much joy. He's eight years old now but hasn't changed very much since we first brought him home. He still eats dog food, begs for treats, and picks on the dogs. In fact, I'm surprised I am able to write this without him crawling all over me *and* the computer, trying to get some personal attention from me.

As with our rescue of Pogo, Jesus came to rescue us: lost, afraid, and stuck in lives of sorrow and sin. He wanted us to know that we are loved, saved, and adopted. Can you imagine what it will be like when He takes us to His home? I can picture myself running, jumping, playing, and eating all the wonderful foods in heaven. Best of all, I'll run up to Jesus for a hug. Just like Pogo brings us so much pleasure, I totally believe Jesus is looking forward to taking us home. With us there, His joy will be complete. Hebrews 12:2 says that Jesus "endured the cross" because we were "the joy that was set before Him."

My heart yearns for that day. *Come soon, Lord Jesus!*

Mona Fellers

Let's Eat!

God has said, "Never will I leave you; never will I forsake you."
So we say with confidence,
"The Lord is my helper; I will not be afraid."
—*Hebrews 13:5, 6, NIV*

And my God will meet all your needs according to the riches of his
glory in Christ Jesus.
—*Philippians 4:19, NIV*

Long before I was a mother, I decided that when my time came to deliver a baby, I wanted it to be an all-natural delivery without the use of any drugs. Also, I would breastfeed my baby. No bottles!

Before my baby girl was born in Alaska, I knew that there was very little help available to me in terms of having a natural childbirth or breastfeeding. Someone suggested that I go to the library for some resource books. I came home with a handbook from La Leche League International.* That book was an excellent help to me. In fact, after I became a first-time mother, that book helped take away any guilt I later had for sleeping with my baby or taking her with me everywhere I went rather than getting a babysitter.

I remember reading how a mother's body lets her know when the baby is hungry, even before the baby cries. But some might wonder why a mother shouldn't just go get the baby to feed *before* the baby starts crying. I read an answer to that in my handbook. The author asked the reader to think about how nice it is to walk into one's house when hungry and discover that dinner is already prepared! The table is already set for the meal. That very thought makes one smile. I loved that visual! And that is what I did for both of my babies. That way they always knew that not only was I close by to hear their cries but also that I would always supply their needs.

Pondering this maternal anticipation of a baby's nourishment needs led me to a spiritual parallel. God is like that! He says, "And it shall come to pass, that before they call, I will answer; and while they are yet speaking, I will hear" (Isaiah 65:24, KJV). God is always close by to hear our cry and meet our needs. What a wonderful God we serve! He will never leave us! He is working on the answers to our problems right now! And He's gone to heaven to prepare a special place for us, with a table already set. It's ready and waiting for you and me. Wow! Let's eat!

Kathy Jo Duterrow Jones

---

* La Leche League International is a nonprofit group that provides women with information and support for breastfeeding.

God's Unimaginable Presence

"When you pass through the waters,
I will be with you;
and when you pass through the rivers,
they will not sweep over you.
When you walk through the fire,
you will not be burned;
the flames will not set you ablaze.
For I am the Lord your God."
—*Isaiah 43:2, 3, NIV*

While teaching at a large university in Southern California, I was contacted by the campus director of a vocational nursing school who wanted my help in lifting the school out of probationary status. The school was on probation due to poor student outcomes, so they could not start any classes.

Knowing that I could help, I accepted the challenge to get the school going again. The school's pass rate was at least 20 percent below the national pass rate. Implementing the plan of correction included improving the academic infrastructure, which meant making changes. Implementing changes could create a lot of stress in the work environment. More often than not, I would not even leave the campus for lunch.

One day, as the stress escalated to the point of becoming an unbearable burden, I decided to go out for a walk and get some lunch. First, I went window shopping, which relaxed me. Since I was feeling hungry, I drove into the drive-through lane of a fast-food restaurant to get some food. I placed my order and then waited in line to get my food.

At the payment window, I asked how much I owed. The lady at the window said, "It is your day today!" I looked at her, stunned, and asked what she meant by that statement. "You don't have to pay anything for your food. It is *your* day today!" I could not believe what I had heard.

"Thank you so much and may you have a good day too," was all I could say. I suddenly realized I'd been trying to carry my burdens alone. Yet God had not left me. He was there with His assurance—through this kind gesture—that His presence with me could conquer any trial.

Many times in the stress of our lives, we overlook the presence of God, who, in His own ways, reminds us that He knows our thoughts and distresses. He says, "Come to me, all you who are weary and burdened, and I will give you rest" (Matthew 11:28, NIV).

Edna Bacate Domingo

Under His Wings

Keep me as the apple of the eye,
hide me under the shadow of thy wings.
—*Psalm 17:8, KJV*

Our front porch is small but has two hooks for hanging baskets. When we bought the house, we were blessed to inherit two Boston ferns from the previous owners. Before winter, I took the ferns down, trimmed them, and stored them in the garage (and sometimes in my bathtub), taking them out on sunny days and watering them periodically. One year in the 1970s, we had a string of sunny days, so I brought the ferns out of their winter dungeon for some fresh air and sunshine.

I had them on the porch when a bird flew directly to one of them for nest-building purposes. But now I was faced with a dilemma. I knew that a cold front was coming in, and I needed to decide whether to take the ferns back into the garage for safekeeping or leave them on the porch so that the bird would have a safe place to have her young. In so doing, however, I would be risking the life of my precious fern should the temperature drop too low. After much thought, counsel, and prayer, I decided to leave the ferns outside so as not to disturb my new feathered neighbors. The next morning a thick layer of frost covered our back deck. My heart sank as I thought of my precious ferns still hanging from the front porch. But then I heard happy little chirps coming from the hanging basket and the flurry of activity coming and going from it. I knew I had made the right decision whether or not my ferns survived.

God has reminded me of a sacrifice much greater than possibly losing my ferns. "For God so loved the world, that he gave his only begotten Son, that whosoever believeth in him should not perish, but have everlasting life" (John 3:16, KJV).

God foresaw that sin's coldness would envelop His treasured, newly formed world. Yet He chose to make the ultimate sacrifice of sending His Son, Jesus, to hang on the cold, cruel cross so that we could have the safety of an eternal home with Him.

Through this experience—though the birds would never know the sacrifice that I risked for them—I caught just a tiny glimpse of the anguish God must have felt making the choice to give His Son for us. Fortunately, we know what our salvation cost our caring Father.

Let's spend some time today thanking Him, because He sacrificed everything for us.

Annemarie Freeman

Providential Meeting

And let us consider one another
in order to stir up love and good works.
—Hebrews 10:24, NKJV

had been looking forward to this day with great anticipation. My very busy daughter, who is a counselor at a large mental-health facility, and I had planned a girls' day with shopping at our favorite thrift stores and also lunch. We arranged our plans to coincide with my husband's attendance at a ministerial meeting at a church in the city where our daughter lived.

As she and I parked in front of the first store, her cell phone rang. Hearing her side of the conversation, I realized she was speaking with a family member who had been having some emotional struggles. When our daughter finished the call, we both knew that she needed to attend to that situation. Reluctantly, we canceled our plans, and she drove me back to the church. My husband, who was leaving for lunch with other ministers, was surprised to see me. After hearing the reason, he suggested I join his group for lunch. He said that Carolyn, a hospice chaplain, would also be attending.

Carolyn and I found many subjects to discuss. She asked me what I did in my spare time. I told her that years ago I had enjoyed knitting and had just recently decided to take up that hobby again. But I said I was looking for a knitting "purpose." Carolyn said her hospice patients could use lap robes. I thought, *I can do that!* Thus began my lap robe ministry. I always pray each robe recipient will be blessed. Carolyn has said each robe has been greatly appreciated and that they are always the right design and color for each particular person.

I intended to keep knitting, but two shoulder surgeries—along with my physical therapists' counsel—informed me I should wait a year. They suggested I use a round loom. Problem solved until I had surgery on both my hands. The occupational therapists said, "Wait a year." I prayed, *What can I do?* Our daughter called and said her mother-in-law, an avid quilter for years, was moving into a smaller residence and needed to find someone who could use three huge boxes of material, full of beautiful fabrics and all color coordinated! I purchased books of simple quilt patterns and am now continuing my lap robe ministry by sewing instead of knitting.

A girls' day with my daughter that had started with disappointment had resulted in a new friendship and a new ministry with many others also being blessed. God knows best.

Laura Hartmann

Unconditional Love

Charity suffereth long, and is kind, . . . beareth all things, believeth all
things, hopeth all things, endureth all things. Charity never faileth.
—*1 Corinthians 13:4, 7, 8, KJV*

When I was five years old, my siblings and I were placed in foster care. Though separated from my biological mom, I always held on to a feeling of togetherness with her in my heart—always looking, hoping, waiting, and expecting her return. In my thirties, I found my mom. What a great joy! In just two short years, however, my joy was overshadowed by her leaving us again.

You see, one day while my mother was still living in Huntsville, Alabama, near my siblings and me, she decided to leave again without a trace. My older sister and I went to check on her at her apartment. Fearing something was wrong when we heard no response, the apartment security officials allowed us to enter her apartment. To our surprise, our mom had packed up everything and was gone. She didn't even leave a note. Though she didn't leave behind young children this time, she left behind her adult children who still needed and longed for their mother's love. But God is a Healer and reminded me in His compassion to keep praying for her.

Then, after almost seven years, Mom called me. Once again I was filled with joy. I looked forward to seeing her again, and she said she was equally looking forward to seeing me too. In August 2013, I visited my mom. I went to see her with no thoughts of the first or second abandonments, just unconditional love. This time I just knew there would finally be a bonding between us. Sadly, the reunion was heartbreaking for me. My mom could not even hug me, although she hadn't seen me in almost seven years. Needless to say, my visit was cut short. After my return home, I had a lot of questions, and my broken heart left me feeling numb. This was the third time I had experienced rejection from my mother.

As I began to let God heal me, He again spoke to my wounded heart. My Father, Savior, and Friend said to me, "I need you to be a channel of My unconditional love to your mother. I need your mother to know 'God commendeth his love toward us, in that, while we were yet sinners, Christ died for us' " (Romans 5:8, KJV). As of today, I still reach out to my mom. She doesn't communicate with me; but that is OK. I am a willing vessel for God's unconditional love to flow through me. Daily I thank Him for His unconditional love for me.

Wanda Misori

It's Time to Dream Again!

"For I am about to do something new.
See, I have already begun! Do you not see it?
I will make a pathway through the wilderness.
I will create rivers in the dry wasteland."
—*Isaiah 43:19, NLT*

"For I know the plans I have for you," declares the LORD, "plans to
prosper you and not to harm you, plans to give you hope and a future."
—*Jeremiah 29:11, NIV*

I had fallen into a fixed routine that I could almost do with my eyes closed. Alone one morning after my devotional time with my prayer partners, I began to meditate on where my ministry was headed. What were God's plans for it? Next I asked myself and God this question, *What do You want me to do, Lord?* I began to reflect on my walk with Him, and I wondered what had happened to my original dream. Had I become so laid back that I was taking things for granted?

A noise interrupted my thoughts, and once again the question surfaced: *What happened to the dream?* I was then taken back to a point in my life when "the dream" was to see my family, loved ones, friends, neighbors, and everyone I met accept the whole Bible truth.

When my family moved to this neighborhood thirty-five years ago, there was no church of our denomination that welcomed black families. We had to travel a long distance to attend church in another state. It wasn't long before God gave us a vision to start a church in our home. We fasted and prayed, and God blessed us with twelve people to start a church company. We were an energetic group and soon accomplished our church-status vision. But now it's time to step forward into the breakthrough that God has for me and my ministry.

Am I the only one who needs a breakthrough—a fresh anointing? Probably not. God has a work for me; and He has a work for you too. It's time for us to follow the dreams that He has put in our hearts. It's time that we ask Him to take the attitudes that have become "oxidized" in our dream and make them fresh again. Words on the front of my journal read, "To Dream Is to Realize Your Purpose." For me to realize my purpose, I have to trust God to give me directions for my life and ministry. I pray that this new beginning will open many doors and opportunities for me.

God has a plan for all of us. The plan often starts with a dream within our hearts. It's time to start to dream again and bring the dream to fruition with God's help!

Marilyn P. Wallace

Surrender! Stop Struggling!

Be anxious for nothing, but in everything by prayer and supplication, with thanksgiving, let your requests be made known to God.
—Philippians 4:6, NKJV

There are some times in life when we wonder what plans God has for us. Then we go through a period of waiting. At this time, the outcome can depend on our attitude toward life. "For as he thinks in his heart, so is he" (Proverbs 23:7, NKJV).

Some people lose courage when things seem dismal. Others struggle hard and fight for what they want to achieve. While nothing is wrong with this, there is a better way. I have fought all my life for what I wanted, and I prided myself on my resilience. After fighting for so long, however, I got tired. I felt so drained that I gave up on my dreams. That was when I let go. "For in the time of trouble He shall hide me in His pavilion; in the secret place of His tabernacle He shall hide me; He shall set me high upon a rock" (Psalm 27:5, NKJV).

Fortunately for me—and it can be for you too—Jesus heard my cries and saw my tears. Just when I thought hope was gone, my Savior took me from a place of danger (physical and spiritual), put a roof over my head, and brought me back to the foot of the cross. "In you, O LORD, I put my trust; let me never be ashamed; deliver me in Your righteousness" (Psalm 31:1, NKJV). When you're living for God, things aren't going to be all smooth and nice, but I can assure you that you can rest comfortably because your future is secure. "Weeping may endure for a night, but joy comes in the morning" (Psalm 30:5, NKJV).

No more fighting for me. Now when my hands go up, it is not in desperation. Rather, they are hands raised to the Lord in praise. When I shout, it is to glorify the Lord. I have decided to let God fight my battles for me. He said, "But seek first the kingdom of God and His righteousness. . . . Therefore do not worry about tomorrow, for tomorrow will worry about its own things" (Matthew 6:33, 34, NKJV).

With God's blessing and the constant guidance of the Holy Spirit, all you can conceive, you can achieve if it is God's will.

Nothing is impossible with an omnipotent God, so surrender to Him now and stop struggling through this life of dread alone.

Kimberly M. H. Henry

Caterpillars and Collard Greens

"The Spirit of the Lord GOD is upon Me,
Because the LORD has anointed Me
To preach good tidings to the poor;
He has sent Me to heal the brokenhearted,
To proclaim liberty to the captives,
And the opening of the prison to those who are bound; . . .
To comfort all who mourn,
To console those who mourn in Zion,
To give them beauty for ashes,
The oil of joy for mourning,
The garment of praise for the spirit of heaviness."
—*Isaiah 61:1–3, NKJV*

You may ask, What do caterpillars and collard greens have in common? In my forty years of life, never have I met anyone who does not enjoy the view of a butterfly effortlessly floating through the sky on a sunshine-filled day; the sight is often mesmerizing. In addition to the butterfly causing little or no negative responses, a pot of perfectly seasoned collard greens is a wonderful addition to any holiday dinner table, especially when paired with a corn muffin.

The truth is, though, that the butterfly does not start out as a beautiful butterfly. Its beauty is in complete contrast to its previous life. This flying delight was once a creepy, fuzzy, wormlike creature that spent its time munching on all it could find until the day it became a chrysalis inside a dark, dreary cocoon. During its tenure in the cocoon, the body of the little caterpillar had to actually disintegrate in order for it to become what we all love and enjoy: a beautiful butterfly.

The same is true with collard greens. Before they were on your plate, surrounded by the festivities of your holiday meal, a collard green was a tiny seed that had to be buried in the cold, dark ground; watered; and cultivated. Even when the seeds have grown up into beautiful green leaves, their flavor is perfected by the first chill of approaching winter.

Does life seem tough right now? Do you feel like you were dealt a bad hand? Like the caterpillar or the green seed, do you feel like you are buried alive in a cold, dark place? Well, keep the faith; God is producing something beautiful in you at this very moment. He who has promised is faithful, and He will give you beauty one day in exchange for all the ashes that life has heaped upon you. One day soon you will soar like a beautiful butterfly and amaze those who thought your story was over.

And by grace, your life will bring glory to God!

Sommer E. Williams

Removing Every Obstacle

"Therefore I say to you, whatever things you ask when you pray,
believe that you receive them, and you will have them."
—Mark 11:24, NKJV

When I saw him at the door, I was filled with concern and confusion. Don had a kitchen towel wrapped around his right wrist. Copious amounts of blood covered the front of his shirt. Vandals had broken a window in the church, and now that same window had fallen in and cut my husband's wrist. He needed transport to the hospital; we couldn't afford the time to wait for an ambulance. When we got to the car, I asked him to unwrap his hand so that I could see how badly it was hurt. The blood spurted onto the ceiling of the car with every heartbeat. His hand just flopped over limp. The main flexor tendon had been cut, and the radial artery was severed.

He applied a tourniquet, using a large bandana handkerchief he'd stuffed in his pocket. It was a kind he never usually carried, but he had felt impressed to take it that morning.

As we began the drive to the hospital more than thirty miles away, we found our progress impeded by traffic from both directions and a car in front of us going twenty-five miles per hour in a forty-five mile-per-hour zone. Don had lost a lot of blood, and we did not have time for this delay. I had the emergency lights on and blew the horn until it literally stopped working. Still that slow car would not pull over! Then I remembered to pray.

I prayed specifically that the Lord would remove all the obstacles out of the way so that we could get to the hospital in time. Don was starting to black out. From the time I prayed until we got to the hospital, no more vehicles slowed our progress. The slowpoke pulled over. Semitrailers were pulled off to the side of the road, and all lanes were clear. The speedometer tapped out at over one hundred miles per hour. Pulling up to the emergency-room entrance, I easily pushed open the door and ran inside to inform them that Don needed help quickly.

After he was safely checked in, I parked the car and attempted to reenter the same door. It would not open. I fumbled around and accidentally hit an alarm button. When the attendant opened the door, I commented that it was a good thing the door hadn't been locked when I went to it the first time. The attendant responded, "Ma'am, that door is *always* locked."

God truly had removed every obstacle so that we could get help when it was needed.

Janice L. Yancheson

Waiting on the Lord

But they that wait upon the LORD shall renew their strength;
they shall mount up with wings as eagles; they shall run,
and not be weary; and they shall walk, and not faint.
—*Isaiah 40:31, KJV*

Just like almost every little girl, I spent most of my days dreaming about getting married, having children, and living happily ever after! Would *he* be a handsome doctor, a well-read lawyer, or a really cute teacher? As a teenager, I often "planned" my wedding: who my bridesmaids, groomsmen, ushers, flower girl, and presiding minister would be. My colors pretty much stayed the same—purple or pink.

Matthew 6:33 states, "Seek ye first the kingdom of God, and his righteousness; and all these things shall be added unto you" (KJV). So I read my Bible every day, attended church weekly, prayed without ceasing (especially for a husband), treated everyone kindly, and accepted church offices. I joined every choir I could, especially the choirs that traveled so that I would have more opportunities to meet my husband!

Now having reached my forties, I decided to do like Hannah in 1 Samuel 1:10, 11: "Crushed in soul, Hannah prayed to GOD and cried and cried—inconsolably" (*The Message*). So I prayed and cried and cried—inconsolably. I could not tell anyone, though; they might think I was crazy or perhaps "high" on something! By now, all the flower girls I wanted were too old, I had new girlfriends, and the choice of officiating pastor had changed numerous times! But wait! Psalm 27:14 was screaming at me: "Wait on the LORD: be of good courage, and he shall strengthen thine heart: wait, I say, on the LORD" (KJV). So I waited for courage and strength.

Does waiting on the Lord increase our confidence—confidence that He will supply the right man in His time? Does waiting give us courage to endure? And does waiting strengthen our hearts and make us ready to receive His perfect gifts? I think waiting on the Lord is the only way to be ready to receive what He wants us to have.

When I was in my early fifties, God provided the Christian man whom I had prayed and inconsolably cried for. God had strengthened my heart and made me fit for the continuing journey. He provided a husband that has taken care of me in good times and bad times. He is attentive, protective, and kind—a husband that makes my heart merry. God's gift was well worth the wait!

Sylvia A. Franklin

Dandelion Corsage

A cheerful heart is good medicine,
but a broken spirit saps a person's strength.
—*Proverbs 17:22, NLT*

Back in college when my husband and I were dating, I invited him to be my date to a school banquet. Shortly after that, we were taking a walk near the campus and saw some dandelions—very long-stemmed dandelions. This happened back in the days when a gentleman always gave his date a corsage to wear with her special dress. Dick took a look at the bright-yellow flowers and joked that maybe he would give me a dandelion corsage.

When the big day arrived, the lobby of the women's dorm filled with young men waiting for their dates to be called down, and corsages were being sent up to the women who were hurrying to get dressed and ready.

I had on my blue evening dress when one of the runners brought me a florist box. When I opened it, there lay a nicely arranged dandelion corsage. I just laughed. Minutes later, another runner came in with a second florist corsage box, saying "Here is another corsage!"

"Don't open it!" I exclaimed. "I don't want to see it!"

I carefully put on the dandelion corsage, checked my appearance, and descended to the lobby. Dick was on the far side of the room; as I walked past all the waiting men, I thought I was getting some strange looks. And Dick looked totally shocked! "Didn't . . . didn't you get the second corsage?"

"No, I didn't see another corsage," I said with a straight face. (Well, I had actually not seen it.) But I finally had to tell the poor, embarrassed man that there had been another corsage and I would go get it.

Needless to say, we have both laughed about this event through our fifty-seven years of marriage. It is always good to have a shared joke. In fact, we are told that laughter is good for our health. Solomon had it right: a cheerful heart does promote inner peace, joy, happiness, and contentment. All of which promotes good physical and mental health. This might have been what John thought about when he wrote, "Dear friend, I pray that you may enjoy good health and that all may go well with you, even as your soul is getting along well" (3 John 2, NIV).

Ardis Dick Stenbakken

Wake-up Call

Casting all your care upon him, for he careth for you.
—*1 Peter 5:7, KJV*

I am used to wake-up calls because I travel most of the year. Our campus guard wakes me at a certain time if I request him to do so when I need to catch a train or a flight.

I have even experienced sudden wake-up calls when having fallen asleep while seated next to a driver who had to jerk suddenly when avoiding a vehicle accident.

Many times we are awakened by a neighbor's loud music, a ringing telephone, or a surprise knock on the door by friends or someone who is in trouble or need.

But I must confess that since my childhood, God has awakened me between four-thirty and five-thirty every morning. Even if I want to sleep, I cannot because God is very punctual in waking me up every day. The most amazing thing is that when I go back to sleep after talking to my heavenly Father, it is the best sleep ever.

I am reminded of little Samuel, whom God awoke from his sleep in order to inform him about the eventual death of Eli's sons. Yes, God can wake us too.

God might just wake you at two-thirty in the morning because He is God, and He knows your blood-sugar level is going down. This is exactly what I experienced one particular morning. I was in a deep sleep, and suddenly at two-thirty my eyes opened, which was an unusual waking time for me. My body was wet, I felt shaky, and I couldn't move my hand. I said, *God, help me to wake my husband.* Then I managed to touch him and said, "Check my sugar level." Immediately, my husband got the glucometer; he was shocked to discover my sugar level was only forty-six! (Normal fasting blood-sugar levels are between seventy and ninety-nine.) He rushed to the kitchen and got some juice and cookies for me. I felt very weak; but after taking the juice, I regained some strength. I drank more juice and felt even stronger.

God cares for us under all circumstances and at all times. Yes, we need a wake-up call from Him when we need to pray or check our blood-sugar levels or when our lives are in any type of danger. We especially need a wake-up call from Him when we are drifting away from what is right—or even running away from God as Jonah did. In these situations, we need an urgent wake-up call from our awesome God. And how He does care for us!

So today, because He cares, I cast all *my* care upon my God who careth for me.

Premila Masih

May 30

The Power of Prayer—Part 1

I sought the LORD, and he heard me,
and delivered me from all my fears.
—*Psalm 34:4, KJV*

ily! Lily, please wake up!" I could hear my mom saying. Though I could hear her, I was unable to respond. I believe I was in a state of shock. My mom noticed my inability to respond and slightly slapped my face. This enabled me to wake up, but my body was completely numb.

Since literally the day I was born, I was an abused child. I was not loved or accepted by my father. Many horrifying events had transpired throughout the years, and now I was thirteen years old. By that point, my dad had become an alcoholic, and the abuse had intensified. Whenever he left home, he would say, "I am leaving; but when I return, blood will run through this house! I will kill all of you, and then I will kill myself."

That day before he left home, he repeated his usual threat. He returned at three o'clock in the morning. I was awake. A cold chill ran down my spine. My throat was dry, and my body was tense. As with many times before, I started to pray, *Please, God, don't let him be able to open the door.* In his excessively inebriated state, my dad would take a long time trying to open the door with the house keys. After about half an hour, he would make it inside the house.

This night, as soon as he came in, he went to the kitchen, grabbed a knife and rushed to my mother's side, screaming, shouting profanities, and telling her he was going to kill her and then their four children. Being the eldest child, I got on my knees and started praying. I prayed to God with intensity. Although young, I could feel strong forces of evil in this conflict.

"Dear Lord, *please* hear my prayer! *Please* don't let Dad kill Mom or kill my siblings—please!" I continued praying into the early morning hours for what seemed to be an endless length of time. The struggle between good and evil continued. Dad would not tire, and I could truly hear the evil in his voice; it was a demon speaking for sure.

We should never live one day without prayer. The Word of God is our daily bread, and prayer is our daily dose of vitamins. We need both in order to survive the war between good and evil that constantly takes place around and in our lives.

Why not call on God right now?

Lily Morales-Narváez

The Power of Prayer—Part 2

Then they cry unto the LORD in their trouble,
and he bringeth them out of their distresses.
—*Psalm 107:28, KJV*

As my inebriated and cursing father menacingly waved the knife at Mother in the early hours of the morning, my knees started to weaken from kneeling for so long on the hard cement floor. My terrified mind started to lose power. I was mentally drained. I remember saying, "Dear Jesus, I am tired! I can't pray anymore. Let Your will be done and not mine. If You want my dad to take our lives, then I surrender my life to You. Amen." I got up and lay back in bed, prepared to die. All of a sudden, I heard the sound of a heavy object hitting the floor and the scrape of metal across the cement floor before something hit the wall. Then complete silence.

I somehow knew that the loud thump was my dad's body when he hit the floor and the metal object was the knife. To be honest, I don't remember whether I praised God at that moment or not. My young mind and body were in shock. This is when my mom came to my room, where my two little sisters and I slept in one bed. She was rousing us so that we could be delivered.

There is power and deliverance through God in prayer! For thirteen years, I lived as an abused child, suffering many severe and stressful moments of anguish; sorrow; and mental, physical, and psychological abuse. Yet, throughout my years of Christian living, I have also vividly experienced the power of God through answered prayers.

I am here today, years later, sharing this with you because I know that there are many women and children out there suffering as I did—some suffering even more. My greatest hope and most sincere prayer is that if you are a wounded soul, you will seek God with all your heart (Jeremiah 29:13). God has promised that those who truly seek Him will find Him. He will hear and He will heal. He will deliver you (2 Chronicles 7:14).

Do not lose hope. Give your heart and soul to God. Look for help—please! And let vitamin B (the Bible) and P (prayer) be your daily doses of spiritual nutriments to ensure your spiritual health. The war against evil can never be won without these two vitamins in our hearts, minds, bodies, and souls. Let's remember always that God is our help: "Then they cry unto the LORD in their trouble, and He bringeth them out of their distresses" (Psalm 107:28, KJV).

Lily Morales-Narváez

June 1

The Power of Prayer

Seek the LORD, and His strength;
Seek His face evermore!
—Psalm 105:4, NKJV

I have been a pastor's wife for the past thirty-six years. Often the journey has not been very easy! But it is still a pleasure to share how God has been involved in experiences that came my way during my lifetime. So let me share one experience with you.

My husband was pastoring a church in Surat (Gujarat, India) in 1989. In November of that year, my second daughter, Meghna, fell sick with malaria and dengue fever—dreaded diseases in those days as well as now.

Little Meghna, almost four years old, was in the hospital for more than a week. Her fever was very high, and she was receiving treatment intravenously. I had three children, and I still had to take care of the other two, a girl and a boy, all while Meghna was in the hospital.

One week into my daughter's hospitalization, the doctor felt he had done all he could to treat Meghna successfully. He called us with some very discouraging news.

"I am sorry to have to say this to you," he began, "but your daughter's outlook is not good. I think it would be wise for you and the family to prepare yourselves in case the worst thing happens. I will continue to do my best, but things don't look good."

That night I went to the Lord on my knees and pleaded earnestly while my husband went to be with Meghna at the hospital. *Dear Father in heaven, please touch Meghna with Your healing hand. I am wrestling with You, Lord, as Jacob did when he was in such deep distress.*

I don't know when I went to sleep, but early the next morning there was a knock on the door. Opening it, I found myself facing my excited husband. "The fever has come down," he said, "and Meghna is hungry! She wanted to eat her favorite flatbread!"

The whole family rushed to the hospital. When the doctor came in, he was shocked to see her smiling and sitting up. After a quick check, he discharged her. Within a few days, we celebrated her fourth birthday! Since then, the years have flown. Meghna is now a dentist in a Christian hospital and married to another dentist, Marvin Hembrom. They have a little son, Marcus.

Dear Lord, always help us to trust You!

Priscila Kandane

Falsely Accused

Eli said unto her, "How long will you be drunk?
Put your wine away from you!"
—1 Samuel 1:14, NKJV

I t is very painful to be accused even if you have truly done wrong. It is worse and more painful when you have not done what you are being accused of. Accusation wounds like an arrow that pierces a sensitive heart. But we are all guilty of the evil of falsely accusing others. Even children of God are not exempt. I have tried to imagine myself in the shoes of Hannah, a barren woman suffering from the emotional and physical abuse of her rival, Peninnah. Hannah was a woman of value who desperately wanted a child of her own, which in her time was considered to be a sign of God's favor. Yet her wicked rival's taunts tormented her day and night. Her agony grew, as she was now considered to be under the curse of God.

In her moments of desperation and utter helplessness, Hannah decided to pour out her sorrow to God in prayer. Rapt in holy communion with her God through silent prayer, she did not notice the presence of anyone else. But Israel's high priest, Eli, had been observing her. He misinterpreted her prayerful pleadings as being the behavior of an intoxicated woman. Sternly he rebuked her, falsely accusing her of something she had not done. Yet Hannah's response and respectful attitude is worthy of emulation by all of us who are falsely accused.

Ellen White writes that instead of getting angry or showing disrespect toward the aged man of God, "with due reverence for the anointed of the Lord, she calmly repelled the accusation and stated the cause of her emotion. 'No my Lord, I am a woman of sorrowful spirit. I have drunk neither wine nor strong drink, but have poured out my soul before the Lord. Count not thine handmaid for a daughter of Belial, for out of the abundance of my complaint and grief have I spoken hitherto.' "* What was the result of Hannah's gentle and kind response in the face of false accusation? She was blessed by the prayer of the accuser. Peace and joy came instead of quarrel and curse. She finally got what she wanted in the gift of a baby boy, Samuel.

Lord, grant me patience and Your wisdom when I am being falsely accused. Help me to forgive my accusers and learn to live in peace with everyone. Show forth Your glory in revealing the truth about my circumstances. In Jesus' name, I pray.

Omobonike Adeola Sessou

---

* Ellen G. White, *Prayer* (Nampa, ID: Pacific Press®, 2002), 132.

June 3

Graduation Day

Not by might, nor by power,
but by my spirit, saith the LORD of hosts.
—*Zechariah 4:6, KJV*

This past summer we celebrated with my young daughter as she received her second doctorate (PhD); this one was in Hispanic languages. Her first doctorate was in law (JD). Because I have a doctorate (PhD) as well, I was able to march with the graduates and sit with my daughter during the ceremony and place on her the hood (a piece of academic clothing that identifies the degree earned and the institution awarding the degree).

Two hundred and eleven doctoral candidates, two hundred thirteen master's degree candidates, and more than two thousand bachelor's degree candidates received diplomas that day. It was a busy day! With so many people graduating, the ceremony had to be fast-paced and efficient. The hooding was too fast-paced. While one graduate was being hooded, the next name was being announced. There was no opportunity for graduates to bask in the glory of the occasion.

What was also disconcerting to me was that at one point in the ceremony, program facilitators told all doctoral students to stand up and yell out the title of their dissertations. That seemed very impersonal, especially since none of the candidates' names were printed in the graduation program. They weren't even listed. Everything about the ceremony seemed minimal.

At most denominational institutions, there is a much larger celebration. Often there are three services: consecration, baccalaureate, and commencement over a three-day period. In some ways, I felt cheated because of the lack of a personal touch for the graduates at my daughter's graduation. It was exciting, however, for her, and the afterparty was great! Friends and supporters had come from all over the United States to celebrate with us.

I reflected on the good news of another graduation day. When we all get to heaven, even though graduation day down here may have seemed impersonal, Jesus will call each of us by our name. He will give us each a golden harp and a palm branch. He will welcome us into His kingdom. It will be exciting to find ourselves there, and the afterparty will be out of this world!

One of my favorite Bible texts is Zechariah 4:6: "Not by might, nor by power, but by my spirit saith the LORD" (KJV). So remember, only God can get you through this race. He will run beside you and help you to the finish, and He will ensure that you graduate, if you stay with Him.

Eva M. Starner

Cows in a Field—Part 1

God saw all that he had made, and it was very good.
—*Genesis 1:31, NIV*

"Cursed is the ground because of you;
through painful toil you will eat food from it all the days of your life."
—*Genesis 3:17, NIV*

In the beginning, life was perfect. The Lord uses the word *good* to describe what He had made; but in our society today if you say something is "good," it might mean "just OK." We've become so bombastic with our language that we need more exclamation points and more outstanding, wild, and cool ways to express our joy, happiness, and approval. Yet the Lord says "good" in a sure, confident, and definitive way. His creation was truly and wholly good! There was nothing bad that existed: no corruption, no pain, and no disappointment. Until, of course, sin entered the picture.

When we think of Eve's being deceived and Adam's defiant act of eating the forbidden fruit—the first act of sin—it's important to remember that with this first sin came all its vileness. The first sin may not seem that bad; Adam took a little bite of the forbidden fruit. How many times have children gone into a cookie jar and eaten a forbidden snickerdoodle? You wouldn't look at your child as a vile murderer for doing so, would you? But that's the deceptive thing about sin. Eternally speaking, one sin is as bad as the next.

Our first parents made the choice to follow the devil, even if they thought it would be only for a moment. Yet the Lord clearly states, "No one can serve two masters. Either you will hate the one and love the other, or you will be devoted to the one and despise the other" (Matthew 6:24, NIV). He also said, "He that is not with me is against me" (Matthew 12:30, KJV). So one actual sin is not comparable to another sin, for the simple act of turning away from God and His love, for even a moment, is the most wicked thing we can do. In that moment, we have become slaves to the devil.

I was driving on a rather chilly spring day. The rain was beating down on my windshield as I passed a field full of cows on a hill. Many had just given birth to wee little ones that couldn't have been more than a few days old, and they were out in the harsh weather. Why did they have to be out in the harsh elements? Then I realized the answer involved something *I* had done!

Naomi Striemer

Cows in a Field—Part 2

Who is a God like you,
who pardons sin and forgives the transgression
of the remnant of his inheritance?
You do not stay angry forever
but delight to show mercy.
—*Micah 7:18, NIV*

In the harsh wind and rain, the newborn calves huddled at the bellies of their mothers, trying to find shelter in the cruel world they had just entered. From inside my cozy SUV with seat warmers, I couldn't look away from the newborns in the pasture. My own little baby was snuggled comfortably in his car seat behind me; protected, at least for now, from the elements of sin in this world. A pang went through my heart. The truth is that the severe weather was not much more bearable for those little animals than it would have been were we standing out in it.

A second pang stung my heart. The reality that jolted me was that the calves' discomfort, pain, and suffering was not their fault! It was *ours*—it was *mine*.

In God's newly created and *good* world, the temperature was never too hot or too cold. All was perfect. No fierce rains beat down on helpless creatures. God gently watered the plants, trees, and grass with dew by night. God had created a perfect environment that brought continued, never-ending joy to every living creature there. But when sin entered the world, life became difficult, not just for humans but also for *all* of creation. Here's the difference though: God has extended to humankind the gift of salvation and eternal life in an earth made new. We are given a way out of this misery and a way back to perfection. But for every other living creature, this is it. They will know only the sinful world that we "created" for them.

Since we have been given a second chance, it is our duty to be grateful and thankful every minute of every day for this undeserved gift. In our gratitude, we are also to be mindful, caring, and loving in our interactions with all of creation. For creation daily suffers the consequences of human sin.

I once read that our first parents wept when they saw the first dying leaf after their sin, which is a concept you and I can hardly grasp today. May we allow God to give us His tender heart!

As I drove far beyond the field of cows on that cold and rainy day, I silently asked the Lord's forgiveness for my part in perpetuating sin. And I thanked Him for all of His goodness to us. Even when we are most undeserving.

Naomi Striemer

A Friend Indeed

"But I have called you friends, for all things that I heard from
My Father I have made known to you."
—*John 15:15, NKJV*

I t was the best and the worst time of my life. The most wonderful thing was happening in our family. The older of our two children, our son (who had returned to our home state of Florida to work), was getting married in Georgia to his sweetheart whom he had met while earning his master's degree at a Christian university in Tennessee. Among other arrangements, I would fly to New York to pick up my nine-year-old nephew, Zaire, and my three-year-old niece, Nylah, to be the Bible boy and flower girl. Family members from all over joined hands to bring this grand affair to pass, including the planned rehearsal dinner with our favorite Haitian dishes.

But darkness blanketed our lives a few weeks before the wedding. First, the wedding photographer, my son's college friend, was found dead at the age of twenty-five. This loss overpowered my son with grief. Soon my brother lost his fight with cancer. Then more darkness fell as a dear colleague received a diagnosis of cancer; our beloved city of Orlando was terror-stricken by a horrible and hateful shooting of its citizens in a club; and a baby visiting a theme park was killed by an alligator. When we thought we could bear no more, my son became ill one week before his wedding. The day before the wedding, as family and friends gathered for the rehearsal dinner, my son was simply too sick to stay the whole time, and his father carried him to the house. My daughter and I, overwhelmed by fear and worry, wept. That evening Zaire's and Nylah's faces mirrored my hurt. By their bedside as I kissed them good night, Nylah looked at me and said, "Auntie Rose, you were crying. Are you sad?" When I gently replied yes, she whispered, "It's OK, Auntie. I'm your friend." I smiled and hugged her. She had spoken kindness and hope into my heart.

I recalled another Friend who was also very close. That faithful Friend was waiting and wanted me to lay my heartbreak at His feet and trust His love for my child. I shared my sorrows with Him that night and throughout the next day at the wedding ceremonies. Jesus held my son through the nuptials, faded our fears into faith, and filled us with courage for the coming days. He had spoken His love through a three-year-old. He is always on our side and is our Friend indeed.

Rose Joseph Thomas

Invitations

"Come, all you who are thirsty,
come to the waters;
and you who have no money,
come, buy and eat! . . .
Why spend money on what is not bread,
and your labor on what does not satisfy?"
—Isaiah 55:1, 2, NIV

Many mornings I find myself waking up and immediately thinking that I am a weak Christian. I desire that the day be easy with no complications, no heartache, nothing difficult to solve, and no excessive thinking required. I just want a peaceful day.

Why is the Christian life so hard sometimes? As I pray, I am reminded by the Holy Spirit and God's Word that there is much I bring to this mind-set. I am an intense person, and I can *invite* worry, anxiety, and complications. I can create a difficult day with no help from anyone else. This self-awareness is a beautiful epiphany! And I praise Him for it. He shows me the self-fulfilling prophecy of my own thinking. Christ lovingly points out where I might invite complication and confusion; He invites me to order and clarity. Where I might invite worry, He invites me to peace. Where I invite ease and comfort, He invites trust and provision.

This is the God we follow. This is the God who knows us better than we know ourselves, and He is always working for our good. He does this with invitation, not demands or control. He invites us to something better. *Oh, thank You, Father, for Your blessed invitations. All I have to do is accept that invitation and enter into the something better.*

From the beginning of Jesus' ministry, when He called His disciples, saying, "Come, follow me" (Matthew 4:19, NIV), to His words in Matthew 11:28, "Come to me, all you who are weary and burdened, and I will give you rest" (NIV), Jesus lovingly invited.

So each morning when I wake, I am given the freedom and opportunity to invite too. Sure, I can keep my eyes focused on my problems and challenges and invite all the negative responses that go with it. Yet there is a great chasm of difference between my own invitation leanings and the invitation of Christ. And when I choose Christ's invitation each morning, that's when the abundant life that God so generously desires to give will be a reality. It is not a reality of circumstances that are always easy or comfortable, but a heart that is abundant with confidence in God. *He* is an invitation worth accepting every day.

Lee Lee Dart

The Secret to Long Life

"With long life I will satisfy him,
And show him My salvation."
—Psalm 91:16, NKJV

A t the time of this writing, she is ninety-four years old with a sharp mind and no significant health challenges. At her ripe old age, my mother, Theresa, is able to recite psalm after psalm, her favorite being Psalm 150. She could recite that psalm from beginning to end without any mistakes and with appropriate expressions. She is convinced that as long as she has breath, she should praise the Lord! Sabbath is her most anticipated day of the week, when she dresses for church and is taken by her son and his family to the little village church that she has attended for the past seventy years.

When asked about the source of her strength and longevity, Theresa replies with a toothless grin, "Faith in God and a healthful plant-based diet." Added to that, she believes that the leaves of the trees are for the healing of the nations. Consequently, she has an herbal remedy for most ailments. Burdock root detoxifies the blood and lymphatic system. Stinging nettle helps with skin allergies, urinary problems, and insect bites. Inhaling peppermint is beneficial to the respiratory system and an antidote for coughs and colds. Garlic is an antioxidant that helps get rid of colds and flu and lowers blood pressure. Aloe vera relieves heartburn and lowers blood pressure. Flaxseed helps with weight loss and lowers cholesterol.

Through the past nine decades, Theresa has learned to exercise unwavering faith in God and His never-failing promises. Just as she has an herbal remedy for most ailments, she also has a Bible promise for every situation in life. She believes that God will never give us more than we can bear (see 1 Corinthians 10:13) and that He will supply our needs (see Philippians 4:19).

Although she has been blessed with longevity, Theresa looks forward to the new heaven and new earth, where there will be no more pain, sickness, sorrow, or aging. She cherishes the glimpse of the New Jerusalem that John the revelator was privileged to see. "I saw the Holy City, the new Jerusalem, coming down out of heaven from God, prepared as a bride beautifully dressed for her husband. . . . ' "He will wipe every tear from their eyes. There will be no more death" or mourning or crying or pain, for the old order of things has passed away' " (Revelation 21:2, 4, NIV). Like Theresa, I long for heaven. How about you?

Gerene I. Joseph

Stepping Out in Faith

Now the LORD had said unto Abram, Get thee out of thy country,
and from thy kindred, and from thy father's house,
unto a land that I will shew thee.
—*Genesis 12:1, KJV*

When my husband and I first got married, we lived in a one-room basement apartment. The space was very small. We were basically living on top of each other. Don't get me wrong, my husband and I were quite content with our home. It was cozy, it was warm, and it was ours. Our little space was also convenient, for we lived close to local transportation, markets, stores, and our parents. We both had jobs. But with an infant, we were struggling financially.

To alleviate our financial burden, my husband toyed with the idea of joining the military. By doing so, he knew that he could better provide for his family. But not everyone agreed with that decision. In fact, many thought that we were losing our minds and perhaps had gone insane. This decision was also a challenge for our families. They could not understand why we would want to take such a drastic step.

We continuously prayed for God's direction. We discussed it between ourselves and came to a conclusion. We wanted a better life for our daughter and ourselves. God was the only one who could help us. We knew that God had the blueprint for our lives, and we needed to allow Him to lead us. Stepping out in faith, my husband joined the military. Soon things were back in perspective; God had a master plan for us.

Ten months after joining the military, my husband, our daughter, and I moved to Virginia. Initially, our families were worried that we were leaving comfort and security behind. Nevertheless, when you take God at His word, He will supply all of your needs. Even though Virginia was new to us, God had provided everything we needed. Our new home was three times the size of our old home. Our daughter had ample space to grow, and we lived comfortably on one income. God provided for us in ways we could not have conceived.

Abraham left the comforts that he was used to, heading to the unknown. God made a covenant with Abraham that as long as he was obedient, He would provide for his needs. Abraham kept God's word and prospered. God's promises are still active and current today. He has never broken His promise; He continuously provides for us each and every day.

Diantha Hall-Smith

Love Conquers All

Love never gives up.
—*1 Corinthians 13:7, GNT*

And now abideth faith, hope, charity, these three;
but the greatest of these is charity.
—*1 Corinthians 13:13, KJV*

Maggie was a four-year-old bichon frise. Her curly white coat and miniature size made her look deceivingly sweet and cuddly. She was a rescue dog in more ways than one. House training was one issue. She was also socially inept. But she loved me almost instantly.

I was a teacher in a one-room school. On the first day of school I left Maggie at home in her crate. When I returned from work, disaster awaited. Her bedding was shredded. Her little mouth was bleeding from her efforts to tear off the screen door of the crate. The next day a muzzled Maggie went to school with me. The students took turns walking Maggie, petting her, and speaking kind words to her. Our training lasted about three months before she stopped leaving puddles inside. The biting issue took less time. My students adored the fluffy little bundle, ignored her growling, and brought her tiny treats. Soon she was whining excitedly when the children came in the classroom door. Then we all took a chance. When I removed her muzzle, Maggie tore around the classroom, stopped at each child, and licked their hands. Love had won.

After my retirement, Maggie liked nothing better than racing around our fields and playing hide-and-seek with our big dog, Patch. The years flew by, and soon it was Maggie's fifteenth birthday. Shortly afterward, she began to have health issues. Little by little, Maggie slipped away from us. She became almost deaf and blind. I carried her everywhere, praying that she would just go to sleep and not wake up. But that didn't happen. On Easter Sunday, she cried all night long.

While I held her in my arms, she snuggled up to me but continued to cry.

At the veterinarian's office the next day, I held Maggie's dear little head. She looked into my eyes as she went to sleep for the last time. The vet put her into a tiny coffinlike box, and we brought her home. Everywhere I turned, there were memories that clutched at my heart. My grief was raw for many days. My doctor told me that losing a much-loved pet was like losing a child. Yet I thank God that He brought into my life the love of my faithful little friend. Maggie taught me that no matter how much effort it takes to save someone or something, it is worth it.

Patricia Cove

Busy

There is a time for everything,
and a season for every activity under the heavens.
—*Ecclesiastes 3:1, NIV*

For some of us, there is never enough time in a day to do all things that we need and want to do. Schedules fill up quickly, work consumes our thoughts at night, family and friends need our attention, and then there's this thing called sleep. How do you fit it all in? What do you let drop? We can all relate. We are serving and leading; our days are becoming busier and busier. We schedule one thing after another after another, leaving us without time to rest or be restored. We are running on empty most of the time.

The Bible teaches us another way to live: to keep our hearts and our minds focused on those things that really matter. The psalmist said, "Show me, Lord, my life's end and the number of my days; let me know how fleeting my life is" (Psalm 39:4, NIV).

God gives us all 24 hours in each day—1,440 minutes. With this amount of time, even if we spend 20 minutes in our personal devotions, we still have 1,420 minutes left for everything else. Isn't that wonderful?

The question is this: How do we make these devotion-time minutes worthwhile in our very packed days? Let me suggest some essentials.

Each day choose where and how you will spend your moments with God, giving Him the time He deserves. Three things that I have been practicing have proven very helpful as I pause to wait on the Lord: (1) meet with God, (2) listen to God, and (3) talk to God. Meeting with God requires commitment; a plan. Listening to God requires time to be still; a pause. Talking to God requires communion; an open heart. We need to accept His invitation, "Come to Me and learn from Me." It is important to put our time in God's hands, especially at the beginning of each new day, making every moment count! As we read in Psalm 39:4, being aware that our days are numbered helps us to focus on the things that bring real happiness, peace, and purpose in life.

With the psalmist, we can also pray, "Lord, remind me how brief my time on earth will be. Remind me that my days are numbered—how fleeting my life is" (Psalm 39:4, NLT).

Raquel Queiroz da Costa Arrais

Scars

But he was wounded for our transgressions,
he was bruised for our iniquities:
the chastisement of our peace was upon him;
and with his stripes we are healed.
—Isaiah 53:5, KJV

Every time I walk up or down the wooden stairs outside, I see scars. Gouges in the steps show where I fell and remind me how the Lord kept me from breaking a leg or a hip there. Every time I get dressed for an outing, I am also reminded of how God cares for me.

After that fall, while in the emergency room, my nylon stockings were bloodied, making me think I would have to throw them away. Yet my heavenly Father takes care of the smallest details in our lives. After rinsing my nylons at home, I looked to see what damage had been done to my sheer, and only, stockings. Surely, there would be some large hole, but there was not even one hole. There should be some runs in the nylon, but there wasn't even one. Then the stockings should be snagged, but again, I couldn't find even one. No holes, no runs, and no snags! Unbelievable! What rejoicing to my heavenly Father! He knew that purchasing another pair would be difficult as the nearest store is 120 miles away (211 kilometers), one way. Then there's the stress of watching out for moose, deer, and bear along the highway. Unlike humans, they usually do not "stop, look, and listen" for oncoming traffic; they just dash across the road, and woe betide anyone in their way!

My leg will always bear the scars from my fall. Yet the scars will remind me every day of the incredible love of God as well as His sacrifice made for each one of us.

In heaven, our scars will not be on our bodies to remind us of earthly happenings. We will have perfect bodies. What a joy to look forward to! Yet with Jesus, it will not be so. When the two disciples were walking from Jerusalem home to Emmaus, a Stranger joined them. They invited Him to join them for the evening meal. When He put forth His hands to bless the food, they were amazed as they saw in His hands the prints of nails. Scars! The scars that will forever remind us of His great love in giving His life for us. Scars for all eternity.

"O Lord my God, I cried unto thee, and thou hast healed me" (Psalm 30:2, KJV).

"Thou art my hiding place; thou shalt preserve me from trouble; thou shalt compass me about with songs of deliverance" (Psalm 32:7, KJV).

Muriel Heppel

Birthday Blessing—Part 1

Thou wilt keep him in perfect peace, whose mind is stayed on thee:
because he trusteth in thee.
—Isaiah 26:3, KJV

It was time to go and work another shift at the hospital. Before leaving my house, I bowed my head and prayed my daily prayer that God would protect me and my patients. I also asked that He would use me to touch someone with His love that day. My hours at work are always wrapped in suspense because I never know what will happen. Working on a labor and delivery unit is sometimes incredibly busy or very slow and boring or even downright scary! As a certified nurse-midwife, I have grown to respect each day because I never know what unique challenges I will face.

This particular evening one of my patients had finally approached the second stage of labor, and it was time to begin pushing. She and her husband had been waiting for this for a long nine months. They were ecstatic about meeting their first baby! They could hardly wait. Labor had been a very long process. They were both exhausted. Yet the excitement of the moment outshone the fatigue.

I introduced myself. The new mommy-to-be was ready to start pushing. None of us knew it would be quite some time before her little bundle of joy entered the world. Two hours went by and the baby was not coming. We tried all the tricks I knew to help the baby rotate and navigate the birth canal: position changes, squats, and the hands and knees position. Nothing was working. It was time to change the plan. The physician I was working with joined the delayed birthday party. She tried forceps. That didn't work. By this time, the new mommy was really tired! She had been pushing for nearly three hours. She tried a few more pushes, but the baby was not coming. Exhausted and still a long way from delivery, we decided to prepare for a cesarean section.

My patient started to cry.

I had been praying silently. I felt impressed to let her know my secret. I gently squeezed her hand and told her I was a Christian and that I had been praying for her. I asked whether she would like me to pray *with* her.

Sherilyn Gibbs

Birthday Blessing—Part 2

In every situation, by prayer and petition,
with thanksgiving, present your requests to God.
And the peace of God . . . will guard your hearts
and your minds in Christ Jesus.
—Philippians 4:6, 7, NIV

For three hours one night, an expectant mother, supported by our medical team in a labor and delivery unit, had tried everything to encourage the baby to come. Since the mother was still a long way from delivery, the doctor and I decided to prepare for a cesarean section.

At this, my patient began to cry. I reached out and tightly grasped her hand as tears welled up in my own eyes. My heart broke as I saw the pain in her eyes.

Before coming to work that shift, I had prayed that God would protect me and my patients. Since the beginning of this woman's struggle, I had been praying silently. I felt impressed to let her know my secret. I gently squeezed her hand and told her I was a Christian and that I had been praying for her. I asked whether she would like me to pray *with* her. "Yes!" she said. I bowed my head and prayed a simple prayer asking God to keep mommy and baby safe. As we wheeled her back to the operating room, I told her I knew God would take care of them. She thanked me. Within a very short time, the baby was screaming and filling his lungs with air. Baby was healthy! Mommy was healthy, and now she could hold the cute little bundle of joy she had been waiting for! We were all so grateful.

Several months later this same patient came to the office for her follow-up visit. "Do you remember me?" she asked.

"Absolutely!" I responded with a smile. We talked about that big day—the long-awaited birthday party. Then she shared something that surprised me. She said, "When you prayed for me, I suddenly had an incredible sense of peace and security that covered me like a blanket." She shared that my prayer made a huge difference. She then shared that she also was a Christian—she pastors a local church! I was very surprised. I'm so thankful I listened to the Holy Spirit that day.

We never know how living our faith will bless others. We are God's hands, lips, and feet. He wants to use us to touch others with His love. As we follow His promptings, we receive the greatest blessing. In this case, I received the *greatest* "birthday" blessing.

Sherilyn Gibbs

Express Yourself!

We have different gifts, according to the grace given to each of us.
—*Romans 12:6, NIV*

Today, in a large chain department store, I stood in the checkout line behind a young mother. Not only did she have a cart full of groceries and a cute little four-year-old girl in the basket of her cart, but she also had a baby carrier containing a weeks-old baby in the front of the cart.

The little girl kept saying, in her loud "outside" voice, "Scooby *Doo*!" The young mother asked her daughter to stop, or at least keep her voice down. The child looked up at her mother and innocently said, "But I need to express myself!"

Of course, I couldn't help but chuckle, especially when the girl's mother responded, "Then please express yourself more *quietly*."

"Scooby *Doo*!" the little girl began repeating, now in an exaggerated whisper. I suspect the main issue was that the child was finding it difficult to share the limelight with her new sibling. But where this little girl had heard about the need to "express" oneself is beyond me!

We may chuckle at the explanation from the little girl, but the truth is that we all have a need to express ourselves, and we do this in different ways. No, not all of us are as vocal or outgoing as this child was. But I do know this: all of us have been given individual talents because Jesus needs us to use them for Him. When we share—in our own ways—what God has done for us, we will experience His peace, joy, and strength and a sense of security. Not only that, but others around us who hear the expressions of our love and appreciation for Christ will experience His peace, joy, strength, and assurance as well.

The fact that Jesus *needs* us is very good news to me! We all need to feel needed. And we *are* needed, for we are beloved children in God's family. "See what great love the Father has lavished on us, that we should be called children of God! And that is what we are!" (1 John 3:1, NIV). God needs us, as His children, to contribute to the welfare and advancement of the family. We are needed members of God's family, and He has given special gifts that we can use to enrich the lives of those around us. Some of us will do so quietly, and others of us may be feeling the need to shout, "Scooby *Doo*!"

Whatever talent God has given you for *His* glory, just go ahead and express yourself!

Grace Keene

Father

"Honor your father and your mother,
that your days may be long."
—*Exodus 20:12, NKJV*

A couple of years after Orlando married Edda, he became very sick with Hodgkin's lymphoma. In those days, there was no treatment for this type of deadly cancer except prayer. His father wished he would become a pastor, but how could this happen now? After Orlando had been in the hospital for forty days with a high fever, his wife by his side, God granted him complete restoration. (Today he is ninety-two years old and can read without prescription glasses!)

If God had not healed my dad, I would not have been born, nor would he have had his exemplary life as pastor, professor, philosopher, and writer! He would not have become a faculty dean, built an elementary school, or written his many books. His hobbies included orchids, fish, stamp collecting, and coins. What an amazing home we had, so full of interesting things: a domestic zoo, fruit trees, music, miniature trains, and cuckoo clocks. What a lovely upbringing full of joy, freedom, and love!

The Lord has planned each of us from our mother's womb (see Psalm 139:16). If we let Him guide and use us, He will make sure that His plans for us are fulfilled each day. When speaking about the family altar, my dad would say things such as, "The family that prays together, stays together." "The family that enjoys recreation together, remains together." "In public, watch your words; at home, watch your temper." "Guard your thoughts." What wise counsel we received from Dad! Truly, he gave us words to live by.

After sixty uninterrupted years of service to the Lord, he retired when he was eighty, having given to thousands a model of excellence in education, leadership, meekness, courtesy, and integrity. He still possesses the same sharp and brilliant intellect he had when he became a professor of mathematics and physics after earning a master's degree in education with highest honors.

Dad is a miracle of God. Like Moses of old, he knows how to listen to the still, small Voice and follow God's lead to complete enormous tasks and use his blessings to bless others.

May you also find the purpose that the *heavenly* Father has for your life here on earth. Until we are all taken together in the clouds of heaven to continue exploring His purposes for us throughout eternity, may we live by the wise instructions that He has given us in His Word.

Marli Elizete Ritter-Hein

June 17

Perceptions

"Do not judge others, and you will not be judged."
—Matthew 7:1, NLT

When I was younger, I used to watch a television show titled *The Rifleman*. It was a fictional story about a widower, Lucas McCain, who moved to the New Mexico Territory with his young son, Mark. He wanted a fresh start in life after his wife died. Of course, as the title implies, he knew how to use a rifle and was very good at doing so.

As a young person watching this show, I did not like it very well. McCain seemed to be a hard taskmaster, and things had to be done right. Of course, a lot of judgments were passed out with the use of his rifle. According to the television episodes, the bad guys deserved justice because they didn't care about doing right. So they experienced frontier justice at its swiftest.

Now years later, I recently happened across this program again. What a surprise I found it to be! It was not anything like I had remembered it. Mr. McCain still had the rifle, of course, and justice was dealt out. Yet I now understand that this father in the story was concerned that his son, Mark, grow up to do right and have a good work ethic.

I'm sure that this television portrayal was true to the lives and desires of many who crossed the Great Plains and struggled to establish new lives and help build their country. Not everything went right. Fires destroyed. Storms and drought affected harvests. Injustice raised its ugly head. But people were also concerned about how their children were brought up. They wanted a place for them to live, work, and grow. How wonderful it must have been to play a part in settling parts of their nation.

Almost fifty years have gone by since I first watched *The Rifleman*. Time and life lessons enable me to see differently than I once did. I no longer see things with the black-and-white judgmentalism of youth. Age has tempered me, and I am now able to look at the whole picture instead of at just one aspect of it. There are still some days I can slip back into old, *old* habits and whip out a "judgment" faster than Mr. McCain could whip out that rifle of his and exact judgment. Thankfully, Jesus reminds me that judgment is not for me to deal out. That's His job.

I am working on letting Jesus, rather than myself, be the director of my "program."

Mary E. Dunkin

We Never Lose

But thanks be to God! He gives us the victory
through our Lord Jesus Christ.
—*1 Corinthians 15:57, NIV*

With my hands in my back pocket, I realized that my money and the receipt accounting for the company's petty cash had been lost! My friend decided we should search the area. As we left to search, someone said, "You won't find it."

"In faith, we will," my friend answered. We met a few minutes later. "I looked everywhere," she said, shaking her head, "I did not find it." I thanked her for her help. We walked a bit, and then she told me, "I have sad news for you." We were at a breast cancer health fair, so I thought the worst.

"Do you have a lump in your breast?" She shook her head. "Is it work?"

"A relationship," she answered. Then she told me that she had broken up with her boyfriend. We spoke about it, and then she said, "You're the only one I've told. I felt impressed to tell you while I was looking for the receipt. I said if God cares about your lost money and receipt worth one hundred and eleven dollars, then He will solve my relationship problem too."

Usually, God speaks to this friend through signs, so I was a bit bummed. I thought, *Was the lost money a sign that her relationship was over?* I told her I would pray for her, and we said good night. Two days later, while having my devotional time, I remembered that I had worn a different pair of jeans when I had placed the money and the receipt in my pocket. I ran for the jeans, and there it all was! I took a picture and sent it to my friend. I had thought the money and receipt were lost; but unknowingly, I had them all along. Yet helping me search had given her an opportunity to share her pain with me and gave me the opportunity to pray for her.

I messaged her: "Sometimes we think we lose but we never lose if we give God our problems and trust Him to take charge. I pray you have good news today and receive the blessings the Lord has for you. Trust Him to take charge as He always does in your life and in your relationship." One week later my friend told me that she and her boyfriend had had a long, teary-eyed, and prayerful talk and had decided to let God take control of their relationship again.

I am so glad we never lose with God!

Kimasha P. Williams

The Light of the World

"You are the light of the world.
A city that is set on a hill cannot be hidden."
—Matthew 5:14, NKJV

I live in a rustic neighborhood in which I enjoy walking. There I experience nature in a profound way: The birds of varying colors and hues busily sing their songs as they fetch their morning meal. Deer in groups of five or six hurriedly prance across the paved areas, trying to get to the nearest underbrush. The spring brings out the best in the crocuses and camellias. I praise God for His awesome gift of beauty, even though sin has marred His creative works. As I walk and admire nature, I repeat passages from psalms, hum songs of praise, or just talk to God.

Each day I pray that I will be a witness for Christ and that my countenance will reflect His lovely face. One day I was walking my last mile and heading for home when I saw Nancy Williams, whom I usually greet. She shouted as she saw me and said she had been praying she would see me. She wanted me to pray for her son, Trent, who was a police officer. I had never discussed religion with her, but she needed a shoulder to lean on. Her son was experiencing difficulty at work and was thinking about quitting the job because his health was being affected. As she spoke, I breathed a prayer that God would put the right words in my mouth.

Right there on the side of the road, we held hands, and I asked that God would change the situation at Trent's precinct by whatever means He deemed best. I did not see Nancy for another two weeks because I traveled out of town. On my return, I met her almost at the same spot on my walk. She shared how God had changed the job situation at Trent's precinct. Some other officers had been transferred to other precincts and one left the job, and now the work atmosphere was much friendlier. Nancy exclaimed, "God sure does answer prayer!"

Why did this neighbor reach out to me? I cannot say, but I trust that my prayer of asking God to shine through me was what my neighbor saw. Jesus told us that we are the light of the world. Whether we are aware or not, people are watching to see how this light shines from us. We should always reflect the Christ of nature in all that we do.

May God help each of us daily to pray, *Lord, let me be a shining light for You everywhere I go.*

Eveythe Kennedy Cargill

Streams of Supply

Bread shall be given him; his waters shall be sure.
—Isaiah 33:16, KJV

Y ou are not going to get ahead in life—anywhere!—by marrying a pastor," my friends sneered at me when I handed them my wedding invitation.

It's been eleven long, beautiful, and glorious years since I married that pastor. And I have to tell you that I have never regretted, even for a moment, my having followed through on my decision to do so.

Life's journey has its stormy times, but they are sweet, too, when you know you are where God wants you to be and with the one to whom He led you. I've enjoyed bountiful blessings from God by being married to a minister of God. Let me share just one of these blessed experiences.

One day my three-year-old son asked me for an apple. He, of course, could not know that because we were at the end of the month, we barely had any money left even for our necessities.

I double-checked in my purse and found it empty, as I had suspected. So I whispered a prayer. "Lord, You are my Provider, and I claim Your promises from Psalm 34:10, which assures me that even though young lions may hunger because they haven't any food, I will not lack any good thing if I continue to seek You. Please send apples for my son."

When I went to church on the evening of that very day, one of our members came to me after the service and handed me a basket full of kiwis, oranges, bananas, strawberries, and—apples! When she shopped for fruit that day, she had been impressed to share some with me.

I was overwhelmed because I had asked God for only apples. Yet the Giver of all good gifts abundantly "rained" all kinds of fruit over us. I couldn't stop thanking Him.

Surely, we serve a Living God who takes personal interest in the well-being of each and every person on earth. I have learned and embraced this truth: when they are faithfully doing His service, God takes care of His children and never lets them down at any cost. His mercies are everlasting, and His faithfulness is new every morning!

Father in heaven, without Your presence in our lives we cannot do anything. Please help us to remember that You are ever present to supply all our needs today.

Esther Synthia Murali

Who Are My Ancestors?

For by him were all things created, that are in heaven, and that are in earth, visible and invisible, whether they be thrones, or dominions, or principalities, or powers: all things were created by him, and for him.
—*Colossians 1:16, KJV*

My mother, Rose, was a zealous genealogy buff. At the age of eighty-five, she would sit at her computer and learn new software that helped her dig into our ancestry and unlock the secrets of those who came before us. She was determined to search the records, even going to a special library in our town that housed immigrant ship records and government documents. These unveiled clues to the lives of our grandparents, great-grandparents, and great-great-grandparents. Some were married, some divorced, and some single. Babies were born and babies died. The motive driving Mother's research was the knowledge that uncovering all these details of the past would help us better know ourselves. It was revealing to find out who our ancestors were. Sometimes we found out things we wish we hadn't.

The genealogy of Jesus in the books of Matthew and Luke are revealing also. Matthew 1 records Joseph's genealogy as the house and lineage of David. Matthew also shows the Jews that Jesus is their Messiah. There are fourteen generations from Abraham to David, fourteen generations from David to the Babylonian captivity, and then fourteen generations to the Messiah's birth. Luke 3's account of Christ's genealogy records Mary's ancestry all the way back to Adam. Luke wrote for the Gentile audience to show how inclusive God's plan of salvation was.

As we read the list of names, we are surprised that not only are there kings and rulers in Christ's lineage, but also names such as Tamar, Rahab, Ruth, and Uriah's wife. How did they get there? Reading further, we realize that everyone listed is a sinner and in need of a Savior.

Continuing on from the birth of Jesus to His second coming, there is a new ancestral list forming that includes all of us who accept Jesus as our Lord and Savior. We need not be confused about where we come from or where we are going. It is all made clear in God's amazing plan of salvation. He wants us to know Him better by believing in Him, which entitles us to become a part of that heritage today!

Karen M. Phillips

Choosing to Die

In every thing give thanks:
for this is the will of God in Christ Jesus concerning you.
—*1 Thessalonians 5:18, KJV*

He was at it again—making remarks that dug into my soul like a knife. He knew all the buttons to push and delighted in leaning on the whole panel! No pleadings on my part induced him to let up. He was "just joking." What was my problem?

My prayers on his behalf soared to heaven daily. So did my prayers for myself. Everything had been done that I could do. I had tried silence. Let him mock and taunt me. I would be quiet. I had tried greater expressions of love through words of appreciation, his favorite cookies, hugs, and inviting his friends over. I had tried pleas on behalf of our common humanity and the humane treatment of another human being. I had tried appeals to his spiritual side. Why would he want to hurt God by such behavior?

I had tried to banish him from our home. If he couldn't be decent, then he shouldn't come on our turf and continue torturing me. I had apologized for my part (whatever it might be) in encouraging or allowing or causing him to be the way he was. There were no more resources I could think of.

And then my merciful God reminded me of the prayer I had prayed not so long ago. *Lord, I want to die to self. Please do whatever it takes; kill that self that rises up in me so often.* How else does one die apart from the snuffing out of life? When I had prayed, my desire was pure and fervent. I really wanted this sanctification. I had offered God my physical life over and over in exchange for my persecutor's salvation, never remembering that it was my own selfish nature that must die daily instead. Pain is a tremendous motivator. If only we can identify what it is that hurts so badly, we'll thrust it away and be free! We want to stand in triumph over "the enemy" just to feel good again or even not to feel at all. No hanging on the cross will do. So we try this, that, and the other until we are exhausted and angry.

But just now my tears are drying. My heart is calm. I am asking for something else.

Lord, teach me to carry today's cross. Teach me to thank You in the circumstances with which you entrust me. Show me how to die with deep love for those who are manipulated by the evil one. And someday let me see my son rise to new life because You and I chose to die.

Brenda Kiš

God's Timing

A cheerful heart is good medicine,
but a crushed spirit dries up the bones.
—*Proverbs 17:22, NIV*

My friend Eslyn and I have shared similar stories. We've had many laughs together over different situations in our lives. We've helped each other through some tough times, so I do understand the emotional challenges she goes through because I've experienced similar episodes myself. I understand what it's like not to have medication on hand during times of distress and sleeplessness.

One particular evening I heard her talking to the pharmacist about her medications. She couldn't afford to pay for them, but she was assured that someone would pay for them. The pharmacy would call when they were ready. Time went by, and no one from the pharmacy called. It was almost closing time, so Eslyn decided to check in with the pharmacy. Thankfully, her medications were paid for and ready to be picked up, but we only had six minutes to get there.

We hurried out of the apartment to get to the pharmacy. Along the way, red stoplights hindered our progress.

At 9:00 P.M., the pharmacy's closing time, we still had another five minutes of driving. I told Eslyn to notify the pharmacist we were on the way. Would they *please* wait?

That particular pharmacist is known for not being compassionate and said he wasn't sure he would wait. As a matter of fact, he reiterated that the pharmacy closes at 9:00. I didn't want to tell Eslyn it was already 9:05 P.M. When we got there, I just said, "Go! Go! Go!" She ran inside as everyone was walking out. To her surprise, when the employees saw her running toward them, they just turned around and reopened the door and gave her the medications in a bag. Isn't God awesome?

Eslyn was very grateful that I had insisted she try to get her medications—and that the Lord had softened the hearts of the employees. Sometimes God waits until it seems all hope is gone, and then He shows up and shows us His favor as only He can.

Many people may not understand what it's like to need medication, but for some—as with Eslyn—it has its place. God knows what we need and when, so I praise Him for His timing that night. He was on time for Eslyn. He'll be on time for you. He's faithful. Trust Him.

Maple Smith

Who Is Calling My Name?

And your ears shall hear a word behind you, saying, "This is the way,
walk in it," when you turn to the right or when you turn to the left.
—*Isaiah 30:21, ESV*

I can pick out my mother's voice in a crowd. I am not saying that she is loud. On the contrary, she is usually rather soft-spoken. But for years, I have heard that sweet voice say my name: in the mornings, calling me to wake up and eat; after school, picking me out of a crowd of children; at the park, when it was time to head home; at home, when we would follow each other from room to room, deep in conversation. We've spent so much time together that I could recognize her voice anywhere. In a similar way, I trust the Lord's voice when making decisions—especially the big ones. Growing up, my mother taught me His voice. She read me Bible stories to help me distinguish right from wrong and played "sermon games" with me so that I would pay attention to the pastor. She made sure I was always at Sabbath School and at youth programs. So growing up, I learned to tell the difference between my selfishness and the little voice of my conscience telling me when I should not do this or that.

As I grew older, the responsibility of spending time with God fell to me. I had to make the choice to read my Sabbath School lesson or to pray before bed or to listen to the little voice telling me what I should or should not do. And every time I forgot to read or did not pray or ignored the little voice, it grew harder for me to make the next decision and to know what God's plans were for me. Yet we are never far from the love of God. So I would return—confused, lost, and seeking guidance—and I would hear that voice that I had been taught to trust.

I cannot explain to you how I know when God speaks to me. It is a strange feeling of calm and certainty that is unmistakable to me. He does not speak to me in the same way He does to my mother or my father, but I know His voice. It led me to choose a Christian university and to go teach in South Korea. It led me to my marvelous husband.

There is a daily choice to be made: to make time to spend with God. I do not always succeed, but I know He is merciful.

Lord, I ask that You remind me each morning to spend time with You and pray that I will stay in tune with Your voice guiding me to my heavenly home.

Sandra P. Gordon

On the Verge of Missing My Flight

In my distress I called to the LORD;
I cried to my God for help.
From his temple he heard my voice;
my cry came before him, into his ears.
—*Psalm 18:6, NIV*

The highway traffic is slowing down, but I should be boarding the plane in less than an hour! I thought. I had worked all day, and my husband had specifically told me that he would pick me up at four o'clock to take me to the airport. I thought that walking outside five minutes before four o'clock would give me enough time to be ready for when my husband arrived, but my bosses were not there to lock up that day. So I had to lock up, shut off the lights, and turn on the alarms. I also had to pick up my luggage downstairs. And that took me fifteen minutes! My husband told me that because I was late, we would now hit rush hour, and we'd better pray that I would not miss the flight. So there we were, in the middle of traffic, crying out to God for a miracle. Time was running out, and it was looking almost impossible for me to catch my flight.

The next day, March 26, would be my father's seventieth birthday. I longed to celebrate with him because he was very sick. I feared that I would not see him alive again. Leaving ten minutes late had caused us to lose almost an hour and a half in rush hour traffic. Then suddenly, God opened up "pockets" in the traffic so that my husband could advance more quickly. I would still need a second miracle though. Would I make it on time?

We arrived at the airport, and I ran to the counter. I did not even have time to grab my suitcase. It was almost time to close the plane's door. I asked whether I could still board, at which point my husband arrived with my suitcase. The clerk did not know what to tell me, but next to her was the supervisor who took my suitcase—although the cargo hold was already closed! She even called the plane's crew so that they would hold the door open. I had only a few minutes to get to the gate, but finally I boarded, grateful to God and my husband for helping me in such a crucial moment. I was able to celebrate my father's birthday, and my eyes now are teary as I remember it, because that was the last time I saw him alive.

God is great! God is powerful! God is merciful! There is no doubt that God is in control. When problems overwhelm us, we need only to trust in His promises and rest on Him. He will hear our prayers and give us answers according to His wisdom.

Damaris Prieto

Threescore and Ten

"Listen to Me, O house of Jacob,
And all the remnant of the house of Israel,
Who have been upheld by Me from birth,
Who have been carried from the womb:
Even to your old age, I am He,
And even to gray hairs I will carry you!"
—Isaiah 46:3, 4, NKJV

On June 26, 1946, I was in oblivion—asleep in a small, comfortable home, being infused with liquid food—indifferent to the evil outside. This changed when a slap made me cry as I was "brought forth in iniquity" (Psalm 51:5, ESV), having been conceived in sin, not appreciating then that I was "fearfully and wonderfully made" (Psalm 139:14, NIV)! This was the first of many slaps that life had for me, and the tears were just a foretaste of more to come. As the years passed, I became acquainted with the One who made me. After thirteen years of life, I decided to serve Him. I've had some really rough spells, but today, after living seventy years, I choose to count my blessings.

I am blessed to do my small part in relieving human suffering on my island of Jamaica. Though often fraught with numerous interpersonal issues, I claim James 1:12: "Blessed is the one who perseveres under trial because, having stood the test, that person will receive the crown of life that the Lord has promised to those who love him" (NIV). Numerous young people have also been blessed with our mutually beneficial relationships. They benefit from the wisdom I've gained throughout my years of experience while their many needs and exploits have taken my intercessory prayer life to new heights.

I was blessed when I first took my son home. In the years that followed, I gained some insight into my adoption by God, and I learned unconditional love. I have been blessed with relatively good health and the means to complete my travel bucket list, enjoying God's handiwork, with no travel disasters on land, sea, or air—except for five days without my luggage! I am blessed because I have set many goals and, with God, have achieved them all.

Sadly, despite innumerable blessings, I have questioned God's will in "bad" times, tried to run ahead of His agenda, and disregarded His promise to answer my prayers (1 John 5:14). Today I do not know God's plan for my future. Nevertheless, while I am able, I will rejoice always, pray continually, and give thanks in all things.

Cecilia Grant

Break your Alabaster Box

As he sat at meat, there came a woman
having an alabaster box of ointment of spikenard very precious;
and she brake the box, and poured it on his head.
—Mark 14:3, KJV

What a joy it is to be a blessing to someone else!

During the time when Jesus walked on the earth, it was customary for someone in a host's family to wash the feet and anoint the head of a guest. In the Bible story of Mary's alabaster box, Mary went beyond this routine ritual of hospitality. She didn't wash the feet of Jesus with a basin of water. Rather, she washed the feet of the Master with her tears. She dried His feet with her long hair. Then she broke the alabaster box of expensive and fragrant ointment over His head.

Mary's example speaks powerfully of what was in her soul: a total devotion and commitment to Jesus. Her will was to give her all and her best of everything to Him. The disciples and others present on this occasion ridiculed her actions and her gift, but she would offer nothing less.

Mary's heart broke for Jesus when she broke the alabaster box of perfume. And Jesus took that broken heart of hers and made her whole by proclaiming that she was no longer a sinner! The unexpected reaction from Jesus silenced all others. He did not judge her present act of extravagance or the follies of her past. Jesus saw her repentant heart and her contrite spirit.

The blessing of giving of ourselves to others lingers over us. Broken people "smell" different because of their humility and love. Being broken before the Lord affects everyone around us. "For we are to God the fragrance of Christ among those who are being saved and among those who are perishing" (2 Corinthians 2:15, NKJV). It is time we break our alabaster boxes open and allow God to work on our hearts, our minds, and our souls. God's Spirit will then pour out of us like the ointment from that broken alabaster box, and its fragrance will fill the world.

Dear Father in heaven, fill us with Your Spirit so that we may be a blessing to those around us. Amen.

Rita Gill

Before You Call

"It shall come to pass
That before they call, I will answer;
And while they are still speaking, I will hear."
—*Isaiah 65:24, NKJV*

t was nine-thirty on Saturday night. The phone rang. I set down the boxes I was about to carry out to the half-filled van and answered the phone. It was Doris, whom I'd recently met at the University of Cincinnati, and she had immediately taken a friendly interest in me. But it was ten-thirty at night her time, and I wondered why she was calling so late. She didn't keep me waiting. "Why didn't you call me while you were up here house-hunting, Rachel?" I had gone to Cincinnati the week before to look for an apartment but didn't think of calling Doris for some reason. I told her I thought my housing was worked out, but by Friday evening, my last option had fallen through.

God had blessed me with a full study fellowship, and I believed He was leading me to go there. I had managed to borrow a van until Monday evening to move my belongings up there—the only chance I would have to do so before school started. So I had prayed over the Sabbath hours and decided after sundown to do the only thing left that I could do, which was pack the van, but I didn't have the slightest idea what to do next. *But maybe Doris knows of something and can help!* I thought, hopeful that God had impressed her to call with an answer to my earnest prayers.

But Doris had no answer. "Every apartment I know of offhand is occupied," she said, "and nobody's moving out any time soon." I felt that sudden burst of hope die. Just then her line beeped. "Just hold on a minute, Rachel," she said, and I was left listening to the silence. My one glimmer of hope had been dashed. *God, why the tease?* I thought in frustration.

"Rachel, you still there?" Doris's voice broke into my thoughts. "You won't believe this, but this is a friend calling to let me know that the tenant in the third-floor apartment of her house just moved out and to keep her in mind if I heard of anyone looking to rent a place. I told her I had someone on the other line that needed a place right away."

Within minutes, everything had been arranged. The rental price was perfect—utilities all included—and based on Doris's unqualified recommendation, the deposit was waived. The lady had planned to have the apartment ready on Monday, but she said it would be ready for me on Sunday afternoon instead. With a grateful heart, I set out for Cincinnati, Ohio, the next morning.

Rachel Williams-Smith

Look Beyond the Face!—Part 1

And we know that all things work together for good to those who
love God, to those who are the called according to His purpose.
—*Romans 8:28, NKJV*

It took me many years to finally begin understanding Romans 8:28 in a practical way. What has helped me most to really understand it are my experiences as a pastor's wife. Ministry is no bed of roses. While there are indeed some lovely and beautiful roses in ministry, there is no rosebush without thorns. I enjoy ministry. I really love it. I think it's the noblest thing a person could do with her life. There is nothing I enjoy more than working for Jesus.

And so, when I became a pastor's wife after nearly seven years of courtship, I felt sure this was what I wanted and thought I was well prepared for this journey. In my mind's eye, all I could see was happiness and a life full of bliss and togetherness. But, alas, I woke up to find that ministry was not as I thought. I found that it was hard, lonely, and sometimes very cold work. Don't get me wrong, for there are joys too. Yet for the purpose of this devotional, permit me to share a portion of my journey, with the hope that it will help to build someone up!

The churches I was privileged to serve as shepherdess seemed to have their own standards of who and what a pastor's wife should be—how she should act and how she should dress. Among their "requirements," a pastor's wife must be a singer, a public speaker, a musician, and an extrovert, and she'd better have perfectly behaved children. And I tried hard to please them! My husband's success was important to me. But was I truly happy doing all of the above? Of course not. I was forced to wear "hats" I hated but did so for the sake of ministry, and the many other sacrifices seemed endless. Yes, ministry has its thorns.

But who, really, is a minister's wife? I see her as being just like any other woman in the church with the same need for salvation. A pastor's wife is not a magician or a superwoman; she is one who loves the Lord enough to give her life in ministry for the saving of souls. But guess what I discovered? She is also human. This means that she can feel sick, sad, mad, and glad.

Many church members don't seem to see her that way. And I sometimes wonder if we pastor's wives at times mislead others into thinking we are heroines! Yet if the truth be told, we are just broken vessels, wanting to be ready for the Potter's house and for His use!

Jacqueline Hope HoShing-Clarke

Look Beyond the Face!—Part 2

But the LORD said . . . , Look not on his countenance . . . ;
because I have refused him . . . ;
for man looketh on the outward appearance,
but the LORD looketh on the heart.
—*1 Samuel 16:7, KJV*

One experience as a pastor's wife stands out in my mind. One Sabbath my baby son was on my lap and my barely two-year-old daughter was leaning against my side as we sat in one of my husband's largest churches for worship. Now as a pastor's wife, I felt I must not show any sadness to others. So over the years, I kept bottled up whatever pain I might be feeling. (Remember, I am superwoman.) I felt it was my duty to put a smile on my face and keep it there. On this Sabbath morning, my face failed me—it betrayed me. As a matter of fact, my face let me down so very badly that a sister in the church came over to me.

"Sister Clarke, if this is how your face must look, it is better you stay home and not come to church." With that, she was gone. I was so embarrassed. I wished I could evaporate like water vapor. Yet it occurred to me for the first time that I could not pretend forever. What was in my heart had eventually come to my face; and I'd thought I was smiling!

Years later now, I am actually thankful to God for that harsh, cold encounter. It helped me to be me, regardless of others' standards for me. After all, I am a child in this universe, and I have a right to be here. I should be free to express how I really feel. Thank God that today I am no longer a hypocrite. I don't need to pretend. God wants us to be honest with our emotions. When the biblical Hannah was burdened, she took her sorrow to church, and her emotion showed. Her sad heart reflected on her face so much so that even Eli the priest rebuked her. But God understood her needs and met them. I am no longer afraid to take my burdens to God. And if God is at church, then I will carry them there—to Him—no matter who observes!

This difficult experience also helped me in my ministry to others because now I am more sensitive to their needs. I no longer look on their faces and draw my own conclusions. I look *beyond* their faces. I am careful because a smiling face does not necessarily mean that a person is happy! If someone looks unhappy, I try, by God's grace, to reach out in my own way to restore joy. If it is something beyond my reach, I refer the person to the care of Jesus by simply breathing a prayer. I still look at faces, but now I also look beyond them.

Jacqueline Hope HoShing-Clarke

I Can't Bear My Husband Anymore!

Call upon me in the day of trouble:
I will deliver thee, and thou shalt glorify me.
—*Psalm 50:15, KJV*

Kartcha was a charming twenty-year-old girl who fell under the spell of a young man from her village. This man, Youssouf, was not a Christian. Very soon Kartcha drew him to her church but then went to settle in his home in the shortest time possible without paying attention to the necessity of marriage rites. Youssouf became a teacher a few years later and so did Kartcha. The couple had three wonderful children. In the course of his professional life, however, Youssouf fell in love with a nineteen-year-old girl. This girl hastened to give him an offspring. When Kartcha learned the news, she flew into a great fury: "I have never, ever felt so humiliated in all my life! Youssouf, you broke my heart!" she sobbed.

That day Kartcha began harboring the desire to abandon her home together with her children. Kartcha could no longer bear Youssouf; she had a lot to gripe about. She could not forgive Youssouf. How could he betray her so? How could she love his latest child, coming from an extramarital relationship? Despite Youssouf's unrelenting pleas for forgiveness, Kartcha would not grant it. She forgot, however, that she was as morally guilty as Youssouf.

Dear friends, we are very often swift to condemn others of the same mistakes we make—the same mistakes for which we also drop to our knees to seek the Lord's forgiveness. This reminds me of the parable Jesus told about the two debtors (Matthew 18:23–35). The debtor who owed much was forgiven after pleading with the master, but this debtor refused to forgive his fellow servant who owed him much less.

When the Holy Spirit impressed Kartcha of her guilt, she broke down and offered a prayer. *Lord, please forgive me. I was wrong! I am as guilty as Youssouf, but now I am so weak. Please help me to make things right. Lend me Your love so I can love this child of adultery as You love me! Amen.* This prayer was the beginning of a new life for Kartcha, Youssouf, and all their children.

Dear sisters, the solution to our problems is only a prayer away! Right now I urge you to seek prayer without further delay!

Koulibaly N'gandia Diata Epse Diarrassouba

Larry's Choice

And I heard a voice from heaven saying unto me,
Write, Blessed are the dead which die in the Lord
from henceforth: . . . their works do follow them.
—*Revelation 14:13, KJV*

Larry, a late shirttail relative of mine, was a hopeless alcoholic with a checkered past. He married a Christian girl and had two sons before divorcing her and walking out of his sons' lives. Eventually, he married another Christian woman. They also had two sons. Though Larry was neither the husband nor father he should have been, his wife and sons faithfully prayed for him. His wife taught the little ones to love Jesus and took them to church. She sacrificed to put them in a Christian school near the army base in post–World War II Germany, where they lived.

Meanwhile, Larry and a few friends who also liked to drink cut a deal with a local bar owner: for a flat fee of five American dollars, they could consume as many drinks in a week as they wanted. Needless to say, Larry always returned home—back at the base—late at night and roaring drunk. One day some of Larry's superiors took him to watch heavy equipment removing a badly mangled army jeep from nearby railroad tracks. "That was *your* jeep, Larry!" they said.

Larry was speechless! He could not recall even having had an accident the night before. Yet here was the proof before his eyes. Nor did he have any idea how he'd gotten back to the base after the accident. Not long after this incident, Larry neglected to pick up his youngest son from kindergarten because he'd been at the bar again. After becoming sober and realizing his serious oversight, he tried to offer an apology of sorts, but his youngest gently interrupted him.

"Daddy," he said sadly, "you love beer more than you love us, don't you?" At that instant, Larry made a choice. The next time his buddies invited him to go drinking, he declined, telling them what his little son had said. In 2006, Larry fully gave his heart to Jesus and was baptized into his praying wife's church. Only Larry, though, seemed to recall the story of the words his little boy had spoken—which had changed his life. Even his son didn't remember.

At the end of Larry's funeral in 2016, a stranger approached the family: "I owe my happy family life to your father. I scoffed when he told me his little boy's comment had changed his life. Yet when I got married and became a father, I remembered it and made Larry's choice too."

Never underestimate the impact for *tomorrow* of your words and choices today.

Dora Hallock

Twice in a Row!

The angel of the LORD encampeth round about them
that fear him, and delivereth them.
—*Psalm 34:7, KJV*

It's been only four days since the Lord saved my husband from a terrible death right on our property. The Lord sent him away from his garden just before allowing a large papaya tree in the backyard to fall right where he had been working. May the name of the Lord be praised!

At 3:50 A.M., I woke up to get ready to accompany my husband to the bus station. He was traveling to Ouagadougou, the capital city of Burkina Faso, by road to hold a church elders' retreat. We had gotten to bed very late the previous night because we had to put things together for the trip. The station is about two kilometers (about a mile) from where we live, so I saw him off and came back to continue my sleep for a while before getting up for the day.

At 5:07 A.M., my husband sent me a message saying that his bus was safely on the road. I had been up for a while and was helping my son get ready for school.

At 7:15 A.M., I was getting ready to go to work. My husband sent me this message: "We have just managed to avoid a serious accident. The brakes of our bus dropped. Again the Lord protected." So I called my husband to find out more. He told me, "Had it not been for the hand of the Almighty, we would have crashed into a fuel tanker."

Yes—a fuel tanker! You and I know what happens when a vehicle hits a tanker full of fuel! I later learned—after the bus passengers' fright had subsided; the brakes were repaired; and everyone, including my husband, was back on the bus to continue the trip—that both the eyewitnesses and the bus driver testified that nothing short of an invisible hand brought that bus safely to a halt just before there should have been an impact with the fuel tanker.

Again, the Lord protected. For the second time in the same week, the angel of the Lord has encamped round about my husband and delivered him from death.

Sisters, our God is still in the business of saving His children—Daniel from the hungry lions, Jonah in the belly of the fish, and my husband from death twice in a row. God can save you too. Commit all aspects of your life into His care today, and He will direct and deliver you.

Tabitha Kra

Training Wheels

As a father pities his children, so the LORD pities those who fear Him.
For He knows our frame; He remembers that we are dust.
—*Psalm 103:13, 14, NKJV*

When I was eight years old, my parents bought bicycles for my younger brother, Lawrence, and me. As my dad put training wheels on each bike, he said the wheels would be removed when summer vacation started. True to his word, my dad removed the wheels on the last day of school. Instantly, my brother could ride his bike, but I couldn't.

Every day for most of the summer, my dad did his best to teach me how to ride my bicycle. Sensing my desire to give up on our daily lessons, my dad told me, "Cheryol, I guess you're not going to learn how to ride this bike." Just hearing that comment kicked my efforts into overdrive. Every day after supper, I practiced riding my bike by myself.

One day I told my brother I was going to the neighborhood school playground to ride my bicycle. When I got to the school yard, I hopped on the bike seat and began to ride. Lawrence was delighted. After hours of racing each other, popping wheelies, and doing other bicycle stunts, my brother told me he wanted to go home to eat lunch. Unfortunately, I didn't know how to stop my bike. Lawrence tried everything he could think of to show me how to stop. But I was afraid that if I tried to stop the bike, I would fall and get hurt. So I kept riding and riding.

Eventually, my brother told me, "Cheryol, I think Dad's home from work. I'm going to go get him." As I saw my dad approach the school, I started crying and told him I didn't know how to stop the bicycle. My dad softly told me to slow the bike down, and he would stop it for me. He promised that he wouldn't let me fall. My dad stood directly in front of the bike and said, "Come on, baby girl, you can do it." When I was within arms' reach, Poppy grabbed the handlebars with one hand and scooped me up safely into his arms. As I sobbed, he kissed my forehead and said, "Little-bit, you did it. You learned how to ride your bike! I'm so proud of you!" I fell asleep in his arms as he carried me and my bike home.

"Fear not, for I am with you;
Be not dismayed, for I am your God.
I will strengthen you,
Yes, I will help you,
I will uphold you with My righteous right hand" (Isaiah 41:10, NKJV).

Heavenly Father, thank You for your promise of protection.

Cheryol Mitchell Johnson

The Great Controversy at River Lwero

If you declare with your mouth, "Jesus is Lord," and believe
in your heart that God raised him from the dead, you will be saved.
—*Romans 10:9, NIV*

Down at the river Lwero, as the sun was quickly dying in the west on the Sabbath of November 26, 2016, the angels in heaven watched in awe as Pastor Lucas Olwayo said to Sister Beatrice, "I now baptize you in the name of the Father, the Son, and the Holy Spirit." As Beatrice was briefly submerged and then raised up, Satan and his army were not happy.

No sooner did Beatrice come out of the water, gasping for air and wiping her face when she suddenly dropped—or rather sank—again in the water. Our joy turned to shock as we watched elders and a deaconess escort the girl to the riverbank. Earlier that month the girl had attended a two-week Women's Ministries evangelistic series under a big tree at the Lwero market. Now she had given her life to Christ and was starting her new walk with Him in baptism. Millicent Odhiambo, a medical officer, had been giving medical treatments to local people during the evangelistic meetings. Seeing Beatrice collapse, Millicent immediately placed her on the ground and elevated her legs to help her blood circulation because there weren't many signs of life.

Everyone watching the scene, whether standing or sitting, was praying for Beatrice while some continued singing baptismal hymns. After all, Jesus had said, "I have come that they may have life, and that they may have it more abundantly" (John 10:10, NKJV). A great controversy was being fought at the river for Beatrice. After a while, her heartbeat resumed, and she was carried into the nearby shade as people praised God, and the baptisms continued. After making his final appeal, the officiating pastor changed out of his baptismal clothes. Yet his final appeal was still ringing in the heart of one man in the crowd. He, too, had attended all the meetings and had studied the Bible lessons. But he had not responded because he was also the pastor of another denomination. Suddenly, he declared, "I want to be baptized!" The officiating pastor and his assistants immediately went back into the river Lwero. When all was finished, Beatrice—now revived and leaping with joy—ran home to tell her parents of her baptism.

That day a great controversy had raged for two souls at the river Lwero. But "whosoever shall call upon the name of the Lord shall be saved" (Romans 10:13, KJV)!

Monica Koko Asca

A Valuable Lesson Reinforced

Even a child is known by his doings,
whether his work be pure, and whether it be right.
—Proverbs 20:11, KJV

One Sunday my oldest son, Greg, along with his wife, Jenelle, and their three children came to visit. I gave five-year-old Avery crayons and paper for drawing pictures or practicing letters and numbers. After a while, she asked to play games on my iPad. She played for fifteen minutes until her little sister, Kennedy, not quite two, came to watch and touch the screen now and then. Jackson, only a few months old, slept peacefully nearby. Upon returning from the kitchen with beverages and snacks, I saw Kennedy scrolling on my iPad. I immediately called out, "What is Kennedy doing?" We adults headed for Kennedy, surprised that she was using my iPad. She was looking at the family pictures in my photo app and scrolling through the pictures.

"How did she get into the app?" I asked. "Where did she learn to do that?"

"Don't know," was the reply from both Greg and Jenelle. Meanwhile Kennedy, oblivious to the conversation, was happily scrolling. It was amusing to watch her scroll and look at the pictures over and over again. We continued watching her antics in bewilderment. Before long, our chatter and laughter woke Jackson, who was his usual happy, peaceful, and content self.

A valuable lesson was reinforced in me—how easily children learn. Kennedy had probably learned tapping, scrolling, and pinching techniques from watching her sister use her iPad mini, or perhaps from seeing Greg or Jenelle on their phones or electronic devices. No one had said "Kennedy, do this or that." She watched, touched, learned, and did.

What else was Kennedy, or any little child or adult for that matter, learning from me? The familiar little children's song "Oh, Be Careful Little Hands" popped into my head. I knew the subsequent lesson well: I am leaving impressions on others by what I see, say, touch, or do at any time, on any day—whether I plan to or not! What a sobering thought that seldom crosses my mind these days!

Does my behavior perfectly exemplify Jesus Christ and His love, or clearly show that Satan has my heart and mind by my hateful words or actions toward others? I pray that it's Jesus—today and always! What about you, friend? Is it Jesus?

Iris L. Kitching

God Will Take Care of Us

*Fear thou not; for I am with thee: be not dismayed; for I am thy God:
I will strengthen thee; yea, I will help thee; yea, I will uphold thee
with the right hand of my righteousness.*
—Isaiah 41:10, KJV

In June 1998, our family went to a Christian college in India so that my husband and two of my daughters could study. At that time, I was working as a high-school biology teacher. After moving, we requested some school employment for me. The administration said they would provide me with some work for a small stipend each month. But it would not be enough to support three family members in school. It was a testing time for us. We did not lose our faith but kept on praying that God would provide for us. Two weeks passed. Then on July 14, two men came to our home. During a conversation, they suggested that I ask the principal of a nearby Christian high school and junior college whether he had a position open.

The next day, at the campus in Salisbury Park, the principal told us he was overstaffed in most sciences, but the school did need a math teacher. I had taught math to my own children when they were small, but it is not the subject in which I was accredited. If I said I couldn't teach it, I'd lose the job opportunity; if I said I could—perhaps I would not do justice to the students at the school. But we were in a dire situation. I asked to see a copy of the math book I'd be using. Much of it looked familiar to me, so I agreed to teach. I was sent to the classroom along with the headmaster, who observed my teaching and the students' responses. As a result, he recommended me to the principal, and I was given three grade levels of science and math to teach.

What a relief for our family! God performed a miracle for us. From that day onward, I became a math teacher. Though it is a long, tiring day with the travel, I have accepted this situation in order to support my family. I have enjoyed my work and have become one of the favorite teachers in that school. With that job, God provided help at a very financially difficult time and showered us with His blessings. I thank the Lord and the principal for helping me to support my family. There has been no interruption in my employment since then and no loss of salary.

God's promises have been fulfilled in my life. His goodness to us has lived out the promise in that old hymn: "God will take care of you." He will care for you too.

Uma Chinnaiah

Sweet Promises

Before they call, I will answer;
and while they are yet speaking, I will hear.
—*Isaiah 65:24, KJV*

As I went about my household duties on a beautiful Thursday, I kept humming a hymn's tune: "Standing on the Promises of Christ My Lord." I felt light-hearted and happy as various promises from the Bible ran through my mind. I was very thankful for the wonderful Bible promises.

In my heart, I whispered a silent prayer, *Lord, I would love to sing the words from this beautiful hymn to welcome the Sabbath.*

Friday dawned clear and bright with this beautiful song still on my heart. As the Sabbath hours approached, I reasoned within myself as to whether I should go to a friend's house to welcome the Sabbath or have Sabbath worship by myself.

The Sabbath hours approached, and I was not able to go worship with anyone, so I prepared for bed early. I was in bed, reading, when I heard my son and his girlfriend arrive. Eventually, they both came upstairs to my bedroom. I was glad to see them. They wanted to have Sabbath worship with me! I was overjoyed! They both climbed in my bed.

Our first song to sing was "Standing on the Promises of Christ My Lord"! I was so happy and thankful to God for not only hearing my heart's desire but also sending company to worship with me! I went to bed so happy with the wonderful reminder that God hears our prayers and fulfills our hearts' desires, according to His divine will.

I woke up on Sabbath morning with a heart full of joy and thanksgiving, still singing the words to that beautiful hymn.

Deuteronomy 31:6 is a precious reminder that our heavenly Father will never leave us nor forsake us: "Be strong and of a good courage, fear not, nor be afraid of them: for the LORD thy God, he it is that doth go with thee; he will not fail thee, nor forsake thee" (KJV).

Sweet, holy Jesus, thank You for being our Father that cares about every aspect of our lives. Please help us to always keep Your wonderful promises in our hearts. May our thoughts always be lifted up through the words of beautiful hymns that remind us of God's many and sure promises.

Jannett Maurine Myrie

Lord, If You Had Been Here

Jesus said unto her, I am the resurrection, and the life: he that
believeth in me, though he were dead, yet shall he live.
—*John 11:25, KJV*

When difficult losses come into our lives and we don't see evidence of God's *immediate* response, we may be confused as to why. The house of Mary, Martha, and Lazarus in Bethany was a happy one. Jesus would go there to rest from His journeys. In that home, He could visit freely with the family. One dreadful day, however, Lazarus, the man of the house, fell sick.

The two sisters sent word to Jesus, saying, "Lord, behold, he whom thou lovest is sick" (John 11:3, KJV). Jesus did not immediately come to Bethany. Lazarus then died. The quest of Mary and Martha to understand the reason why Jesus did not respond to their urgent plea is the quest of many sincere Christians. Why should the righteous suffer if their God is indeed alive?

When Jesus and His disciples arrived in Bethany, seemingly belatedly, Martha hurried out to meet Him and fell before Him, saying, "Lord, if thou hadst been here, my brother had not died" (verse 21, KJV). Although Martha confessed that Jesus could still ask the Father for whatever He wanted, her response to Jesus' consolation was that her brother would rise in the final resurrection (verse 24, KJV).

Mary met Jesus with uncontrollable tears—to the extent that Jesus was equally moved to weep. He then asked where Lazarus had been entombed. Martha showed some unbelief in Christ's power when she reacted with the words, "Lord, by this time he stinketh: for he hath been dead four days" (verse 39, KJV). In spite of her lack of faith, Jesus went forward with the resurrection of Lazarus. After all, He had said, "I am the resurrection, and the life" (verse 25, KJV).

In loss, the two sisters were not left alone. And as long as Jesus reigns upon His throne, we will never be left alone either. He is nearer to you than you can imagine. The suffering of Lazarus was on His heart, but He only tarried so that the glory of God could be manifested.

God may not be as *early* as we would like, but He is never late, in *His* timing, to respond to the problems that are on our hearts. He might not be as early as we would anticipate or wish, but He is never late to deliver. Perhaps God seems to be late in coming to help you right now. Yet through faith, you *can* live in the hope of His presence, though the way seems cloudy and thorny.

Mary Opoku-Gyamfi

Fill Your Mouth With Laughter

He will yet fill your mouth with laughter
and your lips with shouts of joy.
—Job 8:21, NIV

Laughter may indeed be the best medicine after all. In his *Anatomy of an Illness*, published in 1979, Norman Cousins recounts how ten minutes of solid belly laughter would give him two hours of pain-free sleep. Laughter stimulates heart and blood circulation and promotes respiration. It produces deep relaxation, thereby breaking up our tension.

Just putting on a happy face can be rewarding. Working at an extended-care facility in Kokomo, Indiana, as the activity director for three and a half years, I made what I thought at the time was a profound discovery: if I smiled—whether I felt like it or not—I would feel better. I knew I couldn't bless those old people while looking like a grump, so I would paste on a smile. Soon I was actually smiling! In an article published in the *Orlando Sentinel*, Ronald S. Miller states that "if we just assume facial expressions of happiness, we can increase blood flow to the brain and stimulate release of favorable neurotransmitters."* So when I smile, I am releasing neurotransmitters and giving others and myself a better day in the process!

Years ago Pat Nordman had a ministry with parents who had lost children. At the risk of sounding like a heretic, she asked them to keep a good joke book beside the Bible. She explained that there would be days when even the Bible might need to be supplemented with a good laugh that could, at least momentarily, lift the incredible weight of pain and loss. My personal daily shot in the funny bone is Lynn Johnston's comic strip *For Better or Worse*. God bless her for her painkiller insight on family life.

One more bit of advice: Don't stick around negative people. These are what one writer calls "energy suckers." Do yourself a huge favor and find someone positive and funny and enjoy life along with them. God wants us to laugh and enjoy the full range of positive emotions He created. Otherwise, He wouldn't have promised to "fill your mouth with laughter and our lips with shouts of joy" (Job 8:21, NIV).

Laughter and giggling take time and produce little except a joyful life. So let's rattle those funny bones today, and praise our heavenly Father for the wonderful gift of laughter.

Patricia Hook Rhyndress Bodi

---

* Ronald S. Miller, "Laughter: It Really May Be the Best Medicine," *Orlando Sentinel*, October 9, 1990, 34.

July 11

A Light Shines in a Dark Place

The LORD is my light and my salvation—whom shall I fear?
The LORD is the stronghold of my life—of whom shall I be afraid?
—*Psalm 27:1, NIV*

I turned in my bed; it was still dark, so I looked at the ceiling. It was 4:14. *Yes! I can sleep for two more hours!* So with that, I went back to sleep.

Some genius, somewhere and at some time, invented a clock that shines the time on the ceiling. What a marvelous invention! I can see the time without sitting up or having to turn on a light. It is right there on the ceiling in big numbers I can see even without my glasses.

Or, at least, it is there if it is dark in the room. If the sun shines enough in the morning to light up the ceiling, the lighted numbers on the ceiling clock no longer show, and I have to maneuver over to where I can see my bedside clock.

The other morning just as dawn began to creep in, I could still faintly see the numbers on the ceiling, and it made me think about light and darkness and about shining in the dark.

Light is mentioned 263 times in the New International Version of the Bible, and light and darkness is a theme through much of Scripture, such as Isaiah 9:2, "The people walking in darkness have seen a great light; on those living in the land of deep darkness a light has dawned" (NIV). We find this motif over and over, especially in the books written by John. In John 8:12, we read that Jesus said, "I am the light of the world. Whoever follows me will never walk in darkness, but will have the light of life" (NIV). Jesus also said in Matthew 5:14 that we—you and I—are supposed to be a light set on a hill. Even long before Jesus said that, He said the same thing through Isaiah: "I will keep you and will make you to be a covenant for the people and a light for the Gentiles" (Isaiah 42:6, NIV). How do we do that? Psalm 18:28 gives a clue: "You, LORD, keep my lamp burning; my God turns my darkness into light" (NIV).

Thinking about my ceiling light, it seems to me that in a dark world we should be able to be easily seen. But when Jesus comes in, we will disappear and people will see Him instead. That is what I want: for people to see Jesus through me. In Psalm 36:9, we read, "For with you is the fountain of life; in your light we see light" (NIV). I must cling to the promise found in Psalm 119:130: "The unfolding of your words gives light; it gives understanding to the simple" (NIV).

Ardis Dick Stenbakken

Susan's Miracle

The LORD will watch over your coming and going
both now and forevermore.
—*Psalm 121:8, NIV*

When Susan was growing up, she was kind, never got in trouble in school, always went to Sabbath School and church, learned her Bible memory verse each week, and was involved in her church's children's and young people's organizations. You might say she was the perfect child.

In her senior year of Christian high school, she was in a work-study program. One afternoon her boss asked her to work late. Being naïve, she agreed. That night she was the victim of a horrific crime that changed her life. She told no one, but her belief in God was shattered. How could a loving God let this happen?

College classes helped block out some of the memories, and she graduated with a degree in civil engineering. She had stopped going to church, but sometimes she remembered stories from the Bible about miracles. "Give me a miracle, and maybe I'll believe in You again," she told God. Susan got a job where her parents lived and moved in with them. A new job, a new area, memories of what had happened to her, and living with her parents again caused a great deal of stress. She started having trouble sleeping. Her doctor gave her sleep medication with the following instruction: "upon taking medication, go right to bed." One night after taking the medication, she remembered she needed something from a nearby store. On her way home, after leaving the parking lot, something strange happened—she fell asleep!

Meanwhile her parents were home, worrying where she was and what had happened to her. When she finally arrived home an hour later, her face was as white as a sheet! She explained to them she had been driving all that time, asleep. She didn't know where she had gone; but after a long time, something woke her up about a mile from home. "Mom and Dad," she said, "I know an angel was driving my car. Otherwise, I would have had a bad accident. Now I know God loves me, and I believe in Him." Long ago Susan, my daughter, asked God to show her a miracle. In His time, He answered her prayer in an amazing, almost unbelievable way. Her message today to anyone who has stopped believing in a loving God is, "No matter what terrible thing happens to you, don't give up on God because He will not give up on you."

Dalores Broome Winget

It's Worth It to Wait on God!

Trust in the LORD with all thine heart; and lean not unto thine own
understanding. In all thy ways acknowledge him,
and he shall direct thy paths.
—*Proverbs 3:5, 6, KJV*

It all began on the eve of the morning when I surrendered everything to the Lord and asked His blessing. I was embarking on a new journey: the road to a life of being single and content. Content, according to my definition, was being able to serve the Lord as best as I could and knowing that He was the only One who could make my life whole and complete. I grew up in a church and a culture that revered the marriage union. Being unmarried beyond the age of thirty was a cause of anxiety for all. Church members kept saying, "We're praying for you" every time they saw me (as if I were ill). Family members kept saying, "You're waiting too long," which implied singlehood was entirely my fault, though they meant well. I had to hide from some church members and social invitations. The life of singlehood at times became a challenge. But there were many joyful, carefree days as well while being unattached.

Little did I know that God was working behind the scenes. Truly, it is always darkest before the dawn, and joy comes in the morning. I believe the Lord was waiting for me to forget about my own needs and focus on serving Him and others. I became bold in my prayers and told the Lord that the request for a husband was off my list. All I wanted was for *Him* to make sure I was satisfied on this journey of being single and content, if this was His will for my life.

God's love radiates from inside and reflects in our countenances when we are happy spending time with Him and serving others. I believe that as we occupy ourselves with the Lord's business, people—perhaps some man—will be attracted to that light inside that causes our smiles. For the Lord is faithful; His promises are sure. This journey has turned out to be the adventure of my life. At the appointed time, God brought a God-fearing Christian husband into the picture. Jehovah is still able to do exceedingly and abundantly above all that we can ever ask or imagine (see Ephesians 3:20).

I have been led to the "special sauce" that God was specifically preparing for me, for those blessings take time to prepare. No longer am I on the road of being single and content. I am journeying on the highway of being married, merry, and mesmerized by love. Whatever you are waiting on the Lord to do for you, trust that His promises are true. Our God never fails.

Lebrechtta N. O. Hesse-Bayne

Bloom On

"I am the true vine, and my Father is the gardener. He cuts off every branch in me that bears no fruit, while every branch that does bear fruit he prunes so that it will be even more fruitful."
—*John 15:1, 2, NIV*

During a recent tree-trimming endeavor, my father and I had to make some difficult decisions about which branches to keep and which to cut off. As people who physically hurt when we have to saw off parts of living art, we triple gulped and chose to leave a lower branch on a tree that I can see from my favorite spot on my "worship" couch. Since then, I've looked and looked at that tree and decided that limb just doesn't fit now that we've cut some of the others off. It's off balance and not so pretty after all.

In a surprising concurrence with this, I read of Jesus' call to Matthew. I read that "Matthew, 'left all, rose up, and followed Him.' "* No hesitation. No questioning. No thought of his lucrative business exchanged for poverty and hardship. It was enough for him to *be with Jesus*, listen to His words, and unite with Him in His work.

I've been feeling Christ's saw placed at the base of a few limbs of my soul tree, yet I've been pushing it aside, telling Jesus those limbs belong there. Looking at the tree in the backyard with its lopsided shape has helped me to say, "My mistake. The limb doesn't even look good there anymore. It's time for it to go. You were right."

What has stopped me from allowing the limb removal in the past? The discomfort of change. I'm comfortable, albeit lopsided. It's what I know. I guess it's as if Matthew had lingered before answering Jesus' call. When Jesus fills our world, we find we don't miss for long the limbs He prunes, for He grows new, healthy, beautiful limbs with fruit. And fruit's first phase is flowers—oh, how I love flowers! So life *is* better with Jesus' soul gardening. It's everything you never knew you wanted—*and flowers*! It's the truth!

In your worship time, in your commute, in stolen quiet moments, be with God. Make Him your focus, and give Him the go ahead to prune away. Spring is always coming, and with it the blossoms of your soul tree. Bloom on, fellow soul trees, bloom on.

Mary K. Haslam

---

* Ellen G. White, *The Desire of Ages* (Nampa, ID: Pacific Press®, 2002), 273.

An Appointment with the Lord

Very early in the morning, while it was still dark, Jesus got up,
left the house and went off to a solitary place, where he prayed.
—Mark 1:35, NIV

How glad we are when we have an appointment with a loved one, especially if it promises to be a happy one!

Christians must also earnestly long for a daily appointment with the Lord. When one becomes a Christian, he or she becomes a child of God and a member of God's own family. The greatest joy of a child is to have fellowship with a father and know him better. This can be achieved with the heavenly Father when one has daily quiet time with Him.

Quiet time is a special and regular time set aside each day to be alone with the Lord. It enables one to seek the face of God through the reading of His Word and talking to Him in prayer. In Mark 1:35, Jesus Himself set us an example: "Very early in the morning, while it was still dark, Jesus got up, left the house and went off to a solitary place, where he prayed" (NIV).

We need this devotional time for Christian growth because it helps us to know God intimately. We receive inner strength for the day's journey and nourishment for growing into spiritual maturity. Martin Luther once said, "Unless I spend three or four hours with the Lord in the morning, the devil gets the victory throughout the day." Perhaps our devotions do not need to last that long; however, we must make it a point to spend time with our Lord.

In our devotional time, let us search to know what the Bible says to us personally; what it means for our lives; and what its passages teach us about God the Father, the Son, and the Holy Spirit. Also, we can look for relevant promises to claim, for warnings if we are wayward, and for bad examples to avoid. Our joy is compounded when we share with others what we have learned.

Lord Jesus, thank You for giving me the opportunity to fellowship with You each day. Help me to cherish this appointment time and never want to miss it. In Jesus' name, I pray. Amen.

For further encouragement, read Genesis 15:5, 6; Exodus 34:2, 3; Psalm 5:3; and Daniel 6:10. In each text, you can identify the Bible character who kept a daily appointment with God. Then prayerfully ask God what you can learn from their examples regarding your own quiet times with Him each day.

Charity Danso

Three Big Reasons to Smile

There hath no temptation taken you
but such as is common to man: but God is faithful,
who will not suffer you to be tempted above
that ye are able; but will with the temptation also
make a way to escape, that ye may be able to bear it.
—*1 Corinthians 10:13, KJV*

When my husband and I got married in March 1996, we decided to start a family right away since we were in our late twenties. After a few months, we were expecting our first child, and our excitement was out of this world! This joy was crushed, however. After ten weeks, I miscarried. We were told that this was attributable to uterine fibroids. Our second pregnancy progressed well until the twenty-fourth week, when we lost a baby again.

Discouragement set in. Doubts and fears haunted us. Our faith took a hit. The doctor who was monitoring me told me that we should be grateful that I could even conceive. This encouragement I received cautiously. After three years, we were blessed with a baby girl. We were happy beyond words!

After this wonderful blessing, we were more confident, and our faith started to grow again. A short while later I learned I was carrying twins! It was exciting to see the two heartbeats glowing on the imaging machine! This excitement lasted only a few weeks though, when we lost yet another pregnancy. One year later, however, the Lord blessed us with a baby boy! We could not describe the joy and gratitude we felt.

After six months, we moved from Zimbabwe to Côte d'Ivoire to take up a work assignment. As we were settling in Abidjan, I had a severe bout of malaria. The doctor wanted to prescribe some very strong medication, but he insisted I take a pregnancy test before starting the medication. Nonchalantly, I took the test, never thinking I might be pregnant. After all, God had already performed two miracles. You can imagine how totally and happily shocked we were to learn we were expecting our third baby!

Looking back, we realize that our faith should not have been based on physical evidence because, technically, that is not faith (Hebrews 11:1). But God indulges us and blesses us despite our doubts. He is faithful and will not let us be tested above what we can bear (1 Corinthians 10:13). Praise His holy name!

Eugenia Mzikazi Bhebhe

Answers to Prayer

"Before they call I will answer;
while they are still speaking I will hear."
—Isaiah 65:24, NIV

There is no limit to God's ability to help us. Both Ephesians 3:20 and Philippians 4:19 make this promise. After my marriage, I moved to an entirely new state, where the economy was weak. The area where we moved was absolutely destitute! Pastors' salaries were paid once every three months, and that payment was equivalent to only a single month's salary.

Though we needed to set up a new home as newlyweds, all our money was used up for the bare necessities. Since we owned no rice-paddy field, we would buy one bag of rice from my mother-in-law. After a few days, the rice was used up. We had no money or vegetables, and we were completely bankrupt. We would not ask for an advance on our salary.

I remember sitting at home and crying because life had so many problems just as we were starting our married years.

"The Lord will provide," said my husband when I asked him what we could do.

One Friday evening we left early for a church meeting so that we could first visit a few families and pray for them. Locking our door, we turned to see an auto-rickshaw stop in front of our gate. To our surprise, my mother-in-law got down from the rickshaw and walked toward our house with a big rice bag on her head, a vegetable bag in one hand, and a bag of groceries in the other. We were surprised and shocked to see her. We had not told her how badly we needed food or how fervently we were praying for it. Speechless, my husband and I looked at each other with tears in our eyes. When we told her about our situation and asked how she had known to bring us provisions, she was shocked. "I didn't know! I came because I just felt like seeing you both," she said. "And I decided to bring you things as well."

This is how the Lord took care of us before we could ask Him.

The Lord will supply all our needs. "Therefore, I say unto you, What things so ever ye desire, when ye pray, believe that ye receive them, and ye shall have them" (Mark 11:24, KJV). It was that day I realized what a blessing it was to be a pastor's wife. The Lord had chosen us to be a blessing to others as well. Our faith and witness can be a strength to others.

Dear Lord, help us to rest in You and wait patiently for You, praying and not fainting.

Vijay Moses

To Be Organized Or...

The steps of a good man are ordered by the LORD,
And He delights in his way.
—*Psalm 37:23, NKJV*

like organization. I have to organize things before I can get anything else done. When things are organized, I can see them. They make sense to me, and I can work with them. If necessary, I can always make changes later.

Similarly, when something spiritual is presented in a step-by-step approach, I appreciate that—a strategy for prayer, a spiritual-gifts test, things that keep my spiritual life organized. God is in a box, so to speak. I can see and understand what He wants me to do. He has an organized plan, and I follow it. In fact, to accommodate who I am, God makes changes in me—in a *systematic* way—as I go along.

On the other hand, my pastor husband, Stewart, sees most types of structured organization as being "too rigid," cramping his style. Rigid organization puts *him* in a box that feels claustrophobic. If there is only one way to do things—and Stewart doesn't happen to relate to that one way—he becomes frustrated. But the looser the organization, the easier it is for him to work. He needs flexibility to be able to do things in a way that makes sense to him.

Likewise, he doesn't like putting spiritual things in a box either. For him, a step-by-step approach to church growth or personal prayer or an organized sermonic year planner puts God in a box but allows no room for flexibility. The box becomes a cage that has no exit. My husband sees the organization process more like a lump of clay rather than neat packaging in a structured box. Clay is flexible. If something doesn't work right, one can adjust its shape immediately. There are always limitations, of course, but Stewart's perspective allows for more flexibility. Spiritually speaking, if one strategy doesn't work for him in a given situation, it can be adjusted to better fit the needs to be met. God works with him and molds him, according to who he is, changing him into the person He needs my husband to be.

The all-knowing Lord orders our steps. Two different people with two different personalities, yet one God with the same result: people He can use.

Kathy Pepper

July 19

It's All About Relationship

There can be neither Jew nor Greek,
there can be neither bond nor free,
there can be no male and female;
for ye all are one man in Christ Jesus.
—*Galatians 3:28, ASV*

In her public high school, a Christian teacher started an enditnow project (a global campaign raising awareness and advocating for an end to violence against women and children). The high-school students came from different, and difficult, backgrounds: Bulgarian, Turkish, and Roma (a traditionally nomadic ethnic group). Many children came from abusive and/or low-income families. They manifested a high level of aggression in their behavior. When these students learned to communicate in a nonaggressive manner through the enditnow program, the atmosphere in that school changed dramatically.

One day, when invited to speak to these students, I gave each of them a piece of paper that they had to cut into equal pieces. On one paper, they drew something they wouldn't want crawling up their legs. On the second paper, they drew something they didn't like to eat. On the third paper, I asked them to write the name of someone they dearly loved, such as their mom, grandmother, or favorite aunt. Then I asked them to look at the pictures on their first pieces of paper before crumpling and then stomping on the sketches of scorpions, wasps, and cockroaches. With an escalating noise level, the students happily did the same with their second pieces of paper. They loved "hurting" the drawings of what they didn't like to eat. But when I asked them to do the same thing to their third pieces of paper, bearing the name of a loved one, they grew very quiet. "What's the matter?" I asked. "It's nothing more than a name—it's not the actual person." They couldn't bring themselves to harm those third pieces of paper. "But I love this person!" several of them said. What an eye-opening lesson that was for them! It's difficult to hurt someone with whom we have a relationship. It's hard to wish harm on someone we know.

Before hurting someone, we should first learn about their likes and dislikes, pasts, and families. Rather than skin color, background, gender, or age, a love based on relationship manifests itself in true caring, respect, and tolerance. The students and I decided that in the future, before letting ourselves develop bad feelings about someone, we should try to get to know the person better. I hope you and I will make that same decision as well.

Denise Hochstrasser

Best Friends

A real friend sticks closer than a brother.
—*Proverbs 18:24, NLT*

My neighbor and friend, Sandy, moved away last year but came back to stay a couple of nights at our house while finishing up some remaining business. We were both happy to be together in my kitchen while getting a little dinner ready.

For more than fifteen years, Sandy and I have spent many hours in her kitchen and mine, cooking and entertaining and sharing wonderful meals. We both love to cook and try new recipes, especially ones with previously untried or unusual ingredients.

As we worked together on the meal, I was reminded that one of the nicest things about these times together is that Sandy knows where everything is in my kitchen. I don't need to tell her where the foil is kept or where the knives are. She knows which drawer holds the silverware and which cupboard the salad plates are in. It makes for such an easy and companionable experience.

Through the years, whether peeling potatoes or perfecting a roux, we have shared so many things: our joys, our fears for our children and grandchildren, our mutual dedication to volunteer work, and even our childhood memories. Despite the fact that I had not seen Sandy in quite a while, we caught up quickly because we know each other so well.

As humans, it is so important to our overall well-being to feel that we are *known*, that someone truly knows us and accepts us just as we are. Without that kind of acceptance, we face loneliness and isolation.

We are hardwired to be social beings, so it is not surprising that relationships represent one of the most important components of our lives. But as wonderful as our earthly friends can be, Jesus wants to be our very best Friend. He offers Himself as our "go-to" relationship, and He already knows everything about us.

In 1 Corinthians 13:12, Paul tells us, "All that I know now is partial and incomplete, but then I will know everything completely, *just as God now knows me completely*" (NLT; emphasis added). What a joy!

Jesus knows us fully—completely. And He *still* wants to be friends with us throughout eternity!

Linda Nottingham

Just Be Still

Then He arose and rebuked the wind, and said to the sea, "Peace, be still!" And the wind ceased and there was a great calm. But He said to them, "Why are you so fearful? How is it that you have no faith?"
—Mark 4:39, 40, NKJV

Every one of us knows how it feels to be fearful.

Fear brings confusion and chaos into our lives. But a simple faith in Jesus Christ drives fear and anxiety from our lives. When the disciples of Jesus encountered a Galilean storm, the terrifying nature of the storm immediately caused them to fix their eyes on the turbulent waves as they clung tightly to the side of the boat. They feared for their lives when, in fact, all they needed to do was focus on Jesus.

Fear can become crippling. It keeps us from experiencing a deep intimacy with God. It stunts our God-given potential to impact this world for His kingdom. Perhaps worst of all, fear is a sign that we don't trust God. Yet the One who beckons us to place our wholehearted faith in Him has the power to calm the seas. When He opens His mouth, everything is subject to His authority. So instead of allowing fear into our hearts, we need to replace it with a quiet, still, and deep-rooted trust in God. We need to still our hearts and know *He* is the One who calms storms.

In times of trial and affliction and in dark seasons of our lives, let's ask God to remind us to place all our faith and trust in Jesus alone. Let's allow our souls to feed daily on His Word so that the roots of our faith can grow more deeply than any seed of fear.

The promise found in Philippians 4:6, 7 has always been a source of hope for me: "Be anxious for nothing, but in everything by prayer and supplication, with thanksgiving, let your requests be made known to God; and the peace of God, which surpasses all understanding, will guard your hearts and minds through Christ Jesus" (NKJV).

So whatever storm is raging in your life—be it financial, marital, health related, family, or work related—just be still and trust in Jesus Christ. Let Him calm every storm in your heart and mind and life. Ask God to strengthen your faith in Him. If you need an extra dose of His peace in your current season of life, He will lavishly pour it over you.

All you need to do is ask.

Akosua Ntriakwah

He Is an On-Time God

Be still before the LORD and wait patiently for him.
—*Psalm 37:7, NIV*

Each year I travel to the United States for a physical examination, never knowing what to expect but trusting in God. The year 2014 was no exception. Before I left Guyana, I knew that the finance staff of the church department where I worked was invited to a training program in Panama. During my annual medical visit, the doctor requested that I undergo a CT scan. He subsequently advised me there was something suspicious on the scan that needed investigation. He also advised that if it was what he suspected, I would need surgery and treatment because it might be related to some of my earlier medical history. I prayed silently, *Dear Lord, please remove whatever it is. I don't ever want to be put to sleep by anesthesia or have a surgery again.*

After two more medical tests were completed, the doctor ordered a PET scan. If its findings proved favorable, I would be free to travel. I was asked to inform my doctor when the test was completed so that he could follow up. Two days after the PET scan, my doctor called. "What do you expect to hear, Ms. Alleyne?"

"I hope you have good news," I replied.

"The results are negative," he informed me.

I fell on my knees and cried, "Thank You, Jesus!"

During this time, my return flight had to be changed twice; my departure was on the evening the doctor called about my test results. I arrived in Guyana early the next morning. One of my colleagues met me at the airport and handed me a package with documents for the trip to Panama. My daughter-in-law had requested that I spend some time in Trinidad with the family upon my return. When I checked the documents, I discovered that the group with which I would travel was leaving for Panama the next day and would be in Trinidad all day before leaving in the evening. Excitedly, I called my son and arranged for him to meet me the following morning upon my arrival in Trinidad. Then our group arrived in Panama. The program was edifying, and the sites were beautiful. Meeting with God's people from the Caribbean and Panama was so pleasant.

These experiences remind me that when I call on Jesus, all things are possible. In His time, He works things out for our best good. My dear sisters, let us trust Him.

Ruby H. Enniss-Alleyne

Our God Is a Living God

God is our refuge and strength,
an ever-present help in trouble.
—*Psalm 46:1, NIV*

I was sitting on a kitchen stool one Sunday morning, preparing the family's meal. When I tried to get up, I felt a sharp pain at the waist and couldn't walk properly. At the hospital where I was transported, the doctor said that a spinal problem I had developed would necessitate major surgery to replace a disintegrating disk, which was causing painful nerve and walking problems. For more than a year, I could not go to work or church. My husband and I went from one hospital to another, hoping to find a cure that didn't involve surgery; a very expensive surgery, in fact, that had only a 50 percent chance of success. Besides, our family's income would not be sufficient to support it. I wept bitterly, asking God why this should happen to His child. Many others prayed for me, asking God to intervene; but the problem persisted. So, by God's grace, friends and loved ones helped us to raise the necessary funds for the surgery, which was our only possible option.

On the day of the surgery, the doctor sat down on my hospital bed and said, "Sister Vida, everything is set for the surgery, but remember you have only a 50 percent chance of success because we have to go into the area where all the nerves converge."

He asked, "Do you believe in God?" I told him I did. Then he said, "Trust in God, for with Him all things are possible." I quickly responded that since I knew my God lives, I was going to be among the 50 percent of patients whose back surgeries are successful.

After signing the medical agreement form, I began praying fervently that God, who had brought me that far (though He could have removed the offending disk particles), wouldn't let us waste thousands of dollars that we could have used for His work. I told Him I hoped I wouldn't be rendered unable to walk for the rest of my life. In the midst of my emotional trauma, I heard a voice saying, "My grace is sufficient for you, and My strength is made perfect in weakness."

The surgery was performed, and by the grace of God, all the results came out perfectly! I am now able to go about my normal business. I am walking and praising God. I am in agreement with the apostle Paul that all things *do* work for the good of those who love the Lord (see Romans 8:28).

Our wonderful God is able to do more abundantly than we can ask or think.

Vida Linda Gyasi

He Fights for You

"One of you puts to flight a thousand, since it is the LORD your God
who fights for you, as he promised you."
—Joshua 23:10, NRSV

A friend of mine was not feeling well. Within four days, she decided to go to the hospital because the pain was becoming unbearable. Doctors did all the tests they could think of but could not find anything wrong with her. We did not even realize that she had been ill until a month later when I called her. She told me about her health challenges. In that month, she had seen five different doctors and they all told her the same thing—they could find nothing wrong with her.

When we, along with three other friends, visited her, we found she had lost weight worrying about what was going on with her health. She told us she was about to go see a sixth doctor. We asked her whether she had called the pastor to pray for her, to which she answered yes. Then we asked her how much she was praying about her situation. She said that truthfully she was more worried about the illness than anything else.

Before the visit was over, we had all prayed for her and said we would continue praying about her illness. We assured her that the God who knows and sees all would guide the doctors to know what was wrong—or answer in a different way. We began a prayer journey that day, and what a God we serve! Within a few days, our friend was feeling better. By the end of the week, she was having just a few aches here and there. It has been two months now since our prayer together, and God is swiftly healing her. She has gained weight and has more strength than she had during that challenging month. I know she will be completely healed in God's good time.

Most of us, when we face challenges in life, first start thinking of solutions or ways to combat forces that are bringing on these problems. And we think of solutions before getting down on our knees. Our Creator God knows our needs even before we call on Him. He is already fighting for us against whatever the devil is trying to bring into our lives. Sometimes His answer to our pleas is *no.* Yet even then, God is faithful and on our side. Our pain is His; our sorrows are His. Let us trust Him, and put Him first regarding everything that touches us on this earth.

You can trust Him completely with whatever burdens you are carrying and whatever you are going through right now, for He has promised to fight for *you* each day.

Judith M. Mwansa

How She Met the Lord

Believe on the Lord Jesus Christ
and thou shalt be saved, and thy house.
—Acts 16:31, KJV

I come from the background of a Middle Eastern belief system as did both of my parents. My mother, a teacher and the eldest daughter in a big family—*and a religious leader's niece*, was a good wife in that religious culture. She was always veiled and the first to arrive at her place of worship for services. Then her husband became very sick. Her mom, Aissatou, did all she could to get him good medical treatment. By the time I was born in 1969, Dad's health condition had worsened. After many rounds of medication and trips to traditional healers, Mom decided to turn to Christian pastors for help—without informing Dad of what she had in mind. A charismatic church was the only Christian church in their neighborhood.

During a meeting with the pastor, my mother explained the problem. His response was, "Believe on the Lord Jesus Christ and thou shalt be saved and thy household!" Mom was astonished!

What? After spending everything I have to consult traditional healers, how can my husband get healed with just a sentence? OK, I lose nothing by giving it a try, she thought, quietly promising to give her heart to the Christian God in case my father was healed. She began secretly visiting that church to pray on behalf of Dad. Glory to God! Dad recovered, and Mom kept her promise of becoming a fervent Christian. Dad, however, felt humiliated by her change of religions. He insisted she choose between her marriage and her new faith. Without hesitation, she chose to follow Jesus. As a result, she was divorced and was sent away with her nine children.

Later on, God directed her to another church that worshiped on the seventh day of the week, according to the Bible. Nineteen years ago, after a series of Bible studies, she was baptized. Today she is eighty years old and a grandmother to forty-four and great-grandmother to three. She is still very active in her local church in Parakou, Republic of Benin.

I have been greatly influenced by Mom's conversion and her exemplary lifestyle. I can say that her experience and encouragement have made me who I am today. I thank the Lord for using Mom to guide my steps into His fold. Now it is my turn to do the same for my children.

May God especially bless those of you who are leading others to Him!

Mamata Sassou

Beware of Adding to God's Words

The woman said to the serpent, "We may eat the fruit of the trees of the garden, but God did say, 'You must not eat fruit from the tree that is in the middle of the garden, and you must not touch it, or you will die.' "
—*Genesis 3:2, 3, NIV*

One of the first Bible stories I ever learned was the story about what happened in the Garden of Eden with our first parents, Adam and Eve. Though a familiar story, it is also a sad story. The Bible tells us that God had instructed Adam and Eve they could eat of all the beautiful trees in His garden—with one exception. They were not to eat any fruit from one particular tree, which He had placed in the middle of the Garden, "the tree of the knowledge of good and evil" (Genesis 2:9, NIV). Not eating of it was a test of the couple's love for, and obedience to, God. The forbidden tree was also the only place Satan, the devil, was allowed to have access to them. So God had warned Adam, "You must not eat from the tree of the knowledge of good and evil, for when you eat from it you will certainly die" (verse 17, NIV).

When Eve left the side of her husband one day and wandered in the direction of the forbidden tree, Satan, disguising himself as a serpent, engaged her in conversation. He tempted her to eat the fruit from the forbidden tree. In response, Eve told him that God had said they shouldn't eat the fruit and that "you must not touch it, or you will die" (Genesis 3:3, NIV). Of course, the serpent contradicted the words of God, telling Eve that eating the forbidden fruit would open her eyes so that she would be like God, knowing good and evil.

Something I find interesting in this verse is that Eve quoted God's warning but then *added*, "neither shall you touch [the forbidden tree]" (ESV). Why did she think it necessary to add to what God had said? The Bible does not say. Sometimes when we exaggerate something—as Eve did the instructions of God—we perhaps miss the crucial point and then fail, as Eve did. Similarly, the Pharisees levied additional rules, beyond God's instructions, regarding the Sabbath and eventually missed the core essence of the purpose and meaning of the day. Jesus condemned them for doing so.

Each day let's ask, "Lord, help me not miss the real meaning of Your instructions to me. Help me to learn to obey Your commandments, in simplicity, as they are given. Jesus, today help me not to add anything to Your perfect, wise, and holy words."

Jeyarani Sundersingh

Pulling Down Strongholds

The seventh time around, when the priests sounded the trumpet
blast, Joshua commanded the army,
"Shout! For the LORD has given you the city!"
—*Joshua 6:16, NIV*

On July 27, 1985, my mother lay in a hospital in Sunyani, Ghana; this was her fifteenth day in a coma. The sad news about Mom reached some church choir members attending the annual choir rally in that city. As they began petitioning God for Mother's life, someone asked, "We're a choir, so why don't we do what the children of Israel did to bring down their enemy in Jericho?" The idea caught on, and soon more than one thousand choristers were marching around the government teaching hospital where Mother lay. What a spectacle to watch! Hospital staff, onlookers, and patients wondered at the beautiful music. Some passersby asked what was going on. When choir members answered they were singing and praying for their "shepherdess," a pastor's wife, to come out of a coma, some people laughed. Yet others were absolutely amazed by this display of Old Testament faith in a modern-day world. As with Israel of old, the choir sang their way around the hospital seven times, then stood still and sang an additional seven hymns.

At the end of the final song, they shouted in unison, *Amen!* At that auspicious instant, my mother sneezed—a moment that marked the start of her recovery process. She lived an additional twenty-five years, traveling around the country with my dad doing missionary work.

At Mother's funeral in 2010, three women walked up to me. "We are Christians today," they said, "because of what the choristers did in 1985. We were junior nurses at the hospital then." The choir's act of faith, which I also witnessed as a teenager just finishing secondary school, has been my source of strength throughout the years when faced with challenges. God's ways are not like our ways.

I don't know the nature of the "wall" or the enemy you are facing at this moment, but rest assured that with faith, when you sing praises to Him, your challenging wall will definitely come down. One way or another, it will come down and the city will be yours.

Romans 15:4 tells us that "everything that was written in the past was written to teach us, so that through the endurance taught in the Scriptures and the encouragement they provide we may have hope" (NIV). Soon the Lord will give us the Holy City if only we trust and obey.

Esther Joyce Parkins

There Is a God in Heaven

"It shall come to pass
That before they call, I will answer;
And while they are still speaking, I will hear."
—Isaiah 65:24, NKJV

My little brother begged my father to buy a puppy from a total stranger. My father, convinced that the animal was a dog of great pedigree, since he wanted to do his best for my brother, purchased the puppy.

I was too busy celebrating my own little dachshund puppy, Kofie, to pay much attention to Riley, my brother's new puppy. I randomly noted that Riley seemed to be greedy because of the way he ate. Not for one moment did I wonder whether his enthusiastic eating might not be his way of making up for all the days in his young life that he'd had nothing to eat. As Riley grew, we soon observed with disappointment that he was not a dog of pedigree. Rather, he was what one would term a "domestic breed." But he did become very large and protective.

Never spending as much time with him as I did with my own puppy, I eventually became afraid of him. After some time, Riley became sick. It was then that I began noticing him more often. I felt sorry for him. I remembered being upset with my brother and father for not paying more attention to his failing condition. Riley wasn't as loud as he'd been before. He seemed sad and depressed. He became so sick that my family had to isolate him from the other dogs we had.

After I moved, I would see occasional pictures of Riley and hear about his condition. That made me cry. Guilt and pain ate away at me. I should have treated him better. Not wanting him to suffer anymore, I asked God to put him to sleep. And He did.

The very morning after that prayer, I got a message from my sister, saying Riley had finally died. I was more hopeful than I was sad, though. God had shown me that He'd heard me. He had felt compassion for the suffering animal. God had been there crying with me and was just waiting for me to ask Him to help poor Riley out of his pain.

How many times we fail to give those around us the attention and love they long for but don't get! We need to pray thoughtfully for one another because God in heaven definitely hears our prayers. He answers according to His wisdom when we pray for the highest good of others. How important it is to do right by others because we never know whether we will see them again.

Renauta Hinds

What Do Your Words Create?

*Do not let any unwholesome talk come out of your mouths,
but only what is helpful for building others up
according to their needs, that it may benefit those who listen.*
—*Ephesians 4:29, NIV*

"Then God said," and the entire world was created. Wow! That seems to be just about the most amazing thing ever. Imagine if you were standing next to God, blackness all around, empty of any form. Next to you in the darkness, God spoke, and the entire universe was created. Everything sprang up around you from only His spoken word.

The Bible also tells us how God created humans in His own likeness, giving them the power to speak. This means He gave us the ability to be creative when we talk. Think about how words, both positive and negative, have impacted your life. Even if they were spoken years ago, they still remain with you, giving you joy or pain.

If I come home and unload on my family after a long, stressful day, they all respond, and I can visually see their stress levels rising. I even see the change in my children when they hear their parents discussing the stresses of the day. But what a difference I experience if I come home and let the joys and excitement of their day create a new, positive demeanor in me!

By thinking of and looking for ways to use our words to give encouragement, love, and kindness to others, we are building our characters to reflect Christ and point others to heaven.

Ellen White writes, "Bring the sunshine of heaven into your conversation. By speaking words that encourage and cheer, you will reveal that the sunshine of Christ's righteousness dwells in your soul."* King David prayed, "Create in me a clean heart, O God" (Psalm 51:10, KJV). "Let the words of my mouth, and the meditation of my heart, be acceptable in thy sight, O Lord, my strength, and my redeemer" (Psalm 19:14, KJV).

Let this be our prayer that our words will not tear down and destroy but lift up and edify!

Natysha Berthiaume

---

* Ellen G. White, *Reflecting Christ* (Hagerstown, MD: Review and Herald®, 1985), 185.

Our Visual God

Then God saw everything that He had made,
and indeed it was very good.
—Genesis 1:31, NKJV

Our God is a visual God, meaning that He is a God of design, imagery, illustration, vision, and sight. In Genesis 1, we read, "God saw" (verses 4, 31). The sense of sight is very powerful in the words of the Bible. The Bible is made up of words, many words, but these words often create a visual image of what God wants us to know or understand. We find this in stories where, as we read, we visualize the unfolding of events: Daniel in the lions' den, David challenging Goliath, and Peter walking on water, to name a few. But we also find words that, while not telling a story, still create a visual image.

Let me share with you some examples: "For we walk by faith, not by sight" (2 Corinthians 5:7, NKJV). "And Jesus said to them, 'I am the bread of life. He who comes to Me shall never hunger, and he who believes in Me shall never thirst' " (John 6:35, NKJV). "He will not allow your foot to be moved; He who keeps you will not slumber" (Psalm 121:3, NKJV). "But the fruit of the Spirit" (Galatians 5:22, NKJV).

Over and over, we can visualize what we are reading in the Bible. God uses our senses to reinforce His Word in our lives. We see with our eyes, visualize the words in our minds, speak the Word with our mouths, hear the words with our ears, and even use our hands to draw the images we read. And this brings me back to the creative nature of God (see my devotional for April 6). We can read His Word and see what He is saying to our lives. The psalmist says, "Thy word is a lamp unto my feet, and a light unto my path" (Psalm 119:105, KJV).

What do you visualize when you read His words? For me, I see a path called life. The way through life is often dark with many turns and twists, holes, and dangerous corners. Yet a light emanates from my lamp, the Bible. It sheds enough light so that I can walk one step at a time along life's pathway. I can move forward with faith in the One who holds the lamp, leading me safely.

That, my dear sisters, is how you can visualize the Word of God. Spend some time today as you read and meditate on His words for your life. Then you will also be able to see what He is saying to you and be encouraged.

Heather-Dawn Small

July 31

My Modern-Day Miracle

And my God shall supply all your need
according to His riches in glory by Christ Jesus.
—*Philippians 4:19, NKJV*

My friend Brooke, a lovely Christian woman whom I met after moving to Texas from New Orleans during Hurricane Katrina, knew I needed a car. I'd been in a bad marriage and now needed a vehicle. Like Peter, I had begun to sink when I took my eyes off the Master. Our God heard my cry and prayers during the trials I had gone through, for He never leaves us even when we disconnect ourselves from Him by going ahead of His thoughts and plans (Jeremiah 29:11). Unbeknownst to me, Brooke had heard the Holy Spirit say to her heart, *Get Lynda a car.*

One day Brooke was on my mind and in my prayers, so I called her just to say hello. We encouraged each other every time we spoke. Brooke said, "Lynda, I have something to talk with you about, but it's not suitable for the telephone." I was scared. A couple of days went by before we could meet. That's when she told me that her friend Rachel had felt impressed by the Holy Spirit to give her car to someone who needed one. Rachel and her husband were buying a larger vehicle to accommodate their expanding family. Rachel, however, didn't know anyone in need of a car, but she wanted to be obedient to the voice of God. Then Brooke shared my story with her. God had already made provision for me without any one of us knowing what was about to happen. The Holy Spirit spoke to each of us in different ways and at different times for the same purpose. *Wow! How great Thou art!* Rachel was relieved after hearing what Brooke shared.

"Great! It's a go. Let's do it!" was Rachel's response to Brooke. To make a long story short, God supplied my need for a vehicle and restored my peace of mind. I may have been mentally and emotionally abused in the past, but God's promises are sure. In March 2016, God gave me a free 2008 Toyota 4Runner. Rachel and her husband had it detailed and took care of all the paperwork before taking the car to Brooke, who brought my modern-day miracle to me.

I want to encourage you, especially if you have lost, or are losing, hope. Hold on to God's unchanging hands. *Never* give up on Him, because He won't give up on you!

Dear Jesus, I pray that my story will inspire someone who lacks hope. May this person find joy in You. In Jesus' name, I pray. Amen.

Lynda Shepherd

Are You Ready?

"Therefore keep watch,
because you do not know the day or the hour."
—Matthew 25:13, NIV

In 2014, Hawaii was threatened by Hurricane Iselle. As I sat at home waiting for the storm to hit, it occurred to me that there were parallels between what was going on and Jesus' second coming. (Don't you just love how the Spirit uses things from our everyday lives to teach us?)

Before a storm hits, there are warnings. Starting days beforehand, the storm is tracked and its progress shown on the news. People are reminded to be prepared. This includes making sure you have a full tank of gas in your car, a seven-day supply of food and water for everyone in your household, emergency supplies on hand, an evacuation plan, and your property secured. From time to time, the official weather authorities do update the preparation guidelines, but for the most part, the instructions for disaster preparation remain the same. People hear the warnings whenever a natural disaster approaches. Since Iselle came in August, the middle of hurricane season, the storm's approach was no surprise. Yet we are encouraged to have our emergency preparedness kit ready at *all* times of the year because there is no set season for other disasters such as earthquakes or tsunamis. And yet many people were caught unprepared for Hurricane Iselle. Long lines formed at gas stations and stores. Many stores sold out of water and batteries. This frantic situation reminded me of the foolish virgins in Matthew 25 who were not ready with enough oil in their lamps when the bridegroom came to take them to the wedding feast.

When my husband and I first heard about the storm, we weren't concerned. We had food and water. But we realized that we had become complacent. Being prepared is not just having food and water. We needed to make sure we had evacuation carriers for our cats. Trees and plants around our house needed to be trimmed. Our older house is not up to the latest hurricane codes. So I started to wonder whether I was more like the foolish virgins than the wise ones. *Do I have enough oil in my lamp?* I asked myself. *Have I been doing all I can to make sure that my loved ones and I are ready for Jesus' soon return? Am I living in eager anticipation of seeing Jesus face-to-face, or am I distracted by day-to-day living and the problems of this earth?*

How would you answer these questions?

Julie Bocock-Bliss

That Woman!

And above all things have fervent love for one another,
for "love will cover a multitude of sins."
—*1 Peter 4:8, NKJV*

That woman! Calling again to borrow more money! My husband and I both knew that we would never see it again. Already thousands of dollars had accumulated under her name in our personal ledger. Due to a cutback in pay, we were finding it difficult to pay our own bills. While we were having to delay payment on our bills and making significant lifestyle changes, I found that she was purchasing things that we could never hope to possess: a riding lawn mower, a swimming pool, the latest clothing fashions, just to name a few things. Later, when we went back to school and would have appreciated some financial assistance, she never offered to help or pay back what she had borrowed from us.

In spending time with her, I learned that she had an uncompromising zest for life. She also had a strength rarely seen in people, both physically and in determination. She didn't know how to stop once she started something. Other descriptive terms might include clever, greedy, short sighted, and divisive. We put a lot of time and effort into trying to undo the damage caused by her poor choices. It seemed as though she was always stirring the pot and causing problems.

I found myself on my knees, repeatedly asking the Lord to "please change that woman!" One day in the midst of prayer, I heard a still, small Voice that simply said, *I will.* In the same instant, I knew that the Lord was telling me that I was the one who needed to change. In my frustration, I had developed an overriding negativity, bordering on bitterness, toward her. God made me aware that, before she would consider any changes in her life choices, I would need to change first. As a result of this humbling experience, I sensed my attitude toward her softening. Almost immediately, there was a corresponding change in her response to me and toward other people. Gradually, her moral choices began to change for the better.

I thank God for the power of prayer and the Holy Spirit's work on all hearts that are willing to respond to His leading. I thank God for the improved relationship and mutual respect that we were able to develop over the years. I have learned "above all things have fervent love for one another, for 'love will cover a multitude of sins' " (1 Peter 4:8, NKJV).

Janice L. Yancheson

God's Museum

And he [an angel] said unto him [Cornelius], Thy prayers and thine
alms are come up for a memorial before God.
—Acts 10:4, KJV

I looked at the photographs on our dining-room wall—reminders of mission trips to Mozambique, Brazil, and the Solomon Islands. Memories rushed over me: laying brick, hoisting freshly cut and very heavy two-by-ten boards of rosewood and mahogany, watching a woman who tried on glasses suddenly burst into a smile when she can see clearly, seeing a life-threatening wound heal under our care, finding a home for the homeless boy with that wound, learning some of our group sponsored that boy's education at the school we were building, and thrilling as locals and volunteers gave their lives to God. Such joy-bringing memories! Granted, I've taken a few other photos, such as the ones after a car accident. But those photos don't hang on our wall. They were simply evidence—the case settled. I don't need those photos anymore.

This morning I read Acts 10. I pondered verse 4: "Thy prayers and thine alms are come up for a memorial before God" (KJV). God thought about Cornelius's prayers and the good things he'd done. Like looking at special memories, God must have smiled as He thought about this man who prayed and gave of himself to bless others. I thought about God's "museum"—halls of "photographs" and "DVDs" of humans whose prayers and deeds make Him smile. What joy He must feel remembering them! But there are other "photographs," too, I thought: misdeeds, theft, murder, and violence of all kinds. My thoughts then turned closer to home: worry (lack of trust), irritation (anger), and independence (self-centeredness).

Oh, God, I prayed, *I don't want those photos in Your hall of remembrance.*

In a flash, two Bible verses, like an answer straight from God's heart, burst upon mine: "If we confess our sins, he is faithful and just to forgive us our sins, and to cleanse us from all unrighteousness" (1 John 1:9, KJV). "And thou wilt cast all their sins into the depths of the sea" (Micah 7:19, KJV). Just as I throw away undesired photos that have already been dealt with, God throws away the "DVDs" of my sins for which I've asked His cleansing. They're no longer needed. They've already been dealt with.

"Thank You, God!" I exulted. "Help my life to be full of 'photos' You love to remember."

Helen Heavirland

August 4

God Steps In

Fear thou not; for I am with thee: be not dismayed;
for I am thy God: I will strengthen thee; yea, I will help thee;
yea, I will uphold thee with the right hand of my righteousness.
—Isaiah 41:10, KJV

During the 1984–1985 academic year, I was in my last primary-school class, preparing for the high-school entrance examination. Our teachers did their utmost to help us prepare for the exam. Every school day morning we students underwent rigorous review. If a student made a mistake, the result was a smack on the fingertips. With the help of God, I never received a smack during the first quarter of that year. But during the second quarter, I missed an exercise and was smacked. That being my first time to be punished, I cried all morning.

In order to help us do better, teachers ordered us to come for classes on Saturday. Saturday absentees would receive five spankings on Monday morning. Six of us missed the first Saturday's classes and were punished. As I awaited my turn, I saw that each student spanked cried bitterly. But I didn't cry. The whole class was confused. All I did was a little gesture with my hands on my buttocks. Though I wanted to go sit down, the teacher held me back. He shook me and asked, "Is that you, Ayélé? What's wrong?" Actually, he was afraid that I was going to faint following my punishment because I *wasn't* crying. He did not understand that the God I served could make pain disappear. Later he asked why I was absent on Saturday. I seized the opportunity to tell him as much as I could about the biblical seventh-day Sabbath. Then he understood that my conscience wouldn't let me study on God's holy day. After spanking me on three more consecutive Mondays, the teacher said, "No more spankings. I know you are studious. I also know that the God who absorbs the pain of your spankings will also help you pass the examination." Indeed, I passed the examination! God had stepped in and taken my pain.

Dear sisters, the Lord who promised to support us is a promise-keeping God! When we try our best to do His will, He will not fail us. He will come to our aid when we need Him the most. Let us be faithful to him. Let us teach our young ones very early in life to cling to God and His Word. Let us be examples of faith wherever we find ourselves. Then the Lord will say of each of us: "Behold my servant . . . in whom my soul is well pleased" (Matthew 12:18, KJV).

Cherita Ayélé Tenou

Hide, and Seek God

Your word I have hidden in my heart,
That I might not sin against You.
—*Psalm 119:11, NKJV*

For most of us, the word *hide* paints a negative picture, such as small children hiding from their parents when they know they have done something wrong. Adam and Eve hid from God after their first sin (see Genesis 3:8–10). But today I am focusing on "hiding" in a positive way.

As a child growing up on a farm, one of my favorite things to do was hunt for baby kittens. We had farm cats—outside cats to help cut down on the rodent population. In the spring, these cats would have kittens, and their kitten nests were hidden in many places throughout the farm. Many times when I found a kitten nest, the mother cat would then move the kittens to another hiding place. When the kittens were old enough to lap up the milk my dad put out each morning and evening at the dairy barn, I took it upon myself to tame these wild kittens. Doing so resulted in some battle scars on my hands and arms, but it was worth the reward of playing and having fun with the kittens. I dearly loved all those cats and their kittens!

I think of Exodus 2 in the Bible when Jochebed hid her precious son, Moses, in the bulrushes. She was led by God to protect him. God inspired her with an ingenious idea—to prepare a waterproof floating cradle in which to hide her son, thus saving his life. Moses ended up becoming a great leader for God's people.

Joshua 2 tells the story of Rahab hiding the two Israelite spies in her Jericho home. Hiding them was part of God's plan of victory for Israel.

David hid from King Saul (1 Samuel 19–24). This preserved David for the kingship God had planned for him.

God also hides His own. Psalm 27:5 states, "For in the time of trouble He shall hide me" (NKJV). In this age of computer and GPS technology, how comforting to have this promise!

I also think of the phrase in the well-known hymn "He Hideth My Soul" by Fanny Crosby: "He hideth my life in the depths of His love, and covers me there with His hand."

Thank You, Jesus, for hiding my life in the depths of Your love, protecting me from the snares of the devil.

Ginger Bell

Blessed Surprises From a Faithful God

If God is for us, who can be against us?
—Romans 8:31, NKJV

I would like to share my personal testimony of how God helped and led me during a time of trouble in my life. I pray that my testimony will be an encouragement to many who have had similar problems and who need their faith in God strengthened.

I was married in 1999 to a man of a non-Christian belief system. Though we wanted to start a family, I was not able to conceive for three years. One day I came down with a severe fever and was diagnosed with typhoid. The doctor prescribed several medicines for me, and I took them for three days. Yet my temperature did not return to normal.

My husband and I started to worry and cried out to God in prayer. God led us to a good gynecologist. After examining me, she informed me that I was pregnant. Now we had another worry to pray about. In fact, we were panicked! Not knowing I was expecting a baby, I had just taken typhoid fever medicine for the past three days!

The Lord heard our prayers and kept the fetus alive. When the delivery time drew near, the fluids in the womb were much lower than they should have been. Because of this condition, the doctor warned that the baby might not be born alive. Right there on that bed in the operating theater, I cried out to God again. To our surprise and unlimited delight, I delivered a normal, healthy baby boy. According to Luke 1:37, "With God nothing will be impossible" (NKJV).

Sometime after that, I sadly became so busy with my work that I didn't take time to pray. I started neglecting God and His blessings to me. My next three pregnancies ended in miscarriage. Then a doctor who diagnosed me with a thyroid problem told me there was no chance for me to have another baby. Again I went to God in tears. Through much physical and mental anguish, I was surprisingly able to become pregnant. In the fourth month of pregnancy, however, I had serious problems and, according to the doctor, yet another miscarriage. He even gave me medicine to expel the remaining blood clots. "There is no fetus in your womb," he informed me. Yet, somehow, God kept my fetus safe as I cried to Him to work one more wonder in my life. God gave me a baby girl—another blessed surprise from God!

In hope and faith, ask God right now to work on the problematic situations in your life.

Sunila Prasad

Complete Freedom

Submit yourselves, then, to God.
Resist the devil, and he will flee from you.
—James 4:7, NIV

Geckos (small lizards) are plentiful in Florida. They are frequently seen in sunny spots outdoors and are perfectly harmless. It is when they come inside our house that they get into trouble. Often one of them seeks warmth by climbing partway up the doorframe into our sunroom. When the door is opened, it drops down and frequently ends up inside the sunroom. When a gecko gets inside, I try very hard to catch it and put it back outside again as soon as possible. Yet it will often elude me by running away and hiding under the furniture or behind the window blinds. It moves quickly, evading capture. Try as I might, I often can't find it to return it to its outdoor home. This is usually the death knell for the poor little creature. Usually, days later, I will find a dehydrated skeleton under a piece of furniture or in a corner. If only the gecko had submitted to my rescue efforts, I could have given it the freedom it certainly desired.

Often we are like a little gecko that gets inside the house. Our desire for independence, or our stubbornness, leads us to engage in activities that get us into trouble spiritually, financially, socially, or physically. If our minds are bent on freedom through our own efforts, we yield to Satan's seductions. Despite warnings from our family, friends; our own better judgment; and impressions from the Holy Spirit, we often take a path that leads to undesirable consequences. What a mess we can find ourselves in!

Like my intense efforts to provide a path to freedom for the little geckos, there is One who does that for each of us. Our loving heavenly Father seeks to lead and guide us through the Holy Spirit in paths of righteousness. Even when we resist His efforts on our behalf, He doesn't give up on us. He is a God of second chances. When we are indifferent to His promptings, He tries another way to get our attention. His motive for wanting to save us is His great love for us. He created and redeemed us through the sacrifice of His Son on Calvary.

Our best assurance of complete freedom is a personal relationship with Him. This means spending time with Him daily, interacting with Him through Bible study, prayer, and meditation. Doing so melts our resistance to His will, and we delight in following His precepts and commands. Who do you want to control your life?

Marian M. Hart-Gay

Crushed, Not Destroyed

We are hard pressed on every side,
but not crushed; perplexed, but not in despair.
—*2 Corinthians 4:8, 9, NIV*

I remember the challenges that came into our family when I was a young girl. Yet I also remember my parents saying, "The Lord is in control." And He always was—and still is. My heart has been touched as I recall these childhood memories.

In our Christian journey, we often find ourselves bending beneath the impact and pull of pain and suffering's deep waters. These powerful currents come in the form of emotional trauma, disappointments, and betrayal—even by those whom we hold dear to our hearts, even people in the household of God. Our power to survive challenges resides not in us but with God, who dwells within us.

In the year 2000, I was involved in a fatal automobile accident. There were three fatalities in our taxicab—the cab driver and the two other ladies sitting with me in the back seat. I sustained multiple fractures in my arm and was hospitalized for several months. While in the hospital, the attending orthopedic surgeon and his team informed me that they had decided to amputate my arm. The surgeon stated that, per his medical assessment, amputation was the only option. Hence, a date was booked for me to have my arm amputated. Broken and in despair, I could not even imagine how life would be without one of my arms.

My family encouraged me, and together we took this situation before the Lord in prayer for several days. One morning my doctor came to examine me. He ordered several diagnostic tests. After reviewing the findings, he made a strange remark. "Madam," he said, "I had on my mind to amputate your arm, but I think some people must be praying for you. Your hand shows unusual signs of healing. Amputation is no longer necessary."

I agree with the apostle Paul's words that though we may be crushed, perplexed, and in despair, we are not destroyed (see 2 Corinthians 4:8, 9).

As we make our journey heavenward, let us go forward with absolute confidence in the God who has called us in Christ to present our burdened lives to Him. We may appear to be bent, but we don't have to be broken. God will indeed make the bent straight again.

Felicia Pepra-Mensah

When a Sparrow Falls

"What is the price of two sparrows—one copper coin? But not a single sparrow can fall to the ground without your Father knowing it. And the very hairs on your head are all numbered. So don't be afraid; you are more valuable to God than a whole flock of sparrows."
—*Matthew 10:29–31, NLT*

Thwack! The glass behind me shook just a little, and I leaped to my feet, as did the other two people sitting in the room.

"Was that a bird?" my sister, Susie, cried as I rounded the chair I'd just vacated and headed toward the window. I was sure she was right. She was. "Grab a pan and a towel," she said as she opened the door to the deck. I did so, then joined her next to a quivering, paralyzed sparrow lying on its side, dazed and frightened. It could not get up. Susie picked it up gently and placed it in the makeshift nest. We took it inside where it was warm and safe. A colander placed over the pan allowed the bird to breathe and—us to see it. There were no obvious injuries.

Then we prayed for the little thing. "Lord, a sparrow has just fallen," we said. "Please touch it, heal it, and enable it to fly and be free again. Thank You." The little sparrow soon struggled upright and sat on tiny feet. Eventually, it stood up, wobbling. It began to move more easily. We knew it was time. Outside we set the pan on the grass and lifted the colander. The bird took off like a shot for the nearest large tree, where it stopped briefly before flying on steadily.

"Thank You, Lord," we prayed together. "Thank You for being mindful of the sparrow and all other living things. Thank You for being mindful of *us.*"

We went back inside and joined the others in the house, grateful for the recovery and thankful for the lesson. God, who provides for the tiniest, most nondescript of His creatures—and loves them—will not fall down on the job with us. We are His, created and then redeemed by Him at a very, very great cost. There's nothing He would not do for us, and we know that because He has already paid the ultimate price for us.

We will not hit the deck without His noticing; we will not lie bruised and battered without His doing something. He will pick us up, hold us gently, and keep us safe. He will see to our healing, and we will fly again.

Carolyn K. Karlstrom

August 10

I Am Not Alone

Have not I commanded thee? Be strong and of good courage; be
not afraid, neither be thou dismayed: for the LORD thy God is with
thee whithersoever thou goest.
—Joshua 1:9, KJV

I was about twenty-one when I went to visit my parents in our village. The village is located about seven kilometers (about four miles) from the main road, and to get there, we had to pass through another village that had a cemetery at the exit. In other words, the road that led to my village passed through a cemetery. At that time, transport vehicles did not pass frequently, so one had to make the choice between waiting for a vehicle for endless hours or traveling on foot.

One morning I went to the big city with my younger brother, who was ten years old. On our way back to our village, after walking about three kilometers (a little over a mile and a half), my brother started feeling faint. Soon he could no longer continue walking. Thanks to the Almighty, someone came by just then on a motorbike. I begged the driver to take my brother to the village so that he could receive immediate medical attention. "There are only four more kilometers [about two and a half miles]," I said. "I'll walk the rest of the way home."

"No, you won't," insisted my brother. "I'm not going to leave you alone in the middle of this forest!" He knew I was afraid to be out in the bush alone. Yet we had no other option for his sake than to send him ahead of me on the motorbike for treatment.

By nature, I am a fearful person—even when my mother or other adults were around. At that point in the road, I was especially afraid something (a ghost, maybe?) would come out of the brush to attack me. Yet here I was with no other choice than to walk all by myself through that thick forest! I had *never* been as terrified as I was that day. All sorts of ideas and scenes came into my mind as I walked.

Sadly, at that time, I had not yet learned much about the promises of God contained in the Bible. But God stepped into my ignorance and strengthened my feet and heart for the rest of the journey. How well I remember seeing the village huts and my mother running toward me!

Today I know I was not alone on that path—angels were walking by my side. I also know God's angels are with you when you fail to ask for His protection, as in my case.

How should we respond to such lovingkindness? What will your response be?

Adolphine Zian

Let God's Love Shine in You!

And if it seem evil unto you to serve the LORD, choose you this day whom
ye will serve; whether the gods which your fathers served that were on
the other side of the flood, or the gods of the Amorites, in whose land
ye dwell: but as for me and my house, we will serve the LORD.
—*Joshua 24:15, KJV*

Why doesn't somebody show me appreciation for a change? I brooded one evening. This was after a day when my husband had been too busy to hug me even once, when my older son muttered only one-word answers to my questions, and my younger son always needed something from me. Suddenly, the phone rang. A sister in Christ invited me to take part in a women's conference and asked that I prepare some reflections on Joshua 24:15. Though I agreed, I thought, *Maybe this isn't an appropriate time for me to share about that verse since I am so dissatisfied with my own life right now. What could I possibly share on this topic with others?*

As I reread this familiar verse, the pronouns *me* and *my* took on special significance: "*me* and *my* house." Then the Holy Spirit's quiet voice spoke to my heart. *Yes, that is where it all starts—with* you. *Communication with your son starts with you. The atmosphere in your home starts with you. If you are the loving heart in your family, then your whole house will be filled with warmth and love!* In humility, I asked the Lord to forgive me. I had been waiting for others to do something that needed to start with *me*. With tears of gratitude, I thanked God for His example. He was the first to come and approach us with love, kindness, and forgiveness.

That very evening I made the decision to be the first in my family to move toward relationship improvements. I would not wait until my husband approached me. Instead, I would do my best, as often as possible, to approach him with a hug. I would not growl at my sons or wait for them to speak kindly to me. I would be the first to speak to them with overflowing love and show them often how precious they are to me. I would do my best every day to fill my heart with the love of Jesus and then let it shine from me to every individual I met throughout the day.

Today if life's situations are not what you had hoped they would be, then work toward change—starting with *you*! Make a personal decision that you will be the one to love first, forgive first, and care first. When we act as citizens of heaven, God's peace will fill our hearts.

Irina Begas

Searching for Mom

"Can a mother forget the baby at her breast
and have no compassion on the child she has borne?
Though she may forget,
I will not forget you!
See, I have engraved you on the palms of my hands."
—Isaiah 49:15, 16, NIV

My father died when I was about four years old. My mom gave me to a nurse friend of my dad's to raise. When I was six years old, this nurse sent me to stay with her sister, who had no child of her own. I knew her as my "aunt." At the age of fourteen, my adoptive aunt introduced me to a woman with these words: "She is your biological mom." I did not know this woman and felt no connection with her. She spent some time with me and then left the same day. After her visit, I understood why I had been entrusted to the care of a foster parent. My own poor mom, a single parent, was so poor she could hardly make ends meet or care comfortably for my siblings.

After Mom's visit, I began asking myself why she had abandoned me into the hands of a foster parent and had not visited. Growing up with my foster parent had not been easy, but I thank God for His daily providence. The nurse who had sent me to my foster parent was always there to meet my personal needs through her sister. Sometimes, though, I did not receive all the provisions that were given for my daily and personal needs and often suffered because of it.

During my final year of high school, my foster mom suggested I go to my hometown, knowing that I had not been there since my "adoption." Initially, I thought she was joking. But she urged me, so I decided to go. In fact, I was eager to go because I did not know any of my siblings or anything about my hometown. I set off one afternoon toward that town. When I got there, I began the search for my mother. Unfortunately, the name by which I knew her was different from the one by which she was known in the village. So it took me some time before I found her—with the help of a previously unknown aunt of mine. It seemed that Mom had abandoned me, and her living conditions were disappointing and discouraging. Truly, I was much better off, despite the challenges, with my foster mother.

Reflecting on this part of my life, I deeply appreciated the statement in Isaiah 49:15 that says, "Though she [one's own mother] may forget, I will not forget you" (NIV). This assures that God will never forsake or abandon us. He cares for us and is our true "mother."

Evelyn Osei-Bonsu

We Are Our Worst Enemies

Dear friends, if our hearts do not condemn us,
we have confidence before God and receive from him anything we
ask, because we keep his commands and do what pleases him.
—1 John 3:21, 22, NIV

What's going on with this child's face?" My baby girl's face—from the crown of her head to her shoulders—was inflamed, scaly, and bumpy. She had what is known as cradle cap. None of my concoctions for treatment worked. Now, on this Friday morning, the condition took a turn for the worse. And she was supposed to be dedicated in church the next day! *Will my friends think this is a result of something I did?* I wondered. *Should we postpone the dedication?*

When I expressed concern to my husband, he repeated, "Let's keep things in perspective." His response was coming from his reflections about the threatening episodes during my pregnancy that seemed to signal the preterm birth, which had occurred. Yet we still had our baby. What my husband was telling me was, "Be grateful that we even *have* her, instead of focusing too much on her current ailment." Yet, in order to appease me, we took our baby to our physician that same day. The physician assistant shared with us about his own son's episode with cradle cap. When he got it, their family was about to have a family photo shoot. Family members changed positions in the photographs in order to disguise the cradle cap as much as possible. This story is exactly what I needed to hear. It assured me my baby was going to be OK, and we left with a prescription for medicine that would help her heal.

The baby dedication was beautiful. Contrary to my earlier fears, not one of my supportive friends and family members blamed me for my baby's condition. Most of them had also dealt with cradle cap, so they were full of advice. One even shared a treatment with me. I was so happy I had not postponed this event. I had worried needlessly that I would be condemned.

Neither does God condemn but rather desires to help and support us. "We are not left to ourselves to fight the battle against self and our sinful natures in our own finite strength. Jesus is a mighty helper, a never-failing support. . . . None need fail or become discouraged, when such ample provision has been made for us."*

Shevonne Dyer-Phillips

* Ellen G. White, *Our High Calling* (Hagerstown, MD: Review and Herald®, 2000), 88.

Ministering to the Widows

Honor widows who are really widows.
—*1 Timothy 5:3, NKJV*

Each one of us undoubtedly knows a widow. Perhaps you, my friend, are a widow. Yet how encouraging that throughout the Bible God has shown compassion and a sense of protection for widows (*almana* in Hebrew)—women whose husbands have died.

God established social and economic provisions for the security of vulnerable widows in the Old Testament patriarchal culture (Deuteronomy 24:19–21; 26:12, 13; and the book of Ruth). Without these laws, the lives of widows could have been unbearable.

In the New Testament times, widows were often vulnerable and poor (Luke 18:1–7), and Jesus addressed this need.

James says that visiting the orphans and widows is a demonstration of pure religion (James 1:27). And today the family members of widows should be encouraged to honor God by helping them if they cannot support themselves. Younger widows might be encouraged to pursue education and their careers to help better their situations and provide for their futures. In situations where widows may not need any financial support, the church should provide professional and pastoral support. Some professional legal assistance could be extended to widows who have to fight for what is lawfully theirs. Visitation to widows by women of the church should be intentional.

If a widow has children, both men and woman in the church can provide fatherly and motherly care to the children by paying attention to their needs and spiritual development. Godly men and women can assure the children of widows that they have "family" in their churches. With such support, widows may feel their parenting burdens have been benevolently shared.

Many church members, both men and women, sometimes find themselves single through no fault of their own. Should we not help, as we can, these sisters and brothers in Christ? Should we not do what we can to help them grow in faith despite their hardships? Besides, Jesus offers a special warning to those who take advantage of widows (Luke 20:46, 47).

Let us minister to everyone who is lonely and needs us, because they are precious in the eyes of the Lord (Zechariah 2:8).

Christiana Agyenim-Boateng

Franklin, the Foolish Duck

There is a way that seems right to a man,
But its end is the way of death.
—*Proverbs 14:12, NKJV*

I was excited our new home had a pond with one white duck floating on it. As summer waned, we got ready for snow, but one problem remained—our duck. It was obvious why the old owners had left Franklin. He could not be caught. He was happy to come for food, but the slightest move sent him racing back to the pond. As it got colder, we wondered how to get him to shelter. Then the inevitable happened. The temperature dropped, and snow began to fall.

We arrived home to see Franklin swimming around in a tiny ice-free area; the rest of the pond was frozen to the point of his being unable to swim in it. The ice was hard enough for predators to walk on, but not hard enough for us to do so. Then the bright eyes of a fox shone in the darkness one night. I cried, "We've got to save Franklin!" Prakash, my husband, ran for our canoe. Seated in the stern with no life jacket, he bravely launched onto the ice. With a heave, he pushed the paddle, and the boat skidded across the ice, only to break through in a few feet. Repeatedly, the bow lifted onto the forming ice, slid in the direction of the duck, and then crashed into the water.

Franklin jumped out of his small, unfrozen "pool" area and ran across the ice. He was too fast for the clumsy ice boat. Net in hand, Prakash tried to maneuver the boat near Franklin, but each time the duck veered away. We put out food to lure Franklin to shore. He never left the water. Prakash tried roping Franklin, as Prakash is amazingly accurate for a Nepalese "cowboy," but the noose fell short. Finally, we gave up and returned to the house, cold and discouraged. The following morning Franklin's form lay frozen on the ice.

As sad as we were to lose Franklin, it reminded us of a larger picture. We, too, can be like Franklin, enjoying our own way in life as we swim about doing as we please. Yet, as with the ice, sin drives us into a tight and dangerous trap. Only Jesus can rescue us, and He wants to do just that, but we must cooperate with His rescue efforts. Then He can lead us to the shelter.

Next Easter I will buy a duckling and teach him about having a shelter before he heads for the pond. While I'm at it, I'm going to get closer to my Savior who has prepared a wonderful shelter for me!

Sherry Shrestha

August 16

Send Gabriel Now!

"Before they call I will answer;
while they are still speaking I will hear."
—Isaiah 65:24, NIV

My family arrived in Nairobi, Kenya, on August 22, 1990. We were there to serve as missionaries to students of our denomination attending public universities. Ray (my husband at the time) would also serve as the chaplain for our church work in that area. Right before our seven-year mission term ended, we took a family vacation to Mombasa, which is in the coastal region of Kenya. The birthday of our younger son, Andrew, fell on August 16, which was the last day of our trip.

We decided to leave for home early because friends, who had been attacked, beaten, and robbed a few weeks earlier, warned us not to be on that road after dark. But we kept stopping to purchase souvenirs. As the day grew late, my nerves were on edge. Our last stop was at a gas station, where Ray gave a study to the station workers and others filling their cars. Back on the road, we heard a *psueee!* coming from one of our tires. I knew that wasn't good. Ray and Ricky, my older son, got out to change the flat. But they found *two* flat tires!

Oh Lord! Robbers had evidently placed a strip of nail-studded wood on the road. Andrew and I sat in the back seat, shaking and praying, as Ray and Ricky tried to flag down passing vehicles for help. No one stopped, obviously knowing what happened to stopped drivers in this area. I cried out to God, "Lord, have mercy! Send Gabriel *now!*"

Immediately, a large truck with two men screeched to a halt. They begged us to leave with them. Andrew and I, taking the two flat tires, went with them to the same gas station we had just left. Ray and Ricky, though, remained with our truck as I continued to pray for their safety. Instead of simply dropping us off at the gas station and continuing on their way, the two men (angels?) stayed with us, had the tires repaired, and drove us back to where we'd left Ray and Ricky with our vehicle.

Nearing that area, we saw the unbelievable! Another trucker (another angel?), stopping to help, had parked his vehicle *across* the road, blocking traffic on both sides of the highway! Cars and trucks, for at least a mile, were stopped on both sides of the road! At least two dozen people, bearing various weapons, were guarding my son and husband and our truck. While men lifted our truck, others installed the repaired tires. We praised God for sending angels to protect us!

Joan Collins-Ricketts

I Witnessed His Death

For we know that if our earthly house of this tabernacle were dissolved, we have a building of God, an house not made with hands, eternal in the heavens.
—*2 Corinthians 5:1, KJV*

t was an afternoon shift. It was quiet in the unit. This was the first time I had been assigned to this particular unit. I had six patients to take care of. I quickly assessed my patients and planned their care in order to be sure that I would spend just the right amount of time each patient needed.

At the end of the room was a middle-aged woman sitting by the bedside of one of my patients. I quickly learned that she had been there for several days, watching and caring for her husband, who was terminally ill.

Before I could finish my planned care for the day, the lady stood up and whispered to me, "I have not had any meal since yesterday. I have not been home for several days, and I also need to take a shower. Can I leave him to you for now?"

"Certainly," I responded, and she was gone.

During the wait for her return, I had an opportunity to talk with the man. He was responsive and alert. I asked him if there was anything I could do for him.

"I don't know if there is anything you can do for me at this time."

"I can pray for you," I said. Then I asked my patient if he believed in God and in His Son, Jesus, who saves those who have faith in Him. "Do you trust Him?" The man said that he did. "Oh, Lord," I prayed, "may this dear man have peace and comfort in You."

A few minutes later this patient closed his eyes. Hurrying to his side, I saw he was no longer responsive. I called the doctor to come. He verified my assessment. As soon as the doctor had confirmed the man's death, the wife of the newly deceased returned from her quick trip home. We shared what had just transpired.

"Would you like me to call a clergyman?" asked the doctor.

"No," answered his wife. "This nurse has already done the part of the clergy."

Reaching out to others in need is a ministry God has given each of His workers. Our doing so not only blesses others but also enriches the lives of those who reach out in His name.

Esperanza Aquino Mopera

Determined Because God Is Faithful

Let us hold fast the profession of our faith without wavering;
(for he is faithful that promised).
—Hebrews 10:23, KJV

In 2009, I applied to continue my medical studies. It was not until 2013, however, that my professor called and invited me to return to my educational pursuit. Though I hold a degree in sanitary technology, my dream has always been to obtain a doctorate in medical biology. But as the mother of several children and a homemaker, I also have a little job that gives me a meager income. I had presented my desires to the Lord.

During my personal devotions, I prayed privately to be able to attain my goal. My intercessory prayer group at my local church also prayed about it. Then my coursework toward a master's degree started. After a few months—about halfway through the course—my classmates and I took tests and presented the subjects of our respective theses. We were also assigned to various institutions for internships.

At the end of the internship, my classmates were authorized to register for the next stage of their education, but I did not receive that authorization. I was told by some officials that all those applying from my former school had been denied. That was the only reason they gave.

I prayed and fasted. Nothing changed. I kept my frustrations to myself and, with a heavy heart, turned more fervently to the Lord for divine intervention.

I would not let this latest turn of events discourage me. I decided to continue serving the Lord anyway. I resolved to be a better mother for my children. I would continue singing in my local church choir, all the time continuing to cling to the unfailing promises of the Lord.

Around eight-thirty in the evening on March 7, 2017, a professor of the faculty of medicine called to inform me I could resume classes in order to finish the master's degree I had started!

God is faithful! No matter how long it takes, He always answers our prayers. Let us keep trusting Him for divine intervention in any situation we find ourselves. The Lord has a plan for each one of us. Let us grasp the promise that though it might tarry, the Lord's answer will surely come.

Let this assurance encourage us to wait on the Lord while laboring in His vineyard.

Ursula Claudia Essogo 'n' Guettia

God Cares

Casting all your care upon Him,
for He cares for you.
—1 Peter 5:7, NKJV

In past situations when I have lost something, such as my house keys, I became anxious and tense as I tried in vain to find it on my own. I wasted time, energy, and strength when I should have offered a simple prayer and cast my burdens on the Lord.

Prayer is the key to dealing with life's issues, and there is power in it. Once we have tasted and seen how God fulfills His promise, what peace and solace fills our troubled souls!

I recall an incident that happened just after we had moved to a new location in the summer of 2016. We were surrounded with boxes everywhere. Around midnight, we realized that we didn't have my son's passport in hand. We needed it immediately in order to fill out an important form that had to be sent off. Yet there was no trace of the passport.

We all gathered together, prayed, and then began our search anew. We went through all the boxes, looking high and low. Why couldn't we find it? Tired, I started anxiously wondering, *Will we have to lose time and money applying for another passport?* Sleep was trying to kick in, so we called off the search for the night. I prayed and went to sleep, thinking, *What box could it possibly be in?* The next morning I suggested that my son, Andy, look in one small box in particular. Then I went to work with this same petition on my heart. It wasn't until the following morning that Andy was able to tell us the passport was found. Joy overwhelmed our hearts! Even though we had a rough experience, we learned that God is still concerned about us and wants us to claim His promises and experience His goodness.

Today's text is one of my favorites because it assures me I can lay all my burdens and cares on the Lord. He cares for us. He has time for each one of us. Our part in this process is to come to Him and tell Him everything. We have lost the simplicity of life because we are constantly on the go. Being so busy, we sometimes forget our Creator, who is waiting for us to call on Him. As God cared for the people in Bible times, He still cares for us today. We need to ask, seek, and believe in God. He is faithful, and He will always help us in our time of need.

Dear Father, let our prayers be sincere and our faith strong as we cast our burdens on You alone. Amen.

Helen Riches Jacob

A Story to Tell

But he said to me, "My grace is sufficient for you, for my power is
made perfect in weakness." Therefore I will boast all the more gladly
about my weaknesses, so that Christ's power may rest on me.
—*2 Corinthians 12:9, NIV*

Kintsugi is a form of Japanese art that was born in the fifteenth century when a Japanese king accidentally broke his favorite teacup. He loved this vessel and decided to do whatever was necessary to restore it. Since Chinese artisans were already well recognized for this type of repair work, he sent his teacup to them. When he received it back, he was greatly disappointed at the results. He decided to see what Japanese craftsmen could do to mend his teacup. I'm sure the king was delighted with the repair job after the Japanese craftsmen had repaired and lacquered the teacup with a mixture of gold powder and resin, giving the broken vessel a beautiful new look and making it useful once more.

Kintsugi also conveys a philosophy of beautifully restoring that which has been broken. Broken pieces that have been repaired have a story to tell— the story of restoration. In some cultures, a broken object is thrown out and considered useless and unworthy. But this is not how Christ considers people who are broken. When Christ restores our brokenness through His blood, you and I are more precious than silver and gold.

What is the story of your life? Have you ever felt sad, ashamed, or unworthy? Maybe you feel this way because of abuse, rape, addictions, a failed marriage, children far from church, mistakes in your past, or bad decisions. Have you ever felt that you cannot be useful to God because of your past? Here's good news! He loves us so much more than a teacup! He is ready to restore us! "Therefore if any man be in Christ, he is a new creature: old things are passed away; behold, all things are become new" (2 Corinthians 5:17, KJV). Instead of allowing your story to make you feel diminished, let God touch and restore it into something that is useful and worthy.

Build up a ministry with your own experiences that make you unique and special. Tell your story of how the Holy Spirit entered your heart and applied the golden powder that now makes your life shine! "Arise, shine, for your light has come, and the glory of the LORD rises upon you" (Isaiah 60:1, NIV).

Guadalupe Savariz de Alvarado

Jungle Jewel

And we know that all things work together for good to those who love God, to those who are the called according to His purpose.
—*Romans 8:28, NKJV*

At a church camp meeting in the jungles of Sri Lanka, where my pastor husband and I were serving as missionaries, we noticed a little girl in the crowd gathered around our car. Thin and small with sad, forlorn eyes, she looked longingly at the large Winnie the Pooh bear lying in the back window of our car. Our little boy, Stephen, started talking to her, but her attention was focused on the bear in the window. He motioned for her to get into the car, where he handed her the bear. She clasped its soft, furry body to her chest in a big hug.

"Can we take her home?" Stephen asked me. "You know I've been praying for a little sister and now Jesus has answered my prayer!" He locked the doors so his new friend could not "escape." Having learned that another missionary family was caring for the frail, orphaned waif, we asked them, at Stephen's insistence, if the child could visit our home for a few days. They nodded and brought us a small paper bag that contained, sadly, all that the little one owned. When the missionary family contacted us a week later to inquire when they should pick her up, we told them that the heart integration between the three of us and our little jungle jewel had been so thorough that we never wanted to part with her. So we adopted the child as our daughter and as Stephen's sister. When we flew to the United States on furlough, she stood in a large courthouse with four hundred others and was sworn in as a United States citizen; her small hand proudly held a little American flag. What a gift- and balloon-filled celebration we had afterward!

I wish I could say that we all lived happily ever after, but many trials lay ahead, and many tears would be shed. Yet the lessons we've all learned have brought us closer to one another and to our loving heavenly Father. Leonardo da Vinci is credited with saying something like this: "Obstacles cannot crush me; every obstacle yields to stern resolve. He who is fixed to a star does not change his mind."

If you are contemplating the adoption of a little jewel into your family, I'd encourage you to go forward in the Lord. There is no greater calling. You will face difficulties and trials, but "by his wounds we are healed" (Isaiah 53:5, NIV). Moreover, joy awaits you in the morning.

Patty L. Hyland

God Is Always On Time

Now in the fourth watch of the night Jesus went to them,
walking on the sea.
—Matthew 14:25, NKJV

Have you ever prayed fervently about a desperate situation and then had to wait a long time before you saw any evidence that God had heard your prayers and was acting on behalf of your requests? Most of us have. This was also the experience of Christ's disciples.

In Matthew 14, we find a story about Christ's disciples who were in a boat being tossed by the wind and waves in a violent storm on the Sea of Galilee. Finally, when it seemed they were about to perish, Jesus came to them, walking on the water, in the fourth watch of the night. The fourth watch was the last part of the night, just before dawn. This means the disciples had been at sea for many hours in this fierce storm. It appears that Jesus came to them at the last conceivable moment. And when He arrived, He brought them assurance.

This story reminds us that God's delays are not necessarily His denials. Jesus knew what He was doing all along. Why did He wait so long before He intervened? He was possibly waiting until they had exhausted their own resources to save themselves, then they were fully willing to trust completely in Him.

Lifeguards will tell you that often the hardest person to save is the one who is in a state of panic and, in desperation, actually fights the efforts of the one who is trying to save him or her by using correct methods. Yet when an individual is exhausted, when he or she has no energy left, the lifeguard can grab hold of the victim with a grip that doesn't jeopardize either of them and pull that person back to safety.

In the same way, God will sometimes allow us to get to the end of our ropes, to the end of our resources, so that we are in a state of trust that allows us to cling to Him as He chooses the time and way to save us or our situations.

In the storm, the disciples were exhausted and afraid. Are you exhausted and afraid? Listen to Christ telling you personally, "It is I; do not be afraid." In your darkest night, He wants control of your storm-tossed boat to take you to your destination.

Thank You, Father, that Your timing is always perfect.

Cecilia Amoakohene

Life, Hope, and Truth

And she made a vow, saying, "LORD Almighty, if you will only look on your servant's misery and remember me, and not forget your servant but give her a son, then I will give him to the LORD for all the days of his life, and no razor will ever be used on his head."
—*1 Samuel 1:11, NIV*

Have you ever experienced bitterness of soul? If so, you can relate to a woman in the Bible. Her name is Hannah, and her story begins with much anguish and bitterness of soul. Then she prayed to the Lord and made a vow. We can find encouragement in her story.

Hannah was a married woman who had not been able to conceive and bear a child. To make things worse, the other wife, Peninnah, had been able to bear several children. This had given Peninnah a sense of superiority and strength over Hannah. Her mocking had added to the bitterness of Hannah's dilemma. At Passover, Hannah went, in a state of weakness, to the temple to pray. The strong of this world often mock the weak, but God hears and rescues the Hannahs.

Hannah's prayer, when returning to the temple with the son God gave her, addresses the arrogance of the proud, contrasting their small, haughty world with God's knowledge, which is vast and far beyond understanding. "The bows of the mighty . . . are broken," she says, "and those who stumbled are girded with strength" (1 Samuel 2:4, NKJV).

"My heart rejoices in the LORD!" she says. "The LORD has made me strong" (1 Samuel 2:1, NLT). Hannah recognized that her strength came from God and not from herself. She was not proud in *her* strength but rejoiced in *God's* ability to make a weakling strong. Hannah's story gives us insight to God's heart. Hannah's longing for a child was obviously placed in her heart by God Himself. Her husband did not understand why she could not be content with what she had. Even the temple priest, Eli, rebuked her for her passionate prayer, accusing her of being drunk. Though mocked by Peninnah and rebuked by Eli, Hannah was heard by God. He did not chastise her for not being content. He understands our feelings and invites us to bring our requests to Him (Philippians 4:6). Hannah's story also teaches us that God can use human weakness to accomplish great things. Samuel, Hannah's son, grew up to be a great man of God.

Don't give up hope; God is listening. Remember that there is a purpose in everything that God does, even if we don't understand it at the time.

Diana Ocran

The Name of Jesus Is Powerful

"And His name, through faith in His name,
has made this man strong, whom you see and know."
—Acts 3:16, NKJV

The testimony of Abi, a woman of a non-Christian belief system, helps us to understand the powerful nature of Jesus' name. This lady shared an experience she'd had as she counseled her Christian friend, Mary, who was disappointed in life. What an ironic situation! "Trust in the same powerful name of Jesus," she said to her Christian friend. "I did when a serious misunderstanding with my husband nearly ruined our marriage. I had no one to turn to."

In a desperate moment, she decided to pray to the god of her belief system, using his Arabic name. In an attempt to pray with a talisman in her hand, she could not recite the usual prayer. Instead, she heard herself mentioning the name of Jesus repeatedly. As she kept on calling the name of Jesus, a bright light flashed across where she sat meditating. She turned to see whether somebody else was present but saw no one. Then, as she told Mary, she sensed a change.

"All of a sudden, I felt as if a heavy load had been lifted from my heart. My burdens were rolled away, and I was filled with peace and joy. The hatred within me against my husband was gone. I thought that was the end of my story. But to my utmost surprise, the following week my husband bought a new car as a gift to pacify me! What a name!" she exclaimed. "Indeed, there is power in the name of Jesus, so I haven't stopped calling that name."

What an amazing story this is! Jesus cares about everybody. He is wooing the hearts of people all around the world. He urges each of us not to give way to fear and worry.

"Believe in My name," Jesus pleads, "and keep trusting in Me."

The name of Jesus is the ultimate place where we can get relief. Even in the face of new problems that may arise in life, call on Him. Have faith He will hear, for in His name is power.

Harriet Asuboni

He Stands by Me, He Stands by Thee

She said, "No one, Lord." And Jesus said,
"Neither do I condemn you; go and from now on sin no more."
—*John 8:11, ESV*

Word is going around that Janealine is *hamil*," my mother said softly as she drove. (*Hamil* means pregnant in Indonesian.) Janealine, my best friend of nearly a decade, and I shared the same cultural blood. The pieces of a puzzle were coming together: Janealine's weight gain during soccer season, her turning to face the wall when changing shirts, and her sudden quiet spirit! I had noticed but still was uncertain whether she was pregnant. I embraced the shock and remained silent as my mother, seeing an opportunity to scare me away from the same mistake, lectured me.

Janealine was now the talk of the town—"town" meaning the extended Indonesian community. Teen pregnancy was fairly new in our "town's" history. On top of that, every peer and staff member of the Christian boarding school we'd attended together was curious to know where exactly they went wrong. I asked the same question of myself. After the initial shock wore off, I made every verbal and personal commitment to get down on my knees and keep the couple in prayer. But the whole ordeal had been so tragic that I could hardly bring myself to do so. I begged God to help my best friend and be the friend I couldn't be at the time.

Then Janealine asked me to be her bridesmaid. Feeling honored and excited, I turned to see the others she had chosen. Nostalgia accompanied my tears as I saw, among the chosen, girls we had grown up with. They were still by her side after all these years, even during this step in her life.

The scribes and Pharisees brought an adulterous woman to be stoned not just by rocks but also by hateful words and personal judgments. Jesus saw through their sins but did not love His enemies any less. He did not love the adulterous woman less. He stood by her and chose not to condemn her. His forgiveness encouraged her to sin no more and to discover love in Jesus Christ. That love that we have shown to Janealine she now shares with her beautiful baby boy.

When we struggle to show love to those who have sinned, Christ's words and actions force us to ask ourselves, What sins have I committed that are not much different from theirs? Jesus helps us to forgive others as He forgives us.

In Christ's strength, we can love all equally and courageously stand for those in need.

Celine Lumowa

Sitting on the Fence

And Elijah came unto all the people, and said, How long halt yet
between two opinions? if the Lord be God, follow him: but if Baal,
then follow him. And the people answered him not a word.
—*1 Kings 18:21, KJV*

Sitting on the fence is often an easy place to sit. It can be a comfortable place. But it is always a dangerous place to be.

That's the situation in which the children of Israel found themselves in the time of Elijah the prophet. They had fallen into Baal worship and no longer trusted or worshiped the God of their fathers. Despite the fact that the God of Israel was the Creator and had power over the elements and despite the fact that Israel was experiencing a three-year drought, the people still could not make up their minds as to which was the true God—Yahweh, the God of their fathers, or Baal, the idol. They were sitting on the fence.

On the fence is where the devil would like to keep us as life passes us by. Yet the danger is that a person who sits there for too long could be deceived or even forced to make the wrong choice, instead of giving careful thought before making important decisions.

Elijah met with the Israelites and the prophets of Baal. God, through Elijah, wanted to help His people make the most important decision in their lives—to turn back to Him. During the showdown between good and evil atop Mount Carmel (see 1 Kings 18), God proved to them who He is. After Elijah prayed to God, He answered by accepting Elijah's sacrifice and sending fire down from heaven to consume it. They then made their choice to serve the true and Living God, and God relieved the drought in their land.

God has given us His Word, the Holy Bible, and the Spirit of discernment so that with prayer we can make wise decisions instead of wavering between what would ultimately be right and wrong. Sitting on the fence is like coming to a crossroads. Every day we make decisions—sometimes the wrong ones, for which we pay the consequences. Yet whenever we arrive at a crossroads, let's choose not to sit on the fence. Instead of making no decision or a hasty decision, let's go immediately to the Lord in prayer and ask for guidance. Claiming His sure and unfailing promises as we follow His Word will keep us from sitting on the fence.

Ena Thorpe

A Clean Heart

Create in me a clean heart, O God;
and renew a right spirit within me.
—Psalm 51:10, KJV

I fell in love with the season of autumn. It was a relief from the heat of the Michigan summer. I was amazed at the masterpiece of God's magnificent creation displayed in the blazing colors of the landscape around me. When we moved to California, I planted a sapling whose leaves resembled a maple tree. I nurtured it in the hope that one day I would enjoy its beauty. I was not disappointed. In the summer, the thick canopy of the tree provided shade from the hot California sun. As autumn approached, the green leaves slowly turned to gold, crimson, yellow, and orange, dressing the whole tree in the vibrant colors of the season. In the winter, strong winds stripped the tree of its beauty, and brown leaves lay scattered on the sidewalk below. The once-gorgeous tree now stood bare; its naked branches silhouetted against the evening sky.

Years later our backyard lawn retained puddles of water, making it wet and soggy. On a rainy day, the areas around the drainpipes flooded, drowning the nearby plants. Instead of completely draining, the flow through the drainage was just a steady trickle into the street for days, and moss started to grow around the outlet of the drain. I tried to clean the pipe as far as my stick could reach, to no avail. There was a problem somewhere. A landscape contractor addressed the situation. The unearthed pipes revealed that the roots of the tree I had planted had clogged the pipes, preventing the free flow of the water. I had planted a liquid amber tree (whose autumn foliage is colorful), not knowing its aggressive root system could clog drainage pipes and crack sidewalks. I planted the wrong tree in the wrong spot! A bad investment indeed and one lesson learned. The tree had to go! It cost about two thousand dollars to cut down the tree, replace the drainage system, and resod the lawn in order to restore the backyard to its original condition.

Are we like the liquid amber tree, admired for our outer beauty, yet our hearts produce a root system of pride, arrogance, prejudice, and selfishness that could damage our souls? Before any damage is done, let's ask the Master Creator to cleanse our hearts of the unwanted roots so that we can radiate His beauty in our lives.

I love the autumn colors of a liquid amber tree; but going forward, I choose to enjoy its beauty from afar.

Evelyn Porteza Tabingo

For My Good

And we know that in all things God works for the good of those who
love him, who have been called according to his purpose.
—*Romans 8:28, NIV*

On August 23, 2000, I—feet and legs swollen and weighing one hundred sixty-seven pounds—sat on the side of my bed. A sudden thought entered my mind: *She will be deprived of oxygen during the delivery.* For thirty-six weeks, my mind had been bombarded with thoughts that something bad would happen to the baby during the birth. This time the message was specific. Through prayer, I was trying to control the type of birth I would have. I wanted to have another vaginal delivery instead of another C-section.

Today my prayer would change. I gave God control as I prayed, *Lord, do whatever You need to do to save her. Please do not let her suffer any ill effects of the low oxygen and allow her to come home with me from the hospital.*

One of my five hospitalizations during pregnancy turned into a five-day stay as I started dilating. I received medication until the thirty-sixth week to keep me from having contractions. I went into labor a few hours after it was discontinued. God impressed me when to go to the hospital, arriving at the same time the doctor was scheduled to do a tubal ligation. I went into anaphylactic shock from contact with powdered gloves.

My child, Amber, went into respiratory distress. A C-section was performed before the tubal ligation. Her oxygen level was 11 percent (normal being close to one hundred). Despite respiratory support therapy, an IV tube in her head, a feeding tube down her nose, and electrodes on her chest, I believed God would grant my request that my newborn baby would be able to go home with her mom—even though babies in her condition don't usually go home with their moms.

Three days later, on August 28, hospital discharge orders were completed for both of us. Romans 8:28 tells us that God can use anything to work for good in our lives—even anaphylactic shock. If I had had the delivery I wanted, Amber would have gone into distress in the birthing canal and suffered from the low-oxygen level.

Many times we try to control our lives and solve challenges on our own. Whatever your current situation is, give it to Jesus now! He will work it out.

Pauline J. Maddox

No Way! I Am Waiting

Not giving up meeting together,
as some are in the habit of doing,
but encouraging one another—
and all the more as you see the Day approaching.
—Hebrews 10:25, NIV

My husband, Milton, and I are always thrilled to be able to spend time with our granddaughters, Azoya and Kyrah. This past Thanksgiving holiday was no exception. Our home was filled with happy voices and eager feet wanting to explore our new house.

One evening we were left alone with the grandchildren when their parents left for some well-deserved alone time. As it got closer to bedtime, Kyrah became more and more fretful and wanted the comfort of her mom. "Where are my parents?" she inquired. "Where is my mom?" her weak but defiant voice pleaded. She wanted her mom and wanted her right then.

At bedtime, we completed the girls' nightly routine: pajamas on, teeth brushed, bedtime story read, and then prayer. Then Kyrah declared that she wanted to sleep in her mommy's room. I lay down beside Kyrah in an attempt to comfort her because she had refused to go into my room to wait. In fact, she had defiantly said, "*No way*! I'm not going to your room; I'm staying in Mommy's!" It wasn't long before my little darling was fast asleep and I carried her to my room, where I could keep a watchful eye on her. As I later shared the incident with her parents, I could not help but relate Kyrah's defiant "*No way*!" to our present wait for the return of our precious Lord.

No way will I be distracted by the length of time He is taking to return.

No way will I forget His promise of a sure return.

No way will I forget to tell others of His return.

No way will I neglect to be ready.

No way!

As much as we love our grandchildren, their parents love them even more and came back after their event, as promised, to be reunited with them—including Kyrah. Our precious Lord has also promised to return, and He will. Hebrews 10:37 says, "In just a little while, he who is coming will come and will not delay" (NIV). These words are comforting to me.

Dear Lord, help us to wait patiently and in no way be distracted. Thank You for the promise of Your sure return.

Gloria Barnes Gregory

Practical Parenting

Let us search out and examine our ways . . . ;
Let us lift our hearts and hands
To God in heaven.
—*Lamentations 3:40, 41, NKJV*

Zig Ziglar has been credited with saying that parents who serve as good role models for their children will raise positive children. If this is true in the secular world, how much more important it is for Christian parents to be positive role models for their children! God created humankind in His own image, and humans were to reproduce and replenish the earth. Yet sin marred the beauty and character of creation. For this reason, producing men and women with the qualities of God's character has become a delicate task that calls for thinking, dedication, and discipline in the Lord.

Effective parents must be transformed through Christ. The only way to purposefully raise an innocent and vulnerable baby in a world of sinfulness and corruption is for the parents to be converted in Christ. As parents or role models, our characters and spirituality must be guided by the Word of God through prayer and Bible study. The Word of God places images of rightdoing in our minds and helps to separate us from our inherited and cultivated tendencies to wrongdoing.

When we are really converted, we become capable of fashioning and establishing high ideals in the lives of others. Being able to do so depends on our abilities to uphold and to practice the divine principles we have learned from the Word of God. Doing so is our duty as leaders, teachers, and role models to the children in our lives. As we draw inspiration, guidance, and strength from the Holy Spirit on a daily basis, we share—consciously and unconsciously—these blessings with the children we are leading to Christ.

Sharing these blessings leads us to apply the truth highlighted in Proverbs 22:6: "Train up a child in the way he should go, and when he is old he will not depart from it" (NKJV). Training a child in the right path calls for our love, time, and discipline. We must not forget to spend quality time with our children. We need to reflect God's character to our children. And God's encouraging promise in this verse is sure.

What a joy it is to watch our children grow in their life journeys that are leading them into eternity.

Margaret A. Anti

Abide in Me

"He who eats My flesh and drinks My blood abides in Me."
—*John 6:56, NKJV*

I love to cook. I love nutrition. My son calls me a health "wizard," though he does not know the full implications of that word. His point is this: Mom is (mildly) obsessed with healthy cooking.

On my best days, I will sit down and meal plan for a week, looking through recipes and dividing up my shopping list between the three places I'll need to go in order to get each specific item. This planning will take an hour, maybe more if I'm incorporating new recipes. Then there's the grocery shopping that takes at least three hours, or up to five, depending on the temperaments of the three kids that day. After we come home, unload groceries, and put them away, I begin prepping for the week. Throughout that afternoon, and probably for a couple of hours the next day, I will wash, chop, peel, blend, and assemble ingredients until most of the meals either are ready to go or are ready to be put together quickly. While this saves me the time of being in the kitchen for long periods throughout the week, each meal will still take at least a half an hour to get from fridge to table, and then there's the clean-up.

I spend a lot of time thinking about, and working with, food—physical food that will nourish my physical body. Recently, though, I asked myself how much time I spend eating and drinking spiritually. I have my morning devotions (thirty to sixty minutes), family worship, prayer before meals, and family worship at night. But all this time still doesn't really come close to the amount of time I spend each week on my family's physical nourishment. Of course, if you add church services on Sabbaths, that significantly bolsters the total time. Yet how much of that time is intentionally with God and how much is just social interaction with others?

Jesus said that the person who eats His "flesh" and drinks His "blood" *abides* in Him. So if I'm going to eat and drink of Christ, I have to be intentional, just as I am with my daily meals. I have to read, pray, and even memorize His Word. Throughout my day, I make it a point to come to Him through the New Testament and Psalms in my back pocket or the Bible verses taped to a cupboard. To abide does not happen accidentally. It is a continual, intentional choice. Eventually, abiding becomes automatic—a part of you. Like breathing. Like eating.

Jennifer Day

September 1

Flash Reminder

Then Moses stretched out his hand over the sea,
and all that night the LORD drove the sea back
with a strong east wind and turned it into a dry land.
The waters were divided, and the Israelites went through the sea
on dry ground, with a wall of water on their right and on their left.
—Exodus 14:21, 22, NIV

As I absentmindedly reached for the door of our community clubhouse, a blast of cold air whooshed across my face as the automatic double doors sprang wide open.

In a flash, my thoughts spiraled to the amazing night when Moses thrust his staff high above the Red Sea as the pounding hooves of Pharaoh's quickly advancing chariots sent a pulse of fear through the escaping throng. A gale-force wind caught the attention of all in sight as Moses realized that once again he was standing on holy ground. The mighty God of Abraham, Isaac, and Jacob was present; and before Moses rose two walls of water—sucking up what had seemed just seconds earlier to be a sea of despair. Thousands moved forward on dry ground in breathless silence, not wanting the moment of escape to be only a dream.

Strangely, in that instant I felt the storm's fury and the indescribable thrill of mothers and fathers as they sensed freedom within their reach. But as suddenly as this trip-in-time appeared to my silly heart, it evaporated in the cool night air as I made my way to my waiting car, realizing that God still saves.

Twenty years before, a family friend, Dr. Tom, had shared a quote from Ellen White as I prepared to host a servicemen's center in South Korea. As a missionary for many years in various parts of the world, Dr. Tom knew that life could feel very unsafe at times. I was touched by his thoughtfulness, and when I came across an art piece depicting Moses standing above the Red Sea, I felt God's personal assurance that this story needed to be the focal point in the International Servicemen's Center in Seoul, Korea. I knew that God's flash reminder to me and Ellen White's words had mingled to comfort all who entered that home away from home: "The path where God leads the way may lie through the desert or the sea, but it is [always] a safe path."*

Nancy (Neuharth) Troyer

---

* Ellen G. White, *Patriarchs and Prophets* (Nampa, ID: Pacific Press®, 2002), 290.

A Vapor, Then Immortality

LORD, make me to know mine end, and the measure of my days, what
it is: that I may know how frail I am.
—*Psalm 39:4, KJV*

The joys of life beckon us. The sunrise of birth, the bloom of youth, the laughter at picnics, concerts, parties, and the thrill of travel experiences and accomplishments!

But life on this earth doesn't hold just joys. There are the hidden booby traps to our happiness: wounds and then scars from healing, disappointments, and disasters. Yet we travel on, meeting new people and reuniting with old friends. While older family members pass away, younger ones grow up—but not always.

Primrose gave birth to a beautiful baby girl. Friends and family alike adored the new addition to the family. Then one morning not long after, Primrose leaned over the kitchen sink.

"I have a pain in my chest," she complained.

Sadly, this pain was the precursor to a massive heart attack that no one expected to take the life of a charming twenty-eight-year-old woman. Her relatives and friends never dreamed something like this would happen. She died way too young!

For the next three years, Winell, who was living with relatives, took over the faithful care of the little baby girl Primrose had left behind upon her unexpected death. One night Winell, who was so conscientiously caring for Primrose's daughter, went to bed at her usual time. When she didn't reappear in the morning, one of her relatives said, "Winell must have overslept. She'll miss her appointment this morning if she doesn't get up soon. I'll go to her room and find out why she's still in bed." But no one could awaken Winell. During the night, her frail heart had failed her.

Sadly, our life on this sinful earth is like a vapor. It can be present one moment and gone the next.

Yet immortality beckons us. No more gray hair, cancer, heart failure, pain, or death—only joy forevermore in the presence of Jesus, who "will take these dying bodies of ours and change them into glorious bodies like his own" (Philippians 3:21, TLB).

Hyacinth V. Caleb

September 3

Making Choices

For God so loved the world, that he gave his only begotten Son,
that whosoever believeth in him should not perish,
but have everlasting life.
—*John 3:16, KJV*

ronically, I opened yesterday's mail today. In the midst of the mail was a brown business envelope with the words "To Be Opened by Addressee Only" printed on the outside. As I unfolded the contents of the envelope, I quickly discovered what looked like a check for more than four hundred and fifty dollars. There was a legible signature in the lower right-hand corner. But slightly above the anticipated amount to be paid, written in large, bold print, were the words "This Is Not a Check."

The company that had sent me this envelope was willing to grant me the said amount if I were to accede to their terms and agreements that were written on the back of the document in small print. Their monetary gain would have exceeded far more than four hundred and fifty dollars.

More times than I can count, the phone has rung right when I am trying to get done what seems like the impossible. I stop immediately to answer it only to find a telemarketer on the other end of the line. In spite of the fact that my number has been placed on a Do Not Call list, some telemarketers still manage to get through to me. To hear them tell it, they're phoning me because they don't want me to miss out on the "great opportunity" I would have if I took advantage of their product offer. After all, their product would be most beneficial to me. In fact, they can't imagine how I'm currently getting along without it. In reality, I am not the beneficiary of the anticipated transaction. I am the benefactor, and they are the beneficiary.

Satan is using the same strategy today as he did with Eve in the Garden. First, he tries to get our attention. Second, he'll try to make us lose focus. Third, he zooms in, and before we know it, if we aren't careful, we become his prey. He wants to deceive us in any way he can. And he comes in various forms, shapes, and fashions. Fortunately for us, Jesus overcame the world (see John 16:33). God accomplished His plan of salvation through the blood of Jesus, the true Benefactor. And I choose to be His beneficiary. I look forward to claiming my inheritance. How about you?

Father, thank You for the sacrifice of Your Son and for Your mercy, love, and grace.

Cora A. Walker

In His Likeness

And God said,
Let us make man in our image,
after our likeness.
—*Genesis 1:26, KJV*

When I look in the mirror, what do I see?

To be honest with you, I see my mum's lips and complexion. I see my dad's nose and crooked teeth. As much as I look like my mum, I am not as beautiful a woman as she is. My face is broad like my dad's, but, alas, I also have my mum's big Italian ears. I am both of them fused into one.

The Holy Spirit speaks to me now and tells me to look again. He tells me to take a long, hard look at my reflection. And I do so. What do I see?

Well, I think again, *I am looking at a dusty, musty lump of clay, molded into the image of God. Wow! I don't think God looks one bit like me—I'm too ugly!*

Really? the Holy Spirit says to me. *Valerie, are you calling God a liar?*

No, I hasten to respond. *I would never do that.*

The Bible tells me whom I was created to resemble. "So God created man in his own image, in the image of God created he him; male and female created he them" (Genesis 1:27, KJV).

Wow! I have been made in the likeness of God. Yet all this time, Satan has told me lies about myself that have made me feel ugly. He is such a deceiver. Anyone created in God's likeness and image could never be ugly.

The enemy of our souls wants each of us to feel bad about ourselves all the time. If he can get us to believe that we are ugly, perhaps he can get us to stop believing that God truly loves us with such a divine love that mere mortals have not yet been able to understand it—they can only experience it. God's love is so deep that even while we were yet sinners, Christ died for us (see Romans 5:8). He extended His love and grace far enough to embrace us while we were still mired in the ugliness of sin. In God's eyes, sin is what is ugly—not us.

In fact, we are "fearfully and *wonderfully* made" (Psalm 139:14, NIV; emphasis added). So I dare you to look in the mirror and say to the person looking back at you, "You are beautiful. You are unique. God has created you as His masterpiece. You are one of a kind. Remember to thank Him for all He's done for you."

Valerie Fisher Green

Messenger Pigeon

Don't just pretend that you love others: really love them. Hate what is wrong. Stand on the side of the good. Love each other with brotherly affection and take delight in honoring each other.
—Romans 12:9, 10, TLB

On Sabbath morning, July 23, 2016, I entered the sanctuary with a special prayer request on my heart: "God, please let it be true!" I had just read that a world leader, who was a born-again Christian, would turn seventy on his next birthday. Then sacred memories began flooding my soul: I remembered my dad, who was a baby Christian when he slipped away forty-four years ago—at the age of forty-four—from stomach cancer. In our family, we've learned to celebrate every birthday with genuine thanksgiving in our hearts. When anyone turns seventy among family and friends, we consider any years to follow as bonus years.

During the worship service that day, Terry Lynn triggered more precious memories in my heart as she read the children's story. She told about how the American troops during World War I used homing pigeons to send messages back and forth from headquarters to the front lines. Often these birds were shot down by enemy troops. Sometimes, however, they miraculously made it back to their destinations. Terry referenced one decorated pigeon-hero by the name of Cher Ami ("dear friend" in French). Cher Ami was terribly wounded yet somehow managed to keep flying, remaining faithful to his assignment. In so doing, the heroic pigeon helped save "the lost battalion" of the Seventy-Seventh Infantry Division in the Battle of Argonne.

Have you ever envisioned yourself as a messenger pigeon with a mission? I have. I think back to when I began my writing ministry in 1990, more than twenty years ago. To the best of my abilities, I've written and publicly shared what the Holy Spirit has impressed upon my heart. My stories have been shared around the world for God's glory and the expansion of His kingdom.

Like many messenger pigeons, I've been badly wounded at times, but I've kept flying onward, regardless of the pain. I don't give up because clinging to me is a baby bird that can't fly. I am referring to my precious special-needs son, Sonny, who is now thirty years old. Each new morning we take flight with gratitude, in knowing that Jesus is soon coming to take us home. So today Sonny and I will send a message of God's love to this world leader for his birthday.

Deborah Sanders

The Journey

But he that shall endure unto the end,
the same shall be saved.
—*Matthew 24:13, KJV*

In September 2010, after much prayer and consulting with a few academic friends, I decided to pursue a doctoral degree. For whatever reason, I was under the impression that pursuing this degree would take only eighteen months. To my chagrin and surprise, I discovered that was not the case!

Over time, my journey has met with mixed challenges. I experienced the deaths of my mom, my grandmother (who died two months after I started the program), two uncles, four very close girlfriends, and a coworker. I had to take a leave of absence from school for a year and undergo two major surgeries, and I was appointed the personal representative of my mom's estate. Added to this drama was a strong recommendation, within the past three years, to change my research topic and research methods. In the midst all this, I still maintained a full-time job and sound mind.

Finally, years later, I have prepared for my first oral defense and forged forward to finish this degree. As I began the completion phase of this academic journey, I was reminded of the many blessings and challenges that come with our spiritual journeys. Although weary at times, I would claim and stand on God's promises, such as the one in Psalm 121:1, 2. Matthew 24:13 clearly presents the reward for those who endure. There were times when I wanted to quit this academic journey, but the time and financial sacrifices had been far too great. Besides, when I think about the sacrifice Christ made on my behalf, His love propels me to stay in the race.

Quitting this Christian journey is not an option. Seeing Jesus face-to-face is the ultimate prize to look forward to. After years of hard work, I will finally receive my doctoral degree. Unfortunately, when Jesus comes, my degree will be null and void. It will be of no use in heaven, nor will it help me to make it into His kingdom. What matters most is my character and the pleasant words of my Savior saying, "Well done, My good and faithful servant, Barbara. Enter now into the place I have prepared for you."

"But he that shall endure unto the end, the same shall be saved" (Matthew 24:13, KJV). Let's run this race together. The reward is out of this world.

Barbara Stovall

Trust and Accept

Trust in the LORD with all thine heart;
and lean not unto thine own understanding.
—*Proverbs 3:5, KJV*

D o you believe in prayer? It is written in the Bible, "Ask, and it shall be given you" (Matthew 7:7, KJV). If we want to test the validity of prayer and increase our faith, we must begin by asking.

Three months ago I noticed that my attitude toward losing something was different from what it had been in past years. I lost three hundred dollars somewhere in Maine or Massachusetts. I prayed and asked God to help me find my money. No, I did not locate my money that weekend. And no, I did not find that money sent to my mailbox.

Usually, I get very exasperated, discouraged, and extremely frustrated with myself when I lose something, such as a crayon from a box of eight crayons or a book I haven't yet finished reading.

But this time I noticed I responded differently. I found myself saying, "OK, Lord. I guess You must have thought that someone else needed the money more than I did."

The following week I realized the immunizations I needed for an upcoming mission trip with my church would cost me about $120 apiece. During that very same week, while doing laundry, a handkerchief fell in my lap from one of the pockets of a garment. Inside the handkerchief was my lost money. God be praised! If He had answered my prayer earlier, I would have spent the money on something else. God's timing is impeccable. God is never early or late. God is always right on time!

As mentioned earlier, if we want to test the effectiveness of prayer or increase our faith, we must begin by asking for what we want. This, however, does not mean we get anything or everything requested. As sinful humans, we can act immaturely or irresponsibly, and at times, even refuse to follow God's plan. Yet Jesus said that if we ask, we will receive. That is true, but only if we ask for things that are in accordance with God's will (1 John 5:14). God will reply by saying yes, no, or not now but later. God *will* respond!

With the experience of my missing money, God taught me again to really—from deep in my heart—believe His Word and trust Him. I am glad I'm responding differently regarding lost items; but most important, I'm glad I've learned to ask for and accept whatever God decides.

Wilma Feaster Daniels

The Sewing-Machine Miracle

But Jesus looked at them and said to them,
"With men this is impossible, but with God all things are possible."
—*Matthew 19:26, NKJV*

My personal ministry is sewing quilted lap robes for hospice patients. My sewing machine is a basic model with a few decorative stitch options. After each lap robe is completed, I sew a decorative stitch around the sides. The decorative stitches range from simple designs, designated by the number 2 on my stitch dial, to number 19, the most complex and ornate stitch. One lap robe I was finishing merited a number 19 decorative stitch. After completing it, I forgot to turn back the dial on my sewing machine to the straight stitch, which I always do after finishing a project.

Days later, I tried to turn the dial to a higher-level stitch, but it wouldn't move. I turned it harder. *Clunk!* Immediately, I realized something had broken. The machine still sewed, but every stitch was a combination of the stitch before and after it. I took the machine to the repair shop and was assured that the machine could be fixed—with the warning never to force the dial again.

I started another sewing project but noticed the dial would not move past a certain point. I sewed three sides of a lap robe and was just starting the fourth when my husband came by.

"How is your machine working?" he asked. When I told him the dial would not move beyond a certain point, he said, "Let me try." He did and *clunk*! Chagrined, I took the machine back to the repair shop. I explained I had only one side of a lap robe to finish. Now my machine was unfixable, and no other machine there had the stitch I needed.

Upset, I returned home with the unfixable machine and tried the number 2 stitch. It didn't work. I tried other stitches; nothing worked. My husband said, "Have you prayed about this?" I hadn't considered that!

I went into my sewing room and bowed my head. "Please, Lord, help me finish this project." After praying, I glanced over at my unfinished lap robe. I looked at it more closely and saw that I hadn't used the number 2 stitch but rather the number 3 stitch. I turned the dial to 3, sewed a piece of scrap material, and the stitch was perfect! I finished the remaining edge of the lap robe. "Thank You, Lord!"

When my husband and I told the repairman the story, he just smiled. Being a Christian, he knew that with men, things can be impossible, but with God all things are possible (see Matthew 19:26).

Laura Hartmann

September 9

God Prepares the Way

And let us arise, and go up to Bethel;
and I will make there an altar unto God,
who answered me in the day of my distress,
and was with me in the way which I went.
—*Genesis 35:3, KJV*

It was a normal Friday morning in September when I made my usual trip to the grocery store to buy what was needed for the family's weekend meals.

As I exited the store around noon and wheeled the grocery cart to my car, the warm Texas sun beat down. I sensed my usual desire to hurry home to be with my mother, who lived with me. I always hurried to get back home. I knew that she should not be left alone for too long.

I raised the rear lift gate of my car and started putting in my groceries. As I struggled with a bulky watermelon, a balding man in khaki pants and a white shirt walked in my direction from across the parking lot. "Ma'am, I have been shown by God to give you a blessing today. May I help you with your groceries?"

"No, thanks," I responded. "I think I'm OK."

"Well then," he said, "may I return your grocery cart to the stand for you?"

"Sure. That would be fine." He took the cart without further words, and I went on home, not knowing I would recall that incident later.

My husband, Tom, passed away on the afternoon of that very day, sending my mind and emotions into a whirlwind. Only two days later, as I recalled that tragic day again and again, did I remember the man in the parking lot. If he were truly an ordinary man, then God had used him to speak kindly to me. Yet, in my opinion, I believe an angel of God had come to my side *before* the subsequent tragedy to tell me God was with me that day. That encounter was also a reminder that God will be with me forever throughout eternity—throughout whatever I experience in life. God chose to tell me He was with me and in a manner that would forever be seared in my mind for comfort and encouragement.

God is always there for us. God speaks in ways, if we will but listen, that help us know His presence is with us to comfort us. "He healeth the broken in heart, and bindeth up their wounds" (Psalm 147:3, KJV).

Nathalie "Nathy" Regmund

The Joy of Giving

God loves a cheerful giver.
—*2 Corinthians 9:7, NKJV*

Do you ever spend time thinking of all the things you could do if you suddenly received a lot of money? I have to confess that I sometimes do. First, I would put aside 10 percent for tithe, an additional sum for regular church offerings, and set aside even more for special charities or mission projects. Next I would enjoy helping those who could use a little (or large) financial boost. Of course, income tax would take its share of my newfound wealth as well.

It's fun to dream about what we'd do with more money, but I have no rich uncle who might include me in his will. I won't win a lottery because I don't buy lottery tickets. So dreaming is the best I can do. Or is it? Because there are other ways to bring joy to others.

I remember one Christmas when my two older sisters and I were little girls. The family had no money to buy gifts for us. Mother made our clothes, so there were bits of fabric left from our dresses. She pieced them together and made aprons for us, no doubt with a heavy heart, but we loved our "scrappy aprons" and were as happy with them as if they had come from a major department store! Surely, our pleasure was a blessing to her.

Time can be another gift. When my husband, Ted, and I were retiring after many years of being primarily involved in our work and our church, we wanted to do something in our community. Meals on Wheels, which delivers meals to the homebound, was starting a route in our area, so we applied to be involved in the deliveries. After we were interviewed and approved, another couple took us on our new route so that we could learn where to go and how to proceed. Then we were on our own.

We found this outreach very rewarding and delivered meals one day a week for about fifteen years. We got to know and care for many people on our route during those visits. We even recruited several others from our church to join the ranks.

The last time Ted drove the car, just a few weeks before he lost his long battle with cancer, it was to deliver meals to others.

All around us are many people and areas of need. Why not find something you can do just for the joy of giving? Remember that God loves a cheerful giver!

Mary Jane Graves

My Rock, My Refuge

"The rain came down, the streams rose,
and the winds blew and beat against that house;
yet it did not fall, because it had its foundation on the rock."
—Matthew 7:25, NIV

While my husband drives to Branson, Missouri, I enjoy the scenery. Along the drive, we pass walls of rock that frame the road in places. It is a beautiful landscape! I take out my camera and snap photos of things that captivate my attention. On the hard and almost inhospitable surface of these rocks, some trees grow.

How does a plant grow on a rock, of all places, in order to become big and strong? I see how tree roots have made a home in some crack in the rock. I can imagine that many seeds fell at one time onto that rock but could not survive. I think of how that one seed fell right in that crevice. Still it was in danger of not surviving, perhaps because a little bird might want to devour it. Maybe heavy rains would wash it from its hiding place or the scorching sun burn its tender, sprouting leaves. Then there is always the danger of frost. In its survival, however, I see the wisdom of God. Its roots are strongly attached in the rock, and when the strong winds arrive, that little tree can resist them. The Lord provided for its roots to extract all that was good for growth from inside the rock. But He also sends gentle breezes and refreshing rain to strengthen it.

At some point in your life, you may feel like that little tree. You feel like the seed that fell onto the rock—a world that is sometimes hard and indifferent, a world that does not care about you. You feel that illness or pain is about to scorch and destroy your body or that the strong winds of criticism want to rip you from your home or church. You feel the heavy rains—those problems that are pouring over you, attempting to move the roots of your faith.

But do not become discouraged! Remember that blessed tree that is surviving all the dangerous elements while being grounded in the rock. You are very blessed, for your life is affixed to the Rock, who is Christ! Study His Word to deepen your roots of faith. It will nurture your soul and help you resist the storms of life. When life becomes perplexing and complicated, let the Rock hold and protect you. May God's refreshing rain and soft breezes of blessing strengthen us so that we can comfort and encourage our sisters and peers, making their lives more bearable as they learn the beauty of growing and flourishing in Jesus Christ as well.

Damaris Prieto

All but Rahab...

But actually she had taken them up to the roof
and hidden them beneath piles of flax that were drying there.
—Joshua 2:6, TLB

Have you ever had questions about the story of Rahab in the Bible? I have. For example, why should two men from Israel lodge in the house of Rahab, who was a harlot? Were there no princes, elders, or better men and women in Jericho where they could have stayed? And how could God use a sinful woman like Rahab? Yet we have all sinned. God knows us just as well as He knew Rahab (see Psalm 139:4). And He has also chosen us, as with Rahab, to carry out His purposes. Let's look at some positive attributes displayed in the life of that courageous woman.

First, Rahab chose to put her faith in the God of Israel. To the two Israelite spies on a holy mission, she declared, "I know perfectly well that your God is going to give my country to you. . . . For we have heard how the Lord made a path through the Red Sea for you when you left Egypt! . . . For your God is the supreme God of heaven, not just an ordinary god" (Joshua 2:9–11, TLB). Rahab based her faith on the unmistakable power and care of God for His people.

Second, Rahab not only trusted God but also humbled her heart before Him through her obedience. Even though the king of Jericho sent a message to her, demanding to know the whereabouts of the Israelite spies, she risked her life to save the men of God rather than yield to the king of Jericho. May we stand for God in difficult times and be faithful as Rahab was.

Finally, Rahab was unselfish. Not only did she ask for God's mercy on herself when Israel came to conquer Jericho, she also extended the favor of God to her kindred, father, mother, siblings, and the entire household. She also had compassion for others. Oh, how often we become selfish in our prayers. We lack compassion for others.

May we emulate the good example of Rahab. As with Rahab, you may be guilty of one sin or another, having no hope, but God has a purpose for you and for those you love. Listen for His voice and believe.

One day, when He returns to take us home, we will celebrate with Jesus and the saints in heaven. Yet we make the preparations for that time now, while we are on this earth.

May the Holy Spirit touch our hearts so that we can avail ourselves of the Lord's mercies and allow His blessings to overflow from our lives through the kindness that we show to others.

Philomina Edu

Then It Rained

Let them give thanks to the LORD for his unfailing love
and his wonderful deeds . . .
for he satisfies the thirsty.
—*Psalm 107:8, 9, NIV*

Somewhere between lunch and "my next class begins in ten minutes," I stop by the teachers' lounge. Rene, a colleague and friend, stares quietly out the window at the dry Texas grass. We walk together to our respective classrooms. An unexpected health diagnosis has now made Rene a caregiver for her mother. Two weeks ago, as we sat inside the teachers' lounge before the window, Rene confessed, "I feel as if I am traveling through an endless desert with no water in sight. I pray. I wait. I long for an answered prayer or unexpected blessing. I am grateful for what God has given us. I know He is watching over us. I shouldn't feel this way."

I listen and wonder, *How many of us have been through seemingly endless deserts in life?* I have. I understand. In the following weeks, I meet Rene for lunch and gladly take her calls at home when she needs to talk or pray.

One early morning I walk through campus, but I am preoccupied. Today Rene's mother will visit with her doctors. Will she receive good news? Then I see landscapers planting trees next to the window of the faculty lounge where Rene and I sit during lunch. I notice small stacks of flowers and rosebushes that will line the entire building! "It's a good day for planting!" I am startled by a landscaper's loud voice. He points to the sky. "The soil has been dry, and rain is coming."

That night I am awakened by the sound of thunder and hard rain hitting my bedroom window. I pull the curtains aside, and lightning shows me puddles of rain and water on the grass. Beautiful. As I crawl back into bed, I hear a familiar chime from my cell phone alerting me to a text message that has arrived. It's from Rene: "Thank you for your prayers. We got good news at the doctor's office today. It's raining. I believe 'showers of blessings' can both wash our sorrows away and bless and nurture our future." I agree and thank God as I drift back to a deep sleep, cradled by the sounds of drops of grace falling from the sky.

Heavenly Father, let gratitude for all You have done fall from my lips when I walk through deserts of the heart and soul—and constant showers of blessings. I am grateful for the opportunity to share Your love with others.

Dixil L. Rodríguez

I Was in Trouble!

"Nevertheless do not rejoice in this,
that the spirits are subject to you,
but rather rejoice because your names are written in heaven."
—Luke 10:20, NKJV

I was in trouble. I had made reservations for travel for my ministry; but when I went online to the travel company, I couldn't find them! My clue that something was wrong was that the folks who invited me had not received their copy of the receipt with which to reimburse me. I was on hold with the travel company for at least fifteen minutes when I lost the connection. I called back to get in line to talk with a customer-service agent and was put on hold again. I was running out of time. I had things to do and places to be. Being on hold was pushing my schedule that morning.

I fell on my knees and began to pray to the Father for help with my problem. I could think of many bad scenarios, and I wanted to trust God through any of them. I needed to pray for those tickets. But when I prayed with my face to the carpet, I found myself praying for the lost, for the lost in my family and others' families; for the infilling of the Holy Spirit; and for souls to be saved around the world.

I thought, *Why am I praying this and not for my tickets?* Then I remembered that starting the previous week, my husband, Skip, and I had begun praying, along with our entire church, for a very special and powerful infilling daily of the Holy Spirit. I thought, *So this is what it is like to have the mind of Christ. I pray for the lost instead of myself? I have experienced a deep miracle here.*

Then the Spirit brought to mind the passage in Luke 10:20 when Jesus said, "Nevertheless do not rejoice in this, that the spirits are subject to you, but rather rejoice that your names are written in heaven" (NKJV). So I thought, *Of course, God can do things like calm the wind and waves, cast out demons, fix a plane ticket, heal the sick—and we are impressed and rejoice. But when it comes to the miracle of the Holy Spirit making me one with Christ (my name written in heaven), while still giving me freedom of choice, this is the greatest act of God! He can do it for my loved ones, strangers, and the lost too! He is able! This is cause for my ultimate happy dance.*

So I prayed for others, then for my ticket last. What gave me shivers was not finding my reservations (which I did, praise God!) but that the Holy Spirit could transform my mind to become like Jesus' mind—and that my name is written in heaven.

Merrilou Wilder Inks

September 15

Open My Eyes, Open My Heart

"O LORD, I pray thee, open [my] eyes that [I] may see."
—*2 Kings 6:17, RSV*

Our son, Garrick, received his first passport when he was five weeks old. When my husband, Larry, and I filled in the data on international arrival cards, we joked that his occupation was "child." "Being a child is a full-time occupation," Larry declared. "He'll learn how to walk; he'll pound his first birthday cake into crumbs and rub them into his hair. He'll beat on tambourines, crawl into boxes, and blow bubbles. That's his job!"

We relished each step of Garrick's progress: talking, eating bananas, playing in the sandbox, catching frogs, and riding a tricycle. We looked forward to these same delights with our second child. And then Gillian was born with windblown feet, was deaf, had hip problems—and two holes in her heart. She died when she was four months old. We could not have another.

Tears streamed down my cheeks when, in church, a young mother with a plump, smiling baby sat beside me. Slowly, I learned to cope with the sorrow and the change of expectations.

Three years later I no longer actively grieved for a second child, but then Judy, the mother of Garrick's best friend Emily, announced, "I'm pregnant." I could barely tell her I was happy for her family. When she drove home smiling, tears spilled down my face. Larry turned to me, asking what was wrong. "It's fine for people to have one child, but when they have a second . . ." My words trailed off in a welter of guilt and sorrow. All through Judy's pregnancy, I grieved. Emily stayed with us when Judy went into labor, and Garrick jumped with glee to learn of Geoff's birth. I went to the other room to cry. Their family was blessed. We were not.

But as the years pass, I have learned to see our blessings—and to open my heart to them. The three of us could fit into one canoe and paddle 450 miles down the Yukon River. Many of the summers of Garrick's childhood were filled with dirt and digging on his father's archaeological excavations because, as a family of three, we could afford to travel together. Because we had only one child's interests to consider, it was easy to choose books for our nightly story time.

These weren't the blessings I had envisioned, but they are ones that our family received. When my eyes were open to see them and my heart was open to praise, my life was changed.

Denise Dick Herr

Family Reunion

The LORD bless thee, and keep thee:
the LORD make his face shine upon thee,
and be gracious unto thee:
the LORD lift up his countenance upon thee,
and give thee peace.
—*Numbers 6:24–26, KJV*

Recently, members of my extended family gathered together for a memorial service for Aunt Barb, who was my dad's sister. As we gathered in the cemetery that beautiful afternoon, I realized it had been nearly nine years since I had seen some of those standing with me. Several others I hadn't actually seen in almost three decades. The infant I had at that time is almost thirty years old, married, and has an infant of his own. He also has two subsequent siblings. So much time had passed since previous reunions. We were kids who grew up together, seeing each other nearly every weekend and holiday in their homes, ours, or Grandma and Grandpa's. We had shared summer days at the pool and weeks at the beach. Then we grew up, went to separate colleges, got married, and had kids of our own.

We kept in touch through our parents. Dad would tell me what he heard from Aunt Sue or Aunt Barb about this one moving or that one getting a new job or having a new baby. Then came the days when I began hearing about the *next* generation beginning to leave home one by one. Several of them are married, and two even have little ones of their own.

Despite the lapsed years between personal visits, my cousins and I picked up where we left off, catching up on one another's lives. We shared family pictures and heard a story of a surprise visit from a son who has been living in China for three years. I even saw our old babysitter. It was wonderful to reminisce. Despite the fact that we were together for a sad occasion, it was awesome to be together—a great family reunion.

All too soon it was time to part yet again. I was the last one out of the house because I didn't want to say goodbye. It will probably be several more years before we see one another again.

On the road trip home, I began thinking about heaven. Can you imagine the huge family reunion we will be a part of? Aunts, uncles, grandparents, moms, dads, cousins, friends, neighbors, and total strangers—all one great big family coming home—home to be with God and Jesus forever. I don't know about you, but I can't wait! We'll never have to say goodbye again!

Kathy Pepper

Guardian Angel

For He shall give His angels charge over you,
To keep you in all your ways.
—*Psalm 91:11, NKJV*

When I was about six years old, I lived in Bakersfield, California. The summer after second grade my sister was supposed to babysit me while our mom and dad were at work. My sister was thirteen years old and was always thinking up things to do.

She ran around with her school friends and, of course, dragged me along with her. Once she had us climb up on top of an icehouse. Her favorite thing to do was climb up on things that were high. Though she liked to climb, I didn't. I don't like heights.

One afternoon she insisted that we walk down to the railroad yard, which was located about three blocks from our house. It seemed as if many trains were always sitting around on the tracks in the yard. I learned that this yard was a holding place for trains that were not currently in use.

"Say, let's play on some of these trains!" exclaimed my sister with enthusiasm. "Look! That train over there has a caboose on it. Let's climb up in the caboose and pretend that we're riding in a train." Dutifully, I clambered up the steps into the caboose. Suddenly, the wheels of the caboose began to move along its track as the train began to move.

"We've got to jump!" my sister yelled. "The train is already going faster!"

But how could I jump? I was too scared to even move. "You jump first," I said to my sister in a trembling voice. "Then I will jump after you do." My sister jumped, but I was still too fearful to make the leap.

Now she began running alongside the caboose, pleading with me to jump. But I was still nearly paralyzed by fear. My fear only increased as the train picked up even more speed.

Finally, as the caboose passed by some particularly rocky ground, I jumped! Looking back, I know I could have broken both my legs during this leap of a lifetime. Yet I didn't. Truly my guardian angel was with me and delivered me from serious injury. Today I thank God for His angelic protection over my life.

God will always send His angels to look after us when we ask Him for protection each day. God is good to us all the time and always takes care of each of us constantly. I praise Him.

Anne Elaine Nelson

Traveling Mercies

The angel of the LORD encampeth
round about them that fear him, and delivereth them.
—*Psalm 34:7, KJV*

Thank You, heavenly Father, for this new day. Please give me traveling mercies as I drive to town. Amen, and thank You, I prayed before turning on the ignition.

It wasn't far to our little town, but the highway was an exceedingly busy one. Many semitrucks (also called tractor trailers or eighteen-wheelers) travel swiftly along this route on their long hauls to Prince George, about 120 miles from our town. It is, nevertheless, a lovely stretch of road with few homes. But deer, moose, or bear wandering onto the highway and into oncoming traffic have often caused accidents.

My errand list for the morning included stopping at the post office to collect mail and send a letter. Then I would buy groceries and do a little business at the bank before going home.

Soon I had completed my list and began my trip home. The miles slipped by as I negotiated the railroad overpass, drove by two more roads, and was almost at the bridge. At this point, I needed to turn on my signal to notify drivers behind me that I would be making a left-hand turn off the highway onto Dore River Road. Looking in the rearview mirror, I saw a semi coming up behind me very quickly. I now reached my road and was about to turn when—*swoosh*! The semi roared past me on the left side (the driver's side of the car) and drove merrily on his way. When I recovered from the shock of almost being struck, the realization hit me that *death* nearly came knocking! As I slowly drove the rest of the way home, it was with a sense of awe and thankfulness. Surely, my guardian angel had held me back from turning just a split second sooner. How true it is that angels are "all ministering spirits, sent forth to minister for them who shall be heirs of salvation" (Hebrews 1:14, KJV).

I also recalled God's promise to us in Isaiah 65: "And it shall come to pass, that before they call, I will answer; and while they are yet speaking, I will hear" (verse 24, KJV).

Often in our busy lives we forget that we are being watched and guarded by God's care every moment. What an exciting time it will be when we meet our guardian angels in heaven, for they will surely tell of the many times they have interceded and saved us from harm.

Muriel Heppel

September 19

The Marketplace Choir

But as it is written, Eye hath not seen, nor ear heard, neither have entered into the heart of man, the things which God hath prepared for them that love him.
—*1 Corinthians 2:9, KJV*

I have sung in different choirs for several years. When I was in high school, I joined my school choir. I was a member of my local church choir and also the district choir. I also participated in several spiritual concerts and listened to great choirs perform. But I had never been touched by any manner of singing as I was on Wednesday, September 19, 2012.

My husband, who is a pastor, had just been transferred to our church's headquarters in a country foreign to us. I went to the Assigamé market in Togo that Wednesday to purchase some groceries. A large crowd in the form of a circle stood singing a song of praise in the local dialect. I did not understand all the words, but I could distinguish a few: God, praise, glory, and "in heaven." I had never seen such a thing before, so I approached the circle and found that there was a street preacher in their midst who had just finished sharing a message. Now the Marketplace Female Choir, as I nicknamed them, were raising their voices in a song of praise that enraptured everyone. Almost all the sellers and buyers like me were singing along with strength and vigor. I thrilled at this scene and, without realizing it, had a sudden impression about heaven. I imagined how sweet heaven will be when there will be only one faith with thousands and ten thousands of people singing to the glory of God.

The Bible tells us that every day, hour, and minute angels are present before the Lord of hosts singing His praises. The Bible also says that the redeemed shall sing the song of Moses and of the Lamb around the great white throne. Oh, how beautiful it will be when all the redeemed of every age—not just the women of the Assigamé market—will sing to honor Him who created and redeemed us!

Dear sister, I am sure that your mind's eye has also tried to imagine my marketplace choir moment. But what our Lord has prepared for you and me, no eye has ever seen, no ear has ever heard, and it has not entered into the heart of anyone! Let us make this great appointment the object of our lives!

Tabitha Kra

Perplexities

We are hard-pressed on every side,
yet not crushed; we are perplexed, but not in despair.
—*2 Corinthians 4:8, NKJV*

D o you know that the words *perplexed* and *perplexity* are referenced in the Bible a total of eight times, according to *Strong's Concordance*? When I was young, these words never really described situations I was familiar with. As I got older, though, and life's journey became more complex, I found 2 Corinthians 4:8 summed up my feelings over life's puzzling experiences.

During one of those times, after agonizing with the Lord through reflection and trying to figure out things on my own, I started counting ways God has been good to me. Starting with my thumb, I said, "One: He loves me; two: He's in control; three: He has never failed me; four—" I stopped and smiled. I wouldn't have enough fingers to count my many blessings. But it had helped to start doing so because God had made me smile!

I looked up the word *perplexed* in a dictionary. It means "filled with confusion or bewilderment; puzzled." That pretty much described my feelings when I'd attempted to do good and things turned sour. Sometimes, and maybe most times, we bring perplexities upon ourselves. We barrel ahead, thinking we have such good ideas. Yet God's timetable is very different from ours, so we find it hard to wait. Prayerfully waiting, however, can bring such peace!

God doesn't get perplexed over our attitudes of ingratitude because He knows us, but it does hurt Him. We also hurt Him when we take things into our hands, get upset, and fail to lay all our perplexities at His feet. We should not despair or let things crush us. Jesus was "bruised for our iniquities" (Isaiah 53:5, KJV), yet we sometimes expect to be treated better than He was.

God never fails us, but we disappoint Him when we let the perplexities of life get us down. I'd never thought much about that word before—*perplexity*. The words of a great inspirational writer have consoled me when I faced perplexities. She writes, "Take to Him everything that perplexes the mind."*

Father, please give us the presence of mind to look to You for all the perplexing things that are sure to come to us as we attempt to navigate this worldly journey. May we always remember to follow You as our Guide and to lay everything at Your feet—perplexing or not!

Sharon M. Thomas

---

* Ellen G. White, *Prayer* (Nampa, ID: Pacific Press®, 2002), 11.

Peace

"Peace I leave with you; my peace I give you.
I do not give to you as the world gives.
Do not let your hearts be troubled and do not be afraid."
—*John 14:27, NIV*

John 14:27 has become my daily promise over the last years, simply because when you memorize it and you say it aloud, peace comes. This promise comes from Jesus Himself. He desires us to have peace. But what gives us inward calm when our circumstances seem out of control?

One way to develop consistent peace is to learn to live "in the now." We can spend a lot of time thinking about the past or wondering what the future holds, but we can't do much about anything unless our mind is focused on today. When you look to your past as a reference but not as a residence, you give your mind the ability to embrace your reality today.

Another way to find calmness is by controlling our thoughts. Because of God's promises, I can have peace where I am. "Do not be anxious about anything, but in every situation, by prayer and petition, with thanksgiving, present your requests to God. And the peace of God, which transcends all understanding, will guard your hearts and your minds in Christ Jesus" (Philippians 4:6, 7, NIV). It is our choice to invite into our every thought and experience a peace that transcends all understanding.

The Bible gave us the recipe for a peaceful mind in Philippians 4:8, "Finally, brothers and sisters, whatever is true, whatever is noble, whatever is right, whatever is pure, whatever is lovely, whatever is admirable—if anything is excellent or praiseworthy—think about such things" (NIV). This is a real test for our thoughts. Controlling the mind is not something we can do in our own strength. We need to come to God daily, asking for His help. As I replace my own thoughts with His Word, peace takes hold and calmness floods in.

Finally, prayer is another way to have peace. How? When you pray, you are exercising faith in God. The situation you are facing today may not be different tomorrow, but your mind-set changes when you pray. You look at your problem in a different way. Prayer changes you.

If you are feeling anxious and weary today, trust your Father who says, "Peace I leave with you; my peace I give you. I do not give to you as the world gives. Do not let your hearts be troubled and do not be afraid" (John 14:27, NIV). Go, live the day in peace. Provision is already there.

Raquel Queiroz da Costa Arrais

Plumbing Problem!

What? know ye not that your body is the temple of the Holy Ghost
which is in you, which ye have of God, and ye are not your own?
—*1 Corinthians 6:19, KJV*

When I was growing up, I realized pretty early that sports was not one of my gifts. In fact, when we were required to run long-distance cross-country races in high school, it would take quite a while before I could get to the finish line. By the time I got back to the school grounds, my bag would be the only one left on the field. That was because it was so late that even the school custodians had already left the premises. This discouraged me from participating in any sporting activities.

Fortunately, I married a health-conscious sportsman. For domestic harmony, I would agree to go with him for long walks. I would also drink smoothies and eat lots of vegetables and follow the healthy lifestyle he was striving to promote.

The test of my faithfulness and commitment to this healthy lifestyle came when my husband traveled for three weeks. While he was gone, there was no need for me to make fruit smoothies every morning! At last, I could sleep in for an extra twenty minutes! I did not need to take long walks in the hot and humid Ivorian weather. I could freely eat white refined bread, and it tasted so good!

After a week, though, I noticed that I was not feeling as energetic as I normally did. I developed a very sharp pain in my abdomen. I had to be rushed to the hospital by ambulance. After an entire week of investigation, during which time I could not eat or keep anything down, the medical tests showed that my digestive system had been clogged up. These plumbing problems were now aggravating a previous medical condition. All methods to unclog the backed-up toxins failed. Surgery was the only solution.

At that point, I realized that a healthy lifestyle was something I needed to embrace and maintain!

With this experience, 1 Corinthians 6:19 took on a new significance for my life. Indeed, my body *is* the temple of the Holy Spirit and should be kept in good working condition. This alone is now my motivation for living and eating healthfully.

Eugenia Mzikazi Bhebhe

This Beautiful Day

This is the day which the LORD hath made;
we will rejoice and be glad in it.
—*Psalm 118:24, KJV*

What would you consider a beautiful day? Beautiful days are not only sunny days with blue skies and gentle breezes blowing. A rainy day has a loveliness of its own. If you were a flower, would you complain about the weather? Would you recognize the value of rainy days?

We endure cloudy days and rainy days. We get scattered showers. Other days are bright and dry. On some days, the heat is unbearable; stormy days keep us inside, seeking shelter. Winter brings windy, cold, dreary, wet, icy, and snowy days! "If you don't like the weather in New England," Mark Twain is credited with saying, "just wait a few minutes."

Variety is not bad at all. I count it a blessing! Just as flowers need all kinds of weather to grow, we, too, need a variety of weather to bloom into the stunning flowers God intended us to be.

Trials and challenges are part of life. Jesus said, "These things I have spoken unto you, that in me ye might have peace. In the world ye shall have tribulation: but be of good cheer; I have overcome the world" (John 16:33, KJV).

On sunny days, when all seems to go right and life is a breeze, praise the Lord. Are you depressed and irritable every time a few clouds come around? Then let the billows of doubt draw you to God in prayer, where you will find the answers. The Sun of Righteousness keeps His light ever shining beyond the clouds. Let rainy days turn into lessons of faith and trust in our heavenly Father so that we may become stronger as our roots press deeper into His Word. As we walk in obedience to the Word of God, we will be cleansed from sin and remade in Christ's likeness. Let stormy days lead us to seek shelter in His loving arms and claim His promises! On steamy days, let us dwell "in the secret place of the most High" and "abide under the shadow of the Almighty" (Psalm 91:1, KJV).

Through Christ's victory over dark or unpleasant days, we have victory, for we "can do all things through Christ" who strengthens us (Philippians 4:13, KJV).

Sunshine or rain, God bestows His loving care upon each flower. Undoubtedly, as the saying goes, beauty lies in the eye of the beholder. The blessings of each day lie in our ability to understand that the Creator will take care of us, regardless of the weather.

Rhodi Alers de López

Stormy Weather

Now when evening came, the boat was in the middle of the sea, and
He [Jesus] was alone on the land. Then He saw the disciples straining
at rowing, for the wind was against them. Now about the fourth
watch of the night He came to them, walking on the sea.
—Mark 6:47, 48, NKJV

While reading again the story of Jesus walking on the sea to reach the disciples in the storm (Mark 6), the distinction in the watches of the night caused me to stop and ponder. "When evening came" means the time period of the first watch, which was six o'clock to nine o'clock in the evening. This is when the wind comes up and Jesus first saw the disciples "straining" and struggling at the oars. Yet Jesus didn't go out to them until the fourth watch, which was three o'clock to six o'clock in the morning. Even though they were not aware of it, Jesus had watched them through all four watches, which might have been twelve hours.

Earlier that day Jesus fed the five thousand, and great excitement was generated. The disciples were caught up in the fervor and anticipation of the crowd that Jesus was the Messiah and should claim His throne. But it wasn't time for Jesus to be publicly acknowledged. He firmly insisted that His disciples get in the boat and sail away, to go ahead of Him (verse 45). This delay strengthened their faith and taught them valuable lessons. Only then could the disciples separate themselves from error and discern truth.

Whether or not they could physically see Jesus, Jesus saw them. When His followers came to the end of their own resources, they realized it was impossible to overcome the storm by their own strength. Jesus knew the storms they faced and rescued His disciples in His appointed time.

When we face "storms" and "winds" that beat against us, we may be tempted to think that Jesus doesn't see or hear us because help isn't coming as quickly as we feel we need it. But we can rest assured that Jesus knows the circumstances of our lives. He is watching us, and He never leaves us nor forsakes us (Hebrews 13:5).

We can appreciate our stormy-weather experiences as faith-training boot camp. Jesus loves us deeply, even in the midst of darkness. He responds in His perfect timing because He knows what is best. When we let go of our control, we trust Him to be Captain of the boat.

Today may we all rejoice that we have an awesome Savior who is always with us, even in stormy weather, and loves us unconditionally.

Myrna Hanna

God Calls, God Enables!

And whatever you do, do it heartily,
as to the Lord and not to men.
—*Colossians 3:23, NKJV*

In 1999, I had the joy of finishing my undergraduate studies in education at a Christian university in Engenheiro Coelho, São Paulo, Brazil. It was a double joy because my fiancé and I were graduating and getting married on the same day and in the same place. After marriage, my husband, Josiel P. Souza, decided to go into the seminary. So we remained at the university for four more years. I was invited to become an assistant dean of women. I was only twenty-two.

This mission came with great responsibility, but God empowered me to do it. I always tried to do my best. I tried to treat all the dorm girls fairly. It was not easy to know how to balance being their friend with having to be firm in moments that required me to do so.

I really liked to visit the girls in their rooms and pray with them. Larissa, the adoptive daughter of a secretary of the federal government, was one middle-school girl whom I will never forget. She was needy for attention. Her problem was not lack of money, since everything that she wanted financially her dad gave to her. She had difficulty in following the school and dormitory rules. She was not a member of the denomination that operated the school; therefore, everything was new to her. She would visit me in the office and sit in my lap. One day she appeared with her hair dyed bright red. That was the last straw following several rules she'd broken. She would have to be expelled. I was very sad because I knew that her case was very difficult. Then I called my husband, and we took her to a nearby beauty salon to change back the color of her hair. I tried to do everything possible so that she could remain at the school. I prayed with her and gave her advice, but unfortunately, her dad still had to come pick her up. I tried to stay in contact with her for a while after she left, but then we lost touch.

I thank God for the opportunity of having this experience, even though I was very young. I have no doubt that when He calls us, He also enables us to fulfill His calling for our lives. It is a joy to know that wherever I go, I find girls from the time when I was a women's dean. As the girls used to say, "Once a dean, always a dean!"

Dear friend, accept God's calling for your life and do your best, because all other things will also be added to you (see Matthew 6:33). God has a special plan for your life. Trust and accept it!

Débora de Souza

Grace and Mercy

LORD, you alone are my portion and my cup;
you make my lot secure.
—*Psalm 16:5, NIV*

You take a routine exam and expect the results to be as good as usual. But they're not.

Disappointment comes when you least expected it. Full of hope and assuming the best, you open the envelope with the test results, but hope disappears. There you see the word everyone fears: *cancer*! Suddenly, a dark and uncertain tunnel is in front of you. You cannot escape through any shortcut.

In a second, your life has changed. Your priorities change, and your feelings become confused. No matter how strong you thought you were, at this gloomy moment, even the ground beneath your feet feels shaky. Your heart skips a few beats. Your stomach feels as if it is twisting, and tears fall.

What can you do when something over which you have no control is suddenly threatening to destroy you? The only thing you can do is face that black unknown, holding on to the hand of Someone who is stronger than you. Hang on to Someone who knows everything: the way through the darkness and how to give you the strength to face this unexpected journey through uncertainty.

The faith you have in God keeps strengthening through your daily time and relationship with Him. You can fully depend on your eternal Father because He loves you. He suffers with His children.

The medical resources, the drugs, and the treatments that will be best for each case—your heavenly Father has already arranged. He knows what will be best.

When we have exercised faith in God and depended on Him in times of peace, we will know how to exercise faith in Him and depend on Him for strength in times of crisis.

Fear may come, but even that we can surmount by the grace and mercy of a God who has plans for our lives—even if they are, as yet, unknown to us. Trust in God will give us a sense of serenity and safety even when we enter the valley of pain. The solution to our challenges and the relief from suffering may be closer than we think.

Let's trust God's grace and mercy to increase even when struggles grow.

Edit Fonseca

September 27

God Will Provide

"Before they call, I will answer;
And while they are still speaking, I will hear."
—Isaiah 65:24, NKJV

In 2004, my husband felt that God was calling him for the sacred ministry. With that goal in mind, we made plans so that he could begin his studies as a theology major in Engenheiro Coelho, São Paulo, Brazil. In order to get the financial resources to cover his college expenses, he sold religious books as a literature evangelist during every vacation. I went with him on some of his trips.

In January 2006, we went to the city of São Joaquim, Santa Catarina, Brazil, where we were scheduled to stay in the local church. When we arrived, however, we saw the church was undergoing a major renovation, so we could not stay there. That night we asked God to prepare us a suitable place to stay so that we could work more peacefully, since our financial situation was not good.

The next morning, after our worship, we went to speak with the city's health director. After introducing ourselves and explaining our work to her, we asked her to provide a place for us to stay. Immediately upon hearing our request, she made some calls and came back with the following news: "Go see the director of the local hospital, Mr. Carlos. He will help you." Mr. Carlos offered us accommodations in the hospital! Though not excited about his offer, we went to see the ward where we would be staying.

Imagine our pleasant surprise to find that this ward was a brand-new hospital wing with, as of yet, unused rooms. They were new and fresh with clean, fragrant bedding and a clean bath. We could not believe what God had prepared for us! But God's blessings were not yet finished. Mr. Carlos also informed us that we could enjoy a free lunch every day at one of the city's facilities. The night before we had simply asked God for a place to sleep. Now He had given us so much more than we had asked! During those vacation days, we were able to save a lot of money and managed to pay for the semester's tuition.

In 2008, to the honor and glory of God, my husband graduated.

When I remember the extraordinary way in which God has led in all things, I am thrilled with the unmistakable evidence that He cares for us, that He hears and answers our prayers, and that He provides for our needs—even before we have asked Him to meet those needs.

María Regina Werneck Mandeli

In the Garden with Jesus

There shall be no night there: They need no lamp nor light of the sun, for the Lord God gives them light. And they shall reign forever and ever.
—*Revelation 22:5, NKJV*

I have admired women of prayer both in the Bible and in my own life: my mother, Sergeneide, and my mother-in-law, Julia. Then there was my beloved grandmother, formerly Maria das Dores (of pain) but now Maria de Jesus (of Jesus), which was her missionary name.

When I was a child, my grandmother came to visit us every year. The weeks she spent with us were unforgettable, with many trips and bedtime stories. She always brought us popcorn and gifts! But the most important thing was her strong and contagious presence.

One Wednesday evening she got dressed as usual, with her white church clothes neatly ironed. She was wearing a side braid and perfume. My sister, Gabrielle, and I had also put on our dresses to go the church. It was cold, but laughter echoed on the dark street and warmed our hearts. In church, before the sermon, a church elder stood up and asked who was in charge of the special music that evening. Silence and hesitation descended over the place.

Then Grandmother Maria de Jesus took my sister and me by the hand and marched toward the pulpit. She opened her hymnal to a hymn, "The Beautiful Garden of Prayer." Her voice was strong, the silence solemn, and our infant voices sang the celestial tune with her.

I remember the words:

> There's a garden where Jesus is waiting,
> There's a place that is wondrously fair;
> For it glows with the light of His presence,
> 'Tis that beautiful garden of prayer.*

As we sang, the church joined us in praise. It was so beautiful.

Back home, Grandma put us to sleep with a sweet "Sleep with the angels." I know I did, because I knew they had sung with us that special evening. That night I dreamed I was with Jesus in the Garden where there will be no more night, nor cold, nor distances, nor sadness. Very soon we will be with the Lord in that place of eternal perfection.

Sarah Suzane Bertolli Gonçalves

---

* Eleanor A. Schroll, "The Beautiful Garden of Prayer," 1920.

The Good Fragrance of Christ

For we are to God the fragrance of Christ among those who are
being saved and among those who are perishing.
—*2 Corinthians 2:15, NKJV*

I really like perfumes, but I especially like a nicely scented body wash. That is why I always went to specialty stores to buy it. But there was a period when my husband and I went through financial problems. We saved by cutting on superfluous purchases. I immediately thought, *There goes my body wash!* I carefully used my last bottle until it was empty.

The next time we went to the supermarket, I went straight to the personal hygiene and beauty section. After smelling several body washes, I selected one, thinking I was saving money by shopping at the market instead of at a specialty shop. Then I had a very strong impression: *I am the One who takes care of all your needs!* Remembering my husband's request to help him save money, I replaced the body wash on the shelf. I would trust the Lord and forget the matter.

But God did not forget me.

On the following day, when I arrived at the university where I was taking classes, I noticed that a classmate had a bag from a beauty store known for its excellent and quality merchandise. After class, she came up to me and said, "I want to give you a present." I was confused because she was not a close friend of mine, and it was not my birthday either. She continued, "I want to give you a gift as a thank you for having helped me in some difficulties I was having with this class's subject matter." I thanked her, sat down, and opened the package. It's a good thing I sat down—so that I didn't fall backward when I saw she'd given me not only a very good body wash but also several other types of soap! How could she have known? I had never said anything about this to anyone.

I started crying because, at that moment, I remembered the impression that I had felt the day before: *I am the One who takes care of all your needs!* I hugged my classmate and told her what had happened. She was also very touched. I am happy because this turn of events gave me the opportunity to witness about God's love as I shared with her the good fragrance of Christ.

It is wonderful to see God's love for us. After all, the God who created the universe and who sustains the world took care of such a small detail in my life. It is worth trusting and serving a wonderful, caring God like this!

Val Baminger Oliveira

Protected

Because you have made the LORD, who is my refuge,
Even the Most High, your dwelling place,
No evil shall befall you,
Nor shall any plague come near your dwelling;
For He shall give His angels charge over you,
To keep you in all your ways.
—*Psalm 91:9–11, NKJV*

The shimmering light reflecting off the .45-caliber handgun blinded me. A man, who had approached under false pretenses, was now pointing the gun at me, inches from my face, and staring with the coldest light-brown eyes I'd ever seen. *What is happening?* My body was present, but my mind was in complete shock. *Am I going to die? Here?* I silently prayed for protection and help. Slowly turning my head, I saw another guy at the rear passenger door of my car with a gun to my friend's head. He was demanding money.

The next few minutes were a blur of purses being passed to the perpetrators. *God, please help us!* I silently continued to pray. By God's grace, neither man ever saw my purse—full of cash, my month's salary destined for paying bills—tucked into the seat next to me. I did not offer it up either! I remember the guy closest to me sneering and saying, "Don't worry, I'm not going to steal your car." After taking what they wanted from my passengers, the two men jumped into a green Ford Expedition with missing rear license plates—and then they were gone.

Though I was in shock, I believe the Lord laid out my driving route the next few minutes. Gradually, we came upon a trail of items belonging to my passenger friends in the middle of a side street. Evidently, the perpetrators had gone through the purses and jackets before tossing them out their window of "their" vehicle (which matched the description, police later told us, of a car stolen earlier that evening). Believe it or not, my friends, who had not been carrying cash, were able to reclaim all of their personal items! Only a sweater and credit card, which my friend canceled, were never found. After filing the police report, we returned home, shaken but thankful. In Daniel's words, "My God sent His angel" (Daniel 6:22, NKJV).

No matter what danger you may find yourself in, God is never too busy to hear your call for help, and He never sleeps. Whom shall you fear with God on your side? I praise Him each time I think of what could have happened—if it had not been for God's amazing grace and power that stepped in and said, "Not so!"

Sherilyn Flowers

The Cost of Service

Now may the God of hope fill you with all joy and peace in believing,
that you may abound in hope by the power of the Holy Spirit.
—*Romans 15:13, NKJV*

When God called me twenty-two years ago to work in women's ministries and travel from country to country to encourage, nurture, and empower my sisters around the world, I knew I had finally come home. Doing this is where I knew God wanted me to be.

There was also the additional blessing of traveling the world and seeing and experiencing different cultures. World travel is something I dreamed of as a child sitting in my geography and history classes, and God made it a reality. I know many of my friends think I have a dream job, and some may even envy what I do. But there is a cost to traveling the world to minister to others. Today as I sit in a hotel room in Almaty, Kazakhstan, I am keenly aware of that cost. To those of us involved in global ministry, the cost can be physical, emotional, and even spiritual. But today I think of the emotional cost.

A few days ago, while in Kyrgyzstan, I met a dear mother and her children. In her arms, the woman lovingly held a ten-month-old baby boy who was suffering from hydrocephalus (water on the brain). As she nursed him, she told of her desire to see him healed. She knew the doctors could help, but her husband did not believe in doctors. Instead he said that only God could heal their son if that was His plan. It broke my heart to see the pain on her dear face as she asked for prayer. We prayed for her and her son, asking God to change the father's mind so that this beautiful boy would have a chance to live the life that God has planned for him.

I could tell you stories of women in abusive situations, women with terminal health challenges, women who struggle with poverty, and women who can see no hope in life. I listen and pray with each one, but the emotional cost is great. Though deeply desirous to be of more help, I must walk away with tear-filled eyes and a heavy heart, surrendering these precious ones to God who alone can help. Oh, I look forward to the day when God promises no more pain or suffering! We will live a life of eternal joy and even forget those painful things in our pasts.

The Word of God is where I find healing for pain I see but can't resolve. God's promises are my strength. The knowledge of heaven to come is my hope. *Come soon, Lord Jesus!*

Heather-Dawn Small

Scars That Save

He was wounded for our transgressions,
He was bruised for our iniquities . . .
And by His stripes we are healed.
—Isaiah 53:5, NKJV

It's October 2, and I don't care that I have to wear a wig. I'm not bothered by the bald scar on the top of my head. On this day, all I have is thanksgiving for one of the miracles in my life—my precious daughter.

Shortly after I married, doctors told me that I would not bear children due to an internal deformity. Not to be defeated, I prayed, begged, and tried until God granted me my firstborn, Samuel, three years later. This gift renewed my determination to try for another. My husband, who was one of four boys, dreamed of having a baby girl. Even after three pregnancy losses, we hoped, prayed, and even had a name for her: Crystal Rose.

More than four years passed since I had my first child. As I worked in a school, I caught ringworm, which is a dreaded but common fungal infection of the skin that is more bothersome than dangerous. I made a quick visit to a dermatologist. Upon examining me, he discovered the fungus on my arms as well as on my scalp. To decide on a course for medication, he asked whether there was the possibility of a pregnancy because the medications would harm the unborn. I responded that there was always a chance. A blood test confirmed that I was indeed carrying a life! We would need to postpone all treatment until we welcomed the baby safely.

The sweetest baby girl arrived on October 2, but the uncontrolled fungus on my head destroyed the skin, which shed all the hair, leaving a huge scar instead. Sometimes I mourn the loss of my gorgeous, thick hair and envy the hairstyles of my sisters and friends. But I don't mourn today. On this day, I marvel over the miracle of my daughter, now a young lady who chooses to love others more than herself.

I wonder about the scars in my Savior's side and palms. When is He most thankful that He, God and King, chose to leave His throne to die for a sinner like me? Does He marvel over me, glad that He died for me? The thought that you and I can make Him happy amazes me. Nothing can change the scars that remain from His suffering even as He rejoices over us.

I'm humbled by my scar that tells of my commitment to my daughter. And I praise God for the scars that remind Him that I, too, am His very own child.

Rose Joseph Thomas

October 3

Head Lice and Hurricanes!—Part 1

Trust in the LORD with all your heart,
And lean not on your own understanding;
In all your ways acknowledge Him,
And He shall direct your paths.
—*Proverbs 3:5, 6, NKJV*

I am a planner. I like to have a general idea of how things are going to go. Basically, I like order. Now that's not too much to ask, is it? On the other hand, I am realistic enough to realize that plans can certainly change and that there may be some flexibility required on my part in the event that my well-thought-out plans—well, you know—change.

One day in July as I was hurriedly finishing up my duties at the eye surgery center, I noticed a text from my husband, asking me to call him as soon as I could. I called and listened to him explain that the president of our area church work wanted to meet with both of us. I jokingly asked my pastor husband, "Honey, what have you done? We must be in trouble!"

The next day we met with our president and discovered that he wanted me to pray about being considered for the role of prayer and women's ministries director for our geographic region. We prayed, of course, and then I humbly agreed to assume these new responsibilities.

After the area church committee voted me in the following August, I hit the ground running. The "planner" in me went forward at full throttle. I planned two upcoming back-to-back weekend women's retreats. Already they loomed on the horizon, and I had much to do!

The first retreat for 250 Spanish-speaking women came off without a hitch. What a blessed, beautiful, and sunny weekend! I breathed a sigh of relief as I geared up for weekend number two, planning for 260 English-speaking women. I was actually feeling rather confident since all the retreat decorations were already in place from the first retreat. To be honest, I was planning on some pretty smooth sailing right into the next weekend.

And then it happened. A random email delivered on the Tuesday before the retreat. I hate to admit it, but I half-heartedly read the genuine concern reflected in the text: "What are your plans for Matthew?" *Matthew? Matthew who?* I responded with a chuckle. But I wasn't laughing when the response came back that Hurricane Matthew was headed for the East Coast and expected to make landfall in North Carolina by retreat weekend.

There's nothing like an emergency to send us to our knees and to let God be in full control.

Cindy Mercer

Head Lice and Hurricanes!—Part 2

Your mercy, O Lord, will hold me up.
In the multitude of my anxieties within me,
Your comforts delight my soul.
—Psalm 94:18, 19, NKJV

I did what I do best—pray as I plan. And the week of Hurricane Matthew, I planned as I prayed! Even though our retreat location was about 150 miles inland, I began bracing for the weather impacts that we would inevitably experience at the retreat.

By Thursday, I had lost count of the phone calls, emails, and text messages that all asked the same question: "Are we still having the retreat?" My response was a hearty *yes*! My hopes began to sag, though, as cancellations increased. Then that same Thursday I learned that the boarding high school my son attended was temporarily shutting down because of a head lice outbreak. All the kids were being sent home. *Really?* This seriously could not be happening! At least, I would have my son at home to help me stuff two hundred registration bags, right?

So early on Friday, I went to the camp for the retreat, loaded down with goodies for the weekend. Cancellations had plummeted our attendance from 260 to 150. Yes, Hurricane Matthew made landfall. Yes, torrential rain and high winds came inland. And, yes, we lost power at the camp for twelve hours. But praise God for generators and rubber boots! I felt more like a disaster relief coordinator that week than a women's ministries director. At one point, I said, "Between head lice and hurricanes, I'm about done in."

But you know what? God did something that I never could have planned. He showed up and blessed us anyway despite the obstacles. There was a spirit of closeness and openness among the attendees that was palpable. Not one woman complained about the absence of electricity or about sloshing around in soggy shoes or even our droopy hairstyles we so proudly displayed.

I learned a lot more about myself and about ministering to women in that one weekend than I will probably learn in a lifetime, thanks to God's plans—instead of my own. Specifically, I committed to begin claiming God's promises much more than I do! I found that women really want to see one another's transparency; in other words, be real and let God help you navigate your life's storms. Even if they include hurricanes and head lice!

Cindy Mercer

October 5

"To Everything There Is a Season"

To everything there is a season,
A time for every purpose under heaven.
—*Ecclesiastes 3:1, NKJV*

Nowadays who stays at home? Is *anybody* at home? How many families sit down together at meals and thank God for their blessings and then take the time to visit with one another? How many families eat complete, nutritious meals at regular times? Do little children have much, if any, regulated structure in their lives? Do adults even? Are the buildings we live in homes or just houses waiting for people to hurry to them so that they can hurry out again?

Most of us work hard. Some of us are then able to purchase time-saving devices we think we need, but in many cases, we often don't have the time to use. And that time we are trying to save, where does it go? Recently, I pondered the reality that time is a gift we all have—a free gift. No one lacks time; it's always available to each of us. Perhaps we need to learn to slow down and then, instead of spending time, *enjoy* it for a change. It is a gift from God.

Try sitting down in a comfy chair and making a list of *times* that are special to you. I did that. Here are times from my list: First, the most precious time I spend every day is that early hour when I sit in a comfortable spot, reach for my Bible, Bible study guide, a devotional book, and my hymnal. Then I start asking my God to stay close to me throughout that day and help me to be a better person. In that special time, I give Jesus my highest praises and glorify His holy name. I may sing a favorite song and then pray for each family member, others on my prayer list, and whomever the Holy Spirit impresses me to lift up. I then study my Bible and read from my devotional book. I look forward to this treasured time every day. It pushes me heavenward to stand fast in Jesus and His Word and to do His will in my life.

Other special times that I need and want are with my sweet husband and precious daughters and my friends. The Sabbath day is also very special time for me, when I go to church and Sabbath School to worship my Lord God and fellowship with friends who love Him too.

Time is a gift from God. I want to both spend it well and enjoy it with Him and others.

May God bless you as you think about how you are using God's gift of time. Let's remember to thank Him for giving us this gift that we can both spend and enjoy in so many memorable ways.

Joyce Meyer

The Beauty of a Woman

Do not let your adornment be merely outward—arranging the hair, wearing gold, or putting on fine apparel—rather let it be the hidden person of the heart, with the incorruptible beauty of a gentle and quiet spirit, which is very precious in the sight of God. For in this manner, in former times, the holy women who trusted in God also adorned themselves, being submissive to their own husbands.
—1 Peter 3:3–5, NKJV

Contrary to what our culture and the media tell us, a woman's beauty is not merely her outer appearance. Advertisers constantly bombard us with ads about products that are supposed to make us more beautiful—as if we are not already beautiful the way we are. They promote skin creams to hide or eliminate wrinkles, dyes to hide the gray in our hair, and makeup that, in some cases, threatens to mask one's real face. The ads for fancy clothing and jewelry imply that these products will make us more attractive.

None of these things are necessarily wrong in themselves, but we shouldn't feel as if we need them all in order to make us more attractive. Sometimes we are concerned about the way we look and make an effort to groom the outward appearance. Yet God desires us to be even more concerned with how we look *inside*—the real us. This is where the real beauty lives. This is where character is fashioned. Having a pretty face, a perfect figure, and nice accessories means nothing in the light of eternity.

I have three children: two sons and one daughter. My daughter definitely looks beautiful, but her real beauty comes from within. This beauty manifests itself in her character, personality, and kind attitudes as she deals with others.

I believe we need to get past being overly concerned with our outward appearance and concentrate more on what's inside.

We can allow the Holy Spirit to beautify us from the inside out. For when we have God's beauty inside, it reflects on the outside. We then have the natural beauty of a godly woman, and that beauty is eternal.

Lord, may I reflect Your beauty, the beauty of a godly life. Help me care not so much about what's on the outside but, rather, what's inside.

Shakuntala Chandanshive

God Is Into Ironing

That is why, for Christ's sake, I delight in weaknesses. . . .
For when I am weak, then I am strong.
—*2 Corinthians 12:10, NIV*

You make known to me the path of life;
you will fill me with joy in your presence, with eternal pleasures at
your right hand.
—*Psalm 16:11, NIV*

I never thought that I would get such a profound spiritual lesson from ironing a shirt. One day while I was doing my routine ironing, I was praising God that I had gotten a pretty ivory-colored ruffled blouse that week. I was amazed at how God had worked out my weekly schedule and budget to cover not only my expenses but also have this special garment. Halfway through the ironing of this blouse, I saw a brown streak where I'd just ironed. In horror, I rushed my new blouse to the sink to wash off the spot. But when I returned to iron this blouse, the same thing happened—again and again! I cleaned the iron and its steam openings before ironing another shirt. No brown spots. So I returned to my ivory blouse. To my disbelief, the same thing started happening again.

This thought came to my mind: *No matter how much you work and want your life to be perfect, there are some things that are just out of your control. All you can do is your best. Then trust that God's perfection will cover your imperfections. That's all that matters.* I thanked God for helping me to understand that we cannot control the bad things that happen, but we surely can choose on whom we will depend. So I finished ironing my new blouse—with one brown spot that I couldn't get out. I decided I would wear this blouse, a spiritual lesson, to church.

If we ask God for His guidance, He is faithful to provide. If we need understanding, He is loving and will help us. We may be weak; yet covered by God's grace, we can be strong in Him.

Knowing that God takes care of me in that way makes me so happy! So every time I wear that blouse, that remaining brown spot will be a reminder that even if sometimes I have stains from sin in my life, God is there to turn them into something positive and help me to grow from those experiences. I'm glad His Spirit was at the ironing board with me that day.

Lord, thank You because we don't have to fight to be strong. In fact, whatever strength we have always comes from You and Your presence in our lives!

Yvita Antonette Villalona Bacchus

Message From a King

Hezekiah received the envoys
and showed them all that was in his storehouses. . . .
There was nothing in his palace
or in all his kingdom that Hezekiah did not show them.
—*2 Kings 20:13, NIV*

Have you always been a faithful witness for God? If not, we can learn an important lesson from the life of King Hezekiah. He fell gravely ill; his illness was apparently associated with a serious boil. When the prophet Isaiah told Hezekiah that he would die of this sickness, Isaiah also instructed the king to put his house in order. Hezekiah turned his face to the wall, weeping and pleading with God to heal him. He reminded God how he had walked before Him in truth and with a perfect heart. He had tried to do what was right in the sight of God.

The Lord heard the king's supplications. Isaiah assured Hezekiah that in addition to God's healing him, He would grant the king another fifteen years of life. For him, God turned back the shadow on a sundial by ten degrees. The king was healed.

When the Babylonian king heard of this miraculous healing, he sent presents with envoys to visit him. But instead of sharing with the Babylonian envoys all the amazing details of God's special healing touch on—and extension of—his life, King Hezekiah showed them all the treasures that he had in his treasury. Sadly, Hezekiah, not God, received all the glory that day. And his prideful choice had serious national consequences in the years to come.

One commentator wrote,

> The story of Hezekiah's failure to prove true to his trust . . . is fraught with an important lesson for all. Far more than we do, we need to speak . . . of the mercy and loving-kindness of God, of the matchless depths of the Saviour's love. . . .
> . . . What is our influence over these fellow travelers?
> . . . Every day, our words and acts are making impressions upon those with whom we associate.*

Have you used every opportunity to share with others how God has blessed in your life? *Lord, help us to take advantage of every opportunity that we have to be a witness for You because it may be the only chance that we have.*

Betty Lyngdoh

---

* Ellen G. White, *Prophets and Kings* (Nampa, ID: Pacific Press®, 1997), 347, 348.

A Tongue of Faith and Victory

Let God be true, but every human being a liar.
—*Romans 3:4, NIV*

I don't know about you, but sometimes the bad news reports and negative chatter or comments of others around me can be quite overwhelming. Every now and then, there are times that the negativity tries to creep back into my mind to remind me of what's *not* happening, what's *not* right, and what's *not* good right now. It is during those times that I sense and recognize that the enemy is hard at work, trying to get me to doubt and question what I know and believe about Christ and the Word of God. Having suffered and overcome depression years ago while in college, I refuse, in Jesus' name, to go down into that deep, dark pit ever again.

What if I told you that we may be the ones holding ourselves back in Christ, keeping ourselves from experiencing the joy and the victory that God wants for us and has already promised us? If you were to admit the truth, I'm sure that, at some time or another, you and other Christians you know have been guilty of magnifying a problem *over* the power of our Omnipotent God. We have doubted that a problem could be remedied because we believed more in the plans of Satan and his followers as being successful than we did in the favor of our Almighty God to protect us from hurt, harm, or danger. We have walked through days—dare I say, even our whole lives?—with downcast faces and negative words. We have declared that life is not fair and that things will never change for the better, not realizing that we have made a detrimental choice. This is due to our sinful human nature as we engage with and believe those things that we experience with our five senses more than we believe in the holy Word of God.

God's Word has declared to us that "death and life are in the power of the tongue: and they that love it shall eat the fruit thereof" (Proverbs 18:21, KJV). Deuteronomy 30:19 says, "I call heaven and earth to record this day against you, that I have set before you life and death, blessing and cursing: therefore choose life, that both thou and thy seed may live" (KJV).

We must begin taking the power of our tongues very seriously and choose to use our words responsibly. We are to "walk by faith, not by sight" (2 Corinthians 5:7, KJV).

It is only then that we can begin to experience true joy and victory in Jesus.

Shondolyn Young Richardson

With Christ, We Can!

I can do all things through Christ who strengthens me.
—*Philippians 4:13, NKJV*

This is God's desire for your life: a healthy body, mind, and soul. But the path to what we call "wholly" healthy is not always an easy one. It requires choices and decisions. Sometimes we need to make changes in long-term lifestyle and thinking habits, getting rid of those not conducive to vibrant lives. As you face the challenge of living your life according to God's instructions, make this your motto: "I can do all things through Christ who strengthens me" (Philippians 4:13, NKJV). Now is the time to change to a healthier lifestyle.

In 2006, I was diagnosed with cancer; but with much prayer and guidance from the Holy Spirit, I chose to do alternative treatments instead of the conventional way with chemotherapy and radiation. I considered this route after seeing how my brother suffered.

At a wellness center, my daily routine included several hydrotherapy treatments, physical exercise, and a spiritual renewal. Upon returning home, I put into practice the principles I had learned. I concentrated on living the eight natural laws of health, reordering my life to eliminate stressful activities, preparing only natural and unrefined foods, exercising outdoors daily in the fresh air and sunshine, drinking an adequate amount of water, continuing with the hydrotherapy and massage treatments, not overdoing it, learning to relax, and getting adequate rest and good quality sleep. Daily I renew my walk with Jesus and my trust in God. He has truly blessed me.

In my daily prayers, I say, "Lord, I want to do more than just tell people about what I have learned. I want to be a testimony and an encouragement too." When people face trials and call on supportive friends (or we *are* the willing, but weak friend), it is worth remembering that our prayers, encouragements, and advice do not always convey the needed message of support, but our faithful presence does. Sometimes being there is the most valuable gift we can give another.

Life is a gift from God; live it, enjoy it, celebrate it, and fulfill it.

Camilla E. Cassell

October 11

The Lord Is Willing to Hear

He will fulfill the desire of them that fear him:
he also will hear their cry, and will save them.
—*Psalm 145:19, KJV*

I come from a very large Christian family of five sisters (Rhoda, Deborah, Myrtle, Hazel, and Rebecca) and two boys (Michael and Danny Boy). Danny was the youngest of us all and everyone's favorite.

Once Danny attended a party. While there, he fell down and had to be rushed to the hospital.

At the hospital, his doctors diagnosed him with aseptic meningitis. Fortunately, the infection had not reached his brain. But he became paralyzed from the neck down. After that, he had to be carried everywhere. He was only fifteen years old but was almost six feet tall. And he had a strapping personality.

You can imagine how we all, as a family, went immediately to our knees upon hearing the news of our Danny. My widowed mother was a lady of faith and a faithful woman of prayer. One of my sisters and I were in different locations. I rushed to Hyderabad, India, and saw my brother confined to bed with tears rolling down.

With the whole family together at this point, we followed the lead of our mother. Though the doctors treating Danny were not sure whether or when he would walk again, our mother began praying, day and night, that Danny's health and mobility would be restored.

Then the miracle started. First, Danny was able to move one of his hands and then his legs. Believe it or not, Danny was not only standing but walking just three months later! When he finally stood before our family doctor, the physician was overwhelmed.

And the rest of the story? In 2001, Daniel (Danny) married Della Shalini. They have two daughters: Angel, who is fifteen, and Michelle, who is eight.

My dear mother, Mrs. Lalitha Reddy, has passed away. Yet she has left behind a legacy of unceasing prayer and strong faith. Her life was an open book, and we seven children all have a part of her in our hearts and our Christian walk.

Lord, help us to always focus our lives on You through faith and prayer.

Rhoda Shinge

Saved by an Angel

The angel of the LORD encampeth
round about them that fear him, and delivereth them.
—*Psalm 34:7, KJV*

I t was my third year at a Christian college in Alabama where I was a nursing major. I was living in Carter Hall. I had my own room that quarter, room 317, because my roommate had to leave school for lack of funds.

It was nice having a room to myself because I had shared a room all of my life. I had the bed next to the window and the bookshelf was on the wall to the right of my bed. Most of my nursing textbooks were huge and were very heavy to carry. One day I happened to notice that the bookshelf was leaning a bit toward my bed, but I didn't give it much thought. Each day after class I would come back to my room and place the books on the bookshelf, not really paying attention to the fact that it seemed to lean a little further each day.

One night I went to bed as usual. I really don't remember what happened after that. All I know is that I was suddenly in the hallway screaming. Girls came out of their rooms to see what all the commotion was about.

"What happened?" several asked. "Are you OK?" "Did you have a bad dream?"

These were questions to which I had no answer! I had no idea how I'd gotten into the hallway or why I was standing there, screaming and shaking like a leaf.

Then after a while, I ventured back into my dorm room. Only then did I discover what had propelled me out into the hallway. The bookshelf had fallen off the wall and onto my bed, along with my heavy nursing textbooks!

That's when it hit me. Not the bookshelf, but rather, a realization. My guardian angel had somehow taken me out of the bed, opened the door, and left me standing in the hallway. My guardian angel saved my life that night!

Psalm 91:11, 12 makes this promise: "For he shall give his angels charge over thee, to keep thee in all thy ways. They shall bear thee up in their hands, lest thou dash thy foot against a stone" (KJV). Or in my case, lest I get hit on the head by a falling bookcase!

I thank God for my guardian angel that is always protecting me.

Deniece G. Anderson

Don't Lose Sight

Wherefore seeing we also are compassed about
with so great a cloud of witnesses, let us lay aside every weight,
and the sin which doth so easily beset us, and let us run
with patience the race that is set before us.
—*Hebrews 12:1, KJV*

In the book of Exodus, chapter 14, we find the children of Israel afraid because the Egyptian army was pursuing them. They accused Moses of having taken them into the wilderness to die (verses 11, 12). After listening to their accusations, Moses replied, "Fear ye not, stand still, and see the salvation of the Lord, which he will show you to day: for the Egyptians whom ye have seen to day, ye shall see them again no more for ever" (verse 13, KJV).

A few months ago I decided that I wanted to incorporate running into my exercise routine. When I shared my thoughts with my friend Jessica, she eagerly replied, "You should! I will help you!" During the first week of running, Jessica had me start at what she thought was a good beginning pace for me. After watching me, Jessica said, "Robin, you can do more, but you are your own biggest hindrance. You have a mind-set of defeat before you start the run." By the second week, Jessica told me that she believed I could complete a lap around the track, nonstop. As we began our regular warm-up on a nearby hill that overlooked the track, Jessica said, "Robin, look at the track. Don't think about getting out of breath or becoming tired, but rather picture yourself completing the course."

Oftentimes we get so engulfed with life's distractions and with interferences, which might include other's perceptions about us or our own negative mind-set, that we, like the children of Israel, forget and lose sight of the course God has marked for us. Hebrews 12:1, 2 gives us this reminder: "Let us lay aside every weight, and the sin which doth so easily beset us, and let us run with patience the race that is set before us, looking unto Jesus the author and finisher of our faith; who for the joy that was set before him endured the cross, despising the shame, and is set down at the right hand of the throne of God" (KJV).

Lord, You see and know us individually. I pray this morning for the mind-set of Christ, "who for the joy that was set before him, endured the cross, despising the shame." As we run life's course today, help us to do it with You on our minds and without a murmur or complaint. Amen.

Robin C. Cleary

My Brother, My Sister

*If a brother or sister is poorly clothed
and lacking in daily food, and one of you says to them,
"Go in peace, be warmed and filled,"
without giving them the things needed for the body,
what good is that?*
—James 2:15–17, ESV

feel like we should turn back. I mean, we have several backpacks in our trunk for just this reason," I told my husband as we turned off the highway exit and onto a large street.

"Let's do it then," my husband immediately replied. I pulled into an empty parking lot and ran in my church heels to open the trunk and pull out a backpack. A couple of weeks earlier my husband and I had been impressed by the Spirit to no longer drive by anyone who was in need, especially since neither of us is in the habit of carrying cash. So my husband ordered several large backpacks. After asking the church's food bank for supplies, we packed them with food, water, boxed milk, toothpaste, and several other things, along with two slim Christian books. We carried a few backpacks for a week, but we didn't meet anyone in need. Then, as I was stressing about not getting to church on time, especially since my husband and I were both in the choir (and we were already cutting it close to perform with them), we exited the highway, and there he was: a man, standing in the chilly morning air, with a cardboard sign asking for some help. My husband and I were in the middle of a conversation, the light was green, and I admit that, for a moment, I debated whether we had the time.

So there I was, in my Sabbath heels, picking out a backpack from the trunk, getting on the highway in the opposite direction, exiting, and getting back onto the road in the right direction. We finally got off the highway so that I could pull up next to the exit where this man stood. We all have God-given talents, and while mine is not talking to random strangers, my husband's is. I sat in the driver's seat as my husband approached this man with a backpack and a heart full of empathy. I watched with watery eyes as they talked, and then they inclined their heads in prayer. When my husband returned to the car, I learned the man's name was Jack. Jack had been hit by a truck and was going through a rough time.

That morning as I sang with the choir, my heart was full of joy at having been given that opportunity to serve.

Sandra P. Gordon

Hugs From God

Being confident of this very thing, that He who has begun a good work in you will complete it until the day of Jesus Christ.
—*Philippians 1:6, NKJV*

As I was spending time with Jesus one morning, I looked over at my little table and saw six books. I realized that each one had a bookmark in it. Some of the books had the bookmark halfway through the book, others were a third of the way through, and some were almost at the end. Had I really started reading all of these books and not finished even one of them? After a big sigh of disgust and guilt, I methodically looked at each one and thought, *Which one should I finish first?* I decided it should be the one someone in my small group had given me to read a while ago. I remember really getting into this book and how the person who let me borrow it had underlined practically the whole book, because he loved it so much.

I picked it up to read it again, and guess what? The very next chapter was exactly an answer to a prayer I had prayed to God that very morning. It spoke to me loud and clear, and I knew this was a hug from God.

Sometimes we look at our lives and see only chaos, uncompleted projects, failures, and challenges that divert us. But it is good to step back, look at your life, and recalibrate. It might be something as small as deciding to finish what you started. God has not abandoned you! Even in the midst of chaos He is there with a little word of encouragement, a hug, or a gentle push ahead. Wherever you find yourself, He can move you forward in love and encouragement.

"Being confident of this very thing, that He who has begun a good work in you will complete it until the day of Jesus Christ" (Philippians 1:6, NKJV). That is really a faith statement! Put your name in this promise today. If you have accepted the gospel of Jesus Christ, He has begun a good work in you. As you spend time with Him every day in His Word, in prayer, and fellowshiping together with other believers, He is in the process of completing that good work until He comes. Be assured of that! Say this verse out loud. Maybe someone will hear you and think you're nuts. Or maybe someone will hear you and ask you to explain it. Who knows?

I am not going to worry so much about my unfinished books because I will eventually read them. I am going to wake up each day and praise God for what He has started and will complete!

Lee Lee Dart

Being Intentional

The LORD of hosts has sworn saying,
"Surely, just as I have intended so it has happened,
and just as I have planned so it will stand."
—Isaiah 14:24, NASB

If you're like me, you've shaken your head in disbelief at how fast time passes and how quickly the calendar months change as the years fly by. The older I've gotten, the more I'm realizing that life on this earth is so very short in comparison to eternity with Jesus. And there are some areas in this life that are near and dear to me, so if the word *intentional* is not part of my vocabulary, I'm afraid I will have regrets about missed opportunities.

Recovering from a recent flu bug gave me plenty of time to think and read. The word *intentional* popped into my mind. If I'm not intentional with my marriage, grown children, ministry, and certain relationships, there will be no time for them. They may get overlooked or passed by. Like my marriage. My husband and I love each other, but it can be hard to carve out time for just the two of us—to really communicate, to do fun things together, to grow in our understanding of each other, and to cherish each other. The same goes for our adult children who don't live nearby. Sure, we chat on the phone, text, and email, but being together in person is like the icing on the cake. Also, doing outreach as a couple is important to my husband and me. My husband is a pastor, so he's involved in many ways with church members and community folks. I work full time, but I still need to engage with others around me. And then there are other family relationships that need to be nurtured.

So my husband and I became intentional about these areas and came up with specifics that would enhance what is important to us. For our marriage, we intentionally do something together about once a week, such as a work project, fun date, and even outreach activities. Once a quarter we intentionally go somewhere to eat or stay overnight.

I know the Lord Jesus Christ was, and is, intentional about us. He intentionally made the choice to leave heaven and come to this earth on a rescue mission. He intentionally gave up a "rich lifestyle" for a life of poverty. Everything was well thought out and planned; a part of the intentional gift that love gave us— the Lord Jesus. And as we gaze upon His face and realize the depths of that intentional love, our hearts melt and our dearest thoughts will be of Him.

Valerie Hamel Morikone

Fearfully and Wonderfully Made!

I will praise thee;
for I am fearfully and wonderfully made:
marvellous are thy works.
—*Psalm 139:14, KJV*

It was early spring and the perfect afternoon for a walk out in nature. My children and I felt rather adventurous, and we explored newly discovered areas of the nature reserve close to our home. It was fun walking on the old dam walls and scrambling up the low ones.

The natural law of gravity, however, proved its veracity that afternoon in a very painful way—for me, anyway. First, my not-so-young anymore body went up one of the walls. So far, so good. Then it was time for it to go back down again. My children performed what looked like a very easy jump back down the wall.

I'm sure I can do this, I told myself. The moment I landed, however, I knew that I had made a mistake! Ouch! That hurt, and it still does!

As I listened to an audiobook yesterday, with my injured foot still in its brace, something I heard really caught my attention. It went like this: "If a human being is wounded or breaks a bone, nature begins at once to repair the injury. Even before the need exists, the healing agencies are in readiness; and as soon as a part is wounded, every energy is bent to the work of restoration."*

Just imagine that: "Every energy is bent to the work of restoration"! Truly, we are wonderfully and marvelously made!

We have all sustained injuries (some of them as a result of our own doing) or have experienced illness at some point. Yet how faithful our bodies are at the job of restoration! It is our privilege to assist nature in its appointed course by giving our bodies what they need most in times of illness or injury. In the case of my injury—at the time of this writing—I need to give my body more of the rest it needs. And I can also eat certain types of food to help speed up the healing process.

And most important, I can be *thankful* for this marvelous machinery and remain in awe of a great God and Master Designer! A thankful, cheerful heart brings healing to the bones (see Proverbs 17:22)!

Belinda Solomon

---

* Ellen G. White, *Education* (Mountain View, CA: Pacific Press®, 1903), 113.

Living With Hands Open

*"For whoever would save his life will lose it,
but whoever loses his life for my sake will find it."*
—Matthew 16:25, ESV

Recently, my kids and I watched the movie *A Christmas Carol* in the middle of summer. (Don't judge us!) The story features a miserly character willing to sacrifice relationships and comfort to amass wealth. He lives with hands closed, tightly grasping things in clenched fists and starving heart.

The Bible contains a plethora of characters grasping tightly to stuff. The rich young ruler is one such story (Luke 18:18–25). He's studied scrolls, followed rules, and observed ceremonies. He's rich and has a picture-perfect life. Then there's Jesus: simple, common, living hand to mouth. But His hands spread wide open, giving with gratitude, joy, peace, and grace. The rich young ruler, with all his pious comfort, sees something in Jesus that he desperately needs—peace. A way to calm stormy doubts that rise up when night closes in.

"What must I do to be saved?" He's expecting self-salvation solutions. Imagine his horror when Jesus says, "Open your hands; release your death grip on life!" By asking him to surrender all, Jesus isn't talking just about physical comforts. He's asking this ambitious man to release his hold on the traditions, prejudices, and rules that govern his life. To walk with hands open in complete surrender, trust, and service. The ruler went away sad, with hands remaining tightly closed.

Hands-closed living surrounds us. But peace is never found in clenched hands. And salvation has never been about what we can do. Jesus always lived with hands open, raised in blessing, thanksgiving, and trust that came from complete surrender to His Father of every need, conflict, and storm. Open hands extended to those He encountered in everyday living. Hands that offered grace, healing, comfort, and peace without regard to what He received in return.

As His disciples, we are called to live that same life: surrendering all. Offering gratitude even in the impossible. Trusting that God's ways are not our ways (see Isaiah 55:8, 9). Meeting messy life with grace, forgiveness, and hope. Allowing our faith to unfold in a life-giving relationship with God.

What do you hold with clenched hands? What will it take to place these things in God's hands? How will living with hands open in praise, surrender, and gratitude change your life, your relationships, and your spirituality?

Tina Shorey

October 19

The Gift of Peace

Depart from evil and do good; seek peace and pursue it.
—*Psalm 34:14, NKJV*

My childhood was a wonderful time. Our parents were involved in our lives, carefully teaching us responsibility and many skills. We moved to the foothills, where we lived on ranches. Besides learning, we had so much fun with pets and ponies and camping and fishing. We were in the youth group at church. It was a happy, peaceful time.

But when I became a teen, I got caught up in the things other kids (much cooler than I) were doing. And I lost sight of solid values when I joined the wrong crowd. Over time, I made seriously poor choices and never finished college, which is a loss I would regret.

Later, as a young mother, I became reacquainted with the Jesus I knew as a child. I was married to someone I trusted and loved, but it all fell apart, as did a following marriage to a man who later died.

But by then, I knew that my hope was in Jesus, my Savior. Yet all the while, I was still struggling, without much money, to raise three kids to be Christians. I held tightly to Christ's gentle hand and cherished His forgiving Spirit. In so doing, I continued to learn deeper truths from the Bible.

I tell this about my life because I want to encourage you who are struggling in your walk. I want to encourage you to have faith in the only One who can protect and shield you, guide and comfort you. Only He can finally bring you to that place of peace again. If you've never had peace, He will reveal it to you through His patient love. The "still small voice" still speaks today (1 Kings 19:12, KJV), helping us on our journey heavenward, where we will experience perfect joy and redemption. The Bible says, "You will keep him in perfect peace, whose mind is stayed on You, because he trusts in You" (Isaiah 26:3, NKJV).

I grew and was changed by the work of the Holy Spirit. I became a worker in the church, teaching children for about fifty years. I also taught math in a Christian school. This was a special gift from God because I had always wanted to become a teacher.

Sisters, reach out today, and Jesus will rush to greet you and share with you the promise of His peaceful kingdom. He will withhold nothing good from His cherished daughters.

Kathy Peterson

Traveling Mercy—Part 1

The angel of the LORD encamps around those who fear him,
and he delivers them.
—*Psalm 34:7, NIV*

I travel frequently in connection with my work in women's ministries, mostly by myself. All my life I've been fearful of being alone in strange places, especially at night, but I have learned to rely on the Lord to protect me when I am traveling on His business. Often this places me in circumstances I would normally avoid, such as airport and hotel parking lots between midnight and five o'clock in the morning, traveling in foreign countries by myself, and simply being an obviously solitary woman in a hotel.

I will never forget one instance of God's protection when I made a wrong turn—a very wrong turn. After a sleepless night in a hotel in an unfamiliar city, I checked out at four-thirty in the morning and headed to the airport in the rain. On the way to the rental-car return, I turned onto what I thought was a street, but ten feet later the pavement ended and there I was—on a railroad track with the car tires straddling a rail. I tried to back up, but the tires got stuck in six inches of gravel surrounding the tracks. I was totally helpless. I offered a quick prayer, "Now what, Lord?"

It amazes me how in moments of crisis God puts astonishingly logical thoughts in my mind, not only giving me a plan of action but also keeping me from panicking. In this instance, He reminded me that since I didn't know when a train would come, staying in the car where it was dry was not an option. I had to abandon the car and get to safety. I collected my luggage and walked the short distance to the sidewalk where I called the rental-car agency to let them know their car was stuck on the railroad track. The voice on the other end informed me that it was my problem, not theirs, and that I should call the police immediately.

As I waited for the police on that deserted, rain-pounded street, I put away my useless umbrella and simply prayed for protection. Ten minutes later not one, but two police cars arrived. A young officer politely offered to let me wait in the back seat while he assessed the situation. He determined the car had not suffered any apparent damage and called a tow truck.

Actually seeing God at work in response to my prayers reminded me that there is *no* problem too big or complex for Him to resolve! Perhaps we need to remember that more often.

Carla Baker

October 21

Traveling Mercy—Part 2

The Lord is full of compassion and mercy.
—*James 5:11, NIV*

Sitting in the back seat of a police car was a new experience for me. As I waited for the tow truck, as grateful as I was for the shelter from the rain, I felt uneasy. The molded plastic seat was quite low to the floorboard, and there were bars on the windows and no door handles. Taking no chances, I kept the door open slightly while the police officer gently questioned me about how I came to be on the railroad track at 4:45 A.M. When I explained that I was following GPS instructions to the airport and thought I had turned onto a street, he asked whether I had been "partying" all night! I responded that I don't drink and had been attending a religious convention. Polite but unconvinced, he asked to see my driver's license. Thankfully, he didn't write a ticket.

As we waited for the tow truck, I expressed concern that a train might come along and hit my rental car (for which I would have to pay). The police officer said, "We've already notified the railroad, and all trains on that track have been stopped." I thought, *Thank You, Lord.*

Whether from mild shock or from embarrassment having caused such a bizarre situation that was affecting so many, I found myself chattering nonstop to the officer. "Your partner in the other car doesn't have to wait with us. I'm sure he's free to take care of other police business." The officer calmly responded, "We stay together." Undeterred, I asked the officer's name, told him I would pray for him, and informed him the police department in his city was wonderful. He was patient and didn't seem to mind my babbling.

After a very long twenty minutes, the tow truck arrived and pulled my car off the track and onto the street. The truck driver seemed to take pity on me and tested the car, pronouncing it drivable. What a relief! Then he gave me directions to the rental-car return. After thanking the police officer again for his kindness, I was on my way, arriving at the rental-car return just in time to catch the shuttle to the airport.

At the airport, God, who delights in showing compassion to His children, had one more tender mercy for me. Although I had long since given up on catching my flight, I discovered upon reaching the gate that my plane had not yet left! As I rushed onto the plane, breathless, bedraggled, I marveled again at God's amazing grace—even when we make mistakes.

Carla Baker

Walking in His Peace (When God Said Go)

"Go in peace." . . .
"For the LORD is watching over your journey."
—*Judges 18:6, NLT*

In 2014, my husband and I were part of a group of medical and nursing professionals who accepted an invitation to attend a nursing conference in Monrovia, Liberia. It would be hosted by a Christian university in collaboration with the Liberian Ministry of Health. The aim of the conference was to provide updates on different nursing topics identified by the host country and also to distribute medical supplies and school supplies to an orphanage. We were to depart May 21 and return on June 1. As the departure date drew near, an Ebola outbreak was identified in Guinea, West Africa, and eventually crossed the border into rural Liberia.

Three weeks before our departure I visited my physician, who advised me against taking the trip. Since I was the keynote speaker for the conference, I discussed my travel plans with my son, who is a physician. He also advised us not to make the trip. I explained my predicament to two pastors, who prayed with me to make the right decision. I told God that if He saw I would be in danger, then would He please allow my airline-ticket money to be refunded. Days passed, and I heard nothing from the airlines. I trusted God would protect us and made the decision to travel.

At peace with the situation, we made the trip, had a very successful conference, and returned before the Ebola virus reached the capital of Monrovia.

God can provide protection when we are on His mission. His Word says, "For he will rescue you from every trap and protect you from deadly disease. . . . For he will order his angels to protect you wherever you go" (Psalm 91:3, 11, NLT). Furthermore, "Don't worry about anything; instead, pray about everything. . . . His peace will guard your hearts and minds as you live in Christ Jesus" (Philippians 4:6, 7, NLT).

After arriving back home, we learned of cases of Ebola in Monrovia. We were also informed that the room where we had held the conference had been set on fire by someone whose son died of Ebola and who was accusing the health officials of spreading the virus.

Every day while on the trip, I had walked in God's peace, knowing that His promises never fail. Let us continue to trust Him every day of our lives and pray for those countries still suffering the ravaging effects of the deadly Ebola virus.

Lydia D. Andrews

"What Is That in Your Hand?"

Then the LORD asked him, "What is that in your hand?"
"A shepherd's staff," Moses replied.
—*Exodus 4:2, NLT*

For my devotional one morning I'd read about hands and how important they are for reaching out to help others. That same morning God provided an opportunity for me to reach out and touch my neighbor. She and her family had moved onto our street several months before. I intended to go by to welcome her and share a devotional book. My plan was to put it in a pretty little bag and have it ready for delivery, but something always came up to prevent me from carrying out my plan.

One morning I opened the garage door and decided to go walking back and forth in my driveway and on the street in front of my house to get some exercise. It was then that I saw my neighbor putting letters in her mailbox. I called out to her, "Hello, neighbor! How are you? I've been meaning to come by to welcome you, but I kept putting it off for one reason or another. I don't bake cookies, and I hate to cook, but I do write, so I was planning to share a devotional book with you."

She laughed and said, "That's nice." We came closer as we chatted. She shared that she had moved from Milwaukee and that her new job schedule doesn't allow her to attend Sunday School and she misses that. She hoped to change jobs so that she could go back to church.

I told her that my prayer partner and I usually prayed at about five-thirty in the morning. We would pray for God to grant her wish. I also shared the devotional thought I'd read earlier about the importance of hands and how we can use them to reach out and touch or give someone a hug. Right then, I reached out and hugged her and said, "Welcome to our neighborhood." She responded, "Thank you!" Before we parted, I told her that now it would be a lot easier to give her the gift. I am thankful to God for providing me with the opportunity to meet my new neighbor.

As we live our daily lives, we don't know how far reaching our impact will be on the people we meet. I pray that God will always provide opportunities to sow seeds of kindness: smiles, greetings, hugs, or even a book. Who knows? It may be just what a weary person needs along his or her Christian journey. May God use your hand today to touch someone for Him!

Shirley C. Iheanacho

So What's my Value—Really?

So you are . . . God's child; and since you are his child,
God has made you also an heir.
—*Galatians 4:7, NIV*

I notice on the calendar that the appointment for my annual checkup is in a few days. Then I remember that my doctor likes for me to go to the lab the week ahead for the blood draw before I see him. At the time of my appointment, he and I both have in hand a printout of my lab results. It's a paper with medical terms (which I don't understand) on the left and the appropriate range for good health on the right. The center column always catches my eye: "Your Value."

My mind wanders from the numbers on the page that I don't understand to consider my value in God's sight. When I lived in the girls' dormitory at a midwestern Christian college, there was a large mosaic on the wall in the lobby with a Bible verse that read, "The King's daughter is all glorious within" (Psalm 45:13, NASB). My elementary years were spent in Canada, and I grew up singing "God Save the Queen." I've always had a fascination with the royal family, so reading the Bible verse that called me a King's daughter every day caused me to straighten my posture and put a smile on my face as I went to class.

Some days women struggle to feel valuable to anybody. Even accomplished, competent women have down days. But here's a constant that will not change: "I have engraved you on the palms of my hands" (Isaiah 49:16, NIV). Wow! Now that's exciting! My name on God's hand can't be washed off, scrubbed off, or bleached off. That's even better than a tattoo! My name is there for keeps! He promises that He won't forget us ever!

Read what God said about you:

"I have upheld [you] since your birth,
and have carried [you] since you were born.
Even to your old age and gray hairs
I am he, I am he who will sustain you.
I made you and I will carry you" (Isaiah 46:3, 4, NIV).

What more could we want?

"Yet to all who did receive him, to those who believed in his name, he gave the right to become children of God" (John 1:12, NIV). You know, part of the royal family—a King's daughter! Now stand up straight and smile!

Roxy Hoehn

October 25

"Beware of Dogs!"

For false Christs and false prophets shall rise, and shall shew signs
and wonders, to seduce, if it were possible, even the elect.
—Mark 13:22, KJV

She is not your wife! If you insist on keeping her, she will destroy you! You will never recover from this disease." These were the harsh words coming from someone I will call Pastor Sanvi to Emmanuel, his faithful church member. Pastor Sanvi, regarded as a mighty charismatic pastor, was consulted once a week by people searching for the revelation of hidden things.

But Pastor Sanvi had a secret. Emmanuel's marital relationship would be the fifth one he would destroy. He didn't even seem to take into account the impact the breakup would have on Emmanuel's four children. Emmanuel had been married to Adja for ten years—ten years of hard labor for her, ten years of patience, and ten years of love and sharing. Pastor Sanvi had just broken such a union with one of his "revelations" and without any regret. Adja found refuge with an old childhood friend who agreed to keep her for a little while. Unemployed, Adja was neglected by her family and community. Without consulting her, Adja's brothers-in-law separated her from her children, whom they divided up like so many puppies and took them to their homes.

Betrayed, disappointed, and troubled, Adja burst into tears—the kind of tears shed by all disillusioned women. Through it all, however, she did not forget her Maker. She fought her battles on her knees. She prayed His promises. With Psalm 68 open before her, she pleaded, "Oh, God of Israel. You say You are Father to the fatherless and Judge of widows. You set the solitary in families. So please remember me. Do not let me down, I beseech You. We see we have been listening to the devil's agent—a false prophet whose main mission is to divide families. My God, do not allow this mischief! Save my family in the mighty name of Jesus! Amen." This prayer was the turning point in Adja's life.

Dear sister, maybe you or someone you know is being led astray by a false prophet, someone who gives counsel that does not agree with the Bible. I encourage you to go down on your knees, as did Adja, and claim the unfailing promises of our Lord. Always keep in mind that there are dogs and evil workers in this world. You are in the midst of wolves. Therefore, be wise as serpents, and the Lord your God will deliver you from every snare of the evil one.

Koulibaly N'gandia Diata Epse Diarrassouba

God Will Take Care of You

And it shall come to pass, that before they call, I will answer;
and while they are yet speaking, I will hear.
—Isaiah 65:24, KJV

It was July 1995. My husband and I were en route with a tour group to our denomination's quinquennial world church gathering, held that time in Utrecht, Netherlands. The first stop was London, England. Instead of taking the traditional tour, which I had done several times, I opted to spend the time with my family who resided there.

After the denomination's meetings were over, we embarked on an eight-country whirlwind tour. We arrived in Venice, Italy, on July 12. This date happened to be our anniversary. Several of my family members called to extend their best wishes.

On July 13, I received several messages that my family was trying to get in touch with me. This seemed unusual, and my sixth sense moved into first gear. By the time I was able to speak to a family member, I already suspected troubling news. I was informed that my stepfather had succumbed to a massive heart attack.

Our tour group would be in London within a matter of days before returning to the States, so we approached the airline to negotiate a change in itinerary. We were informed we would have to purchase two one-way tickets from London to the States. We were not prepared for this added expense. All members of my family began praying for a reasonable solution.

We made the decision to remain in London and leave the matter in God's hands. Before we reached our destination, however, the airline had called to let us know that we needed to pay only one hundred dollars for the ticket change.

On the day of our departure, we arrived at the airport, rejoicing. Within a matter of minutes before boarding, an announcement was made asking for two volunteers to travel later since the flight was overbooked. In the recesses of our minds, we chuckled with the thought that the airline was overbooked by only two passengers. Of course, my husband and I gladly accepted the offer. We were handsomely rewarded for doing so.

This event reinforced my trust in God, who takes care of even the smallest details of our lives. Today, if you are experiencing challenges that seem insurmountable, have faith in God.

Yvonne H. Donatto

When We Fall

Though he fall, he shall not be utterly cast down:
for the LORD upholdeth him with his hand.
—*Psalm 37:24, KJV*

In recent years, I have undergone two major back surgeries. Not long after the second one, a middle-aged man ran a stop sign and drove his vehicle into mine. Fearful, I made a trip to see the back surgeon. After examining me carefully, the surgeon assured me that what he had accomplished in my most recent surgery had not been disturbed. But he did remind me, "Just take care of your back. Remember you have two fused discs and are missing another between those two fusions."

Not long ago I was visiting my son in another state. He invited me to ride along with him on a quick run to the hardware store to pick up some supplies for his business. With one foot on the running board, I reached up and firmly grasped the handhold so that I would have a steady support as I pulled myself up into the tall truck's cabin. Without warning, the handhold that I was gripping broke loose! Actually, it would probably be more accurate to say that the large piece of heavy plastic panel along the upper right windshield (which the handhold was attached to) cracked and popped out. The sudden release of support, midclimb into the truck, literally reversed my ascent. Gravity took over, and I found myself sprawling on the ground in the sharp, loose gravel. Though my elbow was bruised and I sustained a nasty scrape on my forearm, my first thoughts were of my fragile back and the surgeon's cautionary words to "take care" of it.

"Mom, are you all right?" My very concerned son was quickly by my side and helped me to get slowly to my feet. I took one careful step and was delighted that doing so caused no unusual back pain. Then I took a few more cautious steps. Still no pain. How grateful I was that God had spared me further back injury despite this sudden fall! He must have "cushioned" the impact that the hard, unforgiving ground should have had on my compromised back.

That experience, in addition to the earlier accident, reminds me *where* God positions Himself when we take unexpected spills in life. Speaking of God's children, the psalmist writes,

> The LORD makes firm the steps
>   of the one who delights in him;
> though he may stumble, he will not fall,
>   for the LORD upholds him with his hand (Psalm 37:23, 24, NIV).

Lord, please uphold us with Your hand today.

Harritte Sutton

Too Much Stuff

"Take care! Be on your guard against all kinds of greed;
for one's life does not consist of the abundance of possessions."
—*Luke 12:15, NRSV*

We were leaving the home we'd lived in for sixteen years. My mother and I had had this house custom built to suit our particular needs as wheelchair users. Our home has an awesome view, wheelchair ramps, and wider doorways—and we loved it. Now it had become too spacious for us to manage on our own. We had to downsize. We made the three traditional piles—throw away, give away, and keep. Sorting through the stuff, I realized that I was like the rich fool Jesus had told about while He was on earth. He diagnosed my present situation succinctly: "You have ample goods laid up for many years" (Luke 12:19, NRSV). The spiritual allusion was dire: "So it is with [she] who [stores] up treasures for [herself] but [is] not rich toward God" (verse 21, NRSV).

I realized that instead of clinging to God and being rich through Him, I was greedily holding onto unnecessary stuff. There was, for example, a stately heron statuette melded from anodized metal that had been trendy in the seventies. I could not seem to let it go. Brooding on the silliness of being a hoarder, the words of Job sprang to mind: "Ask . . . the birds of the air, and they will tell you. . . . The hand of the LORD has done this" (Job 12:7, 9, NRSV).

I fell to my knees (metaphorically speaking), as I realized it was time to make changes in my life. Accepting His direction, I heaped everything into a single pile. The very next day an acquaintance of ours stopped by the house. "Please," she begged. "Let me have this," pointing to the metal figurine. "Somehow it reminds me of the grace, beauty, and peace I learned from you and my grandmother." My surprised smile gave her permission. Musing on the day's occurrence, I gazed through the kitchen window. I spotted a motionless heron, staring down at the creek below. And then I had an epiphany. God had given me a better gift than the figurine.

Seeing the heron in real life was the providential, God-inspired blessing I craved and desperately needed. Through nature, God's second book, I learned that I have His real presence close beside me every day. Because of Him, I am very rich. And in heaven, by His grace, I'll have a spacious mansion waiting for me. Everything else is incidental stuff.

Glenda-mae Greene

Somebody Prayed for Me

"Fear not, for I am with you;
Be not dismayed, for I am your God.
I will strengthen you,
Yes, I will help you,
I will uphold you with My righteous right hand."
—Isaiah 41:10, NKJV

My feisty ninety-one-year-old grandma has been living in a New Jersey, United States, nursing home for two years. Prior to that, she lived a full and vibrant life, which included arriving at church before nine o'clock in the morning on Sabbaths for more than eighty years. A prayer warrior, she's always spoken her mind. Earlier this year she was admitted to the hospital with shortness of breath. Upon arrival, her blood pressure dropped. The emergency room doctor told my brother that our grandmother possibly needed to be intubated. That Monday he told me that I needed to visit Grandma.

Upon my arrival, Grandma recognized me but didn't look like her feisty, vibrant self. The doctor recommended putting her in the intensive care unit on a ventilator to keep her alive and her vital signs normal. After four days, the doctor recommended Grandma be taken off the ventilator and start breathing on her own. After consultation with the family and the doctor, we decided to have the ventilator removed at three o'clock in the afternoon on Friday. I contacted and asked Grandma's immediate family (in the states of California, Michigan, South Carolina, Virginia, Maryland, Pennsylvania, New York, and New Jersey) to come so that we could pray as a family. The immediate family and Grandma's pastor were in the room five minutes before they removed the ventilator. We held hands and prayed.

After leaving the room, the doctor said she probably wouldn't be able to breathe on her own for longer than four hours. When I slipped into Grandma's room, the first thing she said was, "I'm *hungry*! Do you realize no one has given me anything to eat for over a week?"

"Grandma," I said, "you've been in the hospital on a ventilator for a week and almost died." One by one, each family member (more than thirty of us) went back in.

After everyone was in the room, Grandma said, "Always remember scripture. It kept me sane while I was on the ventilator." She began singing: "Somebody prayed for me."

As of this writing, my feisty grandma is still alive and living her best life through our Lord and Savior, Jesus Christ. The moral of my story? Let's keep praying for one another!

Andrea D. Hicks

Speaking His Language

Follow the way of love.
—*1 Corinthians 14:1, NIV*

For the past several months, I have taken three sets of controls to bed with me each night. One set of controls lowers and raises the head and foot of my bed, features I need to ease the back pain that plagues me. The other two controls are telephones. I need the telephones so that I can answer my husband when he calls me at all hours of the day or night. He resides in an assisted-living facility—not by choice but to keep him safe. I understand very little of the language he now speaks to me, but I can readily discern when he tells me how much he loves me or how beautiful I am. (Beauty definitely *is* in the eye of the beholder. I know this because I have mirrors in my home and can see for myself what is true.)

"I love you." "You are so beautiful." Language is a powerful tool that we often take for granted. I actually speak two languages: the English language and the language of love.

I recently went to a Mexican restaurant near my home for supper. When I told the waiter I wanted to order à la carte, he responded, "We don't have that." The language of love would not let me laugh. Instead, I said, "Can I just order two *separate* things?" When he nodded, I said, "One bean burrito and some guacamole." When he returned with my order, I was happy. He was happy that I was happy. We were both happy! How easy it would have been for me to make an issue by explaining to him what *à la carte* means. But in this case, doing so wasn't necessary for us to be able to communicate—in the language of love, that is. After all, he was proud of the restaurant and the fact that he could communicate in a second language. I was proud of him too.

As I sat there thinking about language and the art of communication, I thought about what Jesus said in Matthew 7:12: "So in everything, do to others what you would have them do to you, for this sums up the Law and the Prophets" (NIV).

Jesus was the epitome of kindness. He still is. His primary means of communication has always been the language of love. He asks us to communicate in the same way. He knows that doing so isn't always easy for us. In fact, at times, it seems to be a thankless endeavor. Yet He relies on us to be ambassadors of love—for Him.

That's His way. That's His language.

Grace Keene

October 31

Confirmed by God

"To God belong wisdom and power;
counsel and understanding are his."
—Job 12:13, NIV

In October 2014, our family decided to move out of the house we were living in. I had a tentative job offer in Georgia, and I was excited about it. But I would have to find a place for my mom to live. Because of the type of job being offered, Mom could not come live with me. She is eighty-five years old, and I wasn't sure how she would deal with my not being readily available to her. She has lived with me since her divorce in 1997.

An uneasiness took hold of me, and I turned to God for my answer. I said, "God, if this move is what You want me to do, then confirm it." During my time with God one morning, I read my devotional story for that day. Yet it was a caption from the next day's reading that caught my eye. It stated, "Just pack, God will do the rest." Wow! God gave me a direct answer to my prayers, but His ways and mine are different. I continued to pack, but the job I was expecting in Georgia fell through overnight. I was disappointed. Once again I left things in God's hands.

Then on November 2, 2014, in the midst of packing and moving, my mom became ill and had to be hospitalized for six days. On day seven, she was admitted to a rehabilitation center for a month. Now I understand why God closed the door on the job in Georgia. He knew that my mom would need me.

God is awesome! I'm glad He sees ahead into the future and does what's best for us. Yes, I'm still waiting for the revelation of "God will do the rest." Yet I'm sure that whatever it is, it will be for my good and His glory.

God's plan and ours don't always coincide, but He wants to teach us patience. Perhaps He's taking us through a wilderness experience or a season of drought, like the children of Israel went through, so that He can give us a more obvious blessing at the right time. I'm thankful for His consideration of my request. "God, I still need a job. What's the delay? What now, Lord?" He's silent, so I guess that means I'll continue looking for the open door and be patient.

Even though my life is in limbo, I can't wait to see what He's up to. So I continue to pray for peace while I wait on His expressed will. If you are going through a similar situation in some area of your life, I encourage you to cling to the Lord in prayer. He is faithful to keep His promises.

Maple Smith

Popcorn—Part 1

"Let the little children come to me, and do not hinder them,
for the kingdom of God belongs to such as these.
Truly I tell you, anyone who will not receive the kingdom of God
like a little child will never enter it."
—Mark 10:14, 15, NIV

As we head into the part of the year known as the holiday season, I am ever mindful that for some of us the season's joy will be tempered by thoughts of "what might have been." Let me share some of my thoughts with you as well as how a loving God helps me keep going.

As a wife and also the mother of one-year-old Lynnel, I suffered—out of nowhere—a stroke when I was pregnant with our second child, a son. Though I learned to walk again, I lost all letter recognition and vision in my upper right quadrant. Those disabilities impacted my ability to be hired for work ever after. As Lynnel grew a bit older, popcorn fascinated her. And come to think of it, why not? A kernel of popcorn has such potential. When Lynnel was four, my aunt died. "We don't have to be too sad," Lynnel commented, "because one day she's going to just pop right out of her grave like all the popcorn does when we forget to put the lid on."

What a blessing her words would later become to me. For her age, Lynnel had a deep understanding of God. When she got excited, she would stand and wiggle as a wet puppy does. "I love Jesus more than anything in the whole wide world!" she would exuberantly exclaim. Though my mind was on other things in those days, the memory of her joyful exclamations drew me, over time, into a deeper friendship with God. Praise God for the faith of children!

When Lynnel was five and a half, my dad took her, my son, and me in his pickup truck to transport some lovely, quality furniture we'd inherited from Aunt Fifi. My husband and I were excited about adding these treasures to our household. In the predawn hours, Dad grew sleepy from the all-night trip and asked me to drive. I did for about an hour. After falling asleep at the wheel, I crossed the center line and hit the opposite gravel shoulder. Like a barrel, the heavily laden truck rolled down the embankment and into the dry bed of Sour Grass Creek.

Fifty years later, I've long stopped asking God, *Why?* I'm learning to leave the reasons—whatever they are—with Him. His grace teaches me how to cope and to look forward to a future filled with hope because now, as with Lynnel, I, too, "love Jesus more than anything."

Bernie Martin Beck

Popcorn—Part 2

Praise be to the God and Father of our Lord Jesus Christ,
the Father of compassion and the God of all comfort,
who comforts us in all our troubles, so that we can comfort
those in any trouble with the comfort we ourselves receive from God.
—*2 Corinthians 1:3, 4, NIV*

After the accident, I awoke in a hospital intensive care unit (ICU) with my jaw wired shut. As my hospital bed was wheeled out of the ICU, we passed my unconscious five-year-old, Lynnel, in a criblike bed. I thought, *I've got to say goodbye to her!* I was able to prop myself up on my elbow. In my heart, I said, *Goodbye, my precious one.* It was a true God moment. Back in the ICU, my dad saw the doctor look down at my child and cry out, "Oh, my God, *no!*" Dad was broken for the rest of his life, and I have struggled too. Yet I *will* cope (triumphantly) in the ways God has taught me to.

First, I will always give myself permission to acknowledge that grief lingers and that some of the pain may never really go away. Doug, my late husband, used to say, "Time softens pain—it doesn't bite as hard as it used to. Hang on to the good memories." I try to do that.

Second, I'll continue to get professional counseling when I need to get over a bump.

Third, I won't blame anyone anymore—not even myself. I'll also continue to study how I can best cope in order to facilitate healing. I once saw a movie about two young people who committed suicide together. The majority of the movie, though, focused on how the four parents coped with their losses. One became an alcoholic; another, a workaholic. And another said, "I'm going to talk, talk, talk my way through this grief—and I'm going to be present for other grieving people." That was my choice too. How healing that has proven to be!

Fourth, I will accept God's ongoing comfort in ways He offers it. When opportunities present themselves, I will pass on the comfort I have received. I'm willing to stand—bruised, bleeding, and tear stained—before God and man if sharing my experience will help just one more person cope with his or her loss. I don't want my experience to be wasted, and it hasn't been.

Finally, I will respect grieving styles that differ from mine. And mine? Every year on Lynnel's birthday, I take popcorn to her grave. Through my tears and reminiscing, I like to recall my four-year-old's visual about how loved ones will "pop up" out of their graves on resurrection morning. Her long-ago words are *heavenly* comfort to me now. Even so, Lord Jesus, come!

Bernie Martin Beck

Before You Call

"Before they call I will answer;
while they are still speaking I will hear."
—Isaiah 65:24, NIV

There is never a good time for your car to have complete engine failure. I was the general manager of a Christian university's campus radio station, 90.1 FM WJOU, and served as an adjunct professor in the communication department. The engine seized in my car, and I was devastated. It was the worst timing! I had no transportation; and financially, a new car was out of the question. For months, I had to learn how to be patient and wait on rides from family, friends, and even my students. But God is the Great Provider! He already had a miracle in progress.

A few years earlier we had a Pastor of the Year contest at the radio station to celebrate Pastor Appreciation Month. Out of all of the entries, one local ministry stood out from the rest. The pastor and his wife had started an outreach program for men transitioning out of prison that included housing and job-skills training. The program director of the radio station, Jody Jones, and I visited the sweet little church and presented the couple with a beautiful gift basket, and in return, they showered us with love. It was a wonderful day, but I had no idea how important it would be several years later.

One morning, after weeks of uncertainty and inconvenience, I felt very strongly that the Lord was going to make a way for me to get a new car. Nothing had really changed—except for my faith. I decided without any doubt in my heart that God was going to provide. I told my mother, "I need to go to the car dealer to get a car."

Stunned, she said, "A car? Today? You don't have any money!" I repeated what I had said. As a strong woman of faith, my mother looked at the determination on my face and said, "OK! Let's go!"

After speaking with a salesperson and testing several cars, I went inside the dealership to the finance department. I said a silent prayer as I sat at the desk of a nice man and told him my situation. He smiled and quietly said, "You don't remember me, do you?" When I looked puzzled, he continued, "You came to my church and honored my pastor and his wife a few years ago. We appreciate your station so much. Don't worry, ma'am, you *will* get a car today." And I did. "Before you call, I will answer." What an amazing God!

Victoria L. Joiner

Lessons From a Tugboat

The Lord is my strength and song, and is become my salvation.
—Psalm 118:14, KJV

I remember how my children loved to hear stories when they were young. One such story was "Scuffy the Tugboat." Scuffy was a little vessel that worked in the harbor and came to know just how important his work was, even though he was small.

Recently, as my husband and I were sightseeing on the banks of the Port River, we noticed a tugboat stop near where we were sitting. As we were discussing its functions, we glanced the other way to see a huge red cargo ship round the curve in the river, accompanied by another tugboat acting as the pilot boat. Very slowly it approached and almost stopped. It was then that we saw an amazing procedure take place as each tugboat took its position so as to totally control this gigantic ship. One nosed into the bow on one side, and the other seemed to be connected and pulling the other side at the stern. The ship moved slowly forward until it reached where it was to be berthed. The two tugboats then maneuvered it, turning it completely around before coming to the same side and carefully pushing this enormous cargo ship into its berth!

These tugboats were applying what Ecclesiastes 9:10 admonishes us to do: "Whatsoever thy hand findeth to do, do it with thy might" (KJV). While watching the teamwork of the tugboats, Ecclesiastes 4:9 also came to mind: "Two are better than one; because they have a good reward for their labour" (KJV). Much can be learned from teamwork, for when we work together, more is accomplished and with satisfaction.

I also remembered Isaiah 28:26, "For his God doth instruct him to discretion, and doth teach him" (KJV). As tugboat operators need intense instruction in the skills they must perform, we, too, need the divine guidance in all we do in service for God and others. "In all your ways acknowledge Him, and He shall direct your paths" (Proverbs 3:6, NKJV).

What we concluded that day was that whatever you undertake, always do it well, even if you feel inadequate or unimportant. This is what Scuffy the little tugboat learned too.

Lyn Welk-Sandy

The Mighty Hand of God

Behold, the LORD's hand is not shortened, that it cannot save.
—*Isaiah 59:1, KJV*

had already gone through surgery twice, and this was the third time. This time around it was a minor surgery; therefore, there was no cause for alarm. I mounted the surgical table with the confidence I had in my Lord. What happened afterward, I did not see coming. A day after I was discharged from the hospital, I noticed I had a sore throat, but it did not occur to me that it might have something to do with the surgery. After all, I would not have been discharged if there was a problem.

A week later I went back to the hospital for a routine checkup. That was when I realized how I had been saved by the mighty hand of God. The doctor told me what happened just about the time I was awakening from the surgery's anesthesia.

"Never in my life have I been as terrified as I was on the day of your surgery," she informed me.

"What happened?" I asked. According to her, I almost lost my life during that minor procedure. While awakening from the surgery, she said, I had suddenly lacked breath. The only way the medical team could revive me was through intubation. I know that had it not been for the Lord's timely intervention, I would have been counted among the dead. This experience has allowed me to really understand that every aspect of our lives, every minute spent, every new day, is a testimony of God's love toward us. In my case, God gave me another opportunity to live, whereas, in other cases, some people have lost their lives. One thing is sure: I am not more deserving than those who have passed away before me. For Ephesians 2:4, 5 says, "But God, who is rich in mercy, for his great love wherewith he loved us, even when we were dead in sins, hath quickened us together with Christ" (KJV). Paul adds that "by grace are ye saved" (verse 8, (KJV).

I was saved by grace—only by grace! I believe God brought me back so that I could continue to work in His vineyard and contribute to His great mission.

Dear sisters, let us be grateful to our God for every single day. He never gets weary of taking care of us. He always intervenes even in the smallest details of our lives at the right moment when we need Him most. May His name be praised!

Adolphine Zian

The Power of Kindness

Love is kind.
—*1 Corinthians 13:4, NIV*

Throughout the past year, I have been focusing my attention on one special aspect of God's love: His kindness. This has grown my awareness of His practical care for me, and my practical care for others, to a new and richer level. Love is a feeling that can be tucked away in our hearts, hidden like a pearl in an oyster. But kindness puts flesh on the love and brings it to life in the space between people.

Earlier this year I joined an online Christian initiative called "40 acts," which encourages people to do at least one act of kindness a day for forty days. Every day I received some thoughtful inspiration and a kindness challenge: kindness in my home, on my journey to work, around my town, in my office, down my street, and across my world. Being part of this initiative opened my eyes even wider to the great need for kindness every day in every possible and simple way. Finding ways to be kind to others has brightened my own life too. One day I saw a young mother at the top of a long flight of stairs in a department store. She was maneuvering a loaded buggy with one hand and a distressed toddler with the other. I touched her arm gently. "Let me carry the buggy down the steps for you. Then you will have both hands for your little girl."

She sighed, and her whole body relaxed. "Thank you so much! That's so kind of you!"

I waited at the bottom of the stairs. As she settled the toddler back into her buggy, I told her, "You are so patient with her. You are doing a great job as a mom. I hope that you have a lovely day together."

She turned to me with tears in her eyes. "I needed that. It is a lovely day. Now I can see how blue the sky is. It's amazing." It only took a few moments. It cost me nothing. But it gave her hope and comfort and helped her to see the world in a bright new way.

Kindness is a powerful way to change our communities. It is something we can all do every day to make God's love real in this broken and lonely world. It is also one of the best ways to nurture your own happiness and to counteract loneliness and sadness. Why not try doing something kind every day for forty days and see what happens? Ask God to show you how you can share His kindness today.

Karen Holford

Mulberry Warrior Trees

Once more the Philistines came up . . . ;
so David inquired of the LORD.
—2 Samuel 5:22, 23, NIV

Have you ever prayed for the will of God and later faced another similar situation, so you did exactly as you did before, but it didn't work out? I have. David's story in 2 Samuel 5:17–25 shows us why we are out of sync with God's will when we do not ask for it each time.

The Philistines had been the enemy of the Israelites for centuries. For decades, David was sometimes their enemy and sometimes their vassal. But when David was anointed king of all Israel, not simply the tribal chief of Judah, he was no longer an ally, and they invaded Israel.

David asked the Lord whether he should go up against them in the Valley of Raphaim and received the answer that they would be delivered into his hand. The Lord Himself went out before David's army, causing fear and confusion, making it easy to rout the Philistines.

Soon the Philistines returned and spread out again in the Valley of Raphaim. I would naturally think I should do exactly as I had done before, and I would rush out, thinking, *I will victoriously chase them away again.* But not David. He inquired of the Lord for the second time.

The Lord gave different instructions: do not attack straight on, but circle around behind them and wait for the signal to advance quickly. The signal? "The sound of marching in the tops of the mulberry trees" (verse 24, NKJV). Did it sound to David and his mighty men like a mighty angel army was marching to their rescue? Did it give them courage? Did they laugh out loud with joy?

The Philistines heard the disorienting sound of marching in the tops of trees and were once more thrown into chaos. To move forward meant to stumble into the expected Israelite camp. To retreat meant crashing into the approaching . . . what? Reinforcements! But were they friend or foe? Long ago the valley was the home of the giant Rapha, who was an ancestor of Goliath. Were these giants, maybe even ghosts, shaking their swords and spears in the tops of the trees?

When the Israelites attacked from the rear, the panicked enemy fled, never to return.

Did you notice? The Lord gave new instructions. He always does. Just ask Moses how to get water from a rock, or Joshua how to conquer a city, or Jeremiah how to act out a message from the Lord. These stories teach me that God is creative and doesn't do things the same way each time. I must ask for God's will to be revealed every day in every circumstance.

Rebecca Timon Turner

November 8

Perfect Timing!

In all thy ways acknowledge him, and he shall direct thy paths.
—*Proverbs 3:6, KJV*

When I retired in 2008, Walter, my husband, promised that we could move closer to our family, so I immediately started decluttering our home. By 2009, he had totally changed his mind. The thought of physically and emotionally moving was too stressful, and he proclaimed to everybody that he would not move—ever! He loved our home, his retired employment, friends, church, mechanic, barber, grocery store, and the Kansas City Chiefs' football games.

In 2010, when visiting our son and daughter-in-law in Atlanta, Georgia, we saw a subdivision that we loved, but the prices of the condominiums were *way* out of our price range. That trip excited me so much that I called a real-estate agent when we returned home. *It certainly wouldn't hurt to get information*, I thought. Eventually, we invited the real-estate agent to our home. While there, he asked Walter why he wanted to move. He looked up from his newspaper and said, "I don't." I was more than devastated and promised the Lord that if moving was not His will, I would be content living in our clutter-free home. Family and friends joined me in praying for our future as I claimed Philippians 4:6, "Don't worry about anything; instead, pray about everything. Tell God what you need, and thank him for all he has done" (NLT).

In 2011, miracles started happening. Walter got so disgusted with going to the Chiefs football games that he sold our two season tickets that we'd had for forty years. (Thank You, Jesus.) For sixteen seasons, he'd absolutely loved his retired seasonal IRS job until he was put on a special assignment that he hated. At the end of that season, he quit. (Thank You, Jesus.) After living in our cozy home for thirty-three years, the neighborhood started changing, and the property value started going down. Besides, there was too much grass to cut and too much snow to shovel.

The "for sale" sign went up in July 2012, and we visited Atlanta in September. This time a subdivision condo we'd loved in 2010 had been drastically reduced because of the recession and a foreclosure. The price was just right, and our offer was accepted. After living in Kansas City, Missouri, for forty-eight years, we moved to Atlanta just two days before our darling twin granddaughters were born. We are still praising God, from whom all blessings flow!

Lord, in every situation, may I let go and wait on You because Your timing is always perfect!

Shirley Sain Fordham

The Day the Lord Took Control

The LORD will guide you always;
he will satisfy your needs.
—Isaiah 58:11, NIV

Have you ever felt that you could do it all? Sometimes we do things without consulting God first, and then we have to call on Him to save us from life-threatening situations. One of my favorite Christian writers admonishes us to give the direction of our day to the Lord when we first awaken in the morning. One day I learned a lesson that I will never forget: no matter what is at stake, ask God first.

The weather forecast said it would be a bad winter day; however, I didn't heed the warning nor ask God's guidance. I thought that I had enough time to work for a little money! I did everything that I'd planned to do that day and proceeded to return home. It was then I discovered that while I was at work, the weather had grown worse. Heavy snow was falling by then. I became concerned about driving my car that was not in good condition. Nevertheless, I had to get home to my children.

That's when I recognized that I'd made a big mistake relying on myself without consulting God that morning. I needed help—and fast. No other car was on the road; everybody else had evidently obeyed the warning. I remember a quote I'd read: "Human pride and self-sufficiency stand rebuked in His [the Savior's] presence."*

At one point, my car started sliding and spinning in all directions. I prayed to God to forgive me and to help me. He heard my cry, and the car stopped on a mount facing north. I kept praying because I was afraid that the car would overturn. Providentially, it slid back down on the road facing the west, which was the direction in which I was going. I thanked God and promised Him that never again would I try to be Wonder Woman. And about the money I'd wanted so much to earn that day? Well, due to the ice storm that hit later that night, I couldn't use that money until businesses opened a week later!

The Lord will keep His promises if we trust Him, not ourselves, to take care of our needs. Never forget that "angels from the courts above will attend the steps of those who come and go at God's command."†

Flore Aubry Hamilton

---

* Ellen G. White, *The Desire of Ages* (Nampa, ID: Pacific Press®, 2006), 49.

† White, *The Desire of Ages*, 48.

November 10

Earnest and Enduring Empathy

Rejoice with them that do rejoice,
and weep with them that weep.
—*Romans 12:15, KJV*

I received a phone call from one of my best friends, stating that her brother was diagnosed with a high-grade metastatic brain tumor. Heart in my throat, my lungs twist-tied, and my brain refusing to fire, I couldn't process how in the world my friend was going to handle this.

My mind raced back to the past. Two years ago my husband suffered from a brain tumor, and I had been in the same situation. Everything felt empty. I felt empty. Hollow. Shrinking inside myself. Dying inside a bubble of terror, an instant at a time. During that period, a multitude of family and friends stepped up to offer support, sit with us, and pray over us; the outpouring of love was amazing.

I could relate better with my friend because I, too, had undergone the same pain. I could encourage her because I understood brain tumors. I could empathize and agonize with her. Knowing she wasn't alone penetrated her wall of panic and despair. My comforting words changed her perspective because it came from someone who had suffered.

Jesus is our perfect example of empathy. He didn't come to earth to save us as God, detached and gazing down in sympathy and pity. He came as man, born into the trenches, to live and suffer as a human. His empathy makes Him the perfect sacrifice, the perfect bridge between God and us.

The Bible tells us, "For we do not have a high priest who is unable to empathize with our weaknesses, but we have one who has been tempted in every way, just as we are—yet he did not sin" (Hebrews 4:15, NIV).

Empathy requires a willingness to wear the same emotions. If we applied our trench-induced emotions to someone else's trench experience, we could change the church as we change lives. God draws us to certain people, people we're uniquely shaped to help. Look around in your life. Then take the challenge. Put away your sympathy and embrace your empathy.

We don't all share the same life experiences. We never will. But God wants us to identify with the heartbreak of pain and suffering, the shame and rejection and loss of others. Helen Keller wrote, "So long as you can sweeten another's pain, life is not in vain."

Esther Synthia Murali

Veterans of Faith

All these people died still believing what God had promised
them. . . . But others were tortured. . . . Others were chained
in prisons. . . . And others were killed with the sword.
They were too good for this world.
—Hebrews 11:13, 35–38, NLT

During the Korean conflict, my uncle Harry had only one home: the United States Air Force. When on home leave, he bounced between the families of his two sisters, one of them being my mother. During one of his visits to our home, Uncle Harry pulled from his duffel bag a handful of plastic charms attached (by knotted strands of soiled thread) to a small central ring.

"Carolyn, I want you to have this," he said, dropping it into my small outstretched hand. "A little girl in Seoul gave it to me on the street one day. I asked someone to translate what she said. What she had said to me was, 'I want you to have this because you look so sad.' "

Though my uncle chuckled, I knew in my six-year-old heart that a measure of truth lay behind the little girl's words. I, too, had observed Uncle Harry's unexpressed sadness, especially each time our family drove him to the bus depot to catch a Greyhound coach "to Korea." Grandma said Korea was very far away. I knew it only as long, squiggly lines on the map she showed me every day before we knelt to pray for him after Mom and Dad had left to teach.

Dad's youngest brother, another beloved uncle, served in another branch of the military during World War II. Though spared throughout life-threatening combat situations, he, too, returned home changed from when he'd left. Though both uncles are gone now, I often thank God for their sacrifice. In their memory, I pray for other veterans in whose courageous shoes I was never asked to walk. Yet because *they* served, I and many others have greatly benefited.

I am especially grateful for another group of vets that fought along the front lines and often in the face of death. They're listed in Hebrews 11. Take a moment today to read about these men and women who responded to Christ's invitation to serve. Not counting the cost, they answered the call of the Commander who would, and did, pay the ultimate price for them.

Christ calls us into the same service—and into the same close conflict. Will we walk in the footsteps of these veterans of faith: Jochebed, Moses, Rahab, Sarah, Daniel, and Deborah?

May God help us do just that!

Carolyn Rathbun Sutton

"Vengeance Is Mine"

Don't hit back. . . . Don't insist on getting even; that's not for you
to do. "I'll do the judging," says God. "I'll take care of it."
Our Scriptures tell us that if you see your enemy hungry,
go buy that person lunch, or if he's thirsty, get him a drink.
Your generosity will surprise him. . . . Don't let evil get
the best of you; get the best of evil by doing good.
—*Romans 12:17–21*, The Message

In 2006, an Amish community experienced a tragic shooting that resulted in the deaths of five schoolgirls. More shocking than the shooting were the attitudes of forgiveness and generosity the community's families extended to the shooter and his family.

In 2015, a young man attended the Bible study of an African American church in South Carolina, where he murdered nine people during the service. The victims' families also displayed forgiveness toward this young man.

In June 2004, an altercation at a local night establishment resulted in two deaths, which included the life of my middle son being taken. And as with the families of the previously mentioned victims, I also immediately expressed an attitude of forgiveness.

These are just three tragic incidents in the history of our lives. Although our families have never met, we have threads of commonalities. One of these is how to "avenge" these senseless acts of violence. Yet all three families remembered that God is love, God is forgiveness, and according to God, He will handle all vengeance in due time.

Many families have lost loved ones to acts of violence. We know we are living in the final days of earth's history, and as such, we suspect these random, sometimes intentional, acts of violence will only get worse, not better. Losing loved ones under any circumstance is very difficult. But there is hope for those who love the Lord so that we "will not be sad, as are those who have no hope" (1 Thessalonians 4:13, GNT). You see, one day we will look up and see a cloud that is smaller than a man's hand. As it gets closer, we will see Jesus (God the Son) riding on a cloud of angels and blowing the trumpet that calls our loved ones from their graves. We can comfort one another with this thought (see 1 Thessalonians 4:16–18). What a day that will be!

Truly, we can say that the God of heaven will supply all of our needs "with all his abundant wealth through Christ Jesus" (Philippians 4:19, GNT). Our need, as families who have experienced violent acts, is to show how to forgive and then allow God to handle the vengeance.

Mattie E. Johnson

God Is Faithful

"Therefore know that the LORD your God, He is God, the faithful God
who keeps covenant and mercy for a thousand generations with
those who love him and keep His commandments."
—Deuteronomy 7:9, NKJV

Have you ever met someone who had questions about God? I have. Too often Christians think that being children of God makes them immune to the attacks of the devil. They assumed that the storms of life would just by pass them.

The exact opposite, however, is true. The enemy of our souls wants us to lose faith in God's love and doubt His wisdom and care. That's precisely why he attacks the children of God.

Sadly, I have even seen people turn their backs on God and walk out of the church because God did not stop some life storm from coming against them.

Surely, the storms will come, and they will often come when we least expect them. That makes them an even stronger test of our faith. Not one of us wants to experience trouble in life. Yet if we have to go through trials, it would at least be helpful if we could know in advance what to expect. That way we could plan better for this time of difficulties, right? Unfortunately, that is not how it works. Because if we could foresee the future and make provisions for hard times, we would begin to rely on ourselves instead of relying on God. How would our faith ever grow?

God, in His love and mercy, sometimes allows trials in our lives so that our faith in Him *can* grow. How will we react to unexpected challenges: in faith and trust, or with doubts and fear? When the enemy comes in like a flood against us, where will we turn?

The indisputable reality of a walk with the Lord is that He never abandons us even when we feel abandoned. The God of the mountaintop experiences in our lives is the same as the God of the low times in our lives. He is with us in good times and in painful times. Whether suffering during the day or at night, we can still trust His promises, especially the one that assures us that nothing is too hard for Him (see Jeremiah 32:27). Thank God for this faithfulness to supply our every need! Thank God for His promise to never leave us! Thank God for His power to heal, bless, forgive, and wash us from our sins! Thank God for His love, mercy, and goodness.

I thank You, Lord, that in all situations You remain faithful.

Christiana Agyenim-Boateng

The Everlasting Arms

"The eternal God is your refuge,
and underneath are the everlasting arms."
—*Deuteronomy 33:27, NIV*

This morning while reading Mark 9, I saw a beautiful picture of our Jesus. He created a visual aid when He put a little child among the group of disciples surrounding Him. Then Jesus took the child into His arms and told the disciples that anyone who welcomes a little child in His name welcomes Jesus and the One who sent Him (Mark 9:36, 37, NIV). In the next chapter, Mark recounts the familiar story of Jesus welcoming children to come to Him. Again, Mark emphasizes that Jesus "took the children in his arms, placed his hands on them and blessed them" (Mark 10:16, NIV).

Suddenly, I noticed that only Mark mentions Jesus taking children into His arms. Matthew and Luke both tell these same stories, but neither author mentions the fact that Jesus takes children into His arms. Don't you love this picture? Can't you just see Jesus reach out to the little ones, and they respond by climbing onto His lap? What could be more comforting than to feel loving, safe arms around you? Children were the most marginalized class in the time of Jesus. They were not seen as important or contributing members of society—though even slaves contributed. Yet Jesus sees their value and true worth; and He admonishes each of us to become loving and trusting "as a little child" (verse 15, NKJV).

As I was reflecting about the arms of Jesus, I was drawn to a beautiful passage in Deuteronomy 33 that concludes Moses' blessing on the tribes of Israel before his death: "The eternal God is your refuge, and underneath are the everlasting arms" (verse 27, NKJV). There is nothing like the feeling of God's arms around you! Once in an extremely difficult time in my life, I was talking to the Lord and asking Him to comfort me. I opened my Bible, and there it was! "As a mother comforts her child, so will I comfort you" (Isaiah 66:13, NIV).

Our God knows us personally and intimately. He knows our needs and desires. He loves us infinitely and unconditionally. Maybe today you need to feel His strong arms supporting, lifting, and comforting you. He is there for you! Just lean back and rest in those strong arms of love. He will carry you through whatever you are facing.

Myrna Hanna

The Meaning of the Word

My little children, let us not love in word or in tongue,
but in deed and in truth.
—1 John 3:18, NKJV

Have you ever counted the many different nuances and meanings for the word *love*? I have tried, yet this word is rich with different meanings in different settings. Let's first look at a few everyday uses of that word.

Love, of course, can express a deep and tender affection one holds toward another person, such as the love one feels toward family members and friends. We've all said, "I love my sister" or "I love my children." The same word can symbolize a strong emotional bond that one has with a friend: "I love Susie and Tom; they're my best friends." And haven't we heard that same word used to indicate a strong attachment to an object or animal, such as, "I love my camera" or "I love my pet"? We also use the same word to convey our enjoyment of things we see or experience: "I love sunny days, flowers, and rainbows." And do we not also use this word to signify recognition of, and appreciation for, other people's attractive qualities: "I love her kindness and his smile"?

One of the more common uses of the word *love* describes an intense desire or attraction between persons of the opposite sex, though it can also entail a sense of respect, commitment, and devotion: "I love my husband." And my husband knows exactly what I mean because my loving actions toward him back up my words.

Yet what do we mean when we say that we love the Lord? I'm sure the expression of this sentiment indicates not only the meanings mentioned above but also so much more. When we truly love God, do we not also respect Him for who He is as our Creator and Redeemer? When we verbally express our love for Him, we are indicating that we admire, recognize, and appreciate His character. We regard Him with affection as our Father and Elder Brother. Saying we love Him means we are devoted to Him and committed to doing His will. We enjoy fellowship with Him more than anyone else.

The question is, Do our actions back up our words when we say, "I love You, Lord"? Can others see Him at work in our lives? Do I love others, including enemies, as He loves me?

Lord, may my actions clearly communicate to You—and others—my deep love for You.

Rhodi Alers de López

Let Us Watch and Be Ready

"Therefore you also be ready,
for the Son of Man is coming at an hour you do not expect."
—Matthew 24:44, NKJV

After four days at camp meeting, we felt as if our spirits had been rejuvenated. The four of us felt our burdens lifted as we made our way to the railway station to take our train back home.

Since we arrived at the station an hour before our train was to depart, we spent the time in lively discussion about how we had been blessed at camp meeting. In fact, we even passed some of the time singing the songs we'd enjoyed.

Then came the announcement that our train would arrive one hour late! Though a bit tired, we managed to keep up our spirits by chatting and singing. Then came the second announcement: our train would be late by an *additional* hour!

Now that announcement *did* dampen our spirits! In fact, we began to feel uneasy. Our tired bodies longed to stretch themselves out and just go to sleep. The breeze turned chilly, and we began to shiver. One more hour ticked by. No train. By this time, we had become extremely tired, if not a bit grumpy. Waiting became very irksome to us! What was the problem? Just a short time before, we had felt vigorous. Our hearts burned with zeal to witness for the Lord as we sang our songs at the train depot. But as the hours of waiting passed, our whole outlook had changed. Then, finally, after a five-hour wait, there came our train! We rushed to the stipulated platform, clambered aboard the train, and settled, at long last, into our seats.

This experience reminded me of our anticipation of Christ's second coming. Each of us began that waiting and watching full of spiritual vigor. We yearned to witness for Him. Yet I wonder whether the wait has caused us to fall into such a spiritual stupor that we've become more preoccupied with the inconveniences of the wait than with the grand event itself.

The Bible tells us that after the prolonged delay, Jesus will surely come! Will we remain alert and continually watch, making sure we are ready? Or will we become careless about making the necessary preparations as did the five foolish virgins in Jesus' parable (Matthew 25:1–13)?

Jesus is coming soon! Let us be found watching and waiting! Maranatha!

Jeyarani Sundersingh

Sometimes There Is a Reason for the Storm

"You intended to harm me, but God intended it for good to accomplish what is now being done, the saving of many lives."
—*Genesis 50:20, NIV*

Heights with a view of nature's grandeur thrill me with a tranquil calm. So several years ago, when my husband, Ron, said, "Next year we should go to the big island of Hawaii and take a helicopter tour of the Kīlauea volcano," I heartily agreed. I said a prayer for God to guide the trip, then thought no more about it until we got closer to the date.

A few days before leaving, I checked the weather and was slightly concerned that rain was in the forecast the day of the helicopter flight. "Heavenly Father, I just want to mention that we have been planning this trip for a year. Please let there be sunshine," I prayed. We enjoyed some days at a nice beach and then drove around the island toward the volcano.

Sometimes we know a storm is approaching, and sometimes we don't see the storm. It can be the same with the storms of life as in the experience of Joseph, in the biblical book of Genesis, who didn't see the storm approaching in his life. His father, Israel, favored him above his brothers. Every so often Joseph would report a dream he'd had that made him look superior to the rest of the family. This incited strife among his brothers. One day, away from their father, the brothers seized him and sold him to some Ishmaelites; and Joseph eventually landed in prison.

Yet near the end of a life that turned out to be prosperous, Joseph shared that there had been a reason for the storm in his life: "You intended to harm me, but God intended it for good to accomplish what is now being done, the saving of many lives" (Genesis 50:20, NIV).

On the day of our helicopter trip, the sky filled with black clouds from which rain poured. Assuming the worst, I resorted to constant prayer. When we reached the helicopter tour office, they said, "We're having a rain delay; please sit over there." Twenty minutes later: "Now you can go get on the helicopter." Looking up as I approached the helicopter, those black clouds were still in the sky. Then, as if God were addressing my concern, the pilot said, "You're in luck and will have the best view of the bright-red flowing lava because of these dark-black clouds. Had it been blue sky today, the lava would look washed out." Instantly, I thought, *Wow! I was supposed to be in a storm!* And my heart was stilled with a tranquil calm.

Diane Pestes

Where's the Joy?

He maketh the barren woman to keep house,
and to be a joyful mother of children. Praise ye the LORD.
—*Psalm 113:9, KJV*

When my close friend, whom I'll call Wendy, was struggling with infertility, I claimed the promise in Psalm 113:9 on her behalf. I could understand her longing, since I, too, had waited years for a child. Finally, Wendy and her husband had a healthy baby boy, and together we celebrated God's answer to our prayers. But I never thought to claim Psalm 113:9 for myself. After all, I wasn't barren—just single. Waiting for a husband was frustrating, but eventually God fulfilled that desire of mine. By the time Greg and I decided to start a family, I was thirty-nine. Despite being "geriatric" in obstetric and gynecological lingo, I conceived without any trouble.

But when Austin was born, I quickly discovered that the "joyful" part of the verse didn't come automatically. The constant round of nursing, diapers, baths, naps, and playtime, interspersed with cleaning, cooking, and grocery shopping, was exhausting—and that was just on the good days. It was much easier to be a frustrated, anxious, depressed, lonely, or even angry mother of children than a joyful one. I knew things had to change. Fortunately, the rest of Psalm 113 points the way to experiencing joy. The psalm praises God for His incomparable greatness and caring intervention in our lives. I realized that as I focus on God and His blessings, I leave no room for negative thoughts!

I can dwell on the sacrifices I've made to become a full-time mom, or I can thank God for the growth He is bringing into this new phase of my life. I can stew over the ways I think my husband should help out, or I can appreciate the ways he already shows his love. I can berate myself for my failures (like that humiliating moment when I found myself yelling, "Stay down!" at my uncooperative baby on the changing table), or I can pray for God's help to do better next time. I can live in dread of Austin's wails or in anticipation of his smiles. When Austin was only a few months old, I began singing to him every morning: "This is the day that the Lord has made; I will rejoice and be glad in it" (see Psalm 118:24). Soon he would grin when I launched into the familiar melody, but the song was more for me than for him: a declaration of my choice to be a joyful mother even in my not-always-enjoyable circumstances. God is fulfilling His promise!

Rachel E. Cabose

Geraldine

Blessed be the God and Father of our Lord Jesus Christ,
the Father of mercies and God of all comfort,
who comforts us in all our tribulation, that we may be
able to comfort those who are in any trouble,
with the comfort with which we ourselves are comforted by God.
—*2 Corinthians 1:3, 4, NKJV*

As a young woman, I desperately wanted a mentor. In my mind's eye, she was in her fifties, of another race, large bosomed, wise, experienced, and compassionate. I think I named her something like "Geraldine." When I'd bring her my stories of interpersonal drama, wildly fluctuating emotions, heart-stopping fears, and hopeless thoughts, she'd look at me knowingly and gently dispense her counsel. She'd be blessed knowing she helped me, and I'd be blessed being helped. We'd hug. It was awesome. Yet no such mentor appeared in my life, so I struggled through my young-adult years with a mentor-shaped hole in my heart just about the size of Geraldine.

Once my two daughters flew the nest, I decided to return to graduate school for a degree in counseling. In spite of my own need for support, I'd always been the type that found herself listening to endless stories from a seemingly infinite number of people who likewise needed to be heard. *Maybe I can make a career out of this*, I thought. *I seem to have a knack for it.* Three years later I launched my private counseling practice, and it's going strong to this day.

A funny thing happened when I started counseling. The needy woman inside me, the waif who had never been fully mentored—that lost inner child—found solace. I'm not sure of all the hows and whys, except that giving what I'd always craved helped satisfy the yearning. I'm not a large-bosomed woman of another race; I'm just me and, well, modestly endowed. But other than that, *I* am being Geraldine on a daily basis these days.

It would be awesome if there were enough mentors to go around. But the sad fact is, there's a deficiency. This is why I've added counseling and coaching training to my practice—I want to help people be able to help people. I want to help multiply counselors, coaches, mentors, and disciplers in our midst. But I cling to the belief that, should the help not be found, God can fill the deficit. And He does it sometimes by leading us to give the very thing we crave.

Jennifer Jill Schwirzer

Angels' Presence

The angel of the LORD encamps
around all those who fear Him, and delivers them.
—*Psalm 34:7, NKJV*

For He shall give His angels charge over you,
to keep you in all your ways.
—*Psalm 91:11, NKJV*

The challenges of mission work strengthen our faith in God. My husband and I agreed to work, without salaries, in the poorest mission in the northern Philippines. The beautiful scenery with year-round temperate weather made it a home for us. We never went hungry as God provided. Our two daughters were born into our simple life in Baguio City. After seven years of committed service, we moved to metro Manila to work. We found a two-story apartment that had jalousie (louvered) window panels on the first and second floors. One day I was dusting the window panels upstairs, and one of the glass panels fell to the ground below—right where my daughter and other children were playing. I ran downstairs to learn that it had seemed as if someone had pulled my child out of the path of the falling panel so that it wouldn't hit her on the head! I believe angels were protecting those children.

A week later the mission president phoned to tell us a mission house had been finished and asked if we would like to live there. We were very grateful and moved. After lunch one Friday, I was putting my two-year-old daughter to sleep, and my older daughter offered to get a pillow from the bedroom upstairs. My older daughter, not seeing a wooden panel left by the painters, bumped her head on it, lost her balance, and fell down the flight of stairs. On her dangerous descent, her body turned 360 degrees, causing her to come to a halt with her feet hitting the cement floor instead of her head. Surely her guardian angel controlled her fall! I picked her up and cuddled her. Together with the two-year-old, we knelt and thanked the Lord for her guardian angel and the miracle of her safety. In her church's Bible study class the next day, she and I shared her testimony.

In the Psalms, David helps us to understand that angels are always near. Any sign of their presence is beautiful and symbolic evidence of God's omnipotence and omnipresence in our lives. God promised that His angels would camp around us. Should we not remember to embrace this promise and thank Him for His involvement in every circumstance of our lives?

Edna Bacate Domingo

What Really Matters

But every man is tempted, when he is drawn away of his own lust,
and enticed. Then when lust hath conceived, it bringeth forth sin:
and sin, when it is finished, bringeth forth death.
Do not err, my beloved brethren.
—*James 1:14–16, KJV*

On Monday, November 21, I was given an alert by a medical doctor in a hospital. "Ma'am, we will have to operate. You may not make it." Wow! Forty years of life, twenty-four doing the Lord's work, more than sixteen years of professional life, and then just recently married—yet all of this suddenly seemed meaningless at this critical moment.

Within five hours, I was being wheeled, at walk-run speed, to an operating theater. No chance to write a will, make a phone call, or give special instructions to anyone. On that day I understood that life on this planet is a most precious, yet fleeting gift from God. He gives life; He determines its end. What a God of love, patience, and mercy! What forbearance that God, who alone has the final word on anything, still allows us to run around in our sin, madness, foolishness, and self-delusion, thinking we are the ones in charge of our lives.

What causes us to live out what I call the "Nebuchadnezzar syndrome"? As with that proud Babylonian king, we can quickly forget what is truth, even though we are here for only a time. We came into this world with nothing, and we can take nothing out. How then should we pass our time, spend our resources, and live our lives?

The Bible is replete with God's call to His standards, righteousness, and ways. So how do we stand with God? Let's do a heart, mind, and soul audit. No matter how big, bad, bossy, or beautiful, we are mere blades of grass, flowers of the field, and wisps of vapor—here today and gone tomorrow. Nothing on this earth lasts forever except our characters—*if* we respond to God.

At some point in life, many of us have gotten ahead of ourselves. We might have thought we were the best student, spouse, staff member, or employer. But God's Word calls us to examine ourselves. We have no true or lasting value outside of a relationship with God.

I call on us today to realize we are here just for a season. What really matters is how we relate to God, His Word, His work, and His world.

Let us turn our eyes upon Jesus and worship Him!

Keisha D. Sterling-Richards

My Journey of Faith

The prayer of faith will save the sick.
—James 5:15, NKJV

In May 2008, the fingers on my left hand suddenly became numb and then, very quickly, the fingers on my right hand also. The numbness became so bad that I could not zip up my boots or open doors and jars, and I even had difficulty buttoning my clothes. I saw eleven different doctors that year, but no one knew what had caused this problem. Multiple sclerosis and carpal tunnel syndrome were ruled out.

I decided to find a new general physician. After giving me a full physical exam, my new doctor sent me to a neurologist at Michigan State University. This was the third neurologist I had talked to about my condition. As I walked into the clinical center, I had no hope that this new doctor would be able to help me. Imagine my happiness when Dr. Bhanasuelli not only knew what was wrong with me—I had Lewis-Sumner syndrome, which occurs in only six people out of one million—but also had me in treatment within four days. My life changed for the better.

It seems that Dr. Bhanasuelli just happened to have attended Wayne State University in Detroit where Dr. Lewis, who had codiscovered Lewis-Sumner syndrome, taught; she was in his class! So, of course, she recognized my symptoms immediately and knew exactly what to do about them: IVIg (intravenous immunoglobulin) four days each month and 2,000 milligrams of CellCept (an immunosuppressant) daily.

In preparation for a ten-day trip to Bermuda in April 2011, I had my monthly four days of IVIg at the hospital. But to my dismay, I found that my hands and also my feet were numb the entire time I was on my trip. I wanted to be anointed while I was in Bermuda, but our itinerary was so tight that there was no opportunity to schedule an anointing.

When I returned home, however, all the numbness was gone. So my doctor weaned me off the CellCept, and I have not had another IVIg treatment since. In fact, I have been in total remission for six years! My neurologist says it may never come back. She had no explanation for my sudden remission. I did—God knew I had *wanted* to be anointed, and He honored my faith!

Patricia Hook Rhyndress Bodi

"Rejoice Evermore and in Everything Give Thanks"

He made their hearts and understands everything they do.
—Psalm 33:15, NCV

We know that in everything God works
for the good of those who love him.
—Romans 8:28, NCV

My husband, Vladimir, was fifty-six years old. When he became ill suddenly, an ambulance was called. The doctor aboard diagnosed my husband with preinfarction syndrome. That Monday our children and I prayed earnestly. We could visit him for only thirty minutes between noon and twelve-thirty but not again until Tuesday. I was overjoyed to see that Vladimir felt good. The doctor said his condition was stable. On Wednesday, I called the hospital to ask whether I could bring my husband clothes. A doctor said, "Your husband doesn't need anything . . . anymore." I didn't understand. The doctor answered, "He passed away."

"How?" I could hardly speak when the doctor said Vladimir had passed away at ten-thirty the previous evening. "What shall I do?" I asked in shock. He told me to "go to the morgue," and then he hung up. I don't remember how I got to the morgue, the manager of which grumbled about my "coming so late." I told her no one had notified me. Disgruntled, she said she was going to send a memo to the head doctor.

I can hardly remember the funeral. I couldn't use my feet to get up. I remembered a verse in the Bible telling us such things as "rejoice evermore" and "in everything give thanks." I was silently crying out, *How, Lord? How is it possible to rejoice when having lost the person closest to my heart? That would be absurd! Rejoice that we lived together for thirty years and never had a fight? Rejoice that the years when we did everything together flew by way too fast?*

Then a very clear thought came into my mind: *Rejoice not concerning what you have lost, but rather, rejoice and give thanks for what you had.* Though the pain at that moment was too bitter, over time my sorrow became lighter. It became easier to remember the pleasant times.

Now I do thank God for what I had. God is too good and wise to make mistakes, and He won't let the pain in this life destroy us. He says, "I am your Comforter and Helper every day."

Liudmila Verlan

There's Pleasure in Giving

Give and it shall be given unto you; good measure,
pressed down, and shaken together; and running over,
shall men give into your bosom. For with the same measure
that ye mete withal it shall be measured to you again.
—Luke 6.38, KJV

Never will I forget the day when I came across a beggar at a traffic light as I walked along January 15th Avenue in Lome, Togo. I was so moved with compassion that I stopped right in front of him. I didn't usually engage in conversations with beggars; I usually gave them money and then moved on. But that day something was different. I asked Moussa Baba (the name he gave me) a lot of questions. He spoke English but none of the native dialects of Togo. Later he told me that he had been hit by a motorbike four months earlier. A traditional "medical" practitioner gave Moussa Baba treatment in the form of a massage, having no idea that Moussa Baba had sustained a thigh-bone fracture when the motorbike hit him. Now, with no capacity to earn a livelihood, Moussa Baba had sent his wife and twins back to his village in Nigeria. He remained in Lome, begging for alms.

A month later I underwent surgery and wasn't able to physically give the beggar money for his treatments. When I left the hospital, I sent money with someone, asking that they look for him, but they couldn't find him at his usual place. Moussa Baba was later spotted at a place in Zongo, another neighborhood. I provided him with enough money to go to an emergency ward. There an x-ray revealed he needed his limb amputated. The operation would cost 800,000 West African CFA francs (equivalent to 1,200 euros or 1,300 United States dollars).

My surgery cost more, but I understood what Moussa Baba was going through and sent him money for his operation. For about a week, my mother and I prayed in order to raise the amount needed for my surgery. God answered our prayers when my godfather sent me 1,000,000 CFA francs (1,500 euros or 1,680 United States dollars) to help defray my surgery expenses. We both had our surgeries, and today Moussa Baba can move around like any other person. Before he left for his country, I shared Jesus with him in our last conversation.

There are many out there waiting for a demonstration of God's love toward them. Let us always ask the Lord to lead us to the needy. He will provide the means Himself while creating the opportunity for us to share His love with others.

Mamata Sassou

Praise and Thanksgiving

Giving thanks always for all things to God the Father
in the name of our Lord Jesus Christ.
—*Ephesians 5:20, NKJV*

Just before my marriage in 1997, I underwent major surgery for a huge ovarian cyst. The senior doctor at the hospital said it was the largest he had ever seen. The operation was successful. After the wedding, I settled in a different state. Six months after the wedding, everyone was expecting me to conceive a child. They came to the conclusion that because I had undergone a major surgery before marriage I would not be able to conceive. My mother-in-law, who conceived five years after her wedding, also expected me to bear a child within a year. I was so discouraged by the way people in the village talked about those who didn't conceive.

One day my husband left for a meeting, leaving me alone at home. I knelt and prayed to God, literally crying out as did Jacob, "Until You bless me, I will not let You go!" (see Genesis 32:26). I also told God that if He allowed me to birth only one child, could the baby please be a boy? Not only would a baby boy carry the surname of his father but also I could not be blamed for having a girl. God answered my prayer when I conceived that very month! I had faith that the child I was carrying would be a baby boy. I told my husband of my prayer. We prayed together and decided to name the child Giftson, because he would be a son who was a gift from God.

The day came, and lo and behold, my heavenly Father blessed me with a baby boy. He was handsome, chubby, and pink in skin shade, like foreigners we had seen. Everyone who visited said, "You gave birth to a foreign boy!" I could not believe the marvelous way God had blessed our family. Everyone in my family was very happy, and we thank and praise the Lord.

Of course, that child, that gift from God, is a special child to us and to everyone on both sides of our family. And he is such a miracle in my life! What a wonderful God we serve! He is a mighty God who hears and answers our prayers.

I want to praise and thank God for the wonderful miracles He performed in my life. Trust and believe in Him. You will experience His blessings in your life too. "I will praise the name of God with a song, and will magnify Him with thanksgiving" (Psalm 69:30, NKJV).

Dear Lord, help me to be grateful to You for Your wonderful leading. Amen.

Vijay Moses

Strength for Weary Days

"And as your days are, so will your strength,
your rest and security be."
—Deuteronomy 33:25, AMP

Have you ever had one of those days when you get up and consider your to-do list, and then you wonder how you're ever going to make it through your devotions? I have!

I thought that when I was no longer raising small children, I would be in charge of my calendar. I must have been confused! Although these days, I might be considered retired, that's just a category. Retirement means schedules, time lines, flight times—you know the drill! And I'm sure you often wonder, *How will I get all this accomplished today?*

When I was a young mother, I remember my mom telling me, "He giveth strength for the day." I didn't really appreciate what she was saying. In fact, I just plowed through the tasks ahead of me for that day and fell into bed at night exhausted. Everything had been done, yet I didn't realize back then that the Lord was interested in even a frustrated mom with young children.

I am thankful for God's faithfulness and His patience with my slow learning curve. Now I know that whatever the day ahead looks like, He already has it managed for me—if I will keep my hands to myself. He tells me, "Be still and know (recognize, understand) that I am God" (Psalm 46:10, AMP). It's difficult—yea, hard—for someone who likes control to allow God to take charge! Through my study, I have learned that it's not enough to be still; I need to *stop*! Yet who stops when the day's list is staring you in the face? I'm learning that unless I stop, I won't see, hear, and feel God's plan for me.

On those days when I feel overwhelmed and stressed and exhausted at the start of the day, I'm so thankful for a God who makes promises like this: "The eternal God is your refuge, and his everlasting arms are under you" (Deuteronomy 33:27, NLT).

It's so much easier to handle whatever happens when you stop to remember that God's got it! At the end of the day, I find that I'm pleasantly tired but no longer exhausted. I can feel where God's arms have held me and carried me throughout my day.

O what a marvelous God I have!

Wilma Kirk Lee

Disappointment and Blessings

My flesh and my heart may fail,
but God is the strength of my heart and my portion forever.
—Psalm 73:26, NIV

November 27, 2013, was a beautiful day with blue skies and bright sunshine. It had all the makings of an unforgettable day of peace and joy. But as long as we are on this side of eternity, we will have to live with pain, tears, and sadness. On that very day, I received a much-feared confirmation that I had invasive cancer in my left breast. In that moment, my whole outlook on life changed. Everything seemed to crumble.

Jesus knows what we need, and in terrible moments like these, He can calm the anxious heart.

Even when our eyes are blinded by tears of anguish and distress, He takes us by the hand and wipes away our tears. He comforts and strengthens us to face the unknown future and walk through the dark, unknown tunnel that lies ahead.

More medical exams. Surgery. Chemotherapy. Radiation therapy. Finally, medication and an extended treatment. Everything God has provided in terms of medical treatment, we have done. By the grace and mercy of our kind Father, I am still here today, recognizing the blessings that He reserves for His children in every situation.

God's specialty is turning tragedy into blessing. It may seem that He is silent, but His answer is certain, though that may be hard to understand in a moment of anguish.

More important than knowing *why* we are suffering is knowing *how* to respond to it. God will show us how to do that in His time. Our part is to trust and depend on His power.

Just now words from a song, which I sang a lot throughout my crisis, are going through my mind. These words of trust still encourage me during difficult moments. They express the commitment that we can trust God without even knowing what lies ahead. We can trust God on dark days, knowing that His will is best for us.

If you are going through a dark tunnel in your life right now, hold firmly to the hand of Jesus. Let's trust Him always, for His plans are always better than ours.

Edit Fonseca

November 28

An Attitude of Gratitude

Why are you down in the dumps, dear soul?
Why are you crying the blues?
Fix my eyes on God—soon I'll be praising again.
He puts a smile on my face.
He's my God.
—*Psalm 42:11*, The Message

Every once in a while, I wake up feeling a bit down in the dumps. I often blame it on hormonal changes or the weather. I become more sensitive, anxious, vulnerable to crying, and impatient with myself or others. Have you had that feeling? When this happens, I have learned to stop myself and ask, Why am I feeling this way? What thoughts could be triggering these emotions? I have noticed that I can exacerbate those feelings by negativity and stinky-thinking self-talk. The more we focus on ourselves and our down feelings, the worse we feel.

As I talk with women around the world, I find I am not alone. We can make life's burdens twice as heavy by "continually anticipating trouble," which brings "wretchedness" upon ourselves, and casts a shadow over others.* Our lives become depressed and anxious. Not good!

The good news is there is an antidote. It is called *gratitude*! Studies suggest that people who keep a "gratitude list" experience better mental health than those who don't. In fact, while doing research among people who experienced trauma in childhood, I observed that those who cultivate an attitude of gratitude experienced better mental and physical health later in life compared with those who don't. This antidote is not new. In the words of an inspired writer, "Nothing tends more to promote health of body and of soul than does a spirit of gratitude and praise."† When I am down, I like to focus on God's promises. "Let the peace of God rule in your hearts. . . . And be thankful" (Colossians 3:15, NIV).

Take just five minutes to list some of your blessings. At today's end, add three things that went well—and something that did *not* happen that you had dreaded would. Focus on the blessings you have. (If you focus on what you don't have, you will have less.) Repeat this daily.

And if your mind is crowded by pain today, do not try to think. Imagine being embraced by our loving God. Simply *rest* in His arms. Thank Him for His love. Let your gratitude and songs of praise ascend to heaven as a sweet aroma. Then watch God put a smile on your face.

Katia Garcia Reinert

* Ellen G. White, *The Ministry of Healing* (Nampa, ID: Pacific Press®, 2003), 247, 248.

† White, *The Ministry of Healing*, 251.

He Is Faithful

"Therefore know that the LORD your God, He is God."
—Deuteronomy 7:9, NKJV

While growing up, life was a constant struggle. My father died when I was four years old. My jobless mom had no means of caring for my older siblings and me. I was adopted by a wonderful woman, who entrusted me to her sister. That day marked the beginning of my life's journey. People in the sister's house regarded me as filthy and hopeless to the extent that I was not permitted to use household utensils. I lived a lonely life as a child with no shoulder to cry on. I could not share my humiliation with my adoptive mother because she lived far away and eventually traveled abroad. I had no one to share my sorrows with but God.

The only thing that kept me moving forward though my bitter experience was my hope in God—and my high academic performance, which endeared me to my teachers. No communication came from my mother. Though I sometimes did not have enough food or clothes, I never gave up. I trusted that one day my burdens would be lifted—to God's glory—if I remained faithful to Him.

Interestingly, it was my foster parent who had introduced me to God. I took delight in worshiping the Almighty. Participating in worship and church activities became part of me because I loved the story of redemption and especially the freedom found in Jesus. I always looked forward to the Parousia that was to end all human suffering and pain. I prayed and sought the face of the Almighty daily. Once I was able to make a casual visit to my mother. When I saw how poverty had consumed her, I cried all night. With that experience, my dreams of reuniting with her were shattered, but God still had a beautiful design for my life in His time.

After finishing my secondary education, I was invited to stay with the son of the woman who had adopted me. After being in his house for six months, early one morning he handed me an application form to attend a university. That began my success story. By the grace of God, I finished my first degree and have started a master's degree still under His care, all to the glory of God. I have learned that nothing is hard for the Lord. If only we have hope and faith in Him, He will surely turn our lives around for the better to His glory. Our God is faithful indeed. Amen!

Evelyn Osei-Bonsu

His Eye Is on the Sparrow

"Look at the birds of the air; they do not sow or reap or store away in
barns, and yet your heavenly Father feeds them. Are you not much
more valuable than they?"
—Matthew 6:26, NIV

It was a beautiful, sunny winter morning. I was praising God that I was dressed, ready for church, and in the car. But to my dismay, as I turned on the ignition to start the car, the service-engine light came on, indicating that something was wrong with the car. All I could say was, "Lord, here we go again, another unexpected repair bill." Since my mandatory retirement due to my health, I have had one financial challenge after another. I remember times in the past when I would read that a person should save and invest for the future. To my disadvantage, that message did not strike a responsive chord in my mind. I truly believed that I had plenty of time to save for the future. Unfortunately, it didn't work out that way. Because of my physical health, I had to retire early from the nursing profession that I loved, and I was not financially prepared. But we serve a caring and loving God.

Matthew 6:26 has blessed me during times like these when unexpected and unplanned financial challenges have occurred. Whenever I have needed money for car repairs or a broken home heating system, among other things, God has always provided whatever I needed.

I was told that the repairs would cost $320. Over half of that amount was the labor charge alone. I did not have that amount, but I trusted God to come through for me. After telling a friend what I needed, he agreed to do the repairs for only forty dollars' labor charge, if *I* purchased the needed parts. God came through again!

My faith in God increases with each new challenge. I believe that He allows these times of testing so that we will be encouraged to trust in Him. He desires that we move beyond our usual security blankets and comfort zones and abandon ourselves in total trust in Him.

Just as God provides for the birds, we can count on Him to provide for us because He loves us more than the sparrows. Do you believe what Jesus said in Matthew 6:26? I do. If the Creator of the universe cares enough about the humble birds to care for them, why would He care any less about us? I have learned that I am of more value to Him than a sparrow.

Whatever you need, you can trust God to provide it.

Clementine H. Collins

God Rewards Obedience

*His lord said unto him, Well done, thou good and faithful servant:
thou hast been faithful over a few things, I will make thee ruler over
many things: enter thou into the joy of thy lord.*
—Matthew 25:21, KJV

Nestled between the continents of North America and South America lies a small but beautiful country named Belize. It is home to blue oceans and famous Mayan ruins and is the birthplace of my mother, Gwendolyn Joy Flowers. Though born to poor parents who lived in a one-room house, she attended a private school as they struggled to pay her tuition. Her mother, Florinda Trapp, did laundry by hand on a washboard for many families and sold home-baked bread and buns.

My mother became well known in Belize City for receiving top marks and the highest honors in her secondary school. In 1961, she was preparing for the rigorous final exams when she learned that the biology lab and conversational Spanish exams would be held on a Saturday—the day on which she and her family worshiped. If she didn't take those exams, she would fail everything. Her school principal even requested permission from her pastor for my mother to "break her Sabbath" just this one time because the exam dates could not be changed. Mother stood firm.

My grandmother, a woman of deep faith, said, "Everyone is making such a big to-do about a test on Sabbath. Don't they know that God, with all His power, can send a hurricane to wipe out that entire biology lab so no test could be given?" Two weeks prior to the scheduled biology test, the written exams were administered in all the disciplines.

Then on October 31, 1961, the Monday night before the Saturday test date, Hurricane Hattie hit Belize City in Central America. With winds reaching 160 miles per hour, the entire city was destroyed, including the biology lab. I praise God that my mother and family were spared during that horrible ordeal. When the subsequent test results were released in February of 1961, my mother was one of only five students who had passed. She became the first girl to ever receive a full college scholarship in what had been a religious all-boys institution!

God had rewarded her obedience. He still does the same today—no matter how grim a situation. Remain obedient. God sees your struggles, and He will create a safe passage for you.

Sherilyn Flowers

The Essence of the Divine Ordinances

This is He who came by water and blood—Jesus Christ;
not only by water, but by water and blood.
—1 John 5:6, NKJV

"Hi Susan, can I wash your feet during the foot-washing ordinance of humility?" asked Rehana in church one Sabbath.

"No, I am too embarrassed to participate. I haven't done my nails, and I have too many calluses," Susan replied. Heather overheard this exchange.

"And I haven't participated in footwashing for years," Susan added. "I'm not touching other people's smelly feet."

Rehana paused and offered a silent prayer before looking up at her friends. "Let's talk about some symbols in today's Communion and foot-washing services," she suggested. "First, remember the bread that symbolizes Christ's body? Well, in Luke 22:19, Jesus said, 'This is My body which is given for you; do this in remembrance of Me' [NKJV]. His sacrifice takes away the sins of many until His second coming [see Hebrews 9:28]. The second symbol, the wine, reminds us of Christ's humanity and painful death for our sins [1 Corinthians 11:26]."

As her friends listened, Rehana continued. "The third symbol, footwashing, symbolizes Christ's forgiveness and humility, which we are to exemplify [Ephesians 5:25–27]. The fourth symbol, water, points to Christ's divinity and selflessness. First John 5:6 says, 'This is He who came by water and blood' [NKJV]. If blood represents His humanity, then water must represent His divinity. Even in death, He showed He was both divine and human as blood *and* water came out of His pierced side [John 19:34]." Rehana paused before adding, "When we humbly enter the room to participate in footwashing with our sins confessed, we can know that God is humbling Himself along with us. His divinity is passing by. His presence is the essence of the ordinances.

"Susan and Heather," Rehana said thoughtfully, "for a meaningful experience, consider writing your confessed sins on a slip of paper and putting it in the foot-washing bowl. You'll see that the water 'dissolves' away what you wrote. Likewise, God can also make us just as spotless in an instant."

Like water, God's forgiveness flows from His throne to cleanse and renew our hearts.

Suhana Chikatla

"All Things Work Together"

And we know that all things work together for good to those who
love God, to those who are the called according to His purpose.
—*Romans 8:28, NKJV*

In December of 2009, I sat alone in my house, crying. Life, as I'd known it, had just unraveled. I was reeling from a blow: my husband was leaving me. He no longer wanted to be married but desired the freedom to be with someone else. During the months that followed this revelation, I struggled to regain my life, my independence, and my future. I endured many trials, setbacks, highs, and lows. Life became a long process of learning, growing, and wondering on many days and nights whether I would ever be happy again, whether I would ever find love and acceptance the way God intended for us to know it. Many days I questioned whether I was destined to be alone for the rest of my life.

In 2011, the long months of daily wondering, praying, and watching for perhaps the right man to enter my life took a turn for the better. I met a man on a Christian dating site. I knew firsthand that there were a lot of con artists out there and a lot of dishonest people, so I had no hope of any lasting relationship developing. Months went by. This gentleman and I finally met in person. I met his kids, and things fell into place. It appeared this friendship was meant to be.

Fast-forward a few months: I decided to move to Nebraska, where this man (now my husband) lived, from Massachusetts, where I'd lived my whole life. But I would have to do something about the townhouse I'd purchased after my divorce. I tend to worry a lot about how things will work out; in fact, I excel at it! One day as I was stressing out, words from a Bible text came into my mind: "all things work together for good" (Romans 8:28, NKJV). Instantly, I ran and looked up the text in my Bible. It was as though God were standing right next to me, whispering, *Hey, don't worry about things. It will all work out OK. I have brought this about, and I will see you through it.*

From that moment on, I knew I didn't need to worry because God would take care of everything and of me. I have never forgotten how near I felt to Him then and still do now. I recite that verse often when things are not looking good, and I remember His promise to me—to us all.

So the next time you think nothing good can come from a tangled situation, remember that God has promised it can. He works *all* things for the good of His children.

Debra Snyder

December 4

Embrace Your Winter

Now we see a dim reflection, as if we were looking into a mirror, but then we shall see clearly. Now I know only a part, but then I will know fully, as God has known me.
—1 Corinthians 13:12, NCV

I run. And when I say I run, I really mean that I don't walk. It's more of a slow jog with the occasional "stop and smell the roses" moments, such as petting the neighbor's puppy or moving a worm off the sidewalk so that it doesn't get stepped on. Or I actually stop to take in the fragrance of the flowers. I run in all kinds of weather all year long. Since I live in the Midwest, I get my share of rain, sun, sleet, snow, and gusty winds.

This past year I trained for, and completed, two full marathons. Being a creature of habit, I stick to one specific route. On one of my long runs in December, I noticed something new. The now leafless trees revealed a beautiful pond in the middle of my city and a set of old railroad tracks beside it. I stopped, marveling at the fact that even though I'd run by this exact spot at least three times a week for the past several months, only during the dead of winter was I was able to see this treasure. Though there all along, it went unnoticed when leafy trees blocked its view.

When asked to name their favorite season, most people will not say winter. It's cold and dark and lifeless. Yet winter has a purpose. It's a time of rest and revelation. I thought back to the many winters in my own journey: my father's suicide, my grandparents' deaths less than twenty-four hours apart, a family member's prison sentence, and my divorce. Dark, cold days. Yet God used those moments to reveal His grace and power and love in a way that I couldn't have seen before. As so many things and people were stripped away, I have been able to see more clearly, more fully, the God who adores me. I have learned to embrace the winter, to look for the unexpected beauty in the midst of heartache, and to find God.

And now, even when spring returns and the leaves grow back and I won't be able to see the pond anymore, I will know it's still there. God, who always uses our pain-filled winter moments for a purpose, has given me the ability to see something: without winter, the other seasons just aren't as beautiful. Only our Almighty God can take the cold, dark, and seemingly lifeless times we experience and use them to draw us closer to Him. A precious gift indeed!

Amy Bock

Do You Have an Angel?

"Do you think that I cannot now pray to My Father, and He will provide Me with more than twelve legions of angels?"
—*Matthew 26:53, NKJV*

I have the pleasure of being part of a small prayer group. For many years, two friends and I have maintained this group with the purpose of praying for one another in our various situations and even in different locations. We continue to this day even though we now live in different places. We still pray daily for one another and, whenever possible, speak on the phone, communicate online, or meet in person to pray together or share our blessings.

Both of my friends have shared experiences of what they believed were angelic interventions in their lives. I must confess that I sometimes wondered whether the stories they shared about the help and protection of angels were not simply coincidences in life and fruit of a greater desire for divine contact. When I shared with my sister-friends that I had had no such experience but desired to know my angel was with me, they suggested that I pray about it.

Sometime after that our church promoted its first spiritual enrichment seminar. During what would be a period of forty days, the members were encouraged to focus on developing a closer relationship with God. Throughout this time of spiritual renewal, we were encouraged to spend the first hours of the day with God in prayer and study. The night before this seminar was to begin, I went to bed praying that the Lord would have my guardian angel wake me up at five o'clock the next morning (see Isaiah 50:4). I fell asleep and slept like a rock.

Early the next morning, while it was still dark, I awoke to a male voice softly calling my name: "Val." Thinking I was dreaming, I slept a bit more. Again I heard the voice: "Val."

With my eyes still closed, I reached out to touch my husband, thinking he was calling me. Then reality struck. My husband was gone on an overnight trip and was not at home! Suddenly frightened, I sat up in bed and looked at the clock. It was five o'clock; my angel had awakened me!

Tears flowed as my heart raced with joy. How can we doubt there is a God who loves us and wants to reveal Himself to us? On that special day, I learned two very valuable lessons. The first is the importance of taking time for intercessory prayer. The second is that God pays attention to the smallest details of our lives. The angel had called me by my nickname.

Val Baminger Oliveira

Christ, the Master Surgeon

Bless the Lord, O my soul,
And forget not all His benefits:
Who forgives all your iniquities,
Who heals all your diseases.
—*Psalm 103:3, NKJV*

Many of God's children are in desperate need of surgery to maintain life. Some may require emergency surgery; others, elective surgery. In every case, however, it is necessary for them to undergo surgery in order to obtain eternal life.

Jesus is the Master Surgeon. His first patient is scheduled for brain surgery early in the morning. Once inside, Christ removes all thoughts that are contrary to the Word and will of God. Spiritual medication is administered from God's Word to enable the patient to think on "whatsoever things are true, whatsoever things are honest, whatsoever things are just, whatsoever things are pure, whatsoever things are lovely, whatsoever things are of good report" (Philippians 4:8, KJV).

Christ's second patient is in need of a heart transplant. The Master Surgeon has promised to "cast away from you all your transgressions, whereby ye have transgressed; and make you a new heart and a new spirit" (Ezekiel 18:31, KJV). Christ removes the stony heart and replaces it with a heart of flesh (see Ezekiel 11:19).

Last but not least, Christ performs an exploratory laparotomy. (In layman's terms, He makes an incision in the abdomen.) Once inside, He identifies any problem and proceeds to make the necessary corrections. He may discover malice, hurt, hatred, jealousy, anger, deceitfulness, envy, covetousness, and other foreign matter that causes excruciating pain and discomfort. He removes the debris from the abdomen and replaces it with the fruit of the spirit: "love, joy, peace, longsuffering, gentleness, goodness, faith, meekness, temperance" (Galatians 5:22, 23, KJV).

There are diseases that can be treated and healed only by our heavenly Father through His Son, Jesus Christ. You will not get a medical bill in the mail. It was prepaid at the cross. You don't have to be premedicated and taken to an operating room on a gurney. You don't have to go to rehab or make any clinical or doctor's appointments for follow-up care. With His stripes, you are healed (see Isaiah 53:5).

Jesus is the Master Surgeon. All you have to do is call on Him. The call is free, and the phone line is open. He is ready and waiting. Why not make your call now?

Cora A. Walker

Trust in God

What shall I return to the LORD for all his goodness to me?
—*Psalm 116:12, NIV*

I n 2007, I was in my first year of university as a psychology major. Since I needed to work to pay for college expenses and help my husband with the expenses of our home, I studied in the evening. In order to keep the Sabbath holy, I did not attend classes on Friday evening. At the start of the fourth quarter, the dean called me into her office. The academic director was also present. Soberly, she told me I could no longer skip the Friday evening classes. Respectfully, I answered, "According to the Bible, the sundown hours of Friday are part of God's sacred worship day. Though I will comply any way I can with the university's requirements, I must make no concessions that would keep me from worshiping according to the biblical commandment. Being able to study psychology is a dream come true, yet I would abandon my studies if they were to keep me from being loyal to God."

The dean interrupted and said, "You're an excellent student, one of the few I always find studying in the library. I suggest you reconsider your choice. I think God wants you to study."

"Oh, yes," I quickly agreed. "God wants us to advance in knowledge. But He wants us first to be faithful to Him." The dean shook her head and told me I'd never graduate. "With all due respect and God willing," I softly replied, "I think I will." She said, a bit more rudely, that she would not argue about religion with me and that I would be asked to sign a statement acknowledging that the university had offered me guidance on the difficulties I would face by not attending Friday night classes. By signing the statement, I would be promising not to hold them responsible for my not graduating. I said I was willing to sign the statement at any time.

When the academic director left the dean's office, I sat there for a while. The dean looked at me and patiently made sure I had understood what would happen. I asked her to assure me she would do whatever she could to help me. She said she would—until she bumped into school rules. Then there was nothing else she would be able to do. Very clearly, I replied, "When you can do no more for me, God will do it."

I was never called to sign that statement. By God's grace and goodness, I finished my studies and now work as a clinical psychologist. How can I repay God for His goodness to me?

María Regina Werneck Mandeli

December 8

God Is Faithful!

Do not be anxious about anything, but in every situation, by prayer and petition, with thanksgiving, present your requests to God.
—*Philippians 4:6, NIV*

God is faithful, and His words are true. Last evening I discovered a small error in my book that involved only two words totaling seven letters, but what a difference those two words made. Right away, my mind raced with anxious thoughts. I corrected the error and emailed it to the publisher, along with a prayer for God's intervention for the correction to be made before the book was released. I slept relatively well; but upon awakening the next morning, I began to worry again. I was about to phone my book representative to tell her about the email I'd sent earlier when I decided to check my email. There I saw an email sent to me by a friend two days earlier that was still unread. It was a devotional from a book she liked. The author had written that when something makes us anxious, we should talk to Jesus about it. We should bring our petition with thanksgiving and thank Him for the opportunity to trust Him more.

These were profound words and just what I needed to hear at that precise moment. Immediately, I felt at peace and decided to read the statement again. Afterward, I knelt by my bed and petitioned my heavenly Father to forgive my sins, to give me peace of mind, and to handle the problem for me. Oh, the peace of mind we often forfeit when we neglect to take everything to God in prayer.

When I got up, a calmness enveloped me. I found myself smiling at what God had just done. I decided not to call my representative but to leave it in God's hand. That can be difficult to do sometimes. As human beings, we want answers right away, and we take matters into our hands. Today I plan to leave it in God's hand. He knows how to fix it better than I can. To confirm that He would take care of my dilemma, He impressed my prayer-warrior friend to call me. She shared Proverbs 3:5, 6:

> Trust in the LORD with all your heart,
> And lean not on your own understanding;
> In all your ways acknowledge Him,
> And He shall direct your paths (NKJV).

Dear reader, are challenging situations in your life causing you to feel overwhelmed right now? Tell Jesus; He will listen; He will answer when you call. So cast all your cares on Him because He loves and cares for you.

Shirley C. Iheanacho

"Chosen"

But you are not like that, for you have been chosen by God Himself—
you are priests of the King, you are holy and pure, you are God's very
own—all this so that you may show to others how God called you out
of the darkness into his wonderful light.
—1 Peter 2:9, TLB

I sat on the edge of my Southwest Airlines seat. My husband, Don, and I were sitting in a row with three seats, and I was destined to be the middle seat occupant but determined to make it fun. Carefully, I searched the incoming crowd of travelers for just the right one. Someone small and friendly.

As the trail of travelers thinned out, I spotted her, tall and thin, with a big smile on her face. "Hi, would you like to have my aisle seat?" I offered. As with previous travelers responding to my question, this traveler's face lit up. She looked at me more closely.

"Sure, thanks!" She smiled and sat down as I eased over next to Don, sitting comfortably by the window. Through my travels, I have learned that when the airline has a fully booked flight with open seating in three seats to a row it is wise, whenever possible, to choose your neighbor.

Without fail, these weary travelers who end up in the back of a boarding line, for one reason or another, are so happy when offered an aisle seat that it changes the whole atmosphere. My new neighbor felt chosen and was grateful. That afternoon, we exchanged names and learned that Mikaila was returning from her dear friend's graduation in the nation's capital and was headed for her first year in college on a scholarship with a psychology degree on the horizon. She was eager to share and, as always, Don was having fun teasing her.

After the flight, Don caught up with our new friend and former seatmate and whispered, "Chosen!" as he gave her a wink. Mikaila laughed and headed out of the baggage claim area with a smile. I was a little embarrassed at Don's forwardness, but then, surprisingly, my eyes glistened with tears as God interrupted my self-centeredness and whispered in my thoughts, *You are chosen, too, Nancy!* I turned around to focus on that wonderful thought: Jesus, the Creator of the universe, has chosen silly me and many others to be His spokespersons? I, indeed, was grateful, remembering that He called me out of the darkness so that I could walk in His wonderful light. Did you know you are chosen too?

Nancy (Neuharth) Troyer

December 10

Gift Giving

Every good gift and every perfect gift is from above,
and cometh down from the Father of lights,
with whom is no variableness, neither shadow of turning.
—James 1:17, KJV

Ever wonder about all the gift giving that goes on at Christmastime? It's the most commercial holiday in America. In the distant past, one didn't see any Christmas themes in department stores until after Thanksgiving. Now Christmas décor shows up in autumn.

Some Christians say we shouldn't get caught up in this gift-giving pressure. Let's look at that perspective. Think about the gifts God gives us: life, health, friends, family, food, clothing, and transportation, among others. Those are gifts we should never take for granted.

Then there's God's greatest gift given to humankind: Jesus, the Son of God, Messiah, Emmanuel, the Prince of Peace. How many of us could give our son away to a group of people who didn't want him? (I get upset when I hear my boys being criticized.) Think of having to be apart for more than thirty-three years, not knowing whether he would return home again or not. Yet God the Father loved us so much that He did just that. That's why we call it *amazing* grace and love!

Then what did His Son, Jesus, do? He gave Himself up totally for us. He willingly left His perfect environment in heaven to come live among us. He taught people how to live better, fulfilled lives. He healed many of their diseases. By His example, He reflected His Father—His character was a reflection of God. He gave the ultimate gift by dying on the cross and becoming sin for us. He'd rather die than let us go. By giving His life, we may now have the gift of eternal life. It's so hard for us to understand such a precious gift, such a sacrifice.

There are many ways we can thank Him. A few Christmases ago our family members started selecting worthy causes we could give to instead of spending money on gifts for each other. A number of Christian relief ministries have "catalogs" in which specific projects for needy people around the world are pictured and to which one can donate. Does this mean there are no gifts under our tree? No. I still pick up different items throughout the year that are wrapped up so that family members know they are also special to us.

During this season, take a few moments to reflect on how special God's gifts are to you. Especially the gift of His Son. For the love of the world, don't let Him go.

Louise Driver

The Fire That Wouldn't Stay Lit

"For I know the plans I have for you," declares the LORD,
"plans to prosper you and not to harm you,
plans to give you hope and a future."
—*Jeremiah 29:11, NIV*

After a two-week Alaskan cold snap, which included temperatures of zero degrees Fahrenheit (along with wind chills of at least twenty-five below zero), I took the first calm day to clean my chimney. I always clean the chimney before my first fire of the season and felt it needed to be done.

After I cleaned the chimney, my fire started well, but every time I closed the stove door, the fire smothered out. Three times I tried, but I could *not* get that fire to stay lit. I felt chilled and tired from being out in the extreme cold all day, so I gave up and went to bed.

The next evening I cleaned the chimney again. I lit the fire and got it going good, but when I closed the stove door, it smothered out again. The fire behaved as if the chimney were clogged, but I'd cleaned it, remember? I went upstairs to my loft to wiggle the pipe a little to see whether I could dislodge whatever might be stuck in it. Between the floors I had installed a larger pipe with the smaller pipe inside as a heat barrier. I noticed the top of the inside pipe was burned through in a couple of places. So I decided to replace the entire pipe instead of just the damaged piece.

As I pulled out the old pipe, I was speechless at what I discovered! The pipe had been totally destroyed, burned through all the way around! It was hanging almost in two separate pieces, held together only by the thinnest of lacy-looking burnt pipe. I looked in the bottom piece of the pipe. It was totally blocked with creosote. No wonder my fire had smothered out—it had no air!

In more than twenty years of heating with wood and coal, I had *never* had the pipe get completely blocked when I'd brushed out the chimney. Had I *not* cleaned the chimney that Sunday and had the pipe *not* gotten totally blocked by the creosote, the fire would have stayed lit when I closed the door. The flames would have raced up the chimney and out into my loft. I would have already fallen into my normal deep sleep for the night, unaware of the danger, and would probably never have awakened. I am thankful to God for sparing my life that night.

What about you? How about thanking God right now for His often unseen protection?

Sonia Brock

December 12

True Satisfaction

"Listen carefully to Me, and eat what is good,
and let your soul delight itself in abundance."
—Isaiah 55:2, NKJV

There is a verse in the Bible found in Isaiah 55 that says, "Why do you spend money for what is not bread, and your wages for what does not satisfy?" (verse 2, NKJV). This Christmas season, as always, I will spend money on gifts for others. But it is also a hectic time, and feelings of being overwhelmed with all the preparations fill my heart at this "most wonderful time of the year." Even my health can be affected as I succumb to a cold or sickness. Pondering this verse anew, I ask, Does this apply to me and to what I'm doing?

The answer to the first question is yes! I do spend money but that brings only limited satisfaction because I find myself always wanting to purchase more—even for myself. For example, I once needed one shirt for a special event, but I ended up buying three.

Once home I was filled with buyer's remorse. I reprimanded myself for being so foolish as to buy more than I really needed. Again, this Bible verse came to mind, for I had spent money on what does not truly satisfy. *Oh, Lord, forgive me. Will I ever learn?* I reminded myself that I need to allow the Lord to be part of every buying transaction and not just assume I can handle the decision making alone. Obviously, I can't—as evidenced in my last purchase at the store.

I have a good friend named Colleen who is such a blessing to me. Each week we get together on the phone and pray together. Our last discussion was on exerting self-control regarding the different things we discussed, such as food, our thinking habits, and money. We both could identify with the struggles of the other and encouraged each other through heartfelt prayer. We confessed our weaknesses and told God of our desire to make changes, asking for His help.

During this Christmas season as we shop, may we also "buy wine and milk without money and without price" (verse 1, NKJV). May Jesus fill us completely. When we invite the Lord to be in charge of our decisions, only then is it safe to spend money.

True satisfaction will fill our hearts as we partner with the Lord each day!

Rosemarie Clardy

"Welcome Home"

Devote yourselves to prayer,
being watchful and thankful.
—*Colossians 4:2, NIV*

In a lecture hall at work, I observe a colleague deliver the first Lunch and Learn presentation to the faculty on time management. He invites us to complete the Daily Inventory sheet he passes out, mentioning how it helped him realize he was trying to do more things in one day than there were hours. I know that feeling! Back in my office, I send him a congratulatory email on his presentation. Then I glance at the handout, look at the clock, and quickly fill in the inventory. Five hours later, standing in my kitchen, I am appalled at the outcome of my Daily Inventory sheet. Handwriting all over the page outlines the tasks completed and marginal notes indicate follow-ups: commute, teaching, meetings, office hours, grading, editing, student visits, and more. A restless night is my reward for realizing how busy my days are.

At work early the next morning, I read an appreciative email response from my colleague. His closing comments grab my attention: "I hope you have the opportunity to complete the Daily Inventory and notice what was missing. At the end of my day, the truly important things in my life were lacking in cultivation of time. They were routine. Changing that made me more focused. It was as if my heart told my mind: 'Welcome home!' "

I glance at my completed inventory sheet stuffed in my purse. What have I missed? An appointment? A deadline? As I look at the time slots, my eyes get teary. I see what has become a routine, and it pains me: prayer. Nowhere on the handout do I list time spent reading my Bible or having my morning devotions. In fact, when the alarm rings, the first thing that comes out of my lips is a prayer. I pray all day! When I wake up, before I teach, attend a meeting, drive to and from work, I always pray! But yesterday I spent two hours in an accreditation meeting. Yet I did not devote two hours in one sitting to a one-on-one personal meeting with my Savior in the evening. Daily prayer reads as part of my routine. How did this happen?

I see the lesson plans in front of me, waiting for a final review before teaching in an hour. I needn't devote more time to what needs no more time. I close my office door, lock it, and take in the silence. I open a small Bible stowed in my purse and read a psalm out loud. Then I kneel on the hard floor and pray. Just like that, I can hear my heart tell my head: "Welcome home!"

Dixil L. Rodríguez

Multiplying Talents

Whatever your hand finds to do, do it with your might.
—*Ecclesiastes 9:10, NKJV*

And whatever you do, do it heartily, as to the Lord and not to men.
—*Colossians 3:23, NKJV*

One of the things I do for my local church is lead the choir. I can assure you that it did not come automatically to me to go up front and direct a choir. People knew me as a very shy person. Neither am I really a musician or anyone who is learned in music. I like to sing and have been in good choirs and have learned from my choir conductors. Nothing more. Yet when the need arose and no one else was willing to direct a choir, I did it.

During my first year as choir leader, I asked the church to let me be the assistant director because I was not confident. By the second year, I accepted the assignment without hesitation.

When I started out, my daughter (who had had about three years of piano lessons) was already playing for the choir, so she just continued. When she got married in April, she agreed that a youngster, whom I thought we could use as a pianist, would be the best choice.

Although Sean was just about to turn eleven, he could play the piano for the practices and performances. We were both learning. He had two years of lessons, and I had no training in conducting.

At our first Christmas concert, we sang three songs along with two other groups. By Easter of the next year, we performed two songs from Handel's *Messiah* besides other songs we had learned. The following Christmas we had a longer repertoire.

The church choir has now presented several concerts, including *Messiah*, some of John Rutter's compositions, and other musical works. This was possible not because we were great musicians but because we did the best we could for God.

We worked hard, and we prayed hard. Sean is now an accomplished accompanist and a medical student and the accompanist at his medical school. As for me, I can now go up front and give presentations for various meetings. God has blessed us with being able to do more than we used to because we were willing to do a church assignment that was a little challenging for us.

God can really use small talents and multiply them if we give them to Him.

Let us do the best we can as we work and wait for our Lord.

Rosenita Christo

Recovery and Replenishment: A Lesson Learned in Retail

For I have satiated the weary soul,
and I have replenished every sorrowful soul.
—*Jeremiah 31:25, KJV*

An upscale department store chain hired me to work in recovery and replenishment as a seasonal sales associate. The season for which they hired me was the Christmas season. Recovery and replenishment responsibilities include traveling throughout the store during one's work shift and making sure everything is in order and that all products are neatly organized. If an item is missing from its rightful place or if items are depleted from the display, the workers in recovery and replenishment are responsible for restoring the items.

On my first day of working at the department store, I was assigned to the cashmere sweaters display. The sweaters were in demand due to a discount of more than 50 percent. So I spent all eight hours of my shift neatly folding and restocking the cashmere sweaters. Now here's the funny part: No sooner had I neatly organized the cashmere sweaters by color, size, and style, than another customer would come along and sift through the neatly organized stacks. Whether or not the customer chose to buy a sweater, the display was a complete mess again by the time he or she finished browsing. The V-neck sweaters were mixed with the crew-neck sweaters, and the red sweaters were mixed with the green. Inwardly, I would sigh as I went to work restoring the cashmere sweater display to neatness and order.

After about four hours of doing this repeatedly, a lesson emerged in my mind. Is this not what God does for us? No matter how much we mess up in life or fall victim to life's curveballs when the devil desires to sift us like wheat (see Luke 22:31), God is there. His Son, Jesus Christ, is always working to restore us to God's image and make us presentable before the Lord.

Unlike me, God is very patient as He works to restore us. No matter how much we're messed up, He quietly untangles our mixed emotions from the drama and trauma we've endured. He gently restores us to who He has called us to be in this life. When our resources are depleted, He graciously replenishes us with the gifts of time, money, and His love.

Aren't you glad that we serve a God who is in the restoration business?

Alexis A. Goring

December 16

My Guardian Angels

*Surely goodness and mercy
shall follow me all the days of my life.*
—*Psalm 23:6, KJV*

One cold day in December I went outside to warm up my van before going to work. The wind hit me in the chest as a heavyweight boxer might punch his opponent. *What was that?* I wondered, clutching at my chest with its sudden feeling of heaviness. As the week progressed, so did the pain in my chest.

Five days before Christmas, experiencing increasing chest pain and shortness of breath, I anointed my head with oil and asked God to keep me throughout the day and deliver me from the pain. Later that day I decided to go to an urgent-care center. Both the nurse and receptionist said they suspected a heart attack and told me to get to the nearest hospital, which was just down the street. For whatever reason, I drove past the hospital to the next urgent-care center in my town of Pleasantville, New Jersey, United States. When the doctor ran an electrocardiogram test on me, he found something abnormal about the results. He called my husband to come drive me to a hospital. My husband informed him that his youngest daughter had his car but when he got it, he would pick me up. I told the doctor I felt well enough to drive myself home. He walked me to my van and made sure I put on my seat belt. He repeated his orders to go straight home. As I was driving home, I started to get the pain all over again. I prayed, *God just let me get home.*

When I arrived, my husband was waiting at the door and drove me to the nearest hospital in our town. Once I arrived in the emergency room, they admitted me right away. My doctor had called ahead. Once the tests were all done, the doctors in the emergency room concluded that the enzymes in my blood were showing either I had, or was having, a heart attack. Test results also revealed I had a 90 percent blockage. I was subsequently transported by ambulance to the same hospital that I had driven past earlier, the only hospital equipped for cardiac catheterization procedures. As they prepared me for the procedure, I once again prayed that God would be with me and that His hands would cover the hands of the doctors and nurses.

I stand in amazement of God's goodness and mercy. I am also amazed that He sends His guardian angels to protect us even in our foolishness. "For he shall give his angels charge over thee, to keep thee in all thy ways" (Psalm 91:11, KJV).

Avis Floyd Jackson

The Appointed Time

Wait on the LORD: be of good courage,
and he shall strengthen thine heart:
wait, I say, on the LORD.
—Psalm 27:14, KJV

I am not enthusiastic about waiting. Waiting in a doctor's office, in a grocery store line, or for a baby to be born is not always pleasant, but God's Word tells us, "They that wait upon the LORD shall renew their strength" (Isaiah 40:31, KJV). In 1993, I married a young man from a warm and loving family. My husband, a pastor, is the youngest son and the sixth of his seven siblings. All but one gentleman in his family worshiped on Sabbath. We tried to live our faith, praying that the whole family would be in that faith. We prayed and waited.

One day we received a special message. Uncle Kwesi, my husband's uncle, wanted to be baptized after reading about the seventh-day Sabbath. Though his sister, my husband's late mother, had been baptized, he had taken the time to study on his own about the Sabbath, also reading literature about how to have better health through following Bible principles. He was convinced that this was the right time for him to take this step of faith.

We were overjoyed when my husband lowered Uncle Kwesi into the watery grave of baptism and brought him up again. We talked so much about how on resurrection morning, this will be one of the surprises for his mother.

On December 17, 2016, my husband received a phone call. "Brother T. T. got baptized today," said the elated caller on the other end of the line. He quickly put the phone to my ear, and I heard the words repeated by one of my sisters-in-law. I shouted a very loud "Amen!"; then my family smiled, watching me dance for joy concerning the news.

We had prayed and waited for twenty-three years for the time to be "fulfilled" for the baptism. Some who had prayed had already passed away, but they had claimed the promise. Though the answer to prayer had "tarried" (Habakkuk 2:3), God had brought it to pass in His time—as with Adam and Eve, Abraham, and Martha awaiting fulfillment of God's promises.

Today we cry, "How long?" as we wait to be taken to heaven. Yet we will wait patiently, praying and living like Christ. Then at the appointed time, God makes all things beautiful (see Ecclesiastes 3:11).

Dear Lord, help us to know that You will answer our prayers at the appointed time.

Mimonte Dorcas Odonkor

December 18

Longsuffering

With all lowliness and gentleness,
with longsuffering, bearing with one another in love.
—*Ephesians 4:2, NKJV*

Exchange of greetings, pleasantries, small talk, and "Happy holidays!" floated in the tropical air that afternoon in December.

Caribbean people surely have an extra dose of joy within them every Yuletide season, I thought. The apparent spirit of happiness was contagious. It was the Christmas season. People outside a chain department store were waiting to gift wrap purchases for shoppers.

Inside the store, I spent a few minutes before moving toward the cashier. I was glad that I would be next in line to have my purchases rung up and paid for. *Not a long wait*, I thought.

Suddenly, I head a shrill scream come from my right. A child had had to re-shelve an item that he wanted. Now he was not failing to protest—and with a loud voice.

Look out for further temper tantrums, I told myself. The cashier responded to the scream with an understanding smile.

At that instant, I did not look at the child. I was occupied with images of what turmoil one student with this type of behavior could cause in a classroom. I visualized this child as a student being able to upset the equilibrium of a class that had been otherwise engaged in meaningful learning activities.

Tempted to vocalize my thoughts of sympathy with the teachers of "those kids," I cast a quick glance at this child. What I saw elicited sudden concern and sympathy, especially for the woman whom I suspect was his mother. The child appeared to have Down syndrome and was approximately ten years old. I know that parents and guardians of children with disabilities deal with many extra stressors that parents of healthy children don't have. I quickly shifted my previous thinking as I watched the mother pat the child's head after having had to run behind him to bring him back to the checkout line.

Many times we are quick to judge without knowing all the facts. I'm glad I did not verbalize what I thought of the boy's behavior. The Bible encourages us to be "slow to speak, slow to wrath" (James 1:19, NKJV). Let us endeavor to be more longsuffering.

Hyacinth V. Caleb

The Wrong Address?

And we know that all things work together for good to those who
love God, to those who are the called according to His purpose.
—*Romans 8:28, NKJV*

I wanted to give my friend and physical therapist, Martin Iverson, a Christmas present—a fruit basket for his large family. I carefully filled out the order form from a catalog that offered large fruit baskets to be delivered within the week of December 19. I used my friend's business address on his business card as the delivery destination because I didn't have his home address.

The week of the nineteenth came, and I did not hear that Martin had received the basket. Finally, on Friday, I called to ask him whether he had received his gift.

He had not.

I called the company. Someone from the company told me the package would be delivered the next day. I explained that the clinic would be closed on Saturday. The person suggested I tell Martin to pick up his package at the post office the next day.

Upset, I called him and told him that his package of perishable items would be delivered four days late because the post office would be closed on Monday, and the clinic would be closed on Tuesday.

Just hours later I received a triumphant email from Martin: "I got it!"

He explained that I had mistyped the address of the clinic by one numeral. The address I had typed was that of a church where his mother played the piano for their Sunday services. I had addressed the package "To the Iverson Family," so the church had assumed it was for my friend's mother. They had delivered it to her. She brought the fruit basket with her to dinner Friday night, and Martin's family was able to enjoy the fresh fruit on Christmas.

God knew the fruit would not reach its destination in time for Christmas. He therefore allowed my dyslexia to take over as I copied the clinic's address from the business card. The misplaced numeral ensured that my gift of perishable fruit was delivered several addresses away. Martin's mother would receive it in time for the family to enjoy their Christmas present.

God cares about the little things in our lives. And when we give our lives to Him, He takes care of those little things that contribute to our happiness and well-being.

Darlenejoan McKibbin Rhine

My Journey

God is our refuge and strength,
a very present help in trouble.
—*Psalm 46:1, NKJV*

I t was December of 2009 and, like most people, I was getting ready for Christmas. Then I got the news that I had breast cancer. I was devastated. So many questions went through my mind: *Will this be my last Christmas? Will I see the next year through? Who will take care of my fourteen-year-old daughter? How will she cope if I am not around and, likewise, my husband?* I had told a few close friends and church members.

"Jenetta," one sister said to me, "nothing is too big for the Lord."

Finally, I was scheduled for surgery a few days before Christmas. As well as praying for my healing, I prayed for it not to snow because snow had been in the weather forecast. At my preoperation assessment, the nurse assured me, "Don't worry, you will be home for Christmas, even if it takes Santa's sleigh!"

The snow came the day before my operation—a lot of snow. The weather warning was not to travel unless it was absolutely necessary. The night before my operation I was anxious that the weather conditions might prevent the staff from getting to the hospital so that the operation could go ahead. I was also afraid that I would not wake up from the anesthesia. So many things went through my mind that I could hardly sleep.

When morning came, everything was covered with snow. I could not tell where the road was from the pavement, and the temperature had fallen sharply. By six o'clock that morning, my husband had cleared the snow from our car. After several attempts, we finally managed to start our drive. It was dark and bitterly cold. The car was sliding out of my husband's control, but it never entered my mind not to go. I wanted this tumor out of my body! To my relief, when I checked in at the reception desk, I was told the surgeon had arrived. Despite the weather warning, he, too, had traveled from out of town so that my operation could be performed.

I have learned that when we ask the Lord for something, we don't have to tell Him how to answer our prayers. We can leave the answers and resolutions to Him. He is in control of everything, even the weather. When we come to rough, slippery places in life, we can simply be faithful to the Lord, knowing that He will make a way for us through our perplexities.

Jenetta Barker

Do It Now!

"Today, if you hear his voice,
do not harden your hearts as in the rebellion."
—Hebrews 3:15, ESV

Usually, I tackle things in fairly good time. Despite some occasional procrastination, I usually make a list and watch those "cross it off" lines appear as I deal with the task.

One day, however, I purchased a small rug for possible use in the children's Sabbath School room as a decoration. I soon realized that this particular rug would not fit in well nor serve the intended purpose. So it became part of my to-do list, ready in the bag with the sales slip, to take back to the store for a refund.

I carried the bag around in my car for a couple of weeks and finally drove to the department store and headed to the customer-service counter.

"This is one day late," exclaimed the clerk. I didn't realize the full ramification of her statement. She then turned to the manager and asked whether grace could be given me since my return was just one day late.

They conferred, and from past experience, I knew that if they did process my return, they would get in trouble with those in higher positions. They felt they could not honor my request. I thanked them for trying and walked out of the store, pondering the results of my tardiness.

Had I looked at the receipt, I would have seen the thirty-day return policy. As it stood, I now owned a rug that I had no use for.

I learned a hard lesson. Though the lack of a refund was not a huge financial loss, the resulting denial stung my pride and thoughts.

I began to reflect that even deeper things in life could be affected by putting things off, such as the time my husband and I were headed home from a short vacation. Since I wanted to get home sooner than later, we made the choice to forgo an additional few miles to visit some dear, elderly friends. Not long after that, the elderly woman died.

Our failure to stop and visit has stayed in my memory.

There is an even greater decision that needs to be made now, and it affects our eternity. Today is the day of salvation—tomorrow may be too late. Jesus wants a relationship with us now. We don't know about tomorrow, but we do have today.

Valerie Hamel Morikone

My Baby Brother

"But as for me, I would seek God,
And to God I would commit my cause—
Who does great things and unsearchable,
Marvelous things without number."
—Job 5:8, 9, NKJV

My baby brother was born into our family of five when I was five years old. At that time, little did I imagine how much this precious baby would suffer in his life. Though we lived on seventy acres of lovely land, my baby brother became terribly ill with diphtheria. After battling this disease in the hospital for many days, he finally returned home. Though his recovery was slow, God had performed the first miracle in my brother's life.

The second miracle was during a family vacation when my little brother lost his footing in a flooded street and was swept away in the torrents that rushed him through a plughole under a bridge leading to a raging river. God sent an angel in the form of a man, who rescued him from the debris-filled waters and saved his life.

My brother eventually became a teacher and a pastor, serving God for many years in his meek, loving manner. One day I received an email from him that read, "I have colon cancer!"

Instead of losing faith, I remembered how God had spared his life in the past, and I trusted that God would spare his life again. My brother underwent surgery. Unfortunately, one of the surgeons mistakenly cut my brother's ureter, leading to a twelve-day bout of peritonitis. Then he developed septicemia with urine leaking into his lungs, which contributed to renal and cardiac insufficiency and anemia that even eight units of blood were unable to reverse. This led to a forty-day coma and eight months in the hospital.

Yet despite all the human failures and the multiple death prognoses, God heard the pleas of thousands across the world who were praying for him. Thanks to divine intervention, my brother finally came out of his long coma and began the long road toward recovery.

Do you face suffering or sadness, troubles or trials? Remember that Jesus sees us and He cares. Jesus bestows gifts of peace and rest (see John 14:27). Though my brother may never regain all the strength he once had, he will still continue to work for God, making disciples and baptizing them in the name of the Father, the Son, and the Holy Spirit (see Matthew 28:19). And when we join my brother around our Christmas table, we will rejoice in salvation and in the miracles of our Lord.

Marli Elizete Ritter-Hein

God Power!

Having a form of godliness,
but denying the power thereof:
from such turn away.
—2 Timothy 3:5, KJV

I thank God for motorized carts, especially when I shop for groceries. It's easier to ride in a cart (since I have a prosthetic leg) rather than walking and pushing a cart. I have come to realize that a cart's availability and the power gauge flashing "full" do not always mean it has power. Early one morning my husband and I went grocery shopping. With joy, I saw available motorized carts lined up all across the front of the store. *Thank You, God!* I turned one on, and it flashed "full." I unplugged it, got in, and proceeded to shop. My husband and I, as usual, went our separate ways. I hadn't gone far when my cart started slowing down. I checked the digital bar indicating power; the once "full" bar now flashed "empty." A security guard and I decided to make an exchange.

To my dismay, the line of available carts was now down to two! One flashed "empty"; the other one had water on the seat. We made the exchange and I was on my way. Oh no, not again! "Empty"! Now there were *no* more carts available. What should I do? James 4:2 says, "Ye have not, because ye ask not" (KJV). *Well, God, I'm asking for power for this cart, if it's Your will.* After I prayed, the power-indicating bars increased. Whenever the cart slowed down, I prayed.

When I was just about finished shopping, I remembered something on the other side of the store. *Do I chance it?* The bars were low, and doubt set in. When Peter, walking on water, took his eyes off of Jesus, he sank. When Abraham stopped asking Jesus for a certain number of souls in Sodom and Gomorrah to be saved, Jesus stopped saying yes. I decided to go forward even with no power bars left. Praise God! I had enough "God power" to finish my shopping, go through the checkout line, ride to my car, and permit my husband to return the cart to the store.

That day I realized those carts are much like we are. As long as the carts were plugged in to the outlet, they had power, flashing "full." But once under their own power, they began to fail. Like those carts, we must stay connected to the Power Source, Jesus. On our own, we have no power to resist the wiles of Satan. We must "pray without ceasing" (1 Thessalonians 5:17, NKJV). For "the devil, as a roaring lion . . . [is] seeking whom he may devour" (1 Peter 5:8, KJV). How true this is: "Much prayer, much power. Little prayer, little power!"

Mattie E. Johnson

"Fear Not"

"Fear not, for I have redeemed you;
I have called you by your name; you are Mine."
—Isaiah 43:1, NKJV

I love the words of Isaiah 43:1. Why? Because God knows that we face fears every day, yet He tells us never to be afraid. "Fear not" were the very words the angel spoke to Mary, the mother of Jesus (Luke 1:30), and God has been speaking those same words to women ever since. He does not say that dangers don't exist. They do. Sometimes our worst fears come true. Even then, it is the assurance of who God is, what God says, and where God is—by our side—that really matters.

As I pack for a trip to Bulgaria, I am thinking about all the details to which one must attend before leaving home—details that involve planning, prayers, energy, and a good dose of courage since traveling today is so unpredictable. As I think about all these things, I remember this special verse:

"Fear not, for I am with you;
Be not be dismayed, for I am your God.
I will strengthen you,
Yes, I will help you,
I will uphold you with My righteous right hand." (Isaiah 41:10, NKJV)

Courage takes the place of my fears as God reminds me that He is my provision and that I can be content. Contentment is not getting what you want but being happy with what you already have.

Jesus is the only one who can meet our deepest needs and take away our fears as we depend on Him. God is with us, and He will strengthen us in the journey. We also have the assurance of His promise, "I will never leave you nor forsake you" (Hebrews 13:5, NKJV). If He promised, I can claim it. As I close my suitcase after packing for fourteen days on the road, I remember that He is with me and will protect me.

I don't know what you're going to do today or next week, but God will be with you. Take hold of this promise: "Fear not." His presence is the reason you and I need not fear, and the reason we can say, "The Lord is my helper, so I will not fear what man shall do to me" (see Hebrews 13:6).

As you start your day, remember, God has a firm hold upon you. His mighty hand will guide you every step you take. Trust and do not fear! You have God's provision, God's presence, God's promises, and God's protection. So why fear?

Raquel Queiroz da Costa Arrais

Mom's Surprise Christmas Gift

But when the kindness and love of God our Savior was shown,
he saved us because of his mercy. It was not because of good deeds
we did to be right with him. . . .
. . . Those who believe in God will be careful
to use their lives for doing good.
—*Titus 3:4, 5, 8, NCV*

The Word became flesh and made his dwelling among us. We have
seen his glory, the glory of the one and only Son, who came from the
Father, full of grace and truth.
—*John 1:14, NIV*

One Christmas there was little box under our Christmas tree for me from our oldest boy, Jay. I love Christmas surprises, and I could hardly wait until Christmas to open his gift! Jay often had the most interesting surprises—sometimes funny, sometimes strange, and sometimes very nice. I couldn't wait to see what this year's gift would be.

On Christmas Day, I opened the box, took out lots of wrapping paper, then started to take out the little tiny objects: a little cow, a couple of little chickens, several little shepherds, and then a Mary and a Joseph. It was a Nativity scene! I was really excited because I knew just where I would put them—on a special shelf in my kitchen. The little pieces would remind me every time I saw them about the real meaning of Christmas. Mary, Joseph, the shepherds, the wise men, the animals at the manger—but wait a minute, there was something missing! As I looked through the box again, there was no manger and *no Baby Jesus*! Then Jay said to me, "Mom, you're right, Baby Jesus is missing. That's the reason I bought it—the price was marked down."

This unusual Nativity scene I have put on my special kitchen shelf, minus Baby Jesus. When I feel the pressure to go to every party and every open house, taste all the holiday food and treats, get the perfect gift for every single person on the shopping list, wrapping the gifts, and making sure not to forget anyone on the card list, I look at the spot where the missing Baby Jesus should be on the shelf. Then I remember that I often miss the whole point of what Christmas is about—Jesus.

This year let's make sure that the Christ Child, God's greatest gift, isn't missing from your Christmas or mine. Just think of how different this whole world would be if each of us let Jesus be in every thought, deed, purchase, and word. Have a blessed Christmas in Him.

Bonnie R. Parker

December 26

Boxing Day

I have not stopped giving thanks for you.
—*Ephesians 1:16, NIV*

t's Boxing Day and all through *this* house not a creature is stirring, not even a mouse—if we even had one. A mouse, that is," Melissa said, laughing. "We had Christmas. Now it's the day after. Tell me again about Boxing Day. About when you were a girl growing up in Canada."

"Saint Stephen's Day, as it was also called, began in England in the Middle Ages and caught on all around the British Empire. Tradespeople, servants, and the poor could expect a Christmas box," I replied, smiling down into her little face, pink cheeks aglow from the fireplace's warmth. "We each selected something to give away, along with a loaf of my father's homemade bread or mother's date cookies."

"What made you decide to celebrate Boxing Day *before* Christmas this year?" Melissa asked. "Likely much better for the *recipients*, I'd say." She emphasized the word *recipients*.

"I like the tradition of Boxing Day, but having a Christmas box in advance might be much better for the recipients, as you put it." Melissa nodded. "I've never been particularly fixated on things," I continued, "but since the 2014 earthquake I'm more aware than ever that things are just things. What I truly value most by far are my connections with the brains and hearts of others. On my deathbed, I doubt I will be thinking about any things I have ever owned, rather about the brains and hearts I have loved over a lifetime."

"But we *must* celebrate *something* on Boxing Day," Melissa said. "Maybe gratitude?"

"Good idea," I replied. "Let's send a card or email to those for whom we are grateful."

"Or a gratitude box!" On her feet in a flash, Melissa returned with her treasured iPad. "I'll make two lists 'cause they'll be different. Who's first on yours, me?" She giggled.

"The *Reason for the season* tops my list," I replied seriously. "You can be next."

"Same here," she said, equally serious. "You are next on my list. I think everyone needs to pick a Gratitude Day. Can we start a new tradition?" She began typing.

Identify a Gratitude Day. Tell those you love and treasure how grateful you are that they are in your life. Remember to start your list with the *Reason for the season*.

Arlene R. Taylor

Little Mercies

*Don't fret or worry. Instead of worrying, pray. Let petitions
and praises shape your worries into prayers, letting God know
your concerns. . . . It's wonderful what happens when Christ
displaces worry at the center of your life.
—Philippians 4:6, 7, The Message*

To explain about simple faith to some young adults in my care, I told them about my own experience when I was about five and learned that God answers even small requests, like finding my missing doll.

I used to observe the way the sun flooded my bedroom in the mornings and had decided that this was how and when God entered our home. So following the beam that came to the corner of my room, I went behind my door and pleaded with the "Friend" of little children to help me find my doll that I had hunted for, in vain, all day. Lo and behold, as I finished my prayer and opened my eyes, there was my doll right behind me, behind the door!

Fast-forward fifty-plus years: I remember, among other answered prayers, an unforgettable experience at 1:25 A.M. on December 27, 2016.

I have two daughters, both of whom have health challenges, but my younger, though not yet thirty years old, is the one with the greater challenge. She is also more intense in her feelings since she had a major stroke nearly two years ago.

My husband and I took our daughters for a pre-Christmas cruise, and this daughter had taken hundreds of pictures with her phone. We constantly hear about the problems she experiences with the varied phones she has bought over the years. Her greatest fear was realized during the cruise when her phone stopped charging, despite all her efforts. She would lose all her pictures. She was beside herself but asked me to "please fiddle with it" before I went to bed. I did but immediately saw the challenge she faced. I presented this problem to God, asking Him to charge the phone. Such an insignificant prayer to some yet so important to me and my daughter. He said, "Yes." The phone was charged when I checked at 7:45 A.M. As I write, my daughter is downloading her pictures. Truly, no request is too outrageous or trite for our loving heavenly Father!

As the New Year approaches, I know I will be presenting my daughters to Him with trust that He will continue to pour out His mercies, both great and little.

Avery J. Thompson

He Is There All the Time

God is our refuge and strength, a very present help in trouble.
—Psalm 46:1, KJV

There is so much euphoria surrounding the Christmas holidays. One year every family I knew was planning feverishly for the festivities. I had brought our grandchildren (six girls and one boy) to spend the holidays with my husband and me.

On Christmas Day, we had a really good time with the children. There was so much to eat and drink, and the children were so happy, jumping around and shouting with joy. The day went well, without any unfortunate incidents. Then came December 26. Around six o'clock in the evening, I asked the older children to take their baths. After they were done, I went out to the kitchen to fetch hot water from the cooker to transport to the tub in order to bathe the younger ones. As I walked, carrying the hot water, I did not notice that the kitchen floor was wet in a certain place. Unfortunately, I slipped on the moisture, and in the process, the container of hot water poured over me. As a reflex, I shouted, "God save me!" before sending the elder grandchild to call my husband. He came to help me get up to change my clothing. Then I realized I had serious pain from my waist all the way down to my right ankle. When I started to rub saltwater onto the area for relief, I saw—to my surprise and horror—that that whole area was now covered with large, painful blisters. At that particular moment, all I could say was, "God save me from this pain and suffering." My physical anguish was unbearable.

Though taken immediately to the nearest hospital, no one could help me because the facility was not equipped to deal with the serious degree of burns that I had. I was told I needed to be properly treated in a burn unit under special conditions. I was referred to a military hospital. That night, from seven o'clock to eleven o'clock, was like hell for me because of the unspeakable pain. At that hospital, a doctor and two caring nurses gave me some pain relievers. The next five days were very difficult because of the pain, which often brought tears to my eyes.

By the second week, the pain subsided as the blisters began to dry and the dead skin to peel off. I began to have hope once again. I had thought I would be in bed for the next six months; but by the grace of God, I was fully healed (except for a few small scars) by the third week after the accident! Praise God! Our Redeemer lives and rewards those who trust Him!

Adjoa Mawusi Adiaokuk Ekrong Tetteh

Assumption, Faith, and Trust at the Laundromat

Now faith is the assurance (title deed, confirmation) of things hoped for (divinely guaranteed), and the evidence of things not seen [the conviction of their reality—faith comprehends as fact what cannot be experienced by the physical senses].
—Hebrews 11:1, AMP

My trusty, dependable washing machine broke down on Christmas Day, Sunday, my usual laundry day. Our son, Jamie, and his family were leaving Tennessee, United States, on Christmas Day to join us in Texas for a short visit. We expected them to arrive late on Monday. I knew the laundromat would be closed on a holiday, so I would do the laundry the next day. While still at home, I *assumed* the person last using the detergent had tightened the cap. The last person (me) had *not* tightened the cap—or made sure it was securely fastened before we left home.

After our arrival at the laundromat, Stan, my husband, picked up the loaded laundry basket with dirty clothes and detergent and headed toward the door. As I opened the door of the laundromat, I noticed Stan was spilling the contents of the detergent bottle down one of his pant legs. He was not a happy camper! Once inside, he immediately placed the laundry basket on the floor in front of the mega-load washers and then headed for home to change clothes. Next I *assumed* the first row of washers were single-load washers and promptly loaded two loads of clothes. When I lifted the lid to add the detergent and fabric softener, I assumed I'd read the instructions correctly, yet I added the liquids into the wrong receptacles and started the machines. Something didn't seem quite right. I asked the woman behind me whether I had interpreted the instructions correctly. She said "No," and then told me that I was using the mega-load washers. I realized that I was going to have to rewash Stan's clothes in a single-load washer. Enough for assumptions.

Now I chose to exercise faith in the attendant's assistance. Then by faith—not assumption—I was able to trust in the instructions the attendant gave me and to know that the instructions were correct. At home, the repairman assured us our washing machine was beyond repair. Due to the holidays' limited time schedule for delivery and installation of a new washer, I knew I would have to visit the laundromat one more time. My next trip there was without incident—based on the lessons of trust I had learned the previous week.

Thank You, Father, that You are faithful and just so that we can put our trust in You.

Anna Ivie Swingle

Unforgettable Experiences

In everything give thanks:
for this is the will of God in Christ Jesus concerning you.
—*1 Thessalonians 5:18, KJV*

In 2005, I was a childcare assistant at a girls' home in Hortolândia, São Paulo, Brazil, working to earn money for my tuition. That year I finished high school. Caring for thirty girls was a new experience for me. They needed care and affection. The following year I was transferred to work in another home in Engenheiro Coelho, where I also studied at a Christian university, majoring in education. In this home, we had thirty girls (many orphans), four childcare assistants, and one director, whom we called Aunt. I slept in a room with three four- and five-year-olds. One of my favorite memories of this period in my life was a little one falling asleep, hugging me. I would study after they had all fallen asleep, though it was a challenge to balance work and study.

I felt very sad when I saw that some of the girls did not have anyone to come pick them up for vacation. But they were very loved by us and Auntie. During the years I spent working there, I realized how much these girls needed care, attention, and unconditional love. I learned so much during this time. It was a unique opportunity, both for me and for the other girls who worked there, to have a good education, love, and physical and spiritual care. These were brave girls who took advantage of the opportunities given them. When they left the home, they could become successful women and be blessings for church and society.

One of my favorite keepsakes is a gift of appreciation—a cookbook—that one of the little girls at the home gave me. She had won it at her school during a Mother's Day program. In it, she wrote these sweet, tender words: "Auntie Débora: Auntie, I like you. Auntie, I give you this gift with all my heart. Take care of me, please. From: Nazaré." To this day, I keep this book to remind myself of her. I thank God for the opportunity to live with such special girls.

Today may God empower us to do everything He asks of us with a spirit of gratitude and love. If we do, we will certainly receive many blessing from the Lord that will result in greater learning and deeper experiences in our journey with Jesus.

Débora de Souza

The New Year

They are new every morning;
great is your faithfulness.
—*Lamentations 3:23, NIV*

A new year unfolds in our lives—a new chapter soon to be written. A new beginning filled with fragile graces. Optimism arises. Our hopes are renewed. And even when the way is not clear, I never doubt that God's promises for our future are unfolding as He has assured us they would be.

Outside my window, the view of the soon-to-be *January* garden is sweeping and grand. A pure and crystalline newness hangs from trees and bare branches like baubles on a Christmas tree. The atmosphere wears the wings of doves, ashen and soundless. And it seems, too, that the new year moves forward shrouded in a heavenly cloth decorated in jewels of hope, faith, and sacred gladness.

As the early January snows creep in, invited by the slanting winds of winter, the unaccustomed eye may be tempted to see only a garden that has been brutally stripped of its glories. But for the eye that sees far beyond the obvious, there rests genuine loveliness and a treasure chest full of evidence of God's bountiful provisions for man at Creation.

The winter garden rejoices in the beauty of frost and the purification of silence. It rests, but it doesn't die. It remains silent, but it still speaks in a thousand voices.

In the bleakness of January, in the barrenness of the land, and in the silence shed by the nude fingers of winter, we can still find joy, beauty, and evidences of God's amazing love toward His children.

Father, I am like the winter garden, encrusted in the ice and standoffishness of self-unworthiness and sin. Yet You saw in me that shining jewel hidden in the ice. You saw value in me. You removed me from the sins that buried me and hindered my light. You brought me into a life worth living through your salvation.

Like the new year unfolding before us, so we, your earthly children, have been given a clean new slate of opportunities. We start anew.

From now on, may our deeds and lives be witnesses of Your love to those around us.

Olga Valdivia

2019 Author Biographies

Betty J. Adams is a retired teacher in California, United States of America. She has been married for more than sixty-two years and enjoys her children and their families. She has written for her church newsletter and for *Guide*, and she also works for her church's Community Services ministry. She enjoys gardening and scrapbooking. **Jan. 4, May 9**

Christiana Agyenim-Boateng has served in women's ministries in the Southern Ghana Union Conference of Seventh-day Adventists. **Aug. 14, Nov. 13**

Guadalupe Savariz de Alvarado, a psychologist, serves as the Women's Ministries director for the Southern Union Mission of the Euro-Asia Division. She is the mother of two young adult sons and has been happily married for twenty-seven years to Pastor Freddy Alvarado Pimentel. She loves cross-cultural service and ministering to women. Her hobbies include handmade art, sewing, and painting. **Aug. 20**

Cecilia Amoakohene is a new author writing from the Southern Ghana Union Conference of Seventh-day Adventists. **Aug. 22**

Deniece G. Anderson is a registered nurse living in Atlanta, Georgia, United States of America. Her motto is "If I can help somebody as I pass along, then my living shall not be in vain." **Oct. 12**

Sue Anderson is retired from the United States Department of Agriculture, Forest Service, and lives in the Pacific Northwest of the United States of America. She has been married to Chuck for fifty-two years, and they have two married daughters, a granddaughter, two grandsons, and two great-grandsons. Sue enjoys writing and spending time with family and friends. **Jan. 25, May 10**

Lydia D. Andrews is a certified nurse midwife, mother of three adult children, and grandmother of four delightful boys. She and her husband reside in Huntsville, Alabama, United States of America, where she works as a labor and delivery clinical instructor. Her hobbies include reading, cooking, travel, music, and spending time with family. She is involved in the prayer and women's ministries of her church. **Oct. 22**

Margaret A. Anti is a marriage counselor and health educator who holds bachelor's and master's degrees in art. She previously served as the Women's Ministries director for the Central Ghana Conference of Seventh-day Adventists. She is married with three children. **Aug. 30**

Raquel Queiroz da Costa Arrais is a minister's wife who developed her ministry as an educator for twenty years. Currently, she works as an associate director of the General Conference Women's Ministries Department. She has two adult sons, two daughters-in-law, and three adored grandchildren. Her greatest pleasures are being with people, singing, playing the piano, and traveling. **Feb. 5, June 11, Sept. 21, Dec. 24**

Monica Koko Asca, the deputy principal of Kawuondi Secondary School in Kenya, is a teacher by profession who earned a master's degree in Kiswahili. She is a church treasurer at Great Hope Seventh-day Adventist Church in Bondo Station. **Mar. 19, July 5**

Florence L. Ashby lives with her husband in northeast Colorado, United States of America. She works at a nursing home. At her previous church, she was on the church school board for ten years and served as church clerk for seven years. She is the church clerk at her new church. She has two sons, and her husband has one son and one daughter. **Apr. 4**

Harriet Asuboni writes from southern Ghana. **Aug. 24**

Elizabeth Atamian, a Lebanese Armenian, was born in Beirut in 1940 to refugee parents from Turkey. She married Kegham Atamian in 1962 while she was the head nurse at Benghazi Adventist Hospital in Libya. The family eventually had to evacuate and now live in Lebanon. From 1984 to 2005, she taught at Bouchrieh Adventist Secondary School and then volunteered as head librarian and school nurse until June 2014. Fully retired, she now enjoys her grandsons. **Apr. 29**

Yvita Antonette Villalona Bacchus is a graphic designer and violinist. She works in the Music and Communication Departments of her local church. She is grateful for the opportunity to bless and be blessed. Yvita writes from Florida, United States of America. **Jan. 6, Oct. 7**

Carla Baker lives in Maryland, United States of America, and is the director of Women's Ministries for the North American Division of Seventh-day Adventists. She enjoys walking, cooking, reading, and spending time with her three grandchildren. **Oct. 20, Oct. 21**

Jennifer M. Baldwin writes from Australia, where she works in risk management at Sydney Adventist Hospital. She enjoys family time, church involvement, Scrabble, crossword puzzles, and researching her family history. She has been contributing to the devotional book series for twenty-two years. **Apr. 5**

Corletta Aretha Barbar was born in Jamaica, West Indies. She currently resides with her husband, Michael, in Fayetteville, North Carolina, United States of America. She has chaired the Young Women's Ministries Advisory Board, directed the children's choir, helped organize food distribution to the homeless, and served on the Northern California Conference Women's Ministries Advisory Board. She has four degrees and a nursing major. Her hobbies are writing, walking, sightseeing, and singing. **Feb. 20, May 3**

Jenetta Barker lives with her husband and daughter in Bedfordshire, England, and works for a local authority. She enjoys reading, writing, traveling, and spending time with her family. **Dec. 20**

Gyl Moon Bateman and her husband have three sons and live in Michigan, United States of America. She is a registered nurse. Her hobbies are reading, music, cats, visiting friends and relatives, and cooking. She is an active Blue Star Mother since her son served in the army. **Mar. 15**

Dawna Beausoleil, a retired teacher, and her husband, John, live in a retirement community in London, Ontario, Canada. She praises God for the wonderful care with which He has blessed them. **Apr. 27**

Bernie Martin Beck writes from Merlin, Oregon, United States of America. Recently widowed, she has been mother to two and grandmother to five. For nineteen years, she has helped other people "talk, talk, talk" on her Better Life Broadcasting Network show

Journeys 'n Journals (the network's longest running show). Bernie, a church elder, enjoys traveling, local history, and "being there" to support others. **Nov. 1, Nov. 2**

Irina Begas, a new author from the Russian Federation, enjoys singing. **Aug. 11**

Ginger Bell resides in Colorado, United States of America. She and her pastor husband are partially retired. Their two grown children and families live close by and are a delight! She is active in women's ministries on the local and conference levels. Her hobbies include gardening, crafts, antiquing, and being in the beautiful Colorado Rocky Mountains. **Aug. 5**

Sylvia Giles Bennett lives in Suffolk, Virginia, United States of America, with Richard, her husband of more than thirty-five years. She is the mother of two adult children, David and Samantha, and four adoring grandchildren—Kennedy, Derrius, Donte, Davion, and Samy'a. Sylvia, a member of the Windsor Seventh-day Adventist Church, enjoys reading, writing, and caring for the elderly. **Feb. 27**

Natysha Berthiaume lives in Hagerstown, Maryland, United States of America, with her husband, David, and two daughters—Brianna, age eight, and Kianna, age three. She works at the Chesapeake Conference of Seventh-day Adventists, where she is involved with the Women's Ministries and Communication Departments, among others. Her family are active members of the Williamsport Seventh-day Adventist Church, where she has enjoyed being the leader of the Beginner Sabbath School class. **July 29**

Eugenia Mzikazi Bhebhe, an economic and HIV/AIDS specialist, is a Zimbabwean living in Côte d'Ivoire. She is the mother of three children: Sukoluhle, Hlosulwazi, and Siphephelo. She writes on development challenges in Africa. She loves being part of the Seventh-day Adventist women's ministries program. **July 16, Sept. 22**

Moselle Slaten Blackwell is a retired widow. She has two adult children and one granddaughter. In her church, she serves as a deaconess, Sabbath School teacher, and choir member. Her favorite interests are working in the yard; listening to religious music; watching beautiful sunsets; and enjoying a clear, moonlit night sky—all of which speak of God's sovereignty. Moselle writes from Michigan, United States of America. **Mar. 26**

Amy Bock lives in the heartland of the United States of America, where she enjoys reading, writing, volunteering, and looking for God in every moment of life. Her greatest blessings are her teenage kids, Derek and Kylie. Being their mom is pure joy. **Dec. 4**

Julie Bocock-Bliss lives in Honolulu, Hawaii, United States of America. She works in a library, which makes sense since she loves reading so much! She also enjoys traveling and crafts. She thanks God for giving her the time and ability to enjoy these interests. **Jan. 13, Aug. 1**

Patricia Hook Rhyndress Bodi, a long-distance student at Andrews University (completing the theology degree she started in 1956), is active in women's ministries and loves to travel. She lives in Michigan, United States of America. **July 10, Nov. 22**

Rhonda Huffaker Bolton lives in the Pacific Northwest of the United States of America. There she is constantly amazed by the array of fruits and vegetables that the Lord has given us to enjoy. She works in the Religious Liberty Department at the North Pacific Union Conference of Seventh-day Adventists. **Apr. 13**

R. Bowen, a Canadian woman teaching English and living for Christ in Northeast Asia, enjoys traveling, meeting new people, and watching God work to draw others closer to Him. She is supported by her family living in Toronto, Canada, and her international family of prayer across the world. **Mar. 3**

Sonia Brock lives in Palmer, Alaska, United States of America, on a little more than nine acres in a small cabin she built herself. Her dog is her faithful companion. She has been privileged for twenty-three years to drive a school bus in the rugged but beautiful forty-ninth state. She finds service to her church a joy and privilege, whether it's mowing the churchyard in the summertime or greeting at the front door on Sabbaths. **Feb. 13, Dec. 11**

Rachel E. Cabose is a wife, mom, freelance writer, and editor living in rural Charlotte, Michigan, United States of America. She enjoys music, hiking, and ministering to young people. **Nov. 18**

Elizabeth Ida Cain is an administrator at a leading farming company in Jamaica, where she resides. She is a professional florist who enjoys teaching the art and finds spiritual blessings in writing devotionals for women's devotional books. She is looking forward to completing a master's degree in education. **Feb. 8**

Hyacinth V. Caleb was raised in the West Indies and presently resides in Saint Thomas, United States Virgin Islands. University educated in Trinidad and Jamaica, she now teaches high school. This educator loves reading, writing, and working outdoors in her garden. **Sept. 2, Dec. 18**

Florence E. Callender is an author, speaker, speech-language pathologist, and educational consultant who specializes in helping people achieve optimal wellness. She has a teenage daughter and lives in New York, United States of America. **Jan. 19**

Laura A. Canning lives in Berkshire, England. God has gifted her with the art of writing. She enjoys country life, photography, gardening, and her pets. **Mar. 12**

Ruth Cantrell is a retired teacher and counselor from the Detroit Public Schools Community District. She has two adult sons and resides with her husband in Belleville, Michigan, United States of America. She enjoys women's ministry, children's ministry, prayer ministry, reading stories, music, organizing programs, and encouraging other church members. **Jan. 2**

Eveythe Kennedy Cargill, wife of Stafford, resides in Huntsville, Alabama, United States of America. She is a retired teacher and serves on the board of elders at the Oakwood University Church. She has three grandchildren. **Jan. 29, June 19**

Camilla E. Cassell writes from Manchester, Pennsylvania, United States of America. A retired postal employee, she attends Berea Temple Seventh-day Adventist Church and treasures her grandson, Amari. She has compassion for families and feels they should spend time with one another in love and unity, enjoying the gift of life from God. **Apr. 2, Oct. 10**

Shakuntala Chandanshive is the wife of Pastor B. R. Chandanshive, who is the president of Western India Union. She taught for thirty-three years and presently works as the director of Women's and Children's Ministries. In addition, she heads the Shepherdess organization and is the associate director for Education. She loves to sing and tell stories. She has two sons and one daughter and two grandchildren. **Mar. 27, Oct. 6**

Suhana Chikatla, born in India, has two master's degrees and one doctorate. She volunteers in children's, youth, and social leadership positions at her church in Hanceville, Alabama, United States of America. She is an executive council member for the Gulf States Conference Women's Ministries Department. She and her husband, Royce Sutton, have a beautiful two-year-old daughter, Rehana. **Dec. 2**

Uma Chinnaiah and her pastor husband are blessed with two daughters. She taught for twenty years and served as the Women's Ministries director for the East-Central India Union Section. Teaching is her passion. Her hobbies include reading, listening to music, and gardening. **Apr. 18, July 7**

Rosenita Christo formerly taught at the college level. Recently, she also became an associate director for Family Ministries in the Southern Asia Division. She and her husband, Gordon, wrote *For Better or for Worse*, an adult Bible study guide. She loves singing and writing and is the choir leader at her church in India. **Dec. 14**

Rosemarie Clardy enjoys being a stay-at-home mom in North Carolina, United States of America. Her husband plans to retire soon, which will be a new venture for both of them. She is involved in small groups and learning how to knit and crochet. She is getting back to artwork, which was her passion when younger. She would also like to foster animals. **Dec. 12**

Robin C. Cleary is a new contributing author writing from Virginia, United States of America. **Oct. 13**

Sandy Colburn and her husband, Ken, enjoy life in a rural setting in central Tennessee, United States of America, where he is a family practice physician. Together they enjoy gardening, backyard bird-watching, pets, their adult children, and a devotion to their church family and community. **Jan. 26**

Clementine H. Collins, a retired open-heart intensive-care registered nurse, has served in women's ministries for more than twenty-nine years and is currently an assistant to the director of the Women's Ministries Department in the South Central Conference and the Women's Ministries leader for the Ephesus Seventh-day Adventist Church in Birmingham, Alabama, United States of America. She has coordinated the Morning Manna Prayer Ministries since February 2010. She has one adult son, a twenty-three-year-old grandson, and a sixteen-year-old granddaughter. **Nov. 30**

Joan Collins-Ricketts, PhD, MS, BSN, is originally from Jamaica, where she studied nursing at Northern Caribbean University. She is the mother of two grown sons and grandmother to two amazing girls, Rain and Autumn, and one awesome boy, Zaiden. A trained marriage and family therapist who loves the Lord and is passionate about family, she resides in Atlanta, Georgia, United States of America. **May 4, Aug. 16**

Patricia Cove, writing from Ontario, Canada, is a semiretired teacher, church elder, volunteer chaplain, freelance writer, gardener, and lover of outdoor pursuits. Celebrating their sixtieth wedding anniversary in 2017, she and her husband, George, treasure their children and grandchildren. **Mar. 7, June 10**

Martha "Marty" Cunnington lives in the beautiful north Okanagan Valley in the small city of Armstrong, British Columbia, Canada. She and her husband have two grown children. She loves animals, especially horses and dogs. She assists her local church in several departments. **Apr. 30**

Wilma Feaster Daniels is a retired clinical therapist and life coach who enjoys going on mission trips, encouraging individuals through educational seminars, and ushering and greeting at the Breath of Life Seventh-day Adventist Church in Fort Washington, Maryland, United States of America. **Sept. 7**

Charity Danso is a new devotional book contributor writing from Ghana, where she works with women's ministries. **July 15**

Lee Lee Dart is a pastor at the Adventure Seventh-day Adventist Church in Windsor, Colorado, United States of America. This wife and mother of two is passionate about being a conduit of God's love to others. **June 7, Oct. 15**

Jean Dozier Davey and her husband, Steven, live in the beautiful mountains of North Carolina, United States of America. Jean, a retired computer programmer, enjoys family, cooking, walking in the Pisgah Forest, reading, sewing, photography, and encouraging others. **Feb. 18, Apr. 14**

Jennifer Day and her pastor husband, Sean, reside in Alabama, United States of America, with their three small children, who never cease to give them glimpses into the mind and heart of God. **Aug. 31**

Koulibaly N'gandia Diata Epse Diarrassouba holds a bachelor's degree in business communication and a master's degree in modern literature. A part-time French teacher for several years, she is now teaching at the Seventh-day Adventist Secondary School in Bouaké, Côte d'Ivoire. **July 1, Oct. 25**

Edna Bacate Domingo, PhD, MSN, RN, and her husband live in Loma Linda, California, United States of America. She is an associate professor and serves as an elder and as a Sabbath School teacher and superintendent in her church. She has three adult daughters and is blessed with a granddaughter and a grandson. **May 19, Nov. 20**

Yvonne H. Donatto resides in Huntsville, Alabama, United States of America. She enjoys camping, photography, and traveling. She has lived on three continents and vacationed on a fourth. She has been active in the King's Daughters Organization for more than thirty years. She and her husband, Anthony, have two adult children, Yolande and Anthony II, as well as three granddaughters—Ayana, Maya, and Brianna. **Oct. 26**

Louise Driver is the wife of a retired pastor who still preaches almost every Sabbath in the state of Idaho, United States of America. Her sister, three sons, and their families live nearby. She enjoys gardening, reading, and traveling. **Jan. 27, Dec. 10**

Mary E. Dunkin is a daughter, sister, aunt, cousin, friend, caregiver, home economist, Pathfinder, teacher, seamstress, concierge, business owner, writer, and daughter of God. She is most proud of being God's daughter and eagerly waits for Him to return. Until then, she'll keep working. Her home is in New Mexico, United States of America. **Jan. 31, June 17**

Shevonne Dyer-Phillips is a first-time contributing author who writes from Texas, United States of America. **Aug. 13**

Philomina Edu, writing from Ghana, enjoys working with women's ministries. **Sept. 12**

Ruby H. Enniss-Alleyne writes from Guyana and loves young people, athletics, and working in the treasury office at the Guyana Conference of Seventh-day Adventists. She serves as a Youth leader and a Family Ministries leader at her home church, Carmel. She lost her spouse, Ashton, in January 2011. She enjoys her three adult children; daughter-in-law; and adorable grandson, Alaric. **Feb. 16, July 22**

Mona Fellers is the multicounty ambulance inspector in the greater metro area of Denver, Colorado, United States of America. She is married with two daughters, two grandchildren, two dogs, and a cat. She is also the Women's Ministries leader in her church. **May 17**

Maureen Ferdinand is the Women's Ministries leader of the Ambassador Seventh-day Adventist Church and the fund-raising director of the Adventurer Club. She resides with her husband, Ezra, in Fort Lauderdale, Florida, United States of America. They have four adopted daughters and five grandchildren, one of whom one still lives with her. **Mar. 23**

Sherilyn Flowers, born in Belize, now calls Los Angeles, California, United States of America, home. She has authored *Personal Omens Expressing My Soul (P.O.E.M.S.)*, published by Outskirts Press. She loves God. **Sept. 30, Dec. 1**

Edit Fonseca lives in Curitiba, Brazil, and is married to Pastor Otavio Fonseca, with whom she has two sons: Odinilson and Odailson. She served as a leader in women's ministries for fifteen years. Retired now, she still continues working with churches and communities. **Sept. 26, Nov. 27**

Shirley Sain Fordham is a retired educator, a wife, the mother of three married children, and the grandmother of eight. She enjoys her iPhone, family and friends, crocheting, and scrapbooking. She also loves to welcome new members to the West End Seventh-day Adventist Church in Atlanta, Georgia, United States of America. She has learned to occupy well—living, loving, laughing, and learning until Jesus comes again. **Nov. 8**

Sylvia A. Franklin resides in Redlands, California, United States of America, and works as a human resources professional. Now happily married to Joe for ten years, she is the administrative assistant to the Women's Ministries director of the Pacific Union Conference of Seventh-day Adventists. She enjoys people and sharing Christ with them. **May 27**

Annemarie Freeman is an occupational therapist and pastor's wife in Georgia, United States of America. She and her family spent eight and a half years volunteering in Ireland with Adventist Frontier Missions. **May 20**

Ruth Garcia is a new contributing author who writes from Campion Academy in Colorado, United States of America. **Jan. 28**

Sherilyn Gibbs, DNP, CNM, RNC-OB, and her husband, Gary, recently moved to the Pennsylvania Conference of Seventh-day Adventists, of which her husband is the new president. They have two teenage daughters, Carissa and Christina. Sherilyn is a certified nurse midwife and has served women in this capacity for more than twenty years. She enjoys ministry by sharing her musical gifts on the piano, flute, organ, accordion, and voice. **June 13, June 14**

Rita Gill serves in the Northern India Union as the Women's and Family Ministries director. She is married to Pastor Ravi Gill, and she has one son. She has worked as a teacher, understanding counselor, and administrative assistant. She loves to speak to both small and large audiences. Her hobbies are composing poems and writing articles. **June 27**

Joyce Goddard is a retired health professional who served in the East and South Africa mission fields for thirteen years with her pastor husband. She now lives in the United Kingdom with her family. She loves the Lord and enjoys reading, sewing, and traveling to other countries. **Jan. 14**

Sarah Suzane Bertolli Gonçalves lives in Goiânia, Goiás, Brazil. She is the author of elementary-education textbooks with the Brazil Publishing House. She majored in Portuguese and is now working on her master's degree in linguistic studies. She is also a mom and educator. She likes to travel with her kids, Gabriel and Giovanna, and her husband, Robson Gonçalves. **Sept. 28**

Sandra P. Gordon, and her wonderful husband, Eric, study at the University of Arkansas, United States of America. She is working on a PhD in biomedical engineering in order to achieve her dream of teaching at the college level (ideally, her alma mater, Andrews University). **June 24, Oct. 14**

Alexis A. Goring is a journalist who loves people and Jesus Christ. She resides in Maryland, United States of America. Alexis enjoys a good read, but the Holy Bible is her favorite book! **Jan. 18, Dec. 15**

Cecilia Grant is a Seventh-day Adventist medical doctor retired from government service and living in Kingston, Jamaica. Her hobbies are traveling, gardening, and listening to good music. She has a passion for young people, to whom she is always giving advice. **June 26**

Mary Jane Graves, a widow, mother, grandmother, and great-grandmother, is retired and lives in North Carolina, United States of America. She is the librarian in her church and is active in women's ministries. **Apr. 7, Sept. 10**

Valerie Fisher Green is originally from Zimbabwe but now lives in England. She attends West Bletchley Seventh-day Adventist Community Church and loves flower arranging, writing, and spending time with her grandchildren. Since becoming a widow in 2015, she has begun to write devotionals for widows and widowers. **Apr. 9, Sept. 4**

Glenda-mae Greene, a retired university administrator, writes from her wheelchair in the Canadian prairies where she and her mother recently relocated. Writing devotionals is often a postlude to her prayers. **Oct. 28**

Gloria Barnes Gregory is inspired by nature and her precious granddaughters. She seeks to motivate others to make positive life choices. Currently, she and her husband, Milton, serve at the Victory Seventh-day Adventist Church in New York, United States of America. **Aug. 29**

Ursula Claudia Essogo 'n' Guettia, a devoted mother, is also the Health Ministry coordinator at the Niangon Seventh-day Adventist Church and District 3 in Abidjan, Côte d'Ivoire. **Aug. 18**

Vida Linda Gyasi has been the Women's and Children's Ministries director for the Northern Ghana Union Mission since 2014. She holds a degree in land economy and land management. She is a public servant working with the Lands Commission as the regional valuer of the Brong Ahafo Region. She is married and has three children. **July 23**

Dora Hallock lives in beautiful New England, United States of America. She is a clinical nurse specialist in oncology. She is also a pastor's wife, mother of a lovely daughter, and mother-in-law to the husband of the wonderful couple who parent her amazing grandchildren! Her hobbies include walking the beach, sailing, photography, and praying with friends. **July 2**

Diantha Hall-Smith is a daughter of God. She is wife to a devoted Christian husband who serves in the United States Air Force and the mother of two beautiful children. She was born in New York City, New York, United States of America, and has had the honor and privilege of living in and also visiting interesting places, domestically and globally. She enjoys writing, traveling, and spending time with her family. **Feb. 7, June 9**

Flore Aubry Hamilton loves the Lord, and she wants to have a home with Him in heaven. She and her husband, George, live in Huntsville, Alabama, United States of America. They enjoy helping sick people and those with disabilities. **Nov. 9**

Myrna Hanna is assistant vice president for alumni and donor relations at Loma Linda University Health in Loma Linda, California, United States of America. Her favorite things include travel, spending time with family, and encouraging others to make the most of the talents God has given them. **Sept. 24, Nov. 14**

Peggy Curtice Harris, born and raised in the states of California and Washington, has lived in Maryland, United States of America, for the past fifty years. She is a widowed, retired great-grandma and has written fourteen books. She is still active in Destination Sabbath School, prayer ministry, and hospitality outreach in the Beltsville Seventh-day Adventist Church. **Feb. 11, May 14**

Marian M. Hart-Gay lives in Florida, United States of America, with her husband, David. She is a mother, grandmother, and great-grandmother. Knitting and volunteer mission trips are two activities she enjoys. **Feb. 23, Aug. 7**

Cynthia A. HartKnott lives in the United States of America where she works as a victim information and resource advocate for victims of domestic violence. She has been published in the *Encyclopedia of Victimology and Crime Prevention* (Sage Publications) and numerous times in the *Lake Union Herald*. She holds several church offices and is a member of the Community Services crisis network. She enjoys reading, writing, sewing, and trying new recipes. **Mar. 2**

Laura Hartmann and her retired pastor husband live in Goshen, Indiana, United States of America. Retired from secretarial positions, she keeps busy with sewing and knitting lap robes for hospice patients and long-term care residents, volunteering at the Elkhart County jail library, and helping behind the scenes at her local church. She and her husband have three grown children. **May 21, Sept. 8**

Mary K. Haslam is an energetic wife and mother who enjoys photography, fitness, singing, writing, and nearly any distraction from the domestic wonderland of the home. Mary lives in Texas, United States of America. **Mar. 11, July 14**

Helen Heavirland is an author, a speaker, and an encourager who lives in Oregon, United States of America. She has written numerous articles and four books, including *My God Is Bigger*. For more information or inspiration, visit her website, Stories to Inspire, at http://www.HelenHeavirland.com. **May 16, Aug. 3**

Kimberly M. H. Henry is a registered nurse with a specialty in psychiatric nursing. She is a member of the Goshen Seventh-day Adventist Church in the parish of St. Elizabeth, Jamaica, West Indies. **May 24**

Muriel Heppel enjoys the quietness of country living, the wildlife that comes onto her property, entertaining friends, playing Scrabble, and doing church and community service work. Muriel writes from British Columbia, Canada. **June 12, Sept. 18**

Denise Dick Herr was an English professor at Burman University, Alberta, Canada. She enjoys the blessings of reading, travel, and family. **Feb. 22, Sept. 15**

Lebrechtta N. O. Hesse-Bayne is a social economist working in Trinidad and Tobago, where she serves the Lord, working with youth and women and in personal ministries. **Apr. 25, July 13**

Andrea D. Hicks is founder of FOCUS Ministries (Fellowship of Christians Unique and Single). She is also a Women's Ministries director, motivational speaker, beta test coordinator, and quality assurance software engineer for an innovative company for dental professionals. She lives in New York, United States of America. **Oct. 29**

Renauta Hinds of Guyana is a student at the University of the Southern Caribbean in Trinidad and Tobago. She enjoys teaching, writing, drama, art, music, and being an inspiration to anyone with whom she interacts. **Mar. 8, July 28**

Patricia Hines is originally from the Caribbean but has also lived in Orlando, Florida, United States of America. She recently moved to Sebring, Florida. She is a teacher who enjoys music and writing. **Feb. 26**

Denise Hochstrasser is the Women's Ministries director at the Inter-European Division of Seventh-day Adventists and lives in Switzerland. Her vision is that all people can have the same possibilities in life and accept a calling without restriction. **July 19**

Roxy Hoehn is retired in Topeka, Kansas, United States of America, after many happy years leading out in Women's Ministries in the Kansas-Nebraska Conference. She is married to Jim, a retired pastor. She's involved with Sabbath School and social occasions in her local church and has happy times with their eleven grandchildren. **Apr. 11, Oct. 24**

Karen Holford is the Family Ministries director for the Trans-European Division of Seventh-day Adventists in England. She is a qualified marriage and family therapist. She is married to a pastor, Bernie, and they have three adult children and three tiny grandchildren. She enjoys writing and being creative in all kinds of ways. **Nov. 6**

Jacqueline Hope HoShing-Clarke has served in education as a principal, assistant principal, and teacher since 1979. She currently serves Northern Caribbean University as the chair of the Department of Teacher Education. She is married and has two adult children. She enjoys writing and gardening and, most of all, spending time with her grandson. **June 29, June 30**

Patty L. Hyland is a retired teacher; her final position was as an instructor at Rogue Community College in Grants Pass, Oregon, United States of America. She and her pastor husband, Verne, served as missionaries for fourteen years in Sri Lanka and on the island of Palau in Micronesia and have two children. At present, she is a chaplain at Three Rivers Community Hospital in Grants Pass. **Mar. 25, Aug. 21**

Shirley C. Iheanacho resides in Huntsville, Alabama, United States of America, with Morris, her husband of more than forty-seven years. She enjoys visiting the sick and shut-ins, encouraging people, traveling, spending time with her children and grandchildren, and writing. Her newly published book is *God's Incredible Plans for Me: A Memoir of an Amazing Journey.* **Oct. 23, Dec. 8**

Merrilou Wilder Inks is a former vocalist for *It Is Written* Television. She is still singing for the Lord, is an avid vegetable gardener, keeps a few laying hens, and works with her husband in Texas, United States of America. **Sept. 14**

Avis Floyd Jackson lives in Pleasantville, New Jersey, United States of America, and is the mother of five. She does business out of her home and is a party planner. Avis is active in her local church and is a Seventh-day Adventist by calling. **Dec. 16**

Helen Riches Jacob is the Women's Ministries director of the South Andhra Section of Seventh-day Adventists in Andhra Pradesh, India. She and her husband, Pastor Vara Pradesh Jacob, the president of the section, have two sons. She was an English teacher for twenty-six years; she enjoys knitting, crocheting, baking, and music. **Aug. 19**

Joan D. L. Jaensch lives with her husband, Murray, in Murray Bridge, South Australia. She is a mother, grandmother, and great-grandmother. Gardening is her interest. **May 5**

Rachel Privette Jennings attended Pine Forge Academy and graduated from Kettering College of Medical Arts as a registered diagnostic medical and cardiac sonographer. She is a member of Central Seventh-day Adventist Church in Columbus, Ohio, United States of America. She is passionate about theatrical arts. She has acted in, directed, and written plays and also devotional messages. **Mar. 10, May 7**

Cheryol Mitchell Johnson, EdD, is the first woman to be named principal of the largest high school in the state of Missouri, United States of America. She has been an educator for twenty-nine years in both parochial and public school systems. A mentor to teachers and administrators, she is an avid reader and enjoys spending time with friends and traveling with her husband, Steven. **July 4**

Elaine J. Johnson has been married to her best friend for fifty years. They have enjoyed country living in Alabama, United States of America, for the past twenty-five years. She is also active in her small country church. She enjoys writing, reading, and her card ministry. **Mar. 5**

Mattie E. Johnson is a wife, mother, and recently retired educator from the Dayton Public School system, in Dayton, Ohio, United States of America. She spent her last twelve years as a first-grade teacher at the Dayton Boys Preparatory Academy. Currently, she is an elder, the director of the Disabilities Department, and a Sabbath School teacher in the Junior/Earliteen class at the Ethan Temple Seventh-day Adventist Church in the Allegheny West Conference. **Nov. 12, Dec. 23**

Victoria L. Joiner, EdD, has enjoyed a twenty-eight-year career in higher education and broadcasting that has encompassed a variety of administrative and academic pursuits. Currently an assistant professor in the Communication Department at Oakwood Adventist University, she has contributed to *Regional Voice* magazine and *Message*, among many other publications. She hosts a weekly radio program and has two beautiful children, Jennifer and David Miller. **Nov. 3**

Erica Jones is the assistant to the director of Women's Ministries at the North American Division of Seventh-day Adventists in Columbia, Maryland, United States of America. **May 11**

Kathy Jo Duterrow Jones, born in Seattle, Washington, United States of America, has served God in Alaska, Michigan, Maryland, Idaho, and Alberta, Canada. She loves ministering to the needs of others. Her interests include writing, watercolor painting, and camping. **May 18**

Gerene I. Joseph is married to Elder Sylvester Joseph. They have two children, Sylene and Sylvester Jr. She was the director of Children's Ministries and Women's Ministries for the North Caribbean Conference for six years and also served as the director of Education. This musician (piano) and writer of poems is also a certified lay preacher and has conducted one evangelistic campaign. **June 8**

Priscila Kandane, a Women's Ministries director in India, is married to Pastor Ujwal Kandane. She has been blessed with three children. She has taught both primary and high-school levels for the past twenty-five years. She enjoys interacting with women and encouraging them in their spiritual growth. Her hobbies are reading and singing. **June 1**

Carolyn K. Karlstrom is a Bible worker for her home church in the Pacific Northwest of the United States of America. She gives Bible studies, teaches, and preaches. She is also a freelance writer whose articles have appeared in a variety of magazines. She is married to Rick, and they have a sweet black cat named Minuet. **Aug. 9**

Grace Keene was born on December 31, 1935. She grew up in New Rochelle, New York, and attended public schools there. After high-school graduation, she attended Endicott Junior College. She is married to Donald M. Keene; and between them, they have six children. She lives in Ooltewah, Tennessee. **June 15, Oct. 30**

Sonia Kennedy-Brown lives in Ontario, Canada. She recently completed her autobiography, *Silent Tears: Growing Up Albino.* She is active in her church but uses every opportunity to speak on behalf of those who are different and socially ostracized for this reason. For more information, email her at Soniab47@msn.com. **Mar. 6**

Brenda Kiš is a writer and editor for ASAP (Advocates for Southeast Asians and the Persecuted) in Berrien Springs, Michigan, United States of America. She enjoys her two sons and their families in Michigan and Alberta, Canada. **June 22**

Iris L. Kitching enjoys creative endeavors, spoken-word poetry performances, and writing for children. She has worked at the General Conference of Seventh-day Adventists in Maryland, United States of America, for more than twenty years—first in women's ministries, and then in presidential. She and her husband, Will, appreciate the joys of spending time with family and friends. **Mar. 24, July 6**

Betty Kossick is a freelance writer who has been part of seventy-seven books. She has authored three of her own: *Beyond the Locked Door, Heart Ballads,* and *The Manor.* For more information, email her at bkwrites4u@hotmail.com. Betty writes from Florida, United States of America. **Jan. 3, Apr. 12**

Patricia Mulraney Kovalski lives in Collegedale, Tennessee, United States of America. She loves to travel and enjoys her visits with her family in Michigan. She has many hobbies and has been putting on English teas for family and friends since 1997. **Mar. 14**

Tabitha Kra is married to Pastor Emmanuel Kra. They are blessed with two children, Anne and Jonathan. She is currently serving as the Children's and Women's Ministries director for the Eastern Sahel Union Mission in Lome, Togo. She loves reading, traveling, and teaching. **July 3, Sept. 19**

Mabel Kwei, a retired university and college lecturer, did missionary work in Africa for many years with her pastor husband and their three children. Now living in New Jersey, United States of America, she reads a lot and loves to paint, write, and spend time with little children. **Jan. 24, Apr. 17**

Wilma Kirk Lee, a licensed clinical social worker, currently directs the Center for Family Wholeness (CFW), located in Houston, Texas, United States of America. Her husband of five decades is Pastor W. S. Lee. Together they lead out in Family Ministries in the Southwest Region Conference of Seventh-day Adventists. She holds a both a bachelor's degree and a master's degree in social work. **Mar. 20, Nov. 26**

Sharon Long (Brown) retired in 2015 from a thirty-four-year social work career. She is excited to serve God in Edmonton, Alberta, Canada, and abroad. **Apr. 20**

Rhodi Alers de López writes from Massachusetts, United States of America. Her ministry, Expression Publishing Ministries, aims to inspire others to enjoy a closer relationship with Jesus. She's an author, singer, songwriter, and speaker, and she also leads a prayer ministry. **Sept. 23, Nov. 15**

Celine Lumowa wrote her devotional while she was a senior at Campion Academy, Colorado, United States of America, where she worked as a resident assistant in the girls' dormitory. Born in Jakarta, Indonesia, her family moved to America when she was three years old. She grew up in the Adventist Church. Her hope is to someday become a visiting nurse after graduating from college. **Aug. 25**

Betty Lyngdoh is presently working as the director of Women's Ministries for the Northeast India Union of Seventh-day Adventists, in Shillong, Meghalaya, India. She is married to Dr. L. F. Lyngdoh and is the mother of three grown-up sons. In the local church, she is very much involved in Pathfinders and women's ministries. Her husband, sons, and daughter-in-law have been her constant source of support. **Oct. 8**

Pauline J. Maddox is an adult gerontology nurse practitioner working with the health population in Calhoun, Georgia, United States of America. Her capstone article, "Cinnamon in the Treatment of Type II Diabetes," was published in the *Journal of Interdisciplinary Graduate Research* and can be viewed online. It has had more than one thousand downloads globally. **Aug. 28**

María Regina Werneck Mandeli is a psychologist, specializing in psychotherapy of children and adolescents. She is the wife of Pastor Rubens Mandeli; they have a son and live in Sorocaba, São Paulo, Brazil. **Sept. 27, Dec. 7**

Zandile Mankumba is married with four children. She is a qualified teacher. Her hobbies are reading, gardening, and dressmaking. Zandile lives in Côte d'Ivoire, West Africa. **Mar. 13**

Premila Masih serves as the Women's Ministries director for the Southern Asia Division of Seventh-day Adventists and is married to Pastor Hidayat Masih, the vice president and the Sabbath School/Personal Ministries director. A Shepherdess coordinator at Madhya

Bharat and Northern India Union Sections and a teacher for twenty-six years, she loves home decorating, reading, gardening, and making friends. She has two married children and one adored grandson, Brandon Zion. **May 29**

Fabienne Maslet was born in and grew up in Martinique, a French island of the Caribbean. She studied in France and earned a master's degree in engineering in nanotechnology. She is now studying in Trinidad and Tobago for a bachelor's degree in theology and religion. **Feb. 14**

Gail Masondo is a wife, mother of two adult children (Shellie and Jonathan), women's and children's advocate, songwriter, chaplain, Life in Recovery coach, and international speaker. She authored *Now This Feels Like Home.* A New York native, she now resides in Johannesburg, South Africa, with her musician husband, Victor Sibusio Masondo. **Jan. 21**

Nicole Mattson has been working in Adventist education for the past twenty years. She is currently superintendent of Education for the Indiana Conference of Seventh-day Adventists and enjoys living close to her precious grandchildren in southwest Michigan, United States of America. **May 1**

Mary H. Maxson is a daughter of the King, a follower of Jesus, and "Nana" to one grandchild. God chose her to minister at the Paradise Seventh-day Adventist Church in California, United States of America, as an associate pastor for nurture and discipleship. **Apr. 19**

Jenel A. N. Campbell McPherson writes from Baritca, Guyana. She is the wife of a pastor, Mark, and they have a baby boy. Her passion is for young people, with a special emphasis on the needs of young women. She has served in many capacities in her church. **Feb. 4**

Cindy Mercer is a pastor's wife who lives in Morganton, North Carolina, United States of America, where she works part time as a registered nurse. She is passionate about prayer and personal Bible study and enjoys the opportunity to speak at prayer retreats and women's events. For more info, visit the Mercer Ministries website at http://www .mercerministries.com. **Oct. 3, Oct. 4**

Joyce Meyer lives in Colorado, United States of America, with her husband of fifty-one years. She spent many years as a cosmetologist and in-home caregiver. She has three adult daughters and four grandchildren. She is dedicated to God and looks forward with anticipation to His second coming. **Oct. 5**

Wanda Misori, a native of Chicago, Illinois, United States of America, is a family nurse practitioner and assistant professor in the Department of Nursing at Oakwood University. She lives with her husband, Charles, and their five children in Huntsville, Alabama. She is actively involved with women's ministries in her church and enjoys reading and nature walks. **May 22**

D. Reneé Mobley, PhD, is trained in clinical pastoral education and has owned a Christian counseling practice for more than ten years. A member of the National Christian Counselors Association, she does training and also facilitates numerous workshops, seminars, and conferences. She is the mother of two adult women, mother-in-law to the greatest son-in-law in the world, and grandmother to three granddogs. Reneé writes from Alabama, United States of America. **Feb. 24, Apr. 10**

Marcia Mollenkopf, a retired teacher, lives in Klamath Falls, Oregon, United States of America. Her hobbies include reading, writing, and music. She has been blessed to have a growing postcard ministry. **Mar. 28**

Esperanza Aquino Mopera is founder and president of Polio Life Enhancement Organization, Inc., a civic organization in the Philippines that assists polio victims in finding trades or livelihoods to enhance their living conditions. Esperanza writes from Virginia, United States of America. **Aug. 17**

Lourdes E. Morales-Gudmundsson, PhD, is a recently retired university professor of Spanish language and literature who has been published widely in Seventh-day Adventist publications. Though living in California, United States of America, she has presented her "I Forgive You, But . . ." seminar on three other continents. She can be reached at lmorales@lasierra.edu. **Mar. 21, Mar. 22**

Lily Morales-Narváez works for the Texas Conference Adventist Book Center. She earned a bachelor's degree in psychology and writes articles from her home in Keene, Texas, United States of America, for women's devotional books and the *Adventist Review*. She likes to sing, write, and read. She is active in her church and loves her husband and family. **May 30, May 31**

Lila Farrell Morgan writes from North Carolina, United States of America. She is a widow, mother, grandmother, and great-grandmother of one. She enjoys reading, walking, baking, table games, observing nature, and keeping in touch with family and friends. **Mar. 31**

Valerie Hamel Morikone works for the Mountain View Conference in West Virginia, United States of America, and leads out in the Communication and Women's Ministries Departments. She loves to read, cook and bake, and do internet research. **Oct. 16, Dec. 21**

Vijay Moses is the Women's Ministries director of the West Telangana Section of Seventh-day Adventists in India. She is married to G. N. Moses. They have three sons and one daughter. Vijay is very interested in music, enjoys extending hospitality to everyone, and loves to garden. She is also zealous about training women and assisting in their spiritual growth. **July 17, Nov. 25**

Bonnie Moyers lives with her husband in Staunton, Virginia, United States of America. This freelance writer is a mother of two, a grandmother of three, and a musician for several area churches. **Apr. 16**

Sheree Mundy hails from the island of Jamaica but currently resides in Florida, United States of America. She is a nurse educator who has a passion for children. She helps teach a Primary Sabbath School class at her church. **Jan. 9**

Esther Synthia Murali works for Women's Ministries in the South Karnataka Section, in Mysore, India. She is a physiotherapist by profession, but her passion is to minster with her pastor husband. She has a son, Ted, and enjoys playing guitar, painting, gardening, and photography. **June 20, Nov. 10**

Judith M. Mwansa returned to her native Zambia with her husband, Pardon, to reside at Rusangu University after years of church work in the United States of America. Her last ten years were at the General Conference of Seventh-day Adventists, where she worked in the Women's Ministries Department and assisted with the production of these devotional books. She has adult children and one granddaughter and enjoys reading, music, traveling, and spending time with loved ones. **Feb. 12, July 24**

Jannett Maurine Myrie is currently employed at Florida Hospital in Florida, United States of America. She serves as the Women's Ministries director and the Sabbath School superintendent in her church. A proud mother of one son, her hobbies include reading, cooking, going on cruises, and serving as a medical missionary overseas. **July 8**

Anne Elaine Nelson is a retired elementary teacher who authored the book *Puzzled Parents*. She is a widow with four children and eleven grandchildren. She is active in church work as the Women's Ministries leader and an assistant superintendent for Sabbath School. She enjoys music, crafts, photography, and creating memories with her grandchildren. Anne lives in Michigan, United States of America. **Feb. 1, Sept. 17**

Samantha Nelson is a pastor's wife who loves serving alongside her husband, Steve. She is also the CEO of The Hope of Survivors, a nonprofit organization dedicated to assisting victims of clergy sexual abuse and providing educational seminars to clergy of all faiths. She and Steve live in Wyoming, United States of America, and love traveling, hiking in the mountains, and enjoying the beauty of God's creation. **Apr. 22, Apr. 23**

Stacey A. Nicely, a certified and licensed counselor, was born and raised in Jamaica. She studied and worked at Northern Caribbean University before moving to Berrien Springs, Michigan, United States of America. She holds a master's degree in community counseling and is pursuing a doctorate in counseling psychology at Andrews University. She is the testing coordinator at the university's counseling and testing center. **Apr. 24**

Linda Nottingham lives in Florida, United States of America, and teaches an adult Bible study class at her church. She is semiretired but serves as a mentor to female business owners. She was also a 2012 honoree of the Florida Commission on the Status of Women. **July 20**

Akosua Ntriakwah is a Women's Ministries leader in the territory of Southern Ghana Union Conference of Seventh-day Adventists. **July 21**

Diana Ocran is first-time contributing author who lives in Accra, Ghana. She is the Shepherdess International coordinator at the Southern Ghana Union Conference of Seventh-day Adventists, where her husband serves as president. **Aug. 23**

Elizabeth Versteegh Odiyar of Kelowna, British Columbia, Canada, has served God through her church and also managed the family chimney sweep business since 1985. She has twin sons, a daughter, and adorable grandchildren. **Feb. 6**

Mimonte Dorcas Odonkor writes from southern Ghana. **Dec. 17**

Val Baminger Oliveira is a new contributing author who lives in Brazil. **Sept. 29, Dec. 5**

Lyudmyla Oliynyk continually thanks God because she can see His hand in her life, accomplishing His will. She feels called to be a missionary for her church. Currently a four-year theology student, she was born in Ukraine but grew up in Alessandria, Italy. **Jan. 11**

Mary Opoku-Gyamfi writes from Valley View University in Accra, Ghana. **July 9**

Charlotte Osei-Agyeman has served for twenty years as a Women's Ministries director. She has two children, is a retired civil servant, and writes from Ghana. **Feb. 21**

Evelyn Osei-Bonsu writes from southern Ghana. **Aug. 12, Nov. 29**

Sharon Oster is a retired teacher assistant living in Evans, Colorado, United States of America, with her retired pastor husband. She enjoys automobile day trips in the nearby Rocky Mountains. She and her husband have three children and seven grandchildren. **Feb. 28**

Hannele Ottschofski lives in Germany. A speaker for the Hope Channel, she also organizes women's events and has compiled several women's devotionals in addition to publishing her own book, *My Father's Shirt.* **Feb. 2**

Revel Papaioannou and her husband are living their "sunset" years in the biblical town of Berea, Greece, where they enjoy a variety of church work. Revel writes, "Sunsets are so beautiful!" **Apr. 28**

Bonnie R. Parker and her husband, Richard, reside in Yucaipa, California, United States of America. She is a homemaker, a former teacher, and an office manager in her husband's dental office. She enjoys music, writing for the newsletter of her local church, and women's ministries. Her grown sons and their families, including six grandchildren, are a blessing. **Mar. 1, Dec. 25**

Esther Joyce Parkins lives in Ghana. **July 27**

Carmem Virgínia dos Santos Paulo graduated with a degree in languages and literature and is a specialist in linguistics and teaching. She is a health and socioeducational agent. In her free time, she likes to read, sing, and speak of God's love to others. At church, she is the Youth director and the associate Music director. She writes from Brazil. **Feb. 15**

Cathy Payne works in the Education Department of the North American Division of Seventh-day Adventists in Columbia, Maryland, United States of America. She loves spending time with family, friends, pets, and her weekly Bible study group. **Feb. 9**

Karen J. Pearson is the recently retired director of publicity and public relations at Pacific Press® Publishing Association in Nampa, Idaho, United States of America. Her favorite activities include writing and speaking of Jesus. She and her pastor husband have two adult children. **Apr. 21**

Evelyn Gabutero Pelayo, born and educated as a teacher in the Philippines, spent twenty-two years with her husband, Roger, serving as a missionary in Zambia and Madagascar. She enjoys spending time with her two granddaughters, Kai Sofia and Anya Rei. **May 2**

Kathy Pepper is a pastor's wife living in West Virginia, United States of America. She and her husband, Stewart, have a son, two daughters, a daughter-in-law, and one son-in-law. They were blessed with their first grandchild in February 2017. Kathy enjoys working with her husband and graphic design, which she uses in their ministry. **July 18, Sept. 16**

Felicia Pepra-Mensah lectures at Valley View University in Accra, Ghana. **Aug. 8**

Diane Pestes recently authored *Prayer That Moves Mountains*, published by Pacific

Press® Publishing Association. She is also an international speaker who is known for her commitment to Christ and ability to memorize scripture. She resides with her husband in Oregon, United States of America. She can be contacted at her website at http://DianePestes.com. **May 15, Nov. 17**

Kathy Peterson lives in Colorado, United States of America, with Dallas, her husband of twenty-five years. Photography is her passion, especially pictures of her seven great-grandchildren and her beautiful home state. **Oct. 19**

Karen M. Phillips lives in Nebraska, United States of America, and is now remarried to her husband after ten years of divorce. She praises God every day for His amazing love. Together she and her husband conduct a ministry that includes music, Bible studies, and much more. You can check it out at their HeReturns website at http://HeReturns.org. **May 12, June 21**

Birdie Poddar is a retiree who originally comes from Northeast India but now has settled in South India. She has two adult children—a girl and a boy—and five grandchildren. She enjoys gardening, keeping house, cooking, baking, telling stories, writing articles, and composing poems. Birdie also has a handcrafted card ministry for those who need comfort and encouragement. **Jan. 5**

Sunila Prasad is a graduate of Spicer Adventist University in Pune, India. She is married to Mr. Prasad, who is a business graduate. God has blessed them with a son and a daughter. For eighteen years, Sunila worked as an office secretary, but recently she was elected as the Women's Ministries director for the Southeast Andhra Section of Seventh-day Adventists in Andhra Pradesh. Her hobbies include gardening and sharing beauty tips with women. **Aug. 6**

Damaris Prieto lives in Arkansas, United States of America. She is blessed to be the wife of Pastor Luis and the mother of Sandra. She loves photos, reading, and working in women's ministries. **June 25, Sept. 11**

Nathalie "Nathy" Regmund is a new contributing author living in Keene, Texas, United States of America. **Sept. 9**

Katia Garcia Reinert is an advanced practice family nurse practitioner practicing in Baltimore, Maryland, United States of America. Originally from Brazil, she lives in Maryland and serves as an associate director for the Health Ministries Department of the General Conference of Seventh-day Adventists. She enjoys spending time with her nephews and niece, bicycling, hiking, singing, and traveling the world on mission assignments. **Jan. 17, Nov. 28**

Darlenejoan McKibbin Rhine was born in Nebraska, United States of America, raised in California, and educated in Tennessee, earning a bachelor's degree in journalism. She retired from the *Los Angeles Times* newspaper and now lives in the "soggy" state of Washington. A widow with one son, Darlenejoan belongs to the North Cascade Seventh-day Adventist Church and supports the Anacortes Adventist Fellowship company. **Dec. 19**

Shondolyn Young Richardson is a Christian recording artist, speaker, and Women's Ministries area leader for central Alabama, United States of America. She is an elementary school teacher and certified reading specialist. She holds a master's degree in education and is National Board certified in literacy. She and her husband, Michael, have a teenage son and live in Columbus, Mississippi, United States of America. Visit her website at http://www.shondolyn.com. **Oct. 9**

Marli Elizete Ritter-Hein was born into a loving family and grew up in a Christian environment surrounded by nature and animals. What she loves most are family, music, nature, interior decoration, flowers and flower arrangements, reading, and traveling. She and her husband have served God as missionaries in various places. Their two sons are now married. Marli writes from Paraguay. **June 16, Dec. 22**

Dixil L. Rodríguez is a university professor and volunteer chaplain who lives in Argyle, Texas, United States of America. **Jan. 22, Sept. 13, Dec. 13**

Raylene McKenzie Ross, a nurse, is married to Leroy Ross. She writes from Spanish Town, Jamaica. At the time of writing, she is a member of the Spanish Town Seventh-day Adventist Church, where she has served in various capacities over the years, including as the Family Life director. **Jan. 8**

Kollis Salmon-Fairweather is originally from Jamaica, West Indies, but now lives in Florida, United States of America, with her husband. She is passionate about Bible studies and witnessing. She wants to spend her remaining years helping others to know God. **Apr. 3**

Deborah Sanders lives in Alberta, Canada, with her husband, Ron, and son, Sonny. In 1990, God blessed her with a successful writing and prayer outreach ministry, Dimensions of Love. In 2013, she compiled her best stories into a book entitled *Saints-in-Training*. If God wills it to be published, Sonny can use it as a tool to share his testimony for Jesus as he continues to witness. **Jan. 16, Sept. 5**

Mamata Sassou, married and the mother of three, holds two degrees—one being a master's degree in diplomacy and international relations. She deals with conflict management and worked in Kuwait for seven years. After stepping down from her position at the Economic Community of West African States, she worked to support ADRA Niger and women's ministries. She likes traveling around the world as she reaches out to help those in need. **July 25, Nov. 24**

Jennifer Jill Schwirzer, LPC, is a counselor and author residing in Orlando, Florida, United States of America. From Orlando, she directs Abide Counseling and also runs a nonprofit ministry. She hosts a television show, *A Multitude of Counselors*, on Three Angels Broadcasting Network (3ABN). **Nov. 19**

Omobonike Adeola Sessou is the Women's Ministries and Children's Ministries director at the West-Central Africa Division of Seventh-day Adventists in Abidjan, Côte d'Ivoire. She is married to Pastor Sessou, and they are blessed with three children. Her hobbies include teaching, counseling, making new friends, and visiting with people. **June 2**

Lynda Shepherd is a native of New Orleans, Louisiana, United States of America. She now resides in College Station, Texas. She is the mother of two and has one grandson. Jesus Christ is her Lord and Savior; she believes He is the Son of the living Creator God. One of her favorite Bible texts is "I can do all things through Christ which strengtheneth me" (Philippians 4:13, KJV). **July 31**

Rhoda Shinge, wife of Pastor Chandrakant Shinge, has taught English for thirty-five years. She moved to new responsibilities in September 2016 when her husband assumed leadership of the Central Maharashtra Conference. They have two daughters, Mrunal and Meghna, and a son, Dhairyasheel. Their grandchildren are Joshua, Racheal, and Marcus. She loves to sing, write, and conduct family life seminars with her husband. Rhoda writes from Tamil Nadu, India. **May 13, Oct. 11**

Tina Shorey, the codirector of Women's Ministries for the New York Conference of Seventh-day Adventists, United States of America, is a new contributing author. **Oct. 18**

Sherry Shrestha is a family practice doctor living in Berrien Springs, Michigan, United States of America. She and her husband, Prakash, have three grown daughters and their first grandson. Her hobbies include travel, horses, and the natural world. **Aug. 15**

Rose Neff Sikora and her husband, Norman, live happily on their hobby farm in the beautiful mountains of North Carolina, United States of America. She is retired from a forty-five-year career as a registered nurse and volunteers at Park Ridge Health. She enjoys walking, writing, and helping others. She has one adult daughter, Julie, and three lovely grandchildren. She desires that her writing will bless others. **Mar. 29**

Sonya Simms is an avid reader with an interest in fitness. She is a law student and adviser in training at her local Citizens Advice Bureau. She enjoys supporting the youth as a Pathfinder counselor at Luton North Seventh-day Adventist Church in England. In so doing, she also fulfills her passions for the outdoors, creativity, and learning more about God. **Jan. 20, Mar. 9**

Heather-Dawn Small is the director for Women's Ministries at the General Conference of Seventh-day Adventists, in Maryland, United States of America. She has been the Children's Ministries and the Women's Ministries director for the Caribbean Union Conference, located in Trinidad and Tobago. She is the wife of Pastor Joseph Small and the mother of Dalonne and Jerard. She loves air travel, reading, and scrapbooking. **Jan. 1, Apr. 6, July 30, Oct. 1**

Yvonne Curry Smallwood enjoys life's simple pleasures—a colorful sunrise, a crisp autumn day, and time with family members. Her stories have appeared in several publications. She writes from Maryland, United States of America. **Mar. 18**

Maple Smith, a nurse by profession, writes from Huntsville, Alabama, United States of America, though she was born in Guyana, South America. She enjoys spending time with Jesus, family, and friends. In addition to travel, she enjoys gardening and nature. She has held many leadership positions in church and has been married for more than thirty years. She has two adult children. **June 23, Oct. 31**

Debra Snyder is from Shelton, Nebraska, United States of America. She is a medical coder but has a passion for reaching others through her writing. She enjoys leading out in a women's Bible study at her church. This wife and mother of three wonderful children says that her greatest accomplishment is being a mother. **Dec. 3**

Belinda Solomon is the wife of her dear husband, Lincoln, and has two children. She is a newly appointed teacher at an Adventist school in South Africa and coordinates both children's and family ministries for her church. She enjoys cooking, tending her vegetable garden, walking, learning to play the piano, and sewing! **Feb. 3, Oct. 17**

Débora de Souza has a master's degree in science education. She enjoys women's ministries and children's ministries programs and likes to help her husband, Pastor Josiel

P. de Souza, in their pastoral district. The couple has two children: Tiago and Mateus. Her hobbies include traveling and reading good books. Débora writes from Brazil. **Sept. 25, Dec. 30**

Jill Springer-Cato lives in Trinidad and Tobago and works as a technical assistant for the state-owned petroleum company. She is a music minister who also loves working in women's and youth ministries. **Apr. 8**

Sylvia Sioux Stark is an artist who lives in Tennessee, United States of America. Her artwork is displayed in several North American states and also in South America. She enjoys being in the outdoors, hiking, camping, backpacking, and enjoying the work of the Master Artist. She has been published in *Guide*. **Feb. 25**

Eva M. Starner is an assistant professor in the Psychology Department at Oakwood University in Huntsville, Alabama, United States of America. She is a graduate of both Oakwood and Loma Linda Universities. Currently, she has three adult daughters, two sons-in-law, and three wonderful grandchildren. She feels divinely called to her current position and knows that when God opens doors, they stay open! **June 3**

Ardis Dick Stenbakken, now living in Colorado, United States of America, edited these women's devotional books for seventeen years. She did this after retiring as the director of Women's Ministries at the General Conference of Seventh-day Adventists. She and her husband, Dick, love their two children and their spouses and four grandchildren. She is still hoping to find time to once again pursue some hobbies. **Feb. 17, May 28, July 11**

Keisha D. Sterling-Richards, a health-care professional and entrepreneur, is married to Seymour. She rejoices in the Lord and enjoys serving Him and partnering with Him in the King's business. Her passion is service. She also enjoys the Brooklyn Tabernacle, the outdoors, ackee fruit, roasted breadfruit, and avocado. Keisha writes from the beautiful island of Jamaica. **Mar. 16, Nov. 21**

Veon Stewart and her husband, Paul, live in Orlando, Florida, United States of America. She is a mathematics teacher at the Adventist University of Health Sciences, which is associated with Florida Hospital. She is Jamaican by birth and loves to read her Bible. **Jan. 15, May 8**

Barbara Stovall holds an MBA degree and is a research assistant for the Ellen G. White Research Center, Anna Knight Center for Women's Leadership, at Oakwood University in Huntsville, Alabama, United States of America. **Sept. 6**

Naomi Striemer lives in Franklin, Tennessee, United States of America, with her husband Jordan, and dog, Bella. She is a best-selling author, a chart-topping Christian singer and songwriter, and a sought-after speaker who tours around the world singing and speaking. In her spare time, she enjoys baking, board games, and the outdoors. **June 4, June 5**

Jeyarani Sundersingh is a teacher who has served in Adventist mission schools for thirty-five years and been in charge of senior secondary students. Reading is her primary hobby and now writing as well. She currently serves as the Women's Ministries director and Shepherdess coordinator for the Southeast India Union Section of the Southern Asia Division. She loves to serve the Lord. **July 26, Nov. 16**

Carolyn Rathbun Sutton and her husband, Jim, are volunteer field representatives for Adventist World Radio 360. From their home in Alabama, United States of America, she edited this year's General Conference Women's Ministries devotional book, the proceeds of which go to support higher education for women globally. **Mar. 17, Nov. 11**

Harritte Sutton is a mother, grandmother, and great-grandmother living in Tennessee, United States of America. For years, she was the bookkeeper for the paint store and decorating center she and her late husband owned. In addition to church treasurer responsibilities, she assumed receptionist and nursing responsibilities at a hospital and doctor's office. She appreciates her daily time with God. **Oct. 27**

Anna Ivie Swingle—born in California, United States of America, raised in New Mexico, and educated in Texas and Nebraska—is a retired government administrative specialist. This mother of two and grandmother of one loves Jesus Christ and spends time as a volunteer at a hospital. She enjoys family, friends, and traveling. She has been a church clerk, pianist, and organist for more than twenty-five years. **Dec. 29**

Evelyn Porteza Tabingo is a retired cardiac nurse living in Oceanside, California, United States of America. She and her husband, Henry, are from the Philippines and have served as missionaries to East Africa. She enjoys reading, writing, gardening, music, traveling, and spending time with family and her grandchildren. **Apr. 26, Aug. 27**

Arlene R. Taylor recently retired from health care after decades of working with Adventist health facilities. Still living in the Napa Valley of Northern California, United States of America, she devotes her time and energy to brain function research, writing, and speaking. **Jan. 12, Dec. 26**

Cherita Ayélé Tenou is married and blessed with two sons. She works as an administrative secretary at the Eastern Sahel Union Mission in Lome, Togo. She is also a Women's Ministries coordinator in her district. **Aug. 4**

Adjoa Mawusi Adiaokuk Ekrong Tetteh is a new contributing author who writes from Ghana. **Dec. 28**

Rose Joseph Thomas is an educator with the Florida Conference of Seventh-day Adventists in the United States of America. She's married to her best friend, Walden, and they have two children: Samuel Joseph and Crystal Rose. **June 6, Oct. 2**

Sharon M. Thomas is a retired public school teacher in Lancombe, Louisiana, United States of America. She still enjoys working part time and has had a variety of jobs. She enjoys reading, quilting, piano, and playing Scrabble with her husband, Don. **Sept. 20**

Avery J. Thompson currently works at Northern Caribbean University in Jamaica where she served as an associate professor of mathematics and then subsequently as the university registrar for more than seventeen years. She currently works in distance education. She conducts the university church choir and enjoys reading and engaging members of the young adult Sabbath School class. She's been married to Herbert for more than thirty-three years, and they have two adult daughters. **Dec. 27**

Bula Rose Haughton Thompson is a member of the Goshen Seventh-day Adventist Church in the West Jamaica Conference of Seventh-day Adventists. She has been married to Norman for twenty-one years. **Jan. 30**

Ena Thorpe, a retired nurse, resides in Hamilton, Ontario, Canada. She has three adult children and five adorable grandchildren who are her pride and joy. She loves to play

Scrabble and sudoku and attends the Hamilton Seventh-day Adventist Church. **Aug. 26**

Nancy (Neuharth) Troyer is a published author, mother of Steph, and wife of military chaplain Don Troyer. She creates Petal Promise cards, His Voice photo blogs, and Notetaker Sermon Notes in Banning, California, United States of America. **Sept. 1, Dec. 9**

Rebecca Timon Turner is the editorial assistant for the General Conference Women's Ministries Department. She is delighted to have been blessed with a husband and two grandsons in the past two years. She belongs to several small groups, and her mission in life is to encourage her friends to study the Bible deeply. **Nov. 7**

Chinwe Ubani-Ebere, a new contributing author, lives in Georgia, United States of America. **Mar. 4**

Olga Valdivia is a published author and a passionate gardener who lives among the trees and birds surrounding a little white house with black shutters that is located in Idaho, United States of America. This is where she lives and makes a living with her husband. **Apr. 15, Dec. 31**

Wanda Van Putten-Allen, a native of the United States Virgin Islands, resides in Maryland, United States of America, with her husband and two daughters. She is an educator and serves in her church as an Adventurers counselor and member of the Communications Department. **Apr. 1**

Liudmila Verlan is the daughter of a pastor and now the wife of a pastor. She has taught school for forty-seven years and served in her church since the age of fifteen. Ten years of her service involved women's ministries. She also ministered to disabled children and their parents for four years. Liudmila lives in Russia. **Nov. 23**

Carolyn Voss, PhD, is a widow and a retired nurse educator. Her hobbies are sewing, quilting, crafts, walking, golfing, and studying God's Word. Carolyn writes from Harrah, Oklahoma, United States of America. **Jan. 7**

Cora A. Walker resides in Atlanta, Georgia, United States of America. She is a retired nurse, editor, and freelance writer. She enjoys reading, writing, sewing, swimming, classical music, traveling, and spending quality time with her family. **Sept. 3, Dec. 6**

Marilyn P. Wallace and her dog, Precious, live in Panama City, Florida, United States of America. She is a retired educator, church elder, treasurer, and South Central Conference Women's Ministries state director for the Gulf Coast area. She loves to travel and exercise. She is the mother of two children: a son and a daughter (deceased). **May 23**

Anna May Radke Waters, a retired administrative secretary from Columbia Adventist Academy, has served as an ordained elder and greeter. At the top of her long list of hobbies are her eight grandchildren and husband with whom she likes to travel and make memories. She also enjoys doing Bible studies on the internet and responding to prayer requests for Bibleinfo.com. Anna writes from College Place, Washington, United States of America. **Jan. 10**

Daniela Weichhold, originally from Germany, works as an administrative assistant at the European Union headquarters in Brussels, Belgium. During leaves of absence, she has received medical missionary training. She enjoys the outdoors, singing, playing the piano, and cooking. **Feb. 10**

Lyn Welk-Sandy, Mother, Nana, and Great-Nana, is from South Australia and enjoys nature and caravanning in Australia with her husband, Keith. Grief counseling, photography, playing the pipe organ, and hand chiming are some of her favorite activities. **Jan. 23, Nov. 4**

Kimasha P. Williams, originally from St. Maarten, writes from England, where she is doing postgraduate work at the University of Leeds. She enjoys testifying about God's goodness with her family and friends. In church, she is involved in youth ministry, music, and communications—her professional field. **Feb. 19, June 18**

Sommer E. Williams is a senior family service counselor for the Midwest Memorial Group in Detroit, Michigan, United States of America. This loving mother of one has recently begun writing. Her greatest desire is to be always within God's will as He leads in her life. **May 25**

Wendy Williams lives in Ohio, United States of America. Her favorite pastimes are writing, photography, traveling, hiking with her husband, and eating the world's supply of chocolate. **May 6**

Rachel Williams-Smith is a wife, mother, writer, and speaker. She has a bachelor's degree in language arts, a master's degree in professional writing, and a doctorate in communication. She chairs the Department of Communication at Andrews University in Michigan, United States of America. Her book *Born Yesterday* was published by Pacific Press® Publishing Association. **June 28**

Dalores Broome Winget is a retired thirty-year elementary teacher living with her husband, Richard, in Warwick, Pennsylvania, United States of America. This much-published writer has two children and two grandchildren. She enjoys being with family, reading, and traveling. **July 12**

Melanie Carter Winkler has written short stories, articles for magazines, and devotionals. She has a passion for music, writing, and spreading the gospel through the use of her talents. She is involved in children's, youth, and women's ministries at her church. She lives in Western Australia. **Mar. 30**

Janice L. Yancheson is a retired registered nurse and licensed professional counselor. For the past ten years, her husband has been in pastoral ministry in the Murphy district of North Carolina, United States of America. **May 26, Aug. 2**

Adolphine Zian is married and blessed with three children. She is a private sector company manager and the Women's Ministries director for the Côte d'Ivoire Conference of Seventh-day Adventists. She enjoys reading. **Aug. 10, Nov. 5**